Medium of Instruction Policies

Which Agenda? Whose Agenda?

Medium of Instruction Policies

Which Agenda? Whose Agenda?

Edited by

James W. Tollefson
University of Washington

Amy B. M. Tsui
The University of Hong Kong

LEA

LAWRENCE ERLBAUM ASSOCIATES, PUBLISHERS

2004   Mahwah, New Jersey   London

Lawrence Erlbaum Associates, Inc., Publishers
10 Industrial Avenue
Mahwah, NJ 07430

Cover design by Kathryn Houghtaling Lacey

Library of Congress Cataloging-in-Publication Data

Medium of instruction policies : which agenda? whose agenda? / edited by James W. Tollefson, Amy B. M. Tsui.

    p. cm.

Includes bibliographical references and index.
ISBN 0-8058-4277-2 (alk. paper)
ISBN 0-8058-4278-0 (pbk. : alk. paper)
    1. Native language and education—Government policy—Cross-cultural studies 2. Educational, Bilingual—Government policy—Cross cultural studies. I. Tollefson, James W.   II. Tsui, Amy.

LC201.5.M43 2003
306.44—dc21
                                            2003042386
                                                    CIP

Contents

Preface

Since the early 1990s, a revival of interest in language-policy research has contributed to growing awareness that medium-of-instruction policies in education have considerable impact not only on the school performance of students and the daily work of teachers, but also on various forms of social and economic (in)equality. Because much of the daily work that takes place in education involves verbal interaction among students and teachers, medium-of-instruction decisions play a central role in shaping the learning activities that take place in all classrooms and on all playgrounds. Moreover, because educational institutions play such a crucial role in determining social hierarchies, political power, and economic opportunity, medium-of-instruction policies thus play an important role in organizing social and political systems.

In many multi-ethnic and multilingual countries around the world, the choice of a language for the medium of instruction in state educational systems raises a fundamental and complex educational question: What combination of instruction in students' native language(s) and in a second language of wider communication will ensure that students gain both effective subject content education as well as the second-language skills necessary for higher education and employment? Although this question focuses primarily on the educational agenda of providing effective language- and subject-content instruction, medium-of-instruction policies also raise important social and political questions: Which ethnic and linguistic groups will benefit from alternative medium-of-instruction policies? What language policy best fulfills the need for interethnic communication? What policy best maintains a balance between the interests of different ethnic and linguistic groups and thereby ensures an acceptable level of political stability?

This collection of chapters examines the tension between the educational agenda and other underlying social and political agendas in different sociopolitical contexts. In countries where English is the dominant language, debates over the use of the native languages of minority students as media of education center on three questions: For what purposes should mother-tongue education be encouraged and supported by official policy? Should multilingualism and multiculturalism be seen as assets or liabilities? How can ethnic minorities maintain their culture and at the same time not be deprived of their opportunity to gain access to higher education and employment, and to participate effectively in public life as well as in economic activities? In post-colonial countries, the educational agenda of using the most effective medium for education is often driven or clouded by the political agendas of nation building, national identity, and unity, as well as the need to ensure political stability by balancing the interests of different ethnic groups, classes, or political parties. In countries where diglossia or triglossia is evident, either officially or unofficially, the choice of medium of instruction is often a reflection of the sociopolitical and socioeconomic forces at work in the community, as well as a vehicle for the struggle for power among different social groups. The aim of this volume is therefore to unravel the complex social and political agendas that underlie decisions on medium-of-instruction policies.

In selecting the authors and chapters for this volume, the editors have been guided by their belief that medium-of-instruction policies must be understood in connection with social, economic, and political forces that shape education generally. The chapters in this collection demonstrate that medium-of-instruction policies are not only about the choice of the language(s) of instruction, but also about a range of important sociopolitical issues, including globalization, migration, labor policy, elite competition, and the distribution of economic resources and political power. It is the purpose of this collection to explore the links between medium-of-instruction policies and these broader issues. The collection is intended for scholars and other specialists in education, language policy, sociolinguistics, applied linguistics, and language teaching. It is intended for use in graduate and advanced undergraduate courses on language education and language policy.

ACKNOWLEDGMENTS

The editors are grateful to the authors of the chapters in this collection for their efforts to connect medium-of-instruction policies with critically important social, political, economic, and educational issues. Julie Scales contributed her considerable research skills to this volume. Vikki Weston and Winky Mok of the University of Hong Kong provided superb assistance in editing the language of some chapters, formatting the manuscript, and checking the details. The editors are especially grateful to Naomi Silverman of Lawrence Erlbaum Associates, for her support for this project.

—James W. Tollefson
—Amy B. M. Tsui

Contributors

Hassana Alidou, Alliant International University, United States

E. Annamalai, Central Institute of Indian Languages, India

Carol Benson, Stockholm University, Sweden

Saran Kaur Gill, Universiti Kebangsaan, Malaysia

Dylan V. Jones, University of Wales, Aberystwyth, Wales

Kendall A. King, Georgetown University, United States

Marilyn Martin-Jones, University of Wales, Aberystwyth, Wales

Stephen May, University of Waikato, New Zealand

Teresa L. McCarty, University of Arizona, United States

Iluminado Nical, Leyte Institute of Technology, Philippines

Anne Pakir, National University of Singapore, Singapore

Margaret J. Secombe, University of Adelaide, Australia

Jerzy J. Smolicz, University of Adelaide, Australia

James W. Tollefson, University of Washington, United States

Amy B. M. Tsui, The University of Hong Kong, Hong Kong

Vic Webb, University of Pretoria, South Africa

1

The Centrality of Medium-of-Instruction Policy in Sociopolitical Processes

Amy B. M. Tsui
The University of Hong Kong

James W. Tollefson
University of Washington

Most of the studies on medium of instruction, particularly in the 1970s and 1980s, were conducted in the field of bilingual education and focused on the effects of choices of medium of instruction at the micro level, including the classroom and the individual. The studies were motivated by educational concerns. Questions being addressed at the time pertained largely to the effectiveness and efficiency of different models of immersion in the acquisition of the first language and the second language, and in academic achievement in content subjects (for a critique of research on bilingual education, see Paulston, 1980). Although research on language policy sees language-policy issues as very much shaping—as well as being shaped by—the broader social and political issues, most of the earlier studies of medium of instruction had not been situated in the sociopolitical contexts in which they were implemented, and of which they were a part. The emergence in the 1990s of critical linguistics as a field of study focusing on linguistic human rights, and the role of language in power, control, dominance, and equality, has provided new insights and new foci for investigations of language-in-education policies (see, e.g., Fairclough, 1989; Pennycook, 1998; Phillipson, 1992, 2000a; Skutnabb-Kangas, 2000, 2002; Tollefson, 1995, 2002).

This volume makes a case for the centrality of medium-of-instruction policy in sociopolitical processes. The language of a nation, or an ethnic group, is often a symbol of its identity and allegiance, and an embodiment of its values, culture, and traditions. Medium of instruction is the most powerful means of maintaining and revitalizing a language and a culture; it is the most important form of intergenerational transmission (Fishman & Fishman, 2000). It is also the most direct agent of linguistic genocide (Skutnabb-Kangas, 2000, 2002). Medium-of-instruction policy determines which social and linguistic groups have access to political and economic opportunities, and which groups are disenfranchised. It is therefore a key means of power (re)distribution and social (re)construction, as well as a key arena in which political conflicts among countries and ethnolinguistic, social and political groups are realized. Because medium-of-instruction policy is an integral part of educational policy, debates surrounding it necessarily pertain to educational efficacy. All too often, policy makers put forward an educational agenda that justifies policy decisions regarding the use and/or the prohibition of a particular language or languages. Yet, behind the educational agenda are political, social, and economic agendas that serve to protect the interests of particular political and social groups. The tension between these agendas is difficult to resolve, and almost invariably leads to the triumph of the political, social, or economic agenda over the educational agenda. For this reason, we feel that it is important, when examining medium-of-instruction policy issues, to ask and address the questions, "Which Agenda? Whose Agenda?"—hence the title of this volume: *Medium of Instruction Policies: Which Agenda? Whose Agenda?*.

The chapters in this volume address the questions just mentioned in a range of sociopolitical contexts, including minority groups in English-dominant countries, post-colonial countries that have suffered long periods of political and linguistic domination, and countries where ethnolinguistic groups have succeeded in resisting linguistic domination and thereby gained political independence. Accordingly, this book is organized around these contexts. Part I consists of three chapters that focus on the efforts made by linguistic minorities in English-dominant countries to revitalize and maintain their languages, namely the Māori in New Zealand, the Welsh in Wales (United Kingdom), and the indigenous Indians in the United States. Part II consists of five chapters that focus on post-colonial countries and the different paths that they have taken toward nation building through their medium-of-instruction policies. They include Hong Kong, Singapore, Malaysia, India, the countries of sub-Saharan Africa, and the Philippines. Part III consists of three chapters that focus on the conflicts between ethnolinguistic groups, how they were managed, and the political consequences. They cover post-apartheid South Africa, Ecuador, Bolivia, and Yugoslavia. Four recurrent themes can be identified in this volume, and are discussed here under separate headings.

SITUATEDNESS OF MEDIUM-OF-INSTRUCTION POLICIES

All chapters in this volume contextualize the discussion of current medium-of-instruction policies and practices in the history of the development, formulation, and implementation of these policies. The shared understanding is that the interpretation of medium-of-instruction policies, and the debates surrounding them, must be situated in their sociopolitical contexts, which are inseparable from their historical contexts.

The historical reviews provided in the chapters show remarkable similarities in the functions of medium-of-instruction policies. In former colonial states, the colonial language was adopted as a medium of instruction by a small number of schools and made available to an exclusive group of indigenous people. This exclusive group joined the elite of the society who had access to power, wealth, and status, and acted as auxiliaries to the colonizers and as brokers between the colonizers and the colonized. As Pennycook (2002) observes, the spread of western knowledge and values was of equal, if not greater, importance to securing good will toward the colonizers and producing a loyal working force. Consequently, formal education was made available by colonial governments through the indigenous languages (to a greater or lesser extent), either as an alternative, or as a transitional medium of instruction. No matter whether the colonial language or the indigenous languages were used as the medium of instruction, the goal remained the same—to subjugate the colonized. Alidou's account of sub-Saharan Africa, Annamalai's account of India, and Tsui's account of Hong Kong all tell the same story. In English-dominant countries, the history of medium of instruction is no different. The indigenous languages were treated as backward and uncivilized, and seen as something that must be eradicated in order for the country to become modernized. Indigenous people were made to feel ashamed of their own tongue and were penalized for speaking it. They were to be civilized through schooling and the acquisition of another language. This policy of linguistic assimilation, which was part of the machinery of political subjugation, not only deprived the indigenous minorities of the right to speak their mother tongue, but also made it impossible for the indigenous languages to develop into languages that could fully function in all domains. In some cases, it almost led to the demise of the language(s). The indigenous Indians in the United States, the Welsh in the United Kingdom, and the Māori in New Zealand all have undergone the same experience.

The historical background outlined in the chapters in this volume provides a sound basis for appreciating the difficulties faced by post-colonial countries and linguistic minorities in using the mother tongue as the medium of instruction. The lack of opportunity for indigenous languages to develop into languages that could function in all domains has made it necessary for these languages to be standardized and codified before they could be used in domains such as education, law, and government. It has also led to a paucity of teaching materials in the indigenous languages and the lack of a literacy environment for speakers of these languages. The long-standing low status that indigenous languages were accorded, the negative experience with which they were associated, and the prestige that the former colonial languages enjoyed, have together resulted in a lack of confidence in the indigenous languages as adequate working languages, and languages that are suitable for schooling. In many cases, these difficulties have been used as excuses by policy makers for their noncommittal stance toward mother-tongue education. For example, in India and sub-Saharan Africa, the need for codification and standardization of the indigenous languages has been used as the justification for not committing to a definite time frame for implementing mother-tongue education.

LINGUA FRANCA AND LINGUISTIC IMPERIALISM

Another recurrent theme in this volume is that the choice of official languages and the choice of medium of instruction are shaped by political, social and economic forces. In multi-ethnic and multilingual states, decisions regarding which languages should be established as official languages, and which as the medium of instruction, are political decisions that, if ill-managed, can lead to war and bloodshed. Ironically, in many cases the colonial language was chosen as one of the official languages and has often effectively functioned as the dominant working language and the lingua franca. The colonial language is also the dominant or preferred medium of instruction on the grounds that it is ethnically neutral and therefore, theoretically, also politically neutral. Although most post-colonial countries also established ethnic and indigenous languages as the official languages, these languages are often more symbolic than substantive (Fishman & Fishman, 2000). In India, although there are a dozen regional languages that are official languages at the state level in addition to English and Hindi, English continues to play a prominent role. It is used in all three forms of mass media—newspapers, radio, and television—and is the only language taught in all states and in the largest number of schools. In Singapore, English was not only recognized as one of the official languages, it was also selected as the official working language of the country. In Hong Kong and the Philippines, English was retained as an official language alongside the national languages, Chinese and Filipino respectively, and is clearly the preferred medium of instruction. Similarly in sub-Saharan Africa, the colonial languages (English, French, Spanish, and Portuguese) continued to be the official languages after independence, and are used as media of instruction although they are spoken by a very small percentage of the population in these countries. In post-apartheid South Africa, although 11 languages were declared official languages, English is the preferred language of the media and education, and is used almost exclusively as the official language.

The adoption of a colonial language as the lingua franca may be seen as an ethnically neutral move, but it is by no means a politically neutral move. The term *lingua franca*, as Phillipson (2000b) points out, is deceptive: It hides the inequality that is inherent in a system that is supposed to serve both the native and nonnative speakers of the language equally well, but clearly serves some better than others. The asymmetrical power relationship among the official languages in these countries perpetuates social, economic, and political inequality, and favors speakers of the colonial languages, at national, sub-national, and supranational levels. As Phillipson (1992) points out, this kind of linguistic domination, which he terms *linguistic imperialism*, is analogous to economic and military imperialism, except that it is even more pervasive and penetrating because the domination is not just economical but also cultural and ideological. Linguistic imperialism, as Rasool (2000) observes, "continues to circumscribe cultural, economic and political possibilities in the developing world" (p. 60).

LINGUISTIC DIVERSITY: THE RHETORIC AND THE REALITY

The gap between the rhetoric of medium-of-instruction policy and the reality of its implementation is the third recurrent theme. The discourse surrounding language policies is full of phrases such as "respect for linguistic diversity," "rights to mother-tongue education," "promotion of multilingualism," and so forth. As Skutnabb-Kangas (2002) points out, in the policy documents of transnational organizations such as UNESCO, United Nations, the World Bank and the Council of Europe, there is impressive rhetoric about the importance of maintaining all the world's languages because they are part of the heritage of humanity. For example, in late 2001, UNESCO adopted the Universal Declaration on Cultural Diversity, which calls for action against the homogenization resulting from the disappearance of languages. However, behind the beautiful rhetoric there is little commitment to linguistic human rights in education (Skutnabb-Kangas & Phillipson, 1994), particularly the right to mother-tongue education (see also Mazrui, 1997). Articles relating to mother-tongue education are usually vague in their formulation, and contain many more qualified statements than other articles. The 1992 UN Declaration on the Rights of Persons Belonging to National or Ethnic, Religious, and Linguistic Minorities, for example, contains this clause:

> 4.3. States should take *appropriate* measures so that, *wherever possible*, persons belonging to minorities have *adequate opportunities* to learn their mother tongue or to have instruction in their mother tongue. (cited in Skutnabb-Kangas, 2002, emphases added)

Qualifications such as "appropriate," "wherever possible" and "adequate opportunities" allow the state to adopt a minimalist approach to mother-tongue education but still be able to meet the requirements of the policies, which, as Skutnabb-Kangas observes, puts the minorities at the mercy of the state. Similar features can be found in the Council of Europe Framework Convention for the Protection of National Minorities and the European Charter for Regional or Minority Languages, both in force since 1998. It is therefore not surprising that there is no sign of linguistic homogenization abating.

Similarly, in the countries covered in this volume, the declared language policies claim to promote linguistic and cultural plurality, and to provide opportunities for mother-tongue education. However, the lack of commitment on the part of the policy makers is often seen in policy documents that contain exit clauses and qualified statements, the lack of a definite time frame for implementation, the lack of follow-up measures and clear guidance, and a reluctance to provide adequate resources for implementation. This noncommittal stance is motivated by the political agenda of avoiding ethnic conflicts, the economic agenda of exploiting the market of post-colonial countries, and the sociopolitical agenda of protecting the interests of the elite.

GLOBALIZATION, ASSIMILATION, AND ETHNOCULTURAL IDENTITY

The impact of globalization on medium-of-instruction policies is a recurrent concern voiced in this volume. The dominant role of English-speaking countries, particularly the United States, in international economy and politics, and the use of English as the lingua franca on the Internet, have aggravated the pull toward English as a much sought-after commodity, at national, subnational and supranational levels (Phillipson & Skutnabb-Kangas, 1999). In Europe, the move toward integration has made the learning of the major European languages a necessary condition for survival for many of the smaller European countries. The effect of globalization that lead to linguistic and cultural assimilation is particularly evident in smaller states, whose national languages are not among the major languages, and in developing countries, which are keen to remain competitive and play an active role in the international economy.

By equipping the nation with the language(s) of modernization and technological advancement, developing countries are better able to keep abreast of developments in developed countries, and smaller states are able to integrate better with bigger states. But this nevertheless raises the question: What effect does this kind of assimilation have on national and ethnocultural identity? In cases where English is appropriated as the language of the nation, the tension between retaining the culture and values associated with the mother tongue and the adoption of a national identity symbolized by a foreign language is not easy to reconcile. Although globalization can bring about more collaboration amongst countries, it also brings about assimilation of the powerless toward the powerful. The effects of assimilation can be very harmful; it not only exacerbates the existing inequality in power, it may produce nationals who are ambivalent about their own identity, and nations that are stripped of their rich cultural heritage.

SUMMARY OF CHAPTERS

As mentioned earlier, this volume is organized according to the sociopolitical contexts in which medium-of-instruction policies are formulated and implemented. Part I addresses issues confronted by minority linguistic groups in English-dominant countries. The English-dominant countries discussed in this section all had the historical experience of having the languages of the indigenous minorities treated as obstacles to civilization and modernization. The indigenous people were to be civilized through schooling. To this end, they were forced to abandon their own tongue and acquire another, and to assimilate European culture and habits.

Stephen May outlines the history of colonization of the Pākehā (i.e., New Zealanders of European origin) over the indigenous Māori in New Zealand, and provides a detailed account of the efforts made by the Māori to redress the disadvantages that they suffered as a consequence of colonization, and to halt the impending demise of the Māori language (which resulted from the assimilationist policy adopted by the Pākehā). Medium of instruction has been one of the key areas in which the redress is realized. The Māori worked outside the state education system and started an independent movement to establish Māori-medium preschools in the early 1980s, with the aim of reviving traditional Māori knowledge and cultural practices. The success of this movement led to the rapid emergence of Māori-medium education at other levels of education in order to maintain the language acquired in preschool. In 1987, the Māori Language Act was passed and Māori was recognized as an official language of New Zealand. The Māori-medium education policy was motivated by the conviction that total immersion in Māori is the best way to achieve language reversal, to counter the dominance of English that is prevalent in all domains, and to ensure the transmission of cultural practices and behavior. The success of the Māori Language Act led to the Māori demanding significant structural reforms in the state education system, as well as greater autonomy for their people. In 1990, Māori-medium education was recognized as part of the state education system. May observes that Māori-medium education, and the transmission of Māori culture and philosophy through schooling, should not be seen as separatist, but rather as making available to the Māori the same opportunities—social, economic, and political—that have always been available to the Pākehā.

Dylan Jones and Marilyn Martin-Jones examine the development of Welsh-medium education and bilingual education in Wales, where English is the dominant language. They trace the historical context of the educational provision through Welsh and the sociopolitical processes involved. In the late 19th and early 20th century, the Welsh language was considered an obstacle to progress in Wales, and there were moves to eradicate it from the educational system. English-medium education was introduced as a form of intervention to help Wales move forward. Two major efforts were made to resist Anglicization and to maintain the Welsh language: They are to make Welsh the only official language of Wales, and to use it as medium of instruction at all levels of education. Both of these policy changes then led to the formulation of the broader political agenda of self-government for Wales. Welsh-medium education proved successful and attracted students not only from Welsh speaking families, but also from English speaking families. The remarkably successful revitalization of the Welsh language in an English dominant environment was partly due to the good reputation that Welsh-medium schools had established. It was also due to the increased use of Welsh in public institutions in the 1950s and 1960s, which opened up employment opportunities for Welsh speakers. Strong institutional support from local education authorities, the school inspectorate, teacher training institutions, and key educational bodies also played a very important role. The specification in the National Curriculum of Welsh as a Core subject in all Welsh-medium schools and a Foundation subject in all other schools, along with the use of Welsh in public examinations, were important indicators of the currency of Welsh. The passing of the Welsh Language Act in the 1990s ensured that Welsh was recognized as having the same status as English. Jones and Martin-Jones raise two major issues, however, that have yet to be addressed. First, the revitalization of the Welsh language has been achieved mainly through Welsh-medium education at preschool and elementary levels. At secondary level, there has been more demand for English-medium education by native Welsh students, as English is the medium of higher education. This leads to increasing Anglicization, which seems to be inevitable. Second, as Welsh-medium schools have to teach both native and nonnative Welsh students through Welsh, teachers often resort to code switching and code mixing to help students understand the content. Jones and Martin-Jones present an interesting analysis of the patterns of code switching in a mathematics classroom, and highlight the need to conduct classroom-level research to gain a deeper understanding of policy issues.

Although both New Zealand and Wales seem to be moving forward in promoting linguistic diversity, the United States has apparently been moving in the direction of homogenization since the 1980s. Teresa McCarty provides a critical analysis of the history of medium-of-instruction policy in the United States—one of the most linguistically and culturally diverse countries in the world—that serves as a context for making sense of the apparent contradictions in U.S. medium-of-instruction policies. She observes that these contradictions were responses to the political and socioeconomic forces at different times in the history: When linguistic diversity was nonthreatening or even necessary, it was tolerated and even supported—as in the early days of U.S. history, when indigenous languages were instruments for religious conversion and land usurpation, as well as for "civilizing" the children of native Americans, and when the co-existence of multiple European languages helped to spread the ideals of the new government. However, when linguistic diversity was perceived as dangerous—as when Germans were seen as a threat to the country in World War I and the Indians were seen as dangerously uncivilized—it was banned and instruction in languages other than English was prohibited. Likewise, the move toward linguistic homogenization was very much driven by the imagined threat that supposedly came from the shift in the racial and ethnic background of immigrants, from people mostly of European descent, to people of Latin America, Caribbean, and Southeast Asian origin. Evidence of linguistic homogenization is the adoption of English as the official language by a number of states, and the replacement of bilingual education with English-only education (see also, Skutnabb-Kangas, 2002). McCarty points out that such linguistic homogenization reinforces the existing power structure, and further disadvantages non-English speaking children who have been constructed as deficient and underachieving.

The history of the medium-of-instruction policies in New Zealand, Wales, and the United States show that medium-of-instruction policies are never politically neutral. On the one hand, they are reflections of power structures, yet on the other hand they are also agents for changing the power structure. They can be instruments of cultural and linguistic imperialism, but they can also be means for promoting linguistic diversity and cultural pluralism.

Part II of this volume consists of analyses of former colonial states that share the common problem of having to deal with a particular colonial legacy: the prestigious colonial language and its function after independence.

Amy Tsui examines the drastic change in the medium-of-instruction policy in Hong Kong on the eve of the change of sovereignty, and the strong educational agenda that was put forward by the British government to justify mandatory mother-tongue education. In order to make sense of the policy change, Tsui provides a critical analysis of the historical and sociopolitical contexts in which mother-tongue education was mandated. She unravels the various agendas that shaped the medium-of-instruction policy during the colonial period, and points out that the formulation and implementation of the policy were always motivated by a hidden political agenda, despite the fact that it was the economic and the educational agendas that were presented to the people. The prestige of the English language, the power, wealth, and status that have long been associated with it, and the dominant role of English in globalization led to the ironic situation whereby the people of Hong Kong protested vehemently against being educated in their own tongue, and demanded education in the former colonial tongue, even after Hong Kong had gained political independence. Tsui discusses the relationship between the resistance to mother-tongue education and the national identity, or the lack of it, of the Hong Kong people, and argues that the colonial rule seriously undermined the national identity of the Hong Kong people and led to their ambivalent attitude toward their cultural roots and values. Tsui observes that although English-medium education may allow Hong Kong people to achieve a high level of proficiency in English, and hence maintain their competitive edge in international trade and business, it may also sustain a population that is devoid of cultural heritage.

The impact of the predominance of a foreign language on identity, cultural heritage, and cultural values is perhaps even more pronounced when it is actually adopted as a first language, as in the case of Singapore. Anne Pakir gives an account of the successful language planning that the Singapore government systematically and single-mindedly undertook and carried out in order to produce an "English-knowing" bilingual nation. English is learned as the first school language and is the main medium of instruction, whereas one of the official ethnic languages (Tamil, Mandarin, or Malay) is learned as a second language. Despite efforts by the government to ensure that each child learns his or her own ethnic language as a second language, the high economic value of English has led to a language shift whereby English is the predominant language both at home and in the community, especially among the younger generation. The growing economic value of Mandarin since the 1980s, due to China's open door policy in international trade, has motivated the government to selectively educate the brightest students to be equally proficient in English and Chinese as first languages, thereby producing a new English–Chinese knowing bilingual elite. Pakir raises a number of important issues that have arisen from the careful linguistic engineering of the Singapore government, and that have yet to be addressed: the impact of the medium-of-instruction policy on the identity of the Singaporeans and their cultural heritage; the mainte- nance of ethnic languages and the transmission of the cultural values and identities; and the social inequality between the English–Chinese bilingual elite and other bilinguals. She outlines the tension between the expression of a Singaporean identity through English and the expression of an ethnic identity through the corresponding ethnic language; the tension between those referred to in Singapore as the "cosmopolitans" (the embodiment of modern values and principles that has moved the country forward), and the so-called "heartlanders" (the embodiment of traditional values and be- haviors); the tension between achieving high standards of English and maintaining linguistic plurality; and the tension between meeting the eco- nomic needs of the country and social equality.

Among the post-colonial states, Malaysia went through the most radi- cal and thorough change in medium-of-instruction policy. Saran Kaur Gill provides an account of the efforts made by the Malaysian Government af- ter independence to establish national identity and achieve unity through its language policy. Unlike Singapore, where an ethnically neutral lan- guage was adopted as the lingua franca and as an official language, Ma- laysia established Bahasa Malaysia as the official language and the sole medium of instruction for nation building. At the time of Malaysian inde- pendence, having a language of one's own was compared to having a soul and a life. Conscious efforts were made by the government to gradually introduce the use of Bahasa Malaysia as the medium of instruction at all levels of education over a period of 26 years. Unlike in Singapore, India, and Hong Kong, English retained its official language status in Malaysia for only 10 years after independence. After that, it was relegated to a sec- ond language, and from a medium of instruction to a school subject that students did not have to pass. Gill points out that the replacement of Eng- lish by Bahasa Malaysia as the official language and the main medium of instruction succeeded in raising the status of Bahasa Malaysia, and helped the nation to build its national identity. However, this policy poses the challenge of how the Malaysian people can access the most up-to-date knowledge in science and technology, mostly available only in English, in order to realize Malaysia's aspiration to become a developed nation and to play an active role in the international arena. Focusing on higher educa- tion institutions in Malaysia, Gill describes the efforts made by the gov- ernment to meet this challenge by reinstating English as the medium of instruction in higher education, especially in the fields of engineering, sci- ence, and medicine. The change of policy was justified on the same politi- cal grounds as the original policy (i.e., that it is in the best interest of the nation). Strong objections from patriotic Malay intellectuals resulted in a bifurcation in higher education, whereby public institutions of higher education retained mother-tongue medium of instruction, and private institutions of higher education were given the freedom to use English as a medium of instruction. This bifurcation is a compromise that the Malaysian government made in order to balance the economic interests of the nation and the nationalistic sentiments of the intellectuals. Gill outlines the serious social and political consequences of this bifurcation: the creation of a social divide between middle-class children, who can afford private education, and working class children, who can only afford public education; and an ethnic divide between Chinese students, most of whom can afford private education, and the Malay students, most of whom can only afford public higher education. These social and ethnic divides lead to the creation of an elite consisting of graduates of private institutions who have a linguistic advantage over the graduates of public institutions. Drawing on experiences from other countries, Gill makes a case for maintaining a healthy tension between nationalism and internationalization.

In a similar way to Malaysia and Hong Kong, the Indian government also saw the medium of education as an important vehicle for nation building. There was a consensus after independence that English would be replaced by Indian languages in education (as the medium of instruction), as well as in law and administration. However, E. Annamalai points out that there was, in fact, a lack of commitment by the government to change the medium of instruction from English to Indian languages, as evidenced by the lack of a definite time frame for implementation, the inclusion of exit clauses in the policy statements (e.g., "as early as practicable"), and the use of technical justifications, such as the need to codify and standardize the Indian languages before they could be used for learning. The underlying agenda was to avoid conflict between groups with different political interests: between the elite bureaucrats and professionals who wanted to retain English as the language of prestige, and the emerging elite who wanted to empower their own regional languages; as well as between speakers of the regional languages who would benefit from the use of their own languages as media of instruction, and speakers of minority languages who saw English-medium education as a means of resistance against domination by speakers of regional languages. Annamalai points out that the ambivalent attitude of the government opened the door to alternative media of instruction. This perpetuated and intensified social inequality between the middle-class elite, who can benefit from English-medium education, and the masses, who cannot. Annamalai calls for the effective teaching of English as a subject, rather than using it as a medium of instruction. He further proposes that the provision of universal education through the medium of Indian languages should be the top priority of India, where there is a still a very high illiteracy rate.

Whereas Hong Kong, Singapore, Malaysia, and India had all been subject to British rule, sub-Saharan African countries had been under the colonial rule of several European countries, and English, French, Spanish, and Portuguese were the former colonial languages spoken. Hassana Alidou outlines the history of colonization in these countries, and the subjugation of the African people through the imposition of the colonial languages as the dominant or exclusive medium of instruction and through coercive measures used to alienate the children from their mother tongue. Similar to most former colonies, political independence in sub-Saharan Africa has not been accompanied by economic and educational independence. In order to avoid interethnic conflict after independence, the former colonial languages were adopted as media of instruction instead of the national languages, although the colonial languages were only spoken by a small percentage of the population. However, the gap between home language and school language caused serious difficulties in learning and led to ineffective communication in the classroom, low academic achievement, and a high drop-out rate, particularly at primary level. Yet governments in these countries are reluctant to change their policies, and bilingual education, in which the national (or indigenous) languages are used as media of instruction, remains experimental in a small number of schools. One of the major reasons for this is that the sponsors of World Bank projects—who are also former colonizers—are unwilling to fund projects that do not advance their own economic and political interests. Alidou points out that for countries in Africa, where resources are often scarce, the medium-of-instruction policy is further clouded by the continued hegemony of former colonial powers exercised through financial sponsorship.

Illuminado Nical, Jerzy Smolicz, and Margaret Secombe examine the language situation in another post-colonial state, the Philippines, and the apparent quiescence of the Filipino minorities to the imposition of English and Filipino as the national and official languages. They point out that an interpretation of the Filipino minorities' readiness to accept the diglossic situation—which seems to be an exception to the rising resistance against linguistic assimilation by indigenous minorities worldwide—must be situated in the sociopolitical and historical contexts of colonization. The adoption of Filipino/Tagalog as the national language was a political compromise. It was a means to resolve intense ethnic conflicts that could otherwise have led to the adoption of English as the national language because it was considered ethnically neutral. The acceptance of English as one of the official languages was partly an historical consequence of American occupation during which time English was taught and used to the exclusion of all other languages, including the indigenous languages, and partly to avoid domination by the Tagalog speakers. Despite this, the adoption of the Bilingual English Program, which was supposed to resolve the conflict between advocates of English and Filipino, disadvantaged children of non-Tagalog minorities because they were unable to acquire literacy through their mother tongue. Extending an earlier study of high school students from non-Tagalog speaking middle-class families in provincial urban areas, Nical, Smolicz, and Secombe investigated responses from high school students, teachers and parents from two linguistic communities in rural districts of the island of Leyte (Cebuano and Warray) on language attitudes, language use, and language proficiency. Their findings confirmed the findings of their previous study, that behind the (somewhat deceptive) peaceful acceptance of the imposition of one indigenous language over another, there is an underlying tension between Filipino and Cebuano. Nical, Smolicz, and Secombe caution that the tension generated by the assimilationist policy in the Philippines could develop into a more serious ethnic conflict over linguistic equity if multilingualism is not fostered in the school system.

Part III of this volume consists of three chapters that examine the conflicts generated by the asymmetrical power relationship between languages, and the ways in which these conflicts were resolved, or are being resolved.

Vic Webb provides an account of the language situation in post-apartheid South Africa and highlights the social consequence of the continued prestige enjoyed by English. Similar to most multilingual states, post-apartheid South Africa was faced with the challenge of selecting its official languages. To balance the opposing interests of political parties, 11 languages were declared official languages, including two official languages of the apartheid era (English and Afrikaans) and nine major Bantu languages. Webb points out that although the Constitution stipulates that these 11 official languages are of equal status and esteem, and that all citizens have the right to receive education in an official language, or languages, of individual choice, English is used almost exclusively as the official public language and there is little evidence that the stipulated multilingual policy will actually be implemented. The prestigious status of English is most evident in the medium of instruction in schools. Webb presents survey data—comparing the medium of instruction chosen by schools and the home language—that show that English is the home language for only 9% of the population, but that it is the medium of instruction for 80%.

Webb observes that the qualified statements and escape clauses in the language stipulations in the Constitution, as well as the lack of follow-up measures and clear guidance, show a lack of serious commitment to the declared multilingual policy. Webb alerts policy makers to the dire social consequences that will arise if the current situation persists. First, the harmful effects of using a foreign language for learning are not just limited to academic achievement and cognitive growth, but relate to emotional security, sense of self-worthiness, and ability to participate meaningfully in the educational process. Second, the diglossic situation in which English is the prestigious language used for high functions and the language of the Black middle class suggests that the former raced-based inequality in the apartheid era has been replaced by a class-based and even language-based inequality. Webb cautions that this approach could render the stipulations in the Constitution ineffective, and that what is needed is a clearer directive on how the policies should be implemented.

Kendall King and Carol Benson examine the language in education policies in two Andean countries, Ecuador and Bolivia, both of which are still suffering from the strong influence of the Spanish colonial past that discriminated against indigenous languages. Since the 1980s, there has been a move toward greater recognition of the value of indigenous languages and cultures in both countries, as evidenced by the implementation of bilingual intercultural education (BIE). King and Benson provide an account of the shift toward multilingualism and multiculturalism, and explore the gap between policy and practice and the underlying ideological tension and constraints that have contributed to the continued predominance of Spanish-medium education.

In Ecuador and Bolivia, the indigenous people—having been marginalized socially, economically, and politically for a long time under the Spanish colonial rule—have begun to take a more prominent role in the public arena, and to fight for the recognition of their identity, language, and culture. In Ecuador, this has led to legislation incorporating BIE in the school curriculum, and the use of the indigenous language as the medium of instruction. In Bolivia, the recognition of all indigenous languages was legislated, and more recently also intercultural education. King and Benson point out that in both countries there is a gap between policy and implementation, despite the fact that in the Andean countries, policy reforms regarding language in education are part of the broader spectrum of political reforms in which cultural and linguistic pluralism are very much core. They identify a number of causes for this discrepancy, such as human resources and materials constraints, standardization of indigenous languages, different interpretations of bilingualism and interculturalism, and the tension between devolution of power and centralization. Such discrepancies, King and Benson argue, are not indicative of the lack of commitment to equalizing educational opportunities and power relationships. Rather, they are caused by a number of constraints that these two countries have yet to overcome, and by underlying ideological tensions. They are also caused by deep-seated doubts about the adequacy of the indigenous languages as tools for learning and about the maintenance of the indigenous languages through schooling. Such doubts are harbored not only by the Spanish-speaking elite but also by speakers of indigenous languages, and are deeply rooted in the long-standing low status of the indigenous languages, the negative experiences associated with the languages in colonial days, and the prestige that Spanish has always enjoyed as the language of power, status, and wealth. King and Benson point out that despite the problems outlined, important progress has already been made in achieving linguistic equality.

James Tollefson outlines two competing forces that have shaped the language policies of the new states emerging from the disintegration of the Soviet Union and the collapse of the East European communist bloc: the force of ethnolinguistic nationalism on the one hand and the force of globalization on the other. Tollefson explores the tension between these forces in Slovenia, by examining how the effort to protect ethnolinguistic and national identity by the Slovenes in united Yugoslavia led to the political independence of Slovenia, and how after independence, Slovenia had to make adjustments to its medium-of-instruction policies (designed to protect the Slovene language) in order to integrate with the rest of Europe and secure economic survival. Tollefson's account of the struggle between the Serbs and the Slovenes illustrates how medium-of-instruction policy is an arena for power struggle, and how linguistic conflicts have been maximized or minimized to achieve political aims. On the one hand, the imposition of Serbian as the only medium of instruction for all ethnolinguistic groups in Serbia (which intensified the linguistic conflict) was an attempt by the Serbs to advance their own interests under the call for national unity through linguistic uniformity. On the other hand, the Slovenes, by protecting linguistic diversity through a pluralist approach to medium of instruction, paved the way for Slovenia to break away from the domination of the Serbs in Yugoslavia, and gain political independence in order to preserve its own ethnolinguistic identity.

Tollefson further discusses the tension faced by postindependent Slovenia between protecting its national identity and the Slovene language, and the need to acquire other major European languages in order to integrate fully with the rest of Europe. Measures have been taken by the government to ensure that the Slovene language remains the medium of instruction, while at the same time making the learning of foreign languages compulsory. Despite these measures, Tollefson points out that the Slovene language is still under the threat of major European languages because of its limited economic value, which may eventually also affect its use in education. The tension that Slovenia has yet to resolve is common to that faced by countries whose national languages are not among the dominant languages in the wider international context.

In the concluding chapter of this volume, James Tollefson and Amy Tsui summarize the key issues addressed in all the chapters. In particular, they examine the role of medium-of-instruction policies in mediating the tension between the centralizing forces of globalization and state-mandated policies and demands for language rights by ethnic and linguistic minorities.

CONCLUSION

By situating the medium-of-instruction policies of a number of countries in their specific historical and sociopolitical contexts, the discussions in this volume amply illustrate the central role that these policies have played in sociopolitical and economic processes. Choices made in medium of instruction are not purely about educational efficacy but also about social, political, and economic participation, social equality, and human rights. They determine who has access to resources, power, and control, and who does not. They are vehicles for political subjugation of minority groups by dominant groups and the masses by the elites, both at the intranational and the international levels. Decisions on the medium of education also raise important ethical issues. In countries where resources are scarce, the rate of illiteracy is high, and basic education is available to only a small percentage of the population, investment in the use of a foreign language as the medium of instruction is ethically untenable. For example, in sub-Saharan African countries outlined by Alidou, people are deprived of important health information such as how to prevent malaria and HIV/AIDS, because the information is mostly available only in the official languages, which the majority of the population cannot read. The use of a foreign language as the medium of instruction for children who are still struggling with basic expression in that language hampers not only their academic achievement and cognitive growth, but also their self-perception, self-esteem, emotional security, and their ability to participate meaningfully in the educational process. The use in education of a foreign language that alienates children from their own cultural heritage can produce a generation of young people who are devoid of cultural values and the traditions that are constitutive of identity.

With globalization, the world is moving toward greater homogenization linguistically, economically, and culturally. Yet, it is precisely the same force of globalization that has generated resistance against assimilation from minorities groups, and has led to greater tolerance of and respect for cultural and linguistic plurality. Multiculturalism and linguistic diversity, however, should not be just an ideology for containing ethnic conflicts. They should lead to the redistribution of power and provide equal opportunities for ethnic and social groups to participate politically, socially, and economically.

Governments that are seriously committed to the policies of multilingualism and multiculturalism must ensure that conditions for implementation are satisfied. This includes legitimation of policies, adequate provision of resources, and strong institutional support. If these provisions are not forthcoming, multiculturalism and linguistic pluralism will remain rhetorical rather than becoming a reality.

REFERENCES

Fairclough, N. (1989). *Language and power.* London: Longman.

Fishman, J. A., & Fishman, S. G. (2000). Rethinking language defense. In R. Phillipson (Ed.), *Rights to language: Equity, power and education* (pp. 23–27). Mahwah, NJ: Lawrence Erlbaum Associates.

Mazrui, A. (1997). The World Bank, the language question and the future of African education. *Race and Class, 38*(3), 35–48.

Paulston, C. B. (1980). *Bilingual education—Theories and issues.* Rowley, MA: Newbury House.

Pennycook, A. (1998). *English and the discourses of colonialism.* London: Routledge.

Pennycook, A. (2002). Language Policy and Docile Bodies: Hong Kong and Governmentality. In J. Tollefson (Ed.), *Language policies in education* (91–110). Mahwah, NJ: Lawrence Erlbaum Associates.

Phillipson, R. (1992). *Linguistic imperialism.* Oxford, UK: Oxford University Press.

Phillipson, R. (Ed.). (2000a). *Rights to language: Equity, power and education.* Mahwah, NJ: Lawrence Erlbaum Associates.

Phillipson, R. (2000b). Integrative comment: Living with vision and commitment. In R. Phillipson (Ed.), *Rights to language: Equity, power and education* (pp. 264–278). Mahwah, NJ: Lawrence Erlbaum Associates.

Phillipson, R., & Skutnabb-Kangas, T. (1999). Englishisation: One dimension of globalisation. In D. Graddol & U. H. Meinhof (Eds.), *English in a changing world* (pp. 19–36). *AILA Review, 13.* Oxford, UK: The English Book Centre.

Rasool, N. (2000). Language maintenance as an arena of cultural and political struggles in a changing world. In R. Phillipson (Ed.), *Rights to language: Equity, power and education* (pp. 57–61). Mahwah, NJ: Lawrence Erlbaum Associates.

Skutnabb-Kangas, T. (2000). *Linguistic genocide in education—or worldwide diversity and human rights?* Mahwah, NJ: Lawrence Erlbaum Associates.

Skutnabb-Kangas, T. (2002, April 16–20). *Language policies and education: The role of education in destroying or supporting the world's linguistic diversity.* Keynote Address at the World Congress on Language Policies, organized by the Linguapax Institute in co-operation with the Government of Catalonia, Barcelona, Catalonia, Spain. Retrieved September, 2002, from http://www.linguapax.org/congres/plenaries/skutnabb.html

Skutnabb-Kangas, T., & Phillipson, R. (1994). *Linguistic human rights: Overcoming linguistic discrimination.* Berlin, Germany, New York: Mouton de Gruyter.

Tollefson, J. (Ed.). (1995). *Power and inequality in language education.* New York: Cambridge University Press.

Tollefson, J. (Ed.). (2002). *Language policies in education: Critical issues.* Mahwah, NJ: Lawrence Erlbaum Associates.

I

Minority Languages
in English-Dominant States

2

Māori-Medium Education in Aotearoa/New Zealand

Stephen May
University of Waikato

This chapter examines recent developments in Māori-medium education in Aotearoa/New Zealand.[1] In order to focus meaningfully on these developments, we must first situate them critically within the wider historical, social, and political background from which they emerged. This is necessary for two reasons—one related to the particular national context to be discussed, the other to the particular academic discipline in which that discussion takes place.

In relation to the national context under discussion, it becomes apparent that the development of Māori-medium language education is itself both a product and an illustration of a wider repositioning of identity and minority rights issues within this once "British settler society"—particularly, between the indigenous Māori and their European colonizers (see Fleras & Spoonley, 1999; Larner & Spoonley, 1995; Pearson, 1990, 2000). Thus, a critical historical account is vital to understanding the wider social, cultural, and political processes at work here.

In relation to the disciplinary context, it is crucial, in my view, to provide a critical account of the historical/diachronic dimensions of language education policy and practice, because such an approach is central to understanding how particular language ideologies, and the policies and practices that result from them, are created, legitimated and, as is the case here, contested and reformulated (Blommaert, 1999; May, 2001; Woolard,

21

1998). In so doing, one is able "to add to the history of language and languages a dimension of human agency, political intervention, power and authority, and so make that history a bit more *political*" (Blommaert, 1999, p. 5; emphasis in original). My concern with addressing directly these broader social and political issues underlies, prefaces, and shapes the subsequent discussion of Māori-medium education in this chapter.

RETHINKING THE HISTORY OF COLONIALISM

When one significant section of the community burns with a sense of injustice, the rest of the community cannot safely pretend that there is no reason for their discontent. (Waitangi Tribunal, 1986, p. 46)

Until the 1960s, Aotearoa/New Zealand had regarded itself, and been regarded by others, as a model of harmonious "race" relations, a rare success story of colonization. Pākehā (European)[2] New Zealanders, in particular, looked back with pride at a colonial history of mutual respect, cooperation, and integration with the indigenous Māori iwi (tribes). This colonial history began with Pākehā settlement of Aotearoa/New Zealand in the late 18th century, following the voyages of Captain James Cook, although prior to the arrival of the first Pākehā, Māori had been resident in Aotearoa/New Zealand for approximately 1000 years (Walker, 1990). Colonial relations between Māori and Pākehā were subsequently formalized by the British Crown in the 19th century and were interrupted by only brief periods of antagonism, notably the Land Wars in the 1860s. The foundational colonial document, Te Tiriti o Waitangi (the Treaty of Waitangi)—signed on February 6th, 1840, between the British Crown and Māori chiefs—was a surprisingly progressive document for its time. The Treaty specifically attempted to establish the rights and responsibilities of both parties as a mutual framework by which colonization could proceed. Captain Hobson, the Crown's representative, was instructed to obtain the surrender of Aotearoa/New Zealand as a sovereign state to the British crown, but only by "free and intelligent consent" of the "natives." In return, Māori iwi were to be guaranteed possession of "their lands, their homes and all their treasured possessions (taonga)." Consequently, the Treaty came to be commemorated as the central symbol of this apparently benign history. The words "he iwi tahi tātou" ("we are all one people"), spoken by William Hobson at the Treaty's signing, provided its leitmotif. In short, although a White settler colony in origin, the emergence of Aotearoa/New Zealand as a nation-state was seen to have avoided the worst excesses of colonialism. Māori were highly regarded, intermixing and miscegenation were common, and Māori language and culture were incorporated, at least to some degree, into Aotearoa/New Zealand life. Or so the story went.

From the 1970s, a quite different story emerged into the public domain. A generation of young, urban, and educated Māori articulated a history of continued conflict and oppression of Māori by the Pākehā (Sharp, 1990). This theme was to be taken up in subsequent revisionist histories of the country (see Belich, 1986, 1996, 2001; Kawharu, 1989; Orange, 1987; Sinclair, 1993; Walker, 1990). It is beyond the scope of this chapter to detail this newly acknowledged history in any depth, except to say that it soon became clear that the Treaty of Waitangi, for all its potential symbolic significance, was quickly and ruthlessly trivialized and marginalized by Pākehā settlers in their quest for land. Indeed, this quest resulted in almost all Māori-owned land being in Pākehā hands by the end of the 19th century, mostly via illegitimate means. Not surprisingly perhaps, what resulted for Māori were the usual deleterious effects of colonization on an indigenous people: political disenfranchisement, misappropriation of land, population and health decline, educational disadvantage, and socioeconomic marginalization (Stannard, 1989; Walker, 1990).

The cumulative weight of this historical process, allied with the rapid urbanization of Māori since the Second World War,[3] has resulted in ongoing comparative disadvantage for Māori, up to and including the present day. The comparative disadvantages that still face Māori today can be illustrated by, among many other social indices (see May, 2001), their current educational status. Although increasing numbers of Māori have been completing school and pursuing tertiary education, particularly since the 1990s (Chapple, Jeffries, & Walker, 1997), 60% of Māori aged more than 15 years still held no formal educational qualifications in 1991. This compared with 40% for non-Māori. At the same time, Māori were nearly half as likely as the total population to hold a tertiary qualification. This low level of educational attainment is also a key factor in the current disproportionate location of Māori in the lowest levels of the labour market (Davies & Nicholl, 1993).

REDRESSING THE HISTORY OF COLONIALISM

> [T]he education system in New Zealand is operating unsuccessfully because too many Māori children are not reaching an acceptable level of education.... Their language is not protected and their scholastic achievements fall short of what they should be. The promises in the Treaty of Waitangi of equality of education as in all other human rights are undeniable. Judged by the system's own standards Māori children are not being successfully taught, and for this reason alone, quite apart from the duty to protect the Māori language, the education system is being operated in breach of the Treaty. (Waitangi Tribunal, 1986, p. 51)

The recognition of the deleterious effects of colonialism on Māori as a central explanatory variable in their current and ongoing comparative disadvantage in contemporary Aotearoa/New Zealand remains an uncomfortable and contested one for many (Pearson, 2000). Nonetheless, it has resulted in a significant realignment of Māori–Pākehā relations in recent times, not least through the activism of Māori themselves. This has centred on developments in the 1980s that resulted in the reinvestment of the long-ignored Treaty of Waitangi with both moral and political force, principally via the introduction of the notions of biculturalism and partnership into formal public discourse, decision-making, and law (Bishop & Glynn, 1999; M. Durie, 1998; Fleras & Spoonley, 1999; Wilson & Yeatman, 1995). One clear example of this change in direction can be seen in the areas of Māori language policy and, specifically, Māori-medium education.

In 1985/1986, for example, a legal decision concerning the recognition and role of Māori as a language of the state concluded that the Māori language could be regarded as a "taonga" (treasured possession) and therefore had a *guaranteed* right to protection under the terms of the Treaty (Waitangi Tribunal, 1986). In the ruling, the term *guarantee* was defined as "more than merely leaving Māori people unhindered in their enjoyment of the language and culture;" it also required "active steps" to be taken by the guarantor to ensure that Māori have and retain "the full exclusive and undisturbed possession of their language and culture" (Waitangi Tribunal, 1986, p. 29). As a result, in 1987, the Māori Language Act was passed, recognizing for the first time Māori as an official language of Aotearoa/New Zealand.[4]

More significantly still, the 1980s saw the rapid (and highly successful) emergence of Māori-medium education. After more than a century of prejudice and proscription from Pākehā administrators (discussed further in this chapter), Māori language and culture are now being visibly reasserted within education. Moreover, this reassertion has come from Māori initially prepared to work outside the state education system until their language and educational needs, and *rights*, were recognized and acted on.

THE EDUCATIONAL ASSIMILATION OF MĀORI

From the beginnings of the state education system in Aotearoa/New Zealand in the 1860s–1870s, and in line with the broader tenets of colonialism, just discussed, an overtly assimilationist agenda was adopted toward Māori. Accordingly, the teaching of English was considered to be a central task of the school, and te reo Māori (the Māori language) was often regarded as the prime obstacle to the progress of Māori children (R. Benton, 1981). The inevitable result was the marginalization of Māori, and te reo Māori, within the educational process. In particular, Māori have historically had little meaningful influence in educational policy decision-making (G. Smith, 1990a). As Linda Tuhiwai Smith observes, schooling came to be seen as "a primary instrument for taming and civilising the natives and forging a nation which was connected at a concrete level with the historical and moral processes of Britain" (L. Smith, 1992a, p. 6). Ironically, in this process, Pākehā were not only to repudiate and replace Māori language and knowledge structures within education but were also to deny Māori full access to European knowledge and learning.

This was not always so. Prior to the arrival of Pākehā, Māori had practised a sophisticated and functional system of education based on an extensive network of oral tradition, and with its own rational and complex knowledge structure (Nepe, 1991; G. Smith, 1989). Moreover, on European colonization, Māori actively sought to complement their own educational knowledge, and their long-established oral tradition, with "Pākehā wisdom." Largely for these reasons, they turned to the early mission schools. These schools taught only the standard subjects of the English school curriculum, but did so through the medium of Māori. As a result, the period in which these schools were most influential (1816 to the mid 1840s) saw a rapid spread of literacy among Māori in both Māori and English. The initial aim for Māori in incorporating Pākehā learning was one of enhancing their traditional way of life. However, from the 1840s, this outlook was increasingly modified as Māori came to perceive European knowledge as a necessary defence against the increasing encroachment of Pākehā society on Māori sovereignty and resources (Simon, 1992; Williams, 1969). As Ward observes:

> [T]he Māori response to Western contact was highly intellectual, flexible and progressive, and also highly selective, aiming largely to draw upon the strengths of the West to preserve the Māori people and their resources from the threat of the West itself, and to enjoy its material and cultural riches co-equally with the Westerners. (1974, p. viii)

The growing fear among Māori of Pākehā encroachment was, as we have already seen, well founded. It was also to coincide in the 1840s with a change to a more overtly assimilationist policy toward Māori in education. As Barrington and Beaglehole argue:

> Education was to be deliberately out of touch with the Māori environment in the belief that formal schooling could transform the Māori and fit him for a different environment. The Māori was to be lifted from one society to another. (1974, p. 4)

The 1844 Native Trust Ordinance stated, for example, that the "great disasters [that] have fallen on other uncivilized nations on being brought into contact with Colonists from the nations of Europe" would only be avoided by "assimilating as speedily as possible the habits and usages of the Native to those of the European population." The 1847 Education Ordinance Act reinforced this sentiment by making state funding of mission schools dependent on English being the medium of instruction, effectively ending the early practice of Māori-medium teaching. As the Auckland Inspector of Native Schools, Henry Taylor, was to argue in 1862:

The Native language itself is also another obstacle in the way of civilisation, so long as it exists there is a barrier to the free and unrestrained intercourse which ought to exist between the two races [sic], it shuts out the less civilised portion of the population from the benefits which intercourse with the more enlightened would confer. The school-room alone has power to break down this wall of partition … (AJHR, n.d., E–4, pp. 35–38)

This position was further formalized in 1867 when the state established a system of village day schools in Māori rural communities, 10 years prior to the establishment of a parallel public system. Although some privately funded Māori schools remained independent, Māori schooling was now effectively controlled by the state. The Native School system, as it came to be known, operated a modified public school curriculum, with a particular emphasis on health and hygiene. Initially, teachers were expected to have some knowledge of the Māori language, which was to be used as an aid in teaching English. However, by the turn of the 20th century, the Māori language had been virtually banned from the precincts of the schools; the prohibition was often enforced by corporal punishment, which was to continue until the 1950s.

But this was not all. Another theme that came to dominate state educational policy for Māori during this time was their unsuitability for "mental labour" (Barrington, 1992, pp. 68–69). The aim of assimilation was ostensibly "to lift Māori from one society to another" (p. 69), but only as long as they were not lifted *too* high. A key objective of native schooling thus came to be the preparation of Māori for labouring class status; this objective was rationalized largely through racial ideologies (Simon, 1992). The Director of Education, T.B. Strong, observed in 1929 that Māori education should "lead the Māori to be a good farmer and the Māori girl to be a good farmer's wife" (Barrington, 1992, p. 69). Barrington argued that such views

included the assumption that Māori rural communities should be preserved and that Māori should stay within them, a biological and racist assumption that the "natural genius" of Māori lay in manual labour, and a strategy to reduce competition for expanding bureaucratic, commercial and professional positions in urban areas by putting impediments in the way of Māori students. (1992, p. 68–69)

That Māori were to become largely proletarianized after the Second World War, as the needs of industry drew them to the urban areas in rapidly increasing numbers, must be seen as the logical outcome of these educational policies, along with those directed at land alienation (Simon, 1989, 1992).

EDUCATION AND LANGUAGE LOSS

Assimilationist policies in education have also contributed significantly to the rapid decline of the Māori language over the course of the 20th century, despite the fact that the English-only policy of Native schools was not seen initially as in any way threatening the Māori language and culture, and was strongly supported by some Māori (A. Durie, 1999). Since the 1940s, however, there has been a growing concern among Māori about the state and status of the Māori language. In 1930, for example, a survey of children attending Native schools estimated that 96.6% spoke only Māori at home. By 1960, only 26% spoke Māori. The rapid urbanization of Māori since the Second World War has been a key factor in this language decline. Although the Māori language had been excluded from the realms of the school for more than a century, it had still been nurtured in the largely rural Māori communities. The effects of urbanization were to undermine both these communities and the language they spoke. By 1979, the Māori language had retreated to the point where language death was predicted (R. Benton, 1979, 1983; see also N. Benton, 1989).

With this growing realization came an increased advocacy of the need for change in educational policy toward Māori. New approaches to language and education were sought. Assimilation was replaced in the 1960s by a brief period of "integration." Heralded by the 1961 Hunn Report, integration aimed "to combine (not fuse) the Māori and Pākehā elements to form one nation wherein Māori culture remains distinct" (see Hunn, 1961, pp. 14–16). Although an apparently laudable aim, integration proved not so different in either theory or practice from its predecessor. It was less crude than assimilation in its conceptions of culture but a clear cultural hierarchy continued to underpin the model. Hunn, for example, clearly regarded those aspects of the Māori culture that were to "remain distinct" as "relics" of a tribal culture of which "only the fittest elements (worthiest of preservation) have survived the onset of civilisation" (1961, pp. 14–16). Compared with this "backward life in primitive conditions," he argued that "pressure [should] be brought to bear on [Māori] to conform to … the pākehā mode of life" (1961, pp. 14–16), which he equated with modernity and progress.

In the face of mounting criticism from Māori, integration was replaced in the 1970s and 1980s by multicultural education. This latter approach came to be known as "taha Māori" (literally, "the Māori side"). In what was, by now, an integrated state education system, it attempted to incorporate a specifically Māori dimension into the curriculum that was available to *all* pupils, Māori and non-Māori alike. As its official definition outlines: "Taha Māori is the inclusion of *aspects* of Māori language and culture in the philosophy, organisation and the content of the school … It should be a normal part of the school climate with which all pupils should feel comfortable and at ease" (New Zealand Department of Education, 1984a, p. 2; emphasis added). Athough the emphasis was clearly on biculturalism, the approach was also seen as a first step to the incorporation of other cultures within the curriculum along similar lines. As a related publication states: "an effective approach to multicultural education is *through* bicultural education" (New Zealand Department of Education, 1984b, p. 31; emphasis added).

But Māori, perhaps not unsurprisingly, remained sceptical of multiculturalism in the form of taha Māori. One key criticism was that the process of limiting biculturalism to support for "aspects of Māori language and culture" within schools fell far short of the biculturalism that many Māori seek—a biculturalism concerned primarily with institutional transformation and social change. In this sense, multiculturalism was also seen as a useful ideology for *containing* the conflicts of ethnic groups within existing social relations rather than as the basis for any real power-sharing between Māori and Pākehā and, from that basis, other ethnic groups. Second, the peripheral and selective treatment of Māori language and culture does little, if anything, to change the cultural transmission of the dominant group within schooling; this criticism has been directed at multicultural education more widely (May, 1994, 1999). Third, the control of the policy, as with all previous educational approaches, remained firmly with Pākehā educationalists and administrators (Bishop & Glynn, 1999). The very process of cultural "selection" highlights this lack of control for Māori in educational decision-making. However well intentioned it might be, cultural "selection" is a paternalistic exercise that will inevitably reflect more the interests and concerns of Pākehā than those of Māori. Indeed, many Māori educationalists have concluded that the main beneficiaries of taha Māori have actually been Pākehā children (Irwin, 1989; G. Smith, 1990b).

EDUCATION AND LANGUAGE REVERSAL

The effect of these educational policies on language loss among Māori is clearly evident. Currently, more than 9 out of 10 of Aotearoa/New Zealand's 3.8 million inhabitants are first language speakers of English, which means that the country is one of the most linguistically homogeneous in the world today. Even among those of Māori ancestry, only 1 in 10, 50,000 people in all, are now adult native speakers of Māori, and the majority of these are middle-aged or older (Te Taura Whiri i te Reo Māori, 1995).

However, two recent educational developments have begun to halt the process of language loss for Māori. First, the establishment of bilingual schools in the late 1970s saw the beginning of a more positive approach to the Māori language within education, after a century of neglect and proscription. Second, and more significant, the emergence of alternative Māori-medium (immersion) schools, initiated and administered by Māori, during the course of the 1980s, has led to the rapid re-emergence of Māori as a medium of instruction in Aotearoa/New Zealand schools. The latter movement, in particular, has combined with the wider political developments discussed earlier to spearhead the beginnings of what Paulston has described as "language reversal," a process by which "one of the languages of a state begins to move back into more prominent use" (1993, p. 281).

The beginnings of this language reversal within education can be found in the early 1960s, when a formal review of the education system, the Currie Commission, included in its recommendations the teaching of Māori as an optional subject at secondary-school level. This first tentative step to reintroduce te reo Māori into the school curriculum initiated a period of renewed debate on the merits of bilingual schooling in Aotearoa/New Zealand. It was to culminate in 1977 with the first officially sanctioned English–Māori bilingual primary school at Ruatoki, one of the last predominantly Māori-speaking communities in the country. Other schools were to follow, providing primarily a "transition" approach to bilingualism. By 1988, 20 such bilingual schools had been established, predominantly in Māori rural communities. In addition, 67 primary schools and 18 secondary schools by this time operated with at least some bilingual classes, involving approximately 3000 students (R. Benton, 1988; Hirsh, 1990). By 1991, this had risen rapidly to 251 primary schools and 54 secondary schools offering some form of bilingual education to 13,000 primary students and 2500 secondary students respectively (Davies & Nicholl, 1993). By 1996, the overall number of students in bilingual programmes had more than doubled to 33,438, the vast majority of whom were Māori (New Zealand Ministry of Education, 1998). Although these developments have been very encouraging, the rationales for bilingual programmes, and the degrees to which they incorporate Māori as medium of instruction, continue to vary widely (Jacques, 1991; New Zealand Ministry of Education, 1998; Ohia, 1990). This degree of variability and a continuing lack of both teaching and material resources for bilingual education remain an ongoing cause for concern (New Zealand Ministry of Education, 1998; Spolsky, 1987).

Given the developments in bilingual education that the Currie Commission precipitated, it is no doubt ironic that the Commission itself remained deeply ambivalent about any greater role for the Māori language in the educational process (R. Benton, 1981). It certainly did not envisage the development of Māori–English bilingualism in schools in the ways just described (Hirsh, 1990). But if the Currie Commission was surprised by the subsequent development of these bilingual schools and bilingual programmes in light of its own, far more tentative recommendations, it would surely have been shocked at concurrent developments, initially outside the state education system, which have since come to overshadow them significantly. Indeed, much of the growing enthusiasm for bilingual education within state schooling can be attributed to an independent movement for the establishment of Māori-medium preschools—Te Kōhanga Reo—instigated in 1982 by a small group of Māori parents. This movement has been so successful that in the space of just 20 years, it has changed the face of education in Aotearoa/New Zealand, affecting, in the process, all other levels of schooling.

Te Kōhanga Reo

Te Kōhanga Reo—meaning literally, "language nest"—was launched as a movement with the opening of its first centre in April, 1982. At the time of its inception, the continued survival of Māori language and culture was looking bleak. As Irwin states:

> The proposed Te Kōhanga Reo movement, an initiative aimed at reviving traditional Māori knowledge and cultural practices, seemed like an impossible dream to some. Crucial elements which contributed to this doubt were a cultural base which was said to be too fragmented to support such an initiative, and a people whose alienation from this traditional base was considered to be such that they could no longer, nor would they wish to, take part in its reaffirmation. (1990, pp. 115–116)

Yet Te Kōhanga Reo has proved to be, by any comparative measure, a phenomenal success. In 1982, less than 30% of Māori children aged 2 to 4 years participated in early childhood (preschool) education, compared with 41% for non-Māori. By 1991, the Māori participation rate had risen to 53%, largely as a result of Te Kōhanga Reo (Davies & Nicholl, 1993). Indeed, between 1983 and 1993 the growth rate in kōhanga student numbers was 250% (O'Rourke, 1994). This has been matched by the proliferation of kōhanga around the country, so that by 1996 there were 767 kōhanga involving over 14,000 Māori children (New Zealand Ministry of Education, 1998).

The kaupapa (philosophy; set of objectives) of Te Kōhanga Reo can be summarized as follows:

- total immersion in te reo Māori at the Kōhanga Reo,
- the imparting of Māori cultural and spiritual values and concepts to the children,
- the teaching and involvement of the children in Tikanga Māori (Māori customs),
- the complete administration of each centre by the whānau (extended family; see below),
- the utilization of many traditional techniques of child care and knowledge acquisition (Sharples, 1988).

Three aspects of kaupapa can be highlighted as key organizing principles (see Kā'ai, 1990).

1. *Te Reo.* "He kōrero Māori" ("speaking in Māori") is a central organizing principle of Te Kōhanga Reo. An environment where only Māori is

spoken is seen as the best means by which language reversal can be achieved. Only in this way can the current dominance of English in almost every other domain in Aotearoa/New Zealand life be effectively contested. Culturally preferred styles of pedagogy, such as teina/tuakana roles (peer tutoring) and collaborative teaching and learning, also feature prominently in the ethos and practice of Kōhanga (see May, 1994, Metge, 1990, for a fuller discussion).

2. *Whānau*. Te Kōhanga Reo has been, from its inception, a parent-driven and resourced initiative based on whānau (extended family) principles. Kōhanga are staffed by fluent Māori-speaking parents, grandparents and caregivers, often working in a voluntary capacity, and are supported by the wider whānau associated with the preschool. Whānau are usually constituted on traditional kinship grounds but have also come to include, in urban centres, a more generic concept in which criteria for affiliation have moved from kinship ties to that of commonality of interests and/or residence (Nepe, 1991). The latter amounts to a contemporary form of cultural adaptation. The significance of kaumātua (elders) is also highlighted in the whānau structure. Kaumātua are regarded as active participants in the educational process. They are used not just as repositories of knowledge but also as teachers who can model the language, and other forms of cultural practice and behaviour, to Kōhanga children (L. Smith, 1989).

3. *Mana motuhake (self-determination)*. The central involvement of whānau in Te Kōhanga Reo has meant that Māori parents have been able to exert a significant degree of local control over the education of their children. The whānau approach is characterized by collective decision-making, with each whānau having autonomy within the kaupapa (philosophy) of the movement (Irwin, 1990). Meaningful choices can thus be made over what children should learn, how they should learn, and who should be involved in teaching and learning (L. Smith, 1989). Individual whānau are also supported at a national level by the Kōhanga Reo Trust, which was established in the early 1980s to develop a nationally recognized syllabus for the purposes of gaining state funding. This latter objective was achieved in 1990. Prior to this, kōhanga had been almost entirely funded by whānau themselves. Although state funding presents some contradictions here (see later discussion), the principle of "relative autonomy" (G. Smith, 1990a, 1990b, 1992) remains a key feature of Te Kōhanga Reo.

Te Kōhanga Reo represents a major turning point for Māori perceptions and attitudes about language and education. Its success has also had a domino effect on the provision of Māori-medium education at other levels of schooling, as kōhanga graduates have worked their way through the school system over the course of the last 20 years. This is particularly evident at the primary (elementary) level with the development of bilingual schooling, already discussed, and the emergence of Kura Kaupapa Māori (examined shortly). These developments are also now beginning to extend to higher educational levels, with the establishment in 1993/1994 of the first Wharekura (Māori-medium secondary schools) and Whare Wānanga (tertiary institutions) (O'Rourke, 1994). By 1997, there were four Wharekura and three Wānanga (A. Durie, 1999; New Zealand Ministry of Education, 1998).

Kura Kaupapa Māori

The primary (elementary) level Kura Kaupapa Māori (literally, "Māori philosophy schools") provide us with a representative example of the ongoing gains being made by Māori-medium education. The first Kura Kaupapa Māori, entirely privately funded, opened in February, 1985. Five years of political advocacy by Māori followed before a pilot scheme involving six Kura Kaupapa Māori was approved for state funding in 1990. With the success of this scheme (see Reedy, 1992), rapid development has occurred. By 1999, 59 Kura Kaupapa Māori had been established, serving approximately 4,000 students, with five new kura being approved each year (New Zealand Ministry of Education, 1998).

The development of Kura Kaupapa Māori is largely attributable to the success of Te Kōhanga Reo and the increasing demand that it created for Māori-medium education at the primary level. The inability of the state education system effectively to meet these demands (beyond the limited options provided in bilingual programmes described earlier) had led by the mid-1980s to the advocacy of Kura Kaupapa Māori as an alternative schooling option. A principal concern of kōhanga parents was to maintain the language gains made by their children. Kura Kaupapa Māori, in adopting the same language and organizational principles as Te Kōhanga Reo, could continue to reinforce these language gains within a Māori cultural and language-medium environment. More broadly, the importance of "relative autonomy" and "community control" featured prominently in the advocacy of Kura Kaupapa Māori during the 1980s and 1990s (see G. Smith, 1992, 1997). Te Kōhanga Reo had served to politicize Māori parents with regard to the education of their children (G. Smith, 1990b; L. Smith, 1989, 1992b); the advocacy of Kura Kaupapa was a natural extension. In 1984, for example, the Māori Education Conference brought together Māori teachers, community leaders, and educationalists from across the political spectrum to discuss Māori educational concerns. The consensus from the conference was that only significant structural reform of the state education system could change the educational circumstances of Māori children. If this did not occur, the Conference urged "Māori withdrawal and the establishment of alternative schooling modelled on the principle of Kōhanga Reo." In 1988, another hui (conference) produced the Mātawaia Declaration, which states:

> ...our children's needs cannot be met through a continuation of the present system of Pākehā control and veto of Māori aspirations for our children. It is time to change. Time for us to take control of our own destinies. We believe this development is both necessary and timely.[5]

These calls from Māori for greater autonomy and structural change within education were to coincide with the reorganization of the state education system in 1988/1989. The national reforms emphasized parental choice, devolution, and local school management. Although many of the changes that have resulted can be seen as problematic (see Dale & Ozga, 1993), the reforms did provide Māori with a platform to argue for separate recognition of Kura Kaupapa Māori. Initially, the government responsible for the reforms was reticent to apply its own rhetoric of local control to the Kura Kaupapa Māori case. However, after a considerable degree of prevarication, and as a result of consistent and effective lobbying by Māori, Kura Kaupapa Māori was eventually incorporated into the (1990) Education Amendment Act as a recognized and state-funded schooling alternative within the Aotearoa/New Zealand state education system. The principles that have since come to characterize it can be summarized as follows (see G. Smith, 1992, pp. 20–23; see also Bishop & Glynn, 1999):

1. *Rangatiratanga (relative autonomy principle).* A greater autonomy over key decision making in schooling has been attained in areas such as administration, curriculum, pedagogy, and Māori aspirations.
2. *Taonga Tuku Iho (cultural aspiration principle).* In Kura Kaupapa Māori, to be Māori is taken for granted. The legitimacy of Māori language, culture and values are normalized.
3. *Ako Māori (culturally preferred pedagogy).* Culturally preferred forms of pedagogy are employed, such as peer tutoring and collaborative teaching and learning. These are used in conjunction with general schooling methods where appropriate.
4. *Kia piki ake i ngā Raruraru o te Kainga (mediation of socioeconomic difficulties).* Although Kura Kaupapa Māori (or education more generally) cannot, on its own, redress the wider socioeconomic circumstances facing Māori, the collective support and involvement provided by the whānau structure can mitigate some of its most debilitating effects.
5. *Whānau (extended-family principle).* The whānau structure provides a support network for individual members and requires a reciprocal obligation on these individuals to support and contribute to the collective aspi-

rations of the group. It has been very successful in involving Māori
parents in the administration of their children's schooling.

6. *Kaupapa (philosophy principle)*. Kura Kaupapa Māori "is concerned to
teach a modern, up to date, relevant curriculum (within the national
guidelines set by the state," G. Smith, 1990b, p. 194). The aim is not the
forced choice of one culture and/or language over another, but the provision of a distinctively Māori educational environment that is able to
effectively promote bilingualism and biculturalism.

SOME CAVEATS

A number of caveats need to be outlined briefly. First, it must be reiterated
that education cannot compensate for society (May, 1999, 2001); this reality
is recognized by those directly involved in Māori-medium education. As I
argued at the outset, the developments in Māori-medium education must
be situated clearly within the wider social, economic, and political framework of change that has occurred in Aotearoa/New Zealand over the last
20 years. This change has had, at its heart, the restoration of the Treaty of
Waitangi to its central role in mediating Māori–Pākehā relations, along with
the related notion of biculturalism as its leitmotif.

Second, it is important to counter in advance a criticism often levelled
at such developments—namely, that they are separatist and/or a simple
retrenchment in the past. On the contrary, nothing in the development of
Māori-medium education precludes the possibilities of cultural change
and adaptation. The specific aim of Māori-medium education is, in fact, to
accomplish this very process, *but on its own terms*. The crucial question
then becomes one of control rather than retrenchment or rejection. Te
Kōhanga Reo and Kura Kaupapa Māori provide the opportunity for
Māori parents, working within national curriculum guidelines, to change
the rules that have previously excluded Māori language and culture from
recognition as cultural and linguistic capital in schools, and beyond.
Māori knowledge and language competencies thus come to frame, but do
not exclude, those of the dominant Pākehā group, and they are themselves
the subject of negotiation and change. The stated outcomes of Kura
Kaupapa Māori clearly highlight this process of mutual accommodation,
with their emphasis on bilingualism and biculturalism. As Graham Smith
(1990b) argues, "Kura Kaupapa Māori parents...want for their children
the ability to access the full range of societal opportunities" (p. 194). Moreover, Kura Kaupapa Māori remains only one option among many and, at
this stage at least, still very much a minority one. In 1996, for example,
only 2.3% of Māori school students were enrolled in a kura; the vast majority remain in the mainstream, predominantly monolingual education system. Proponents of Kura Kaupapa argue that the crucial point is that

Māori-medium education is made available as a legitimate schooling choice, not that it is the answer to everything.

Third, the incorporation of Te Kōhanga Reo and Kura Kaupapa Māori into the state system does present some contradictions, particularly with regard to the notion of relative autonomy. Although state funding has underwritten these initiatives and, crucially, facilitated their expansion, there is an increasing possibility of state encroachment and appropriation on what were originally local whānau-based initiatives. However, it would seem that the benefits of state involvement outweigh their disadvantages. In particular, the state education system is now beginning to address the critical shortage of material and teaching resources for Māori-medium schools, and for bilingual initiatives more broadly. This has already led to the rapid expansion of Māori–English bilingual training programmes within teacher education and a slow but steady expansion of Māori language-teaching material, both of which augur well for the long-term future of Māori-medium education. Incorporation within the national curriculum and assessment framework has also lent legitimacy to Māori-medium initiatives. This legitimacy has been reinforced by initial assessments that suggest that the academic progress of children in Kura Kaupapa is comparable to their mainstream peers, while providing the added advantage of bilingualism (Hollings, Jeffries, & McArdell, 1992; Keegan, 1996; Reedy, 1992).

Fourth, there remains the ongoing issue of the relative lack of institutional/educational support for the languages and cultures of other ethnic minority groups within Aotearoa/New Zealand. These groups comprise small, albeit long-standing Asian (e.g., Chinese, Indian) and European language communities (e.g., Dutch, German, Greek, Polish). Pasifika peoples (e.g., Samoan, Tongan, Cook Islands Māori) have also increasingly migrated to Aotearoa/New Zealand since the 1960s. South East Asian refugees (particularly from Cambodia and Vietnam) came in the 1970s, whereas more recent Asian migration, reaching its height in the mid-1990s, has come from Japan, Singapore, Hong Kong, Korea, Malaysia, and Taiwan. At present, the language and education provision for such groups remains very limited, the result largely of the predominance of English in Aotearoa/New Zealand and, the reemergence of Māori aside, the ongoing valorization of English as both the preeminent national and international language. Consequently, both an assimilationist imperative and a subtractive view of bilingualism are clearly still apparent in the majority of language policies, as well as language-education policies, aimed at ethnic minority groups (R. Benton, 1996; New Zealand Ministry of Education, 1994).

That said, a more accommodative viewpoint has been advanced in recent years that recognizes a responsibility (and need) for more active state support of the first languages of other ethnic minority groups, particularly within education. Thus, the New Zealand Ministry of Education in the early

1990s made the following assurance: "students whose mother tongue is a Pacific Islands language or a community language will have the opportunity to develop and use their own language as an integral part of their schooling" (1993, p. 10). In this respect, Māori-medium education appears to have provided a template that other minority groups are moving to adopt (see Bishop & Glynn, 1999, pp. 86–96). These developments are reflected in the nascent emergence of comparable Pasifika preschool language nests (modelled on Te Kōhanga Reo). In 1993, 177 such language nests, enrolling 3877 children, were receiving government funding (R. Benton, 1996). At the very least, such developments indicate that the promotion of Māori-medium education need not be at the expense of other ethnic minority groups in Aotearoa/New Zealand. Indeed, such developments may well be instrumental in facilitating the latter's expansion along comparable lines, albeit perhaps not quite to the same extent, given the specific status of Māori as an indigenous group (see Kymlicka, 1995; May, 2000, 2001 for further discussion).

CONCLUSIONS

There is still much to be accomplished in language and education in Aotearoa/New Zealand. There is even more still to do with respect to redressing the long comparative disadvantages faced by Māori as a result of the historical consequences of colonization. However, in the areas of language and education, Te Kōhanga Reo and Kura Kaupapa Māori represent, for the first time since the signing of the Treaty of Waitangi in 1840, a genuine educational alternative that meets the terms outlined in the Treaty of "guaranteed [and active] protection" of their taonga (treasures)—in this instance, Māori language and culture. The aims of Kōhanga Reo and Kura Kaupapa are also contributing to Aotearoa/New Zealand's slow move towards a genuinely bilingual and bicultural society. As Graham Smith (1990b) concludes:

> The advent of Te Khōanga Reo and its politicizing effects on Māori parents has created a new interest and optimism in regard to Māori language and culture revival and survival. Kura Kaupapa Māori is a manifestation of [this] renewed Māori interest in schooling and education. The opportunity to capitalize on the potential of Kura Kaupapa Māori should not be lost in terms of...meeting Māori needs and aspirations related to language and cultural survival, and in terms of building a fair and just New Zealand society in the future. (p. 195)

Finally, I wish to return directly to the concerns with which I began this chapter—namely, the importance of adopting a critical and diachronic approach to both the national and disciplinary contexts within which debates on minority language-medium education are situated. It is clear that Smith's observations on Te Kōhanga Reo and Kura Kaupapa Māori address directly the broader national context of Aotearoa/New Zealand. As for a disciplinary equivalent, this can be found in Tollefson's observation that:

> the struggle to adopt minority languages within dominant institutions such as education … as well as the struggle over language rights, constitute efforts to legitimise the minority group itself and to alter its relationship to the state. Thus while language [education] planning reflects relationships of power, it can also be used to transform them. (1991, p. 202; see also 1995)

What the comments of both Smith and Tollefson also clearly highlight is just what is at stake—historically, socially, economically, and politically—in debates around minority language-medium education. If the example of Māori-medium education in Aotearoa/New Zealand is anything to go by, it is certainly much more than many had at first expected.

REFERENCES

AJHR. (n.d.). *Appendices to the Journals of the House of Representatives 1858–1939.* Wellington, New Zealand: Author.

Barrington, J. (1992). The school curriculum, occupations and race. In G. McCulloch (Ed.), *The school curriculum in New Zealand* (pp. 57–73). Palmerston North, New Zealand: Dunmore Press.

Barrington, J., & Beaglehole, T. (1974). *Māori schools in a changing society.* Wellington: NZCER.

Belich, J. (1986). *The New Zealand wars.* Auckland, New Zealand: Auckland University Press.

Belich, J. (1996). *Making peoples.* Auckland, New Zealand: Allen Lane.

Belich, J. (2001). *Paradise reforged.* Auckland, New Zealand: Allen Lane.

Benton, N. (1989). Education, language decline and language revitalisation: The case of Māori in New Zealand. *Language and Education 3,* 65–82.

Benton, R. (1979). *Who speaks Māori in New Zealand.* Wellington, New Zealand: New Zealand Council for Educational Research.

Benton, R. (1981). *The flight of the Amokura: Oceanic languages and formal education in the South Pacific.* Wellington, New Zealand: New Zealand Council for Educational Research.

Benton, R. (1983). *The NZCER Māori language survey.* Wellington, New Zealand: New Zealand Council for Educational Research.

Benton, R. (1988). The Māori language in New Zealand education. *Language, Culture and Curriculum, 1,* 75–83.

Benton, R. (1996). Language policy in New Zealand: Defining the ineffable. In M. Herriman & B. Burnaby (Eds.), *Language policies in English-dominant countries* (pp. 62–98). Clevedon, England: Multilingual Matters.

Bishop, R., & Glynn, T. (1999). *Culture counts: Changing power relations in education.* Palmerston North, New Zealand: Dunmore Press.

Blommaert, J. (1999). The debate is open. In J. Blommaert (Ed.), *Language ideological debates* (pp. 1–38). Berlin: Mouton de Gruyter.

Chapple, S., Jeffries, R., & Walker, R. (1997). *Māori participation and performance in education: A literature review and research programme.* Wellington, New Zealand: Ministry of Education.

Dale, R., & Ozga, J. (1993). Two hemispheres—both New Right? 1980s education reform in New Zealand and England and Wales. In B. Lingard, J. Knight, & P. Porter (Eds.), *Schooling reform in hard times* (pp. 63–87). London: Falmer Press.

Davies, L., & Nicholl, K. (1993). *Te Māori i roto i nga Mahi Whakaakoranga. Māori Education: A statistical profile of the position of Māori across the New Zealand education system.* Wellington, New Zealand: Ministry of Education.

Durie, A. (1999). Emancipatory Māori education: Speaking from the heart. In S. May (Ed.), *Indigenous community-based education* (pp. 67–78). Clevedon, England: Multilingual Matters.

Durie, M. (1998). *Te Mana, Te Kāwanatanga: The politics of Māori self-determination.* Auckland, New Zealand: Oxford University Press.

Fleras, A., & Spoonley, A. (1999). *Recalling Aotearoa: Indigenous politics and ethnic relations in New Zealand.* Auckland, New Zealand: Oxford University Press.

Hirsh, W. (1990). *A report on issues and factors relating to Māori achievement in the education system.* Wellington, New Zealand: Ministry of Education.

Hollings, M., Jeffries, R., & McArdell, P. (1992). *Assessment in Kura Kaupapa Māori and Māori language immersion programmes: A report to the Ministry of Education.* Wellington, New Zealand: Ministry of Education.

Hunn, J. (1961). *Report on the Department of Māori Affairs.* Wellington, New Zealand: Government Printer.

Irwin, K. (1989). Multicultural Education: The New Zealand response. *New Zealand Journal of Educational Studies, 24,* 3–18.

Irwin, K. (1990). The politics of Kohanga Reo. In S. Middleton, J. Codd, & A. Jones (Eds.), *New Zealand education policy today: Critical perspectives* (pp. 110–120). Wellington, New Zealand: Allen and Unwin.

Jacques, K. (1991). *Community contexts of Māori-English bilingual education: A study of six South Island primary school programmes.* Unpublished Ph.D. thesis, University of Canterbury, Christvhurch, New Zealand.

Kā'ai, T. (1990). *Te hiringa taketake: Mai i te Kōhanga Reo ki te kura. Māori pedagogy: Te Kōhanga Reo and the transition to school.* Unpublished master's thesis, University of Auckland, New Zealand.

Kawharu, I. (Ed.). (1989). *Waitangi: Māori and Pākehā perspectives of the Treaty of Waitangi.* Auckland, New Zealand: Oxford University Press.

Keegan, P. (1996). *The benefits of immersion education: A review of the New Zealand and overseas literature.* Wellington, New Zealand: New Zealand Council for Educational Research.

Kymlicka, W. (1995). *Multicultural citizenship: A liberal theory of minority rights.* Oxford: Clarendon Press.

Larner, W., & Spoonley, P. (1995). Post-colonial politics in Aotearoa/New Zealand. In D. Stasiulus & N. Yuval-Davis (Eds.), *Unsettling settler societies* (pp. 39–64). London: Sage.

May, S. (1994). *Making multicultural education work.* Clevedon, England: Multilingual Matters.

May, S. (Ed.). (1999). *Critical multiculturalism: Rethinking multicultural and antiracist education*. London and New York: Routledge Falmer.

May, S. (2000). Uncommon languages: The challenges and possibilities of minority language rights. *Journal of Multilingual and Multicultural Development 21*(5), 366–385.

May, S. (2001). *Language and minority rights: Ethnicity, nationalism and the politics of language*. London: Longman.

Metge, J. (1990). *Te Kōhao o te Ngira: Culture and learning*. Wellington, New Zealand: Learning Media, Ministry of Education.

Nepe, T. (1991). *Te toi huarewa tipuna. Kaupapa Māori: An educational intervention system*. Unpublished master's thesis, University of Auckland, New Zealand.

New Zealand Department of Education. (1984a). *Taha Māori: Suggestions for getting started*. Wellington, New Zealand: Department of Education.

New Zealand Department of Education. (1984b). *A review of the core curriculum for schools*. Wellington, New Zealand: Department of Education.

New Zealand Ministry of Education. (1993). *The New Zealand curriculum framework*. Wellington, New Zealand: Learning Media, Ministry of Education.

New Zealand Ministry of Education. (1994). *English in the New Zealand curriculum*. Wellington, New Zealand: Learning Media, Ministry of Education.

New Zealand Ministry of Education. (1998). *Nga Haeata Mātauranga: Annual report on Māori education 1997/98 and direction for 1999*. Wellington, New Zealand.

Ohia, M. (1990). The unresolved conflict and debate: An overview of bilingual education in New Zealand secondary schools. *SAME Papers*, 111–132.

Orange, C. (1987). *The Treaty of Waitangi*. Wellington, New Zealand: Allen and Unwin.

Ó Riagáin, P. (1997). *Language policy and social reproduction: Ireland 1893–1993*. Oxford: Clarendon Press.

O'Rourke, M. (1994). Revitalisation of the Māori language. *The New Zealand Education Gazette, 73*, 1–3.

Paulston, C. (1993). Language regenesis: A conceptual overview of language revival, revitalisation and reversal. *Journal of Multilingual and Multicultural Development 14*, 275–286.

Pearson, D. (1990). *A dream deferred: The origins of ethnic conflict in New Zealand*. Wellington, New Zealand: Allen and Unwin.

Pearson, D. (2000). *The politics of ethnicity in settler societies: States of unease*. New York: Palgrave.

Reedy, T. (1992). *Kura Kaupapa Māori research and development project: Final report*. Wellington, New Zealand: Ministry of Education.

Sharp, A. (1990). *Justice and the Māori: Maori claims in New Zealand political argument in the 1980s*. Auckland, New Zealand: Oxford University Press.

Sharples, P. (1988). *Kura Kaupapa Māori: Recommendations for policy*. Auckland, New Zealand: Te Kura o Hoani Waititi Marae.

Simon, J. (1989). Aspirations and ideology: Biculturalism and multiculturalism in New Zealand education. *Sites, 18*, 23–34.

Simon, J. (1992, November). *State schooling for Māori: The control of access to knowledge*. Paper presented to the AARE/NZARE Joint Conference, Deakin University, Geelong, Australia.

Sinclair, K. (Ed.). (1993). *The Oxford illustrated history of New Zealand.* Oxford, UK: Oxford University Press.

Smith, G. (1989). Kura Kaupapa Māori: Innovation and policy development in Māori education. *Access 8,* 26–43.

Smith, G. (1990a). The politics of reforming Maori Education: The transforming potential of Kura Kaupapa Māori. In H. Lauder & C. Wylie (Eds.), *Towards successful schooling* (pp. 73–87). London: Falmer Press.

Smith, G. (1990b). Taha Māori: Pākehā capture. In J. Codd, R. Harker, & R. Nash (Eds.), *Political issues in New Zealand education* (2nd ed., pp. 183–197). Palmerston North, New Zealand: Dunmore Press.

Smith, G. (1992, November). *Tane-Nui-A-Rangi's legacy: Propping up the sky: Kaupapa Māori as resistance and intervention.* Paper presented to the AARE/NZARE Joint Conference, Deakin University, Geelong, Australia.

Smith, G. (1997). *Kaupapa Māori as transformative practice.* Unpublished doctoral dissertation, University of Auckland, New Zealand.

Smith, L. (1989). Te reo Māori: Māori language and the struggle to survive. *Access, 8,* 3–9.

Smith, L. (1992a, November). *Ko taku ko ta te Māori: The dilemma of a Māori academic.* Paper presented to the AARE/NZARE Joint Conference, Deakin University, Geelong, Australia.

Smith, L. (1992b). Kura kaupapa and the implications for curriculum. In G. McCulloch (Ed.), *The school curriculum in New Zealand: History, theory, policy and practice* (pp. 219–231). Palmerston North, New Zealand: Dunmore Press.

Spolsky, B. (1987). *Report of Māori-English bilingual education.* Wellington, New Zealand: Department of Education.

Stannard, D. (1989). *Before the horror.* Honolulu: University of Hawaii Press.

Te Taura Whiri i te Reo Māori, (1995). *He Taonga te Reo.* Wellington. New Zealand. Te Taura Whiri i te Reo Māori [Māori Language Commission].

Tollefson, J. (1991). *Planning language, planning inequality: Language policy in the community.* London: Longman.

Tollefson, J. (Ed.). (1995). *Power and inequality in language education.* Cambridge, UK: Cambridge University Press.

Waitangi Tribunal. (1986). *Findings of the Waitangi Tribunal relating to Te Reo Māori and a claim lodged by Huirangi Waikerepuru and Nga Kaiwhakapumau i te Reo Incorporated Society (Wellington Board of Māori Language).* Wellington, New Zealand: Government Printer.

Waite, J. (1992). *Aoteareo: Speaking for ourselves. A discussion on the development of a New Zealand languages policy.* Wellington, New Zealand: Learning Media, Ministry of Education.

Walker, R. (1990). *Ka Whawhai Tonu Mātou: Struggle without end.* Auckland, New Zealand: Penguin.

Ward, A. (1974). *A show of justice: Racial 'amalgamation' in nineteenth century New Zealand.* Auckland, New Zealand: Auckland University Press.

Williams, J. (1969). *Politics of the New Zealand Māori: Protest and cooperation.* Auckland, New Zealand: Auckland University Press.

Wilson, M., & Yeatman, A. (Eds.). (1995). *Justice and identity: Antipodean practices.* Wellington, New Zealand: Bridget Williams Books.

Woolard, K. (1998). Introduction: Language ideology as a field of inquiry. In B. Schieffelin, K. Woolard, & P. Kroskrity (Eds.), *Language ideologies: Practice & theory* (pp. 3–47). New York: Oxford University Press.

Endnotes

1. Aotearoa (land of the long white cloud) is the indigenous Māori name for the country now known as New Zealand. Māori first settled in New Zealand towards the end of the Pacific migrations that occurred from the 2nd to the 8th centuries AD (Walker, 1990). The term *New Zealand* itself derives from the Dutch origins of the "first" European explorer to sight the country in the 17th century. The conjoint use of the two names is becoming increasingly common and specifically recognizes the bicultural origins of the country.

2. *Pākehā* is the Māori term for New Zealanders of European origin. Its literal meaning is "stranger," although it holds no pejorative connotation in modern usage

3. Prior to the Second World War less than 10% of Māori had lived in cities or smaller urban centres. Currently, 82% of Māori live in urban areas (Te Taura Whiri i te Reo Māori, 1995). Māori have thus undergone what is perhaps the most comprehensive and certainly the most rapid urbanization process in modern times.

4. This legal recognition of the language is still somewhat limited. In particular, the right to use or to demand the use of Māori in the public domain does not extend beyond the oral use of the language in courts of law and some quasilegal tribunals (R. Benton, 1988). Nonetheless, it still stands as the *only* example where the first language of an indigenous people has been made an official state language (see May, 2001). The Act also provided for the establishment of a Māori Language Commission, Te Taura Whiri i te Reo Māori. Closely modelled on the Irish Bord na Gaeilge (see Ó Riagáin, 1997), the Commission's role is to monitor and promote the use of the language, although its staff and resources are limited. A recent Draft National Languages Policy has continued these positive developments by highlighting, as its top priority, the reversal of the decline in the Māori language (Waite, 1992), although as yet further action in implementing the Draft report has not been forthcoming (R. Benton, 1996).

5. Unfortunately, the declaration is not available in any published form. It is therefore not possible to provide a reference for the quotation.

3

Bilingual Education and Language Revitalization in Wales: Past Achievements and Current Issues

Dylan V. Jones
Marilyn Martin-Jones
University of Wales Aberystwyth

Our contribution to this volume focuses on Wales, specifically on the social and political processes involved in the development of Welsh-medium[1] and bilingual education and on contemporary debates about the nature and extent of this hard-won educational provision. Our purpose is to draw attention to the complexity of attempts to change and develop educational provision in bilingual and multilingual settings and to consider the impact of such changes on bilingual teachers and on the different groups of learners with whom they are working. In keeping with the broad aims of this volume, we also emphasise the need to understand educational language choices and the policy decisions that are taken at national, regional, or even school level, with reference to the specific social, demographic, political, and economic processes at work in those contexts.

Our approach is thus broadly similar to other research on language in education in bilingual and multilingual settings, developed since the 1990s, which has sought to incorporate a critical, historical component (e.g., Heller,

1994, 1999; Jaffe, 2001; Martin-Jones, 2000; Martin-Jones & Heller, 1996; May, 2001; Tollefson, 1991, 1995). There is, of course, another longer established and still dominant strand of research on bilingual education and language learning in bilingual and multilingual settings (one that is still quite influential in Wales), in which the main concerns are describing and classifying different types of bilingual education programs, documenting different learning outcomes, and identifying factors (e.g., learner variables or teaching "methods") likely to have bearing on the development of language proficiency. However, as Heller and Martin-Jones (2001) have argued:

> Educational choices in such settings, whether regarding structures, programs, practices or materials, are clearly much more than choices about how to achieve linguistic proficiency. They are choices about how to distribute linguistic resources and about what value to attribute to linguistic forms and practices. They are choices that are embedded in the economic, political and social interests of groups and that have consequences for the life chances of individuals. (p. 419)

Our account of the rapid growth of Welsh-medium and bilingual education in the second half of the 20th century therefore will include reference to the social, political, and legal dimensions of the struggle over the initial establishment of this provision, the different interest groups involved, and the contribution made by Welsh-medium education to the creation of a new "linguistic market" (Bourdieu, 1977) in Wales. It will also consider the demographic, cultural, and ideological dimensions of recent attempts to consolidate and further develop Welsh-medium and bilingual education. We begin by charting the wider sociolinguistic and historical context, identifying the factors leading to the decline of the Welsh language in the late 19th and early 20th century, and documenting some of the ways in which Welsh speakers began to mobilize around the language and to campaign for Welsh-medium education.

THE SOCIOLINGUISTIC AND HISTORICAL CONTEXT

Industrialization, Social Change, and Language Shift in Wales

By the start of the 20th century, English had become the dominant language in Wales, and the language vested with the greatest power and authority. This was the period when Britain's empire-building project was at its height and when a global political and economic order, dominated by English speakers, had been established (Phillipson, 1992). Prior to this, in the latter half of the 19th century, Wales had seen an era of intense industrialization, based primarily on the extraction and exploitation of mineral resources such as iron ore, coal, and slate. This had, in turn, led to immigration, urbanization, and the creation of an urban working class, particularly in the south and north east of Wales (Williams, 2000). The relative geographic isolation of Wales had also been significantly reduced by the establishment of a transport system designed to facilitate the export of iron ore, coal, and slate and to provide easier access to Ireland. The railway routes ran east to west from England to Ireland, via the northern and southern coasts of Wales (Williams, 2000). The emigration of Welsh speakers in search of employment followed these routes in the late 19th and early 20th centuries, although the scale of migration from Wales was much lower than that from Scotland and Ireland in the same period (Williams, 1971). Instead, there had been a significant internal, rural–urban migration.

Increased intervention by the British state in different domains of Welsh public life had an impact on the Welsh language, notably in education. A succession of government reports on the state of education in Wales associated the Welsh language with backwardness and with the prevalence of riots in the 1830s and 1840s (Davies, 1999, p. 43). English-medium education was seen as a desirable form of intervention to combat these "ills." This view was expressed most forcefully in the 1847 report of a government Committee of Enquiry into the role of Welsh in education in Wales. The three Anglican Commissioners who had been appointed to this Committee argued that, "The Welsh language is a vast drawback to Wales, and a manifold barrier to the moral progress and commercial prosperity of the people. It is not easy to over-estimate its evil effects" (Roberts, 1998, p. 204). The content of the report aroused considerable anger in Wales and came to be known as *Brad y Llyfrau Gleision* (The Treachery of the Blue Books; Roberts, 1998).

In the latter half of the 19th century, disputes over the form of religious education in state primary schools created some delay in the advent of English-medium education in some localities in Wales. However, by 1870, a complete network of English-medium schools had been established. The Education Act of 1870 set up local school boards that were charged with ensuring the availability of primary education in areas not managed by voluntary bodies (Davies, 1999). A decade later, universal primary schooling was introduced and attendance became compulsory. This educational legislation, in the latter years of the 19th century, is often viewed as a turning point for the Welsh language. From this time onwards, children in Wales received education through the medium of English from the age of 5 years old. Moreover, the practice of punishing children for speaking Welsh at school, in the corridors, and on the school playground was widely reported.

Considering the level of state intervention in public life, the far reaching effect of the imposition of English-medium schooling and the social upheavals brought about by industrialization and urbanization in the late 19th and early 20th centuries, it is remarkable that the Welsh language survived at all. Its survival is generally attributed to two main factors: (a) the internal pattern of migration, mentioned earlier, that led to the redistribution of many Welsh speakers from rural to urban areas within Wales; (b) the development of Welsh Non-Conformity (religious denominations outside the established Church in Wales; Williams, 2000). The networks of Welsh chapels (of different denominations) that became established across rural and urban areas of Wales served not only as places of religious observance, but also as institutions organising social welfare and Sunday schools (Welsh language and literacy classes, for children and adults). In addition, they provided the ground on which social and cultural activities, such as *eisteddfodau* (competitions in music and poetry) could be fostered.

Despite the vitality of the Non-Conformist movement, by the beginning of the 20th century, the sociolinguistic fortunes of the Welsh language were clearly on the wane. The evidence for this comes from the decennial census. Records stretch back as far as 1891 and, in the 20th century, a robust tradition of research relating to the census data was developed in Wales by cultural geographers (see, e.g., Aitchison & Carter, 2000; Jones & Williams, 2000; Pryce & Williams, 1988).

The data from the decennial censuses, plotted in Fig. 3.1, show how, during the 100 years from 1891 to 1991, the overall number of Welsh speakers peaked at 977,366 in 1911 before contracting to 510,920 in 1991. During the

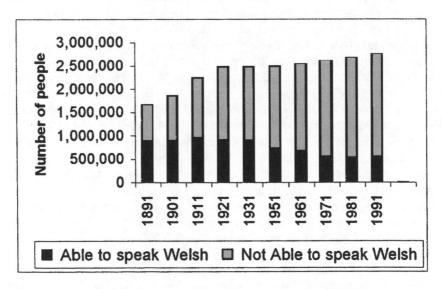

FIG. 3.1. Proportion of the total population in Wales able/not able to speak Welsh. Data are from the decennial census. There was no general census of the population in 1941, during World War II (see Davies, 1999).

same period, the proportion of the overall population who reported as being able to speak Welsh also dropped from 54.4% to 18.7% (Davies, 1999).

There were, however, significant regional variations, with much higher percentages of Welsh speakers being recorded in Welsh heartland areas such as Gwynedd, in the north west of Wales (61% of the local population in 1991) and Dyfed, in the south west of Wales (43.7% in 1991). The map in Fig. 3.2 shows the proportion of the population able to speak Welsh in different regions of Wales in 1991. At the time of writing, we await the publication of the census data for 2001.

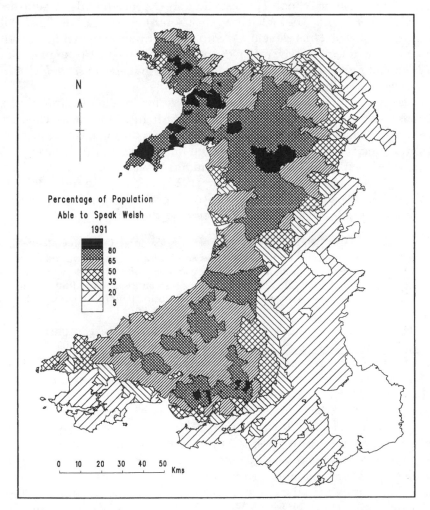

FIG. 3.2. Map of Wales showing proportion of the population able to speak Welsh in 1991. Data are from the decennial census (source: Aitchison & Carter, 2000, p. 95).

Resistance to Anglicization

The main public resistance to the process of anglicization came from a small minority of Welsh intellectuals: ministers from Non-Conformist chapels, university teachers, writers, and publishers. One of the most prominent of these was O.M. Edwards, a university teacher who served as the first Chief Inspector for Schools in Wales from 1907 to 1920. He played a key role in changing attitudes towards Welsh in the schools and in developing a curriculum that was relevant to local Welsh communities (Evans, 2000). He was also one of the first to challenge the practice of punishing children for speaking Welsh at school. His son, Ifan ab Owen Edwards, established *Urdd Gobaith Cymru* (The Welsh League of Youth) in 1922 (Löffler, 2000; Williams, 2000). The *Urdd* developed into an important national movement that continues to play a key role in the promotion of the Welsh language and Welsh culture via a range of extracurricular activities and *eisteddfodau* for children and young adults in Wales.

Despite the efforts of pioneers such as these, institutional life in Wales became increasingly dominated by English during the inter-war years. The first major challenge to this sociolinguistic order during these years came from a group of Welsh intellectuals who formed *Plaid Genedlaethol Cymru* (the Welsh National Party) in 1925. Saunders Lewis, a playwright and academic, was to become the leader from 1926 to 1939. From the outset, the founders of *Plaid Genedlaethol Cymru* were centrally concerned with the promotion of the Welsh language. Their objective was:

> To keep Wales Welsh-speaking, that is, to include: (a) making the Welsh language the only official language of Wales and thus a language required for all local authority transactions and mandatory for every official and servant of every local authority in Wales; (b) making the Welsh language a medium of education from the elementary school through to the university. (Butt, 1975, p. 14)

The setting of these language policy objectives at this early stage in the nationalist movement was to have a far-reaching influence on Welsh language promotion for the remainder of the 20th century. As Williams (2000) states: "It is not an exaggeration to claim that much of the language-related activity since the 1920s has been a playing out of the agenda set by early *Plaid Cymru* leaders" (p. 20). Broader political goals were, at first, subsumed by the campaign for the language. It was only in 1932 that self-government for Wales was included in the broad political program of the Party (Williams, 2000).

The 1950s and 1960s saw the mobilization of a much wider range of the Welsh-speaking population around the language. One particularly significant development in the language movement was the creation in 1963 of *Cymdeithas yr Iaith Gymraeg* (The Welsh Language Society). This was founded in response to a radio lecture by Saunders Lewis, entitled

"*Tynged yr Iaith*" (The Fate of the Language). The main aim of *Cymdeithas yr Iaith Gymraeg* was to engage in direct campaigning around language issues in different domains of Welsh institutional life: in the law courts, education, the media, and local government. It soon became the leading organisation within the language movement and, because of its capacity to mobilise individuals and local organisations, it registered major successes and became a significant force for change within the sociolinguistic order in Wales (Phillips, 1998, 2000).

THE WELSH LANGUAGE IN EDUCATION: A BRIEF HISTORY

From the Early Campaigns to "Normalization"[2]

In the campaign for Welsh-medium education, Welsh-speaking parents became key players. In 1939, a group of parents succeeded in establishing the first *Ysgol Gymraeg* (Welsh School) in the university town of Aberystwyth. This was, initially, an independent primary school with seven pupils that was supported by the *Urdd*, although it later gained statutory status. Five years later, provision was made under Section 76 of the Education Act of 1944 for local education authorities (LEAs) to open Welsh-medium schools, so as to accommodate parental demand. The first state-funded primary school opened in 1947 in Llanelli, Carmarthenshire. Six others had opened in south and north east Wales by 1950 (Baker & Jones, 2000; Davies, 1999; Reynolds, Bellin, & ab Ieuan, 1998).

The main aim of these early Welsh-medium schools was to serve children from Welsh-speaking homes. However, in the 1960s, the Welsh schools began to attract increasing numbers of children from homes where English was spoken, particularly in the anglicized areas of south Wales. The motivations of these parents for choosing Welsh-medium education were diverse: In some cases, Welsh was a heritage language in the family; in other cases, parents were attracted by the ethos of some local Welsh schools and by the high quality of education offered in them (what has recently been described as "their competitive edge" [Reynolds et al., 1998]). There is also evidence from sociological research in South Wales that the increase in the number of parents choosing Welsh-medium schooling reflected a fundamental reassessment of the value of the Welsh language within the changing social and economic conditions of the area, particularly in the former coal mining valleys. Alongside the industrial decline, the 1950s and 1960s saw a steady increase in the use of Welsh in public sector institutions and, thus, an opening up of new employment opportunities (Williams & Morris, 2000).

From their inception, the Welsh-medium and bilingual schools attracted teachers and head teachers who were committed to the promotion of Welsh. Early on in the campaign for Welsh-medium education, the formation of a professional teachers' association, *Undeb Cenedlaethol Athrawon Cymru or UCAC* (The National Union of the Teachers of Wales), provided an important means of achieving coordination between local groups of teachers and parents across Wales who were seeking to exert pressure on LEAs to increase Welsh-medium provision (Williams & Morris, 2000).

In anglicized areas of Wales, parental demand for Welsh-medium schooling was strengthened through the creation of Welsh-medium nursery schools. These schools came to be known as *Ysgolion Meithrin* (The Welsh Nursery Schools). By 1970, there were 60 such schools, all organised on a voluntary basis. In 1971, a national organisation called *Mudiad Ysgolion Meithrin* (The Welsh Nursery Schools Movement) was established at the national *Eisteddfod* in Bangor (Baker & Jones, 2000; Davies, 1999).

Although parental demand was instrumental in the establishment of Welsh-medium and bilingual primary schools, at the secondary level, the initiative came from particular LEAs (Bellin, 1984). The county formerly known as *Sir Fflint* (Flintshire) led the way by founding the first two bilingual secondary schools: *Ysgol Glan Clwyd* in 1956 and *Ysgol Maes Garmon* in 1961. Shortly after, the first bilingual secondary school in south Wales was opened at Rhydfelen in the county of Glamorgan in 1962. As Baker (1993) indicated, Flintshire's initiative represented "the beginning of institutional change in Welsh secondary education" (1993, p. 81).

As Welsh-medium and bilingual provision became a significant dimension of statutory provision in Wales, institutional support increased. Support was received from school inspectors and advisors, from teacher training institutions, and from a number of key educational bodies. As Baker & Jones (2000) observed:

> Part of the equation for success in bilingual education in Wales was the quality enhancement role played by Her Majesty's Inspectors for Education in Wales, local authority advisors and inspectors, pioneering head teachers and teacher trainers, plus institutions such as the Welsh Language Board, the Welsh Joint Education Committee (WJEC)[3] and the Schools Council in Wales. (p. 120)

This institutional support proved to be particularly important in assisting in the establishment of new Welsh-medium and bilingual schools and in the development of appropriate curriculum materials. It also paved the way for the introduction of Welsh-medium public examinations. As Fig. 3.3 shows, there has been a steady increase in the number of pupils entered for public examinations at both 16+ and 18+ through the medium of Welsh. As Baker (1993) has pointed out, the use of Welsh in formal examinations has become "an important indicator of the currency and market value of Welsh" (p. 7).

By the 1970s, Welsh-medium and bilingual education had become quite widely established, albeit with regional variations across Wales. We describe

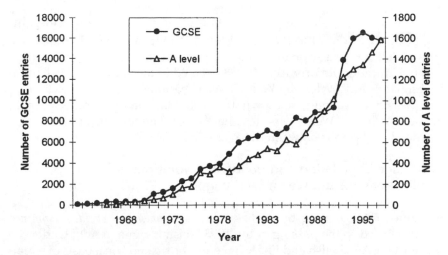

FIG. 3.3. Examinations through the medium of Welsh. The graph is based on Welsh Joint Education Committee (WJEC) examination entries (Welsh Office, 1985, 1991, 1995). Only a very limited number of examinations are offered through the medium of Welsh by other examining boards. Up to 1987, the GCSE numbers are based on the combined number of Welsh-medium candidates sitting the Ordinary (O) level and the Certificate of Secondary Education (CSE). From 1988, these examinations were replaced by the combined General Certificate of Secondary Education (GCSE). The A level has remained as the main academic qualification at 18+ throughout this period.

some key aspects of this variation in the next section of this chapter. According to Williams (1993, cited in Reynolds et al., 1998), this was a period of "normalisation," during which Welsh-medium and bilingual education gained legitimacy, although it was still beset with practical difficulties, such as shortage of curriculum resources. The 1980s then saw further significant changes, as we will show in the following section.

The Impact of the Educational Legislation of the 1980s

Under the Conservative governments of the 1980s, state provision for education in England and Wales began to be restructured along market lines. The Education Act of 1980 obliged LEAs to allow for parental choice of school. Reynolds et al. (1998) explain the significance of this change for Welsh-medium and bilingual schools in Wales as follows: "In the 1944 framework, responding to the wishes of parents for Welsh-medium education had been merely permissible, but in the new framework, parental power and expectations were raised" (p. 8). In response to this legislation, there was further parental demand for an increase in Welsh-medium provision. In another significant development, the 1986 Education Act gave school heads and governing bodies relative autonomy from LEAs by shifting budgetary control to the school level. Parents and people from local communities were also given greater powers on school governing boards.

The Education Reform Act of 1988 ushered in the National Curriculum in England and Wales. In Wales, Welsh became a Core Subject in all Welsh-medium schools, along with English, Mathematics, and Science. In all other schools, Welsh was designated as a Foundation Subject, to be learned by all pupils between the ages of 5 and 16.

Language Legislation and Political Devolution: Implications for the Welsh Language

Sustained campaigning by bodies such as *Cymdeithas Yr Iaith Gymraeg* eventually led to the passing of the 1993 Welsh Language Act.[4] Under the terms of the Act, Welsh and English were to be treated "on a basis of equality" in public sector institutions in Wales. This Act represented a major step forward in policy-making with regard to the Welsh language, though it is important to note that its scope did not extend to the private or the voluntary sectors. The body charged with overseeing the implementation of this Act was the Welsh Language Board. All public sector bodies, including schools and LEAs, are now required to submit Welsh language schemes to the Board indicating how they plan to treat Welsh "on a basis of equality" with English. The Board has a department that deals specifically with the advancement of Welsh-medium and bilingual education.

The last major development that we touch on here is the one that has the potential to bring about the greatest changes in the status of the Welsh language. At the turn of the 21st century, Wales entered a new political era. After a historic vote in favour of devolution, the *Cynulliad Cenedlaethol Cymru* (The National Assembly for Wales - NAfW) was established in May 1999, in Cardiff, the capital city of Wales. This major political change opened up new opportunities for language policy development, including the further development and funding of Welsh-medium and bilingual education. It remains to be seen whether the new political class in Wales is able to grasp these opportunities and develop new strategies for supporting Welsh-medium and bilingual education.

THE WELSH LANGUAGE IN EDUCATION IN CONTEMPORARY WALES

Nursery Provision

Most Welsh-medium education at the preschool level is still provided by *Mudiad Ysgolion Meithrin* (MYM). There are now over 950 MYM groups throughout Wales, subdivided into two kinds of playgroups: (a) *Cylchoedd Ti a Fi* (You and I Circles) give opportunities to children from birth to school age to play within an informal Welsh setting. Parents and guardians can also socialise and, if they wish, learn Welsh with their children as part of a program called *Cymraeg i'r Teulu* (Welsh for Families); (b) *Cylchoedd Meithrin* (Nursery Circles) are aimed at children between the ages of 2 ½ and 5 years old. These promote the education and development of children through the medium of Welsh during their preschool years (Welsh Language Board, 1999).

Primary and Secondary Schools

Welsh-medium and bilingual education are provided at the primary and secondary levels by two main types of schools that are commonly referred to as *designated* and *traditional* bilingual schools. Taken together, these schools represent a significant proportion of the educational provision at these levels. During the 2000–2001 school year (NAfW, 2001), 440 out of a total of 1,631 primary schools (27%) were using Welsh as the sole, main, or partial medium of education, and 52 out of 229 secondary schools (23%) were classified as Welsh-medium schools.

Designated bilingual schools, the *Ysgolion Cymraeg* (Welsh Schools), have mainly been established in the more anglicized urban areas of Wales and offer pupils a Welsh-medium alternative to the local English-medium school. Welsh is the main medium of instruction in these schools. As in other regions of Europe such as Catalunya (Catalonia; Arnau, 1997) and Euskal Herria (The Basque Country; Garmendra & Agote, 1997), the provision in these schools, at primary level, is similar to the early immersion programs first developed in Quebec. Most pupils come from English-speaking homes but learn Welsh within a school environment where the teachers are fluent bilinguals (Bellin, Farrell, Higgs, & White, 1999). These schools build on the preschool experiences that many children will have had within MYM nursery schools and playgroups and, for pupils attending these designated bilingual schools, this is the primary opportunity they have to learn and develop their Welsh. Designated bilingual schools teach most (if not all) aspects of the curriculum through the medium of Welsh.

Nearly all of the *traditional* bilingual schools are to be found in Welsh rural heartland areas where there is often a significant proportion of native speakers of Welsh in the local population. (These schools are sometimes referred to as *natural bilingual schools*. Native Welsh speakers who attend traditional (or natural) bilingual primary schools are introduced to the formal study of English from age 7 onward. Informally, however, pupils learn English through regular exposure to it via the media, local peer groups, and family networks. By the time they enter secondary school at age 11, most native Welsh speakers are reasonably bilingual and biliterate. Over the years, many traditional bilingual secondary schools have been able to offer 50% or more of the curriculum through the medium of Welsh. More recently, guided, in some instances by strong LEA language policies, they have offered an increasing number of subjects through the medium of Welsh; this has led to challenging organisational dilemmas. In the penultimate section of this chapter, we take a close look at one particular type of organisational dilemma, which pertains to the complexities involved in the provision of Welsh-medium education for learners with diverse levels of proficiency in Welsh.

CURRENT ISSUES

The Role of Welsh-Medium and Bilingual Education in Language Reproduction

In the final decades of the 20th century, although the Welsh language gained greater official recognition in education and in other arenas of public life, it came under increasing threat in homes and local communities. Whereas the number of pupils attending Welsh-medium schools and learning Welsh as a second language has continued to increase, the number of children who acquire Welsh as a first language has continued to decline. According to recent National Assembly statistics, only 6.3% of children aged 5 to 11 years old are reported as speaking Welsh at home (NAfW, 2001). Census data from the early 1990s provide further revealing insights into patterns of language reproduction in the family. According to the 1991 census figures, 92% of families where both parents spoke Welsh were passing the language on to their children. However, in households where only one parent spoke Welsh, the language transmission picture was very different. Only 48% were passing Welsh on to their children (Baker & Jones, 1999).

Those who have assumed a language planning responsibility within the Welsh Language Board have identified the issue of language transmission in the family as an area where initiatives are urgently required. Their main objective is to promote language awareness among parents and to provide information, advice, guidance and support to new parents on the advantages of early bilingualism (Welsh Language Board, 2000, p. 98). The census data for the year 2001 may indicate whether the language transmission figures have remained relatively stable for the past decade or whether there has been a further downturn.

What the current language statistics reveal is that language reproduction is taking place outside the home, in the nursery schools, and playgroups organised in the voluntary sector and in the Welsh-medium and bilingual primary schools. All primary schools in Wales are now required to keep records for the National Assembly relating to children's home language backgrounds and their fluency in Welsh. The records for 2000–2001 indicate that 19.5% of children were placed in the "Welsh first language" (or fluent) category and 80.5% were placed in the "Welsh second language" category at Key Stage 1 of the National Curriculum[5] (children aged 5–7) (NAfW, 2001). The figures are broadly comparable for Key Stage 2 (18.1% and 81.9% respectively).

When the percentage of children placed in the "Welsh first language" category is set against the 1991 census figures for the Welsh-speaking population as a whole, shown in Fig. 3.1 (18.7%), we can see that Welsh-medium and bilingual education at nursery and primary levels is playing a significant role in language revitalization. However, concern has recently been voiced (Baker & Jones, 2000; Welsh Language Board, 1999, 2000) about the proportion of pupils recorded as being fluent speakers of Welsh, who are opting for predominantly English-medium schooling at secondary level. The proportion is currently estimated to be about 40%, although there are regional variations. There is even greater discontinuity at the post-16 level, but this is partly due to the paucity of Welsh-medium provision at university level and in further education colleges (post-16 institutions that offer a range of full and part-time vocational and academic qualifications; Baker & Jones, 2000; Heath, 2000).

Anglicization within the Secondary School Population

The increasing use of English by native Welsh students, particularly in the recreational spaces of their lives at school has recently generated considerable concern from both teachers and parents. As a result of the continued expansion of the immersion programs of the more anglicized areas of Wales and the teaching of Welsh as a second language, the number of second-language Welsh speakers appears set to increase still further during coming years. There is little comfort, however, if this is achieved whilst first-language Welsh speakers in Welsh heartland areas are increasingly caught up in a tide of anglicization.

Concerns about the long-term consequences of this process of anglicization have led to calls for strengthening current educational policies and for more to be done to encourage those who currently speak Welsh to continue to do so. In some cases, the debate has focused on the way in which the curriculum is organised within Welsh-medium schools and on the percentage of the curriculum that is delivered through the medium of Welsh. Advocates of what may be termed "stronger" Welsh language policies argue that Welsh-speaking pupils who attend traditional bilingual schools and those who choose to attend designated bilingual schools should be encouraged, or even required, to take subjects such as mathematics and the sciences through the medium of Welsh. Others who challenge this position argue that pupils will inevitably have to switch to English if they are to continue to study mathematics and/or the sciences in higher education, even within Wales, and therefore they should be given the option to study these subjects in English, even within designated Welsh-medium schools. As was highlighted by a recent case involving a designated Welsh-medium secondary school in West Wales, professional and parental opinion appears to be divided on this issue. (See the following article, in the Welsh press, on this topic: "Ail-agor dadl iaith yn ysgolion Sir Gâr" [Re-opening the language debate in Carmarthenshire], *Golwg*, May 3rd, 2001).

The local debates seem set to continue. In the meantime, suggestions that consideration should be given to alternative bilingual approaches that do not involve a strict separation of languages across different areas of the curriculum do not appear to have made much impact on schools to date.

The Increasingly Diverse Intake in Traditional Bilingual Secondary Schools

The third issue has to do with the diverse student intake in traditional bilingual secondary schools. These schools are, for the most part, small schools based in rural areas where pupils have little or no choice as to which school they attend. Therefore these schools must cater for all pupils within their catchment area. In addition to providing for pupils who are Welsh-speaking, these schools also must provide for those with only limited proficiency in Welsh, as well as those whose parents have recently moved into the area. Many of these pupils have missed out on the opportunity to develop their Welsh through Welsh-medium primary education. At the same time, as we indicated earlier, many of the traditional bilingual secondary schools have been extending their Welsh-medium coverage of the curriculum. The combination of learners with highly divergent levels of proficiency in Welsh presents a major challenge to the organisation of this Welsh-medium provision. The dilemmas lie, in particular, in decisions about the grouping of students for work in different areas of the curriculum and about the use of language in the classroom.

Let us take first the decisions about the way students are grouped. One option is to group students according to their linguistic competence and/or their language preference. An alternative possibility is to form ability groups, or sets, according to the students' aptitude for the particular subject in question. A third possibility is to group students in a fashion that ensures a range of linguistic backgrounds and aptitudes.

Many traditional bilingual schools group students according to linguistic criteria during the first years of secondary schooling but move toward grouping by ability as students approach the time when they will take national examinations at 16+. This is particularly true for mathematics, where examination papers at 16+ are currently tiered for three different ability levels and are based on different mathematical curricula. Preparing a mixed ability mathematics class for the external examinations at 16+ is a challenge that most schools take steps to avoid. Students taking external examinations in Wales must, however, choose to do so through the medium of either Welsh or English. They indicate their language preference when they register for the examination. Candidates are allowed to have both the Welsh and the English versions of examination papers on their desks, if their teachers consider this to be helpful to them, but they must answer in either Welsh or English (following their declared language preference). During the later years of secondary schooling, students thus need to be quite clear about which language they are going to adopt as the language for these examinations.

However, the grouping of students by ability in the later years of secondary schooling creates bilingual classrooms characterised by complex communicative practices and patterns of language choice. These patterns are discussed in detail in the ensuing section.

COMMUNICATIVE PRACTICES AND LANGUAGE CHOICE IN WELSH-MEDIUM CLASSROOMS

In this section, we examine more closely the complexities involved in providing Welsh-medium education to students with diverse levels of proficiency in Welsh at the classroom level. Within such classrooms, the teachers work bilingually, alternating between Welsh and English as they speak, working with monolingual and bilingual curriculum materials and writing in both languages on the board. Students have the option of responding to teacher questions, making notes, using texts, and undertaking exercises in the language of their choice. Some students are able to communicate in both languages whereas others are primarily proficient in English. The interactional practices of bilingual classrooms such as these provided the focus of recent research by Dylan Jones (Jones, 1997, 2000). In the following discussion, we provide insights gleaned from this research and we present a jointly conducted analysis of teaching–learning episodes selected from the larger corpus of audiorecordings made during the study.

Doing Mathematics Bilingually

The fieldwork for the study was undertaken by Dylan Jones in five traditional bilingual secondary schools in two Welsh counties during the Summer and Autumn terms of 1998. The schools were aware that the project was primarily concerned with bilingual mathematics lessons. At the time, part of Dylan Jones' role within the Department of Education at the University of Wales Aberystwyth involved initial teacher education and the preparation of secondary mathematics teachers for work in such bilingual contexts. As a result, he was familiar with the schools (and many other similar schools throughout Wales) and he knew all of the eight teachers who participated in the project from previous professional contact. He had previously taught mathematics in similar classroom conditions himself prior to moving into university teaching, and it was his understanding of the challenges of such contexts that had prompted him to undertake the study.

He made a 1-day visit to each school and observed two bilingual mathematics lessons in each one. Notes were made about any handwritten text on the board or any features of the teacher–student interaction that would not be evident from the audiorecordings. In each school, it was possible to hold brief conversations with the pupils, usually immediately before or after the lessons that were being observed. In three schools, it was possible to conduct semi-structured interviews with the head of the mathematics department. Ongoing conversations with all the teachers who participated also helped to inform the study and to establish, for example, the particular characteristics of the teaching groups that were observed. All the teachers were willing to provide copies of worksheets that they used with the pupils.

In the remainder of this section, we present our analysis of two episodes of bilingual classroom interaction recorded during a mathematics lesson with a Year 8 class (age 12+) in one of the schools involved in the wider study. This was a high-ability class. Most of the students were bilingual but the majority had opted to study mathematics predominantly through the medium of English. Three students had only limited proficiency in Welsh. Our aim in considering this episode is to draw attention to the ways in which the teachers' and students' language choices and codeswitching contributed to the negotiation of meanings within the ongoing flow of bilingual talk about mathematical concepts. Codeswitching practices such as those we highlight here were also observed in the nine other classes in the study.

Extracts 1 and 2 that follow are taken from a class on percentages. The class had already done some work on percentages during previous lessons and the teacher was going over some of this work. (The transcription conventions employed in these two extracts are set out at the end of the chapter.) Extract 1 is taken from the beginning of the lesson. It started with a teacher monologue (lines 1–9). This was then followed by four Initiation–Response–(Feedback) (IR(F)) exchanges between teacher and students (lines 10–22). The routine structuring of the teacher–student interaction by means of IR(F) exchanges was broadly similar to patterns first identified in a secondary school context by Sinclair and Coulthard (1975). The only difference here was that the codeswitching between Welsh and English provided an additional dimension of complexity to the structuring of the discourse and to the meaning-making processes that the teacher and the students were engaging in.

Extract 1*

1 T: **reit pawb yn dawel...sh ... reit ni'n mynd nôl heddiw dros y**
       right everybody quiet ... sh ... right we're going back today over the

       gwaith ar ganrannau work we did on percentages
       work on percentages

       [A WHISTLING NOISE INTERRUPTS PROCEEDINGS]

   T: **pwy bynnag sy'n chwibanu ... stopiwch e**
       whoever's whistling ... stop it

       [TURNING TOWARDS ONE OF THE PUPILS]

       Brian ...**reit ddechreuon ni wers ddiwethaf... mae gwaith cartref**
       right we started last lesson... you have some homework

5   **gyda chi fydda i'n dod rownd i wneud yn siŵr eich bod wedi gwneud y**
       I'll be coming round to make sure that you've done the

       gwaith cartref yn dda... ar ddiwedd y wers we went on to writing one
       homework well... at the end of the lesson

       number as a percentage of another **un rhif fel canran o rif arall... mae rhai**
       one number as a percentage of another ... some of

       ohonoch ddim yn siŵr beth i'w wneud yn fy'ny' ... awn ni nôl dros
       you are not sure what to do there ... we'll go back over

       rhywbeth ... marciau prawf right... you do tests and you get your marks back
       something ... test marks

       [TEACHER WRITES " 7/40" ON THE WHITE BOARD]

10   **marc fel yna** seven out of forty **shwt allai newid hwnna i ganran**
       a mark like that   how can I change that into a percentage

---

*__Transcription Conventions__
T   Teacher
P(s)   Pupil(s)
Plain font   English utterances
Bold font   Welsh utterances
Italics   *Translation of Welsh into English*
" "   Text written on the board
[ ]   [DETAILS FROM FIELDNOTES]

        how can I change that into a percentage ... **i ganran**
                                      to a percentage

   P: halve it then times it by five

   T: **reit... hanneru fe** three and a half over twenty then what did you
       right ... halve it

       say you do

15 P: times it by five

   T: **tablu gyda phump** hundred on the bottom. what do you get on
       times it by five

       the top **beth yw'r rhif ar y top**... three and half times five... Brian or
                       what's the number on the top

       Richard

   P: seventeen and a half

20 T: seventeen and a half

   P: percent

   T: seventeen and a half per cent

Codeswitching Within Turns at Talk

If we take a close look at this brief stretch of bilingual talk, we see that there were 17 switches between languages. Fourteen of these switches occurred within a single turn, that is, while one speaker was holding the floor. All of these intra-turn switches occurred in the teacher's talk. This is perhaps not surprising given that the teacher held the floor most of the time and took the longest turns at talk. The teacher had a fluent command of both Welsh and English, so her frequent codeswitching was not due to lack of proficiency in either language. A more plausible interpretation of this pattern of bilingual talk (and one confirmed later through discussions with the teacher) is that she was accommodating the different levels of proficiency in Welsh among the students in the class. The teacher was also attending to the fact that a majority of the students had opted to study mathematics using English as their main learning medium, although this traditional bilingual school has a strong Welsh ethos. A further point to note about the teacher's intraturn codeswitching is that it occurred primarily during Initiations, particularly those addressed to the whole class (as in lines 10–11).

If we now consider some of the individual switches in Extract 1, we can see what communicative functions they served and what specific meanings were being contextualised. In this part of our analysis, we draw on Gumperz's notion of *contextualisation cue* (1982, p. 13). Contextualisation cues are any choices of verbal or nonverbal forms within a communicative encounter that interlocutors recognise as "marked," that is, choices that depart from an established or expected pattern of communication. Contextualisation cues range from phonological, lexical, and syntactic choices to different types of codeswitching and style shifting. They also operate at the prosodic, paralinguistic, kinesic, and gestural level. An interactional sociolinguistic approach to classroom discourse foregrounds the ways in which teachers and learners draw on contextualisation cues and on the background knowledge that they bring to their communicative encounters. These cues and knowledge resources are seen as the key means whereby participants in bilingual teaching–learning encounters negotiate their way through an interaction, make situated inferences as to what is going on, and work out their respective discourse roles.

From the growing body of research on bilingual classroom discourse, we know that teachers and learners routinely use codeswitching (and the contrast between codes) as an additional meaning–making resource in the ongoing flow of classroom talk (Martin–Jones, 2000). For example, codeswitching is used to demarcate different kinds of discourse: to signal the transition between preparing for a lesson and the start of the lesson; to specify a particular addressee; to distinguish "doing a lesson" from talk about it; to change footing or to make an aside; to distinguish the reading aloud of a text from talk about it; to distinguish classroom management utterances from talk related to lesson content, and so on. In this classroom, the teacher was using code contrast in three broad ways:

1. *Doing classroom management and procedural talk.* At the beginning of the extract, we see that the teacher used code contrast as a means of distinguishing classroom management utterances and procedural talk about lesson content from talk about lesson content. In line 3, when she had already begun talking about lesson content in English, she did a brief aside in Welsh. This was a classroom management utterance. She

asked a student who was whistling to stop. The direction of the switch here, from English to Welsh, was significant because it evoked the wider Welsh ethos of the school. Most of the classroom management and procedural talk in this classroom took place in Welsh.

2. *Reiterating points.* Five of the 14 intraturn codeswitches in the teacher's talk served as a means of reiterating what had just been said in the other language. Three points made in Welsh were made again in English (lines 2, 9, and 11) and two points made in English were made again in Welsh (lines 6/7 and 16/17). The points were not all translated word-for-word; some were reformulated in a slightly different way. Whether planned or unplanned, this communicative strategy appeared to be serving as a means of keeping the lesson content accessible to all groups in the class, regardless of their linguistic proficiency.

3. *Referring to numbers and calculations.* In line 10, the teacher switched to English in the middle of a Welsh utterance when referring to the "test score" she has just written on the board. Here, and elsewhere in this lesson, the teacher and the students codeswitched into English on lexical items referring to numbers or calculations in the middle of a predominantly Welsh utterance. The prevalence of codeswitches into English on numbers and calculations in this and the following extract of classroom talk reflects a wider tendency among Welsh speakers. Switches such as these can, perhaps, be seen as sociolinguistic traces of a period when all children learned mathematics through the medium of English and when English predominated in the financial transactions of adults.

Codeswitching Across Turns

Three of the 17 codeswitches in Extract 1 occurred across speaker turns. The first was a switch into English by one of the students in response to a question that ended in Welsh (line 12). This [female] student was doing two things at once in this utterance: answering a question *and* saying something about her language preference. The teacher responded in Welsh (line 13), codeswitching across turns again to provide a Welsh version of what the learner had just said. By reiterating what the learner had said, the teacher was signalling her acceptance of the response but, at the same time, she was perhaps also addressing the students for whom Welsh was the preferred language. One effect of this communicative strategy was that she was explicitly teaching the Welsh way of saying what the student has just said. The third codeswitch across turns served a similar function (line 15). Again, the feedback to the student's English utterance was given in Welsh.

Extract 2

[THE TEACHER WRITES "27/45" ON THE BOARD]

1 T: **un arall ... dau ddeg saith allan o bedwar deg pump** ... twenty
       another one ... twenty seven out of forty five

       seven out of forty five ... I want to change that into a percentage ...

       how can I change that into a percentage... **unrhyw ffordd i**
                                                  any way

       chi'n gallu meddwl am ... dim ots os yw e'n gweithio neu
       you can think of ... it doesn't matter if it works or

5   **beidio**... Carwyn
       not

   P: **rhannu da naw**
       divide by nine

   T: **rhannu da naw** ... divide by nine ... Patrick ... divide by nine
       divide by nine

   P: three

   T: three

10 P: and five

   T: and five... **tri dros bump ... Lisa ... shwt allai gael hwnna mas o**
                   three over five ... Lisa ...   how can I get that out of a

       gant nawr
       hundred now?

   P: **tablu fe gyda** twenty
       multiply it by

   T: **mae rhai ohonoch chi'n siarad ... tablu gyda ugain** . ... multiply
       some of you are talking ... multiply by twenty

15   by twenty **tri ugain**
                  three twenties

P: sixty

T: good ... **chwe deg y cant** ... sixty per cent
     sixty per cent

Extract 2 is taken from the same lesson just a few minutes later. Another "test score" has just been written on the board. Here, we see four full teacher–student IR(F) exchanges. The second exchange (lines 7–11) was more complex than the others because the teacher gave brief feedback (line 9) in the middle of the student's response by echoing what the student had just said.

There are 10 codeswitches in this extract, nine of which are intra-turn switches. Again, all these are in the teacher's talk. The one codeswitch that occurs across turns (line 16) is similar to the one in the previous extract: an English response by a student to a question posed primarily in Welsh. The communicative functions served by the teacher's codeswitching are also similar to those discussed with reference to Extract 1. The teacher switches into Welsh to make a classroom management utterance (line 14). She also uses codeswitching as a means of reiterating particular points. Four of the nine intra-turn switches are from Welsh to English (lines 1, 7, 14, and 17) and one is from English to Welsh (line 11). The latter is a one-word switch where the teacher provides the Welsh version of a numeral that has just been referred to in English by a student speaking primarily in Welsh.

What emerges quite clearly in Extract 2 is the contrast between the way in which the teacher addresses individual learners and the way in which she addresses the class as a whole. As indicated earlier, longer teacher turns addressed to the class as a whole (e.g., long Initiations in a three-part IR(F) exchange) tended to be characterised by codeswitching between Welsh and English. But in addressing individual students, the teacher employed the student's preferred language, signalling her awareness of his or her language background and preference. Thus, in line 5, she nominated a student (Carwyn) who had a preference for using Welsh; the exchange with him unfolded in Welsh. The teacher then nominated a second student (Patrick) in line 7, and that exchange unfolded in English. After this, a third exchange occurred with Lisa in Welsh.

The feedback from the teacher to all three of these learners was followed by a codeswitch into the other language, as if students with a preference for the other language were, again, being included in the conversation. This complex pattern of participant-related code alternation is a common feature of bilingual classroom situations where learners have different levels of linguistic proficiency (Martin-Jones, 2000).

ETHNOGRAPHIC CLASSROOM STUDIES IN MEDIUM-OF-INSTRUCTION POLICY RESEARCH

In this chapter, we have charted the remarkable successes of the long-sustained campaign for Welsh-medium and bilingual education in Wales. We have also drawn attention to some of the contemporary debates about Welsh-medium and bilingual provision. In addition, we have taken a close look at some of the communicative challenges that face teachers and learners in the daily cycles of teaching and learning in bilingual classrooms. In the section of the chapter where we dealt with current debates and controversies, we mentioned that calls that have been made for interventions of various kinds, to preserve what has been gained and to further expand Welsh and bilingual provision. We also showed that these calls for intervention have come from various sources: from those most closely involved in language planning within the educational system, and from people outside of education who are prominent in the cultural and political life in Wales and are deeply concerned about the future of the Welsh language. Some have called for more bilingual provision and have recommended different ways of organising this provision (Baker & Jones, 2000; Williams 1995). Others have called for clearer language separation across the curriculum at the secondary level. Yet others have argued that there should be more Welsh-medium provision and less bilingual provision.

However, before any major interventions are made in the current system of Welsh medium and bilingual education in Wales, we argue that we need to develop a greater understanding of the linguistic and social processes at work in day-to-day cycles of life in schools in different regions of Wales, in classrooms and playgrounds alike. As Baker and Jones (2000) have rightly observed:

> Bilingual education is ultimately dependent for its success on grounded activity in classrooms, interactions between teachers and students, between collaborative and competitive groups of students, and the provision of stimulating and well-structured curriculum resources. (p. 121)

An additional strand of research is now needed in educational settings in Wales. The existing body of quantitative research draws effectively on language data from the decennial census and from school-based records published by the National Assembly for Wales. We have ample experience of this type of research in Wales. It has helped to provide a clear overview of developments within different sectors and to capture national and regional trends. But we also need to know more about the complexities on the ground in different school settings, particularly the specific communicative challenges facing teachers and learners in classrooms—challenges that stem from particular ways of organising bilingual provision. Small-scale studies of a qualitative and ethnographic nature can begin to fill this research gap.

If we take the immediate concerns of teachers, parents, and students as a starting point in defining a research agenda, it would seem that two broad areas of qualitative and ethnographic research need to be developed: (a) classroom-based research, carried out in close collaboration with educational practitioners; and (b) research with secondary-school students that takes account of different dimensions of their lives at school, inside and outside the classroom. We elaborate next on what we see as priorities for each of these types of research.

Classroom-based research should investigate bilingual discourse practices in classrooms where teachers and learners face communicative challenges such as those in the secondary mathematics class we described here. Such research should be interdisciplinary, involving subject specialists as well as linguists, and it should address the role of language in learning across the curriculum. In addition to providing in-depth insights into the complex communicative processes at work in such classrooms, this research should seek to understand the ways in which everyday experiences of talk and learning shape students' commitment to the development of their capabilities in spoken and written Welsh. As Heller (1996) has observed, research on bilingual classroom discourse provides "a window onto the opportunities and obstacles that bilingual education presents to different kinds of students, as well as a glimpse at the strategies that teachers and students use to deal with them" (p. 157).

Research with secondary-school students should build on the fertile ground already mapped out in the survey work carried out by Gruffudd (1996, 2000), by combining ethnographic observation with audio-recording of young people's spontaneous talk in the recreational moments of their lives, as well as in more formal learning contexts. Among the aims for this research should be insight into the values that guide students' everyday actions and language choices and the ways in which language practices are bound up with students' cultural activities and their involvement in peer group networks. As yet, we do not have in Wales any ethnographic studies of conversational interaction among students of secondary-school age or young adults that are comparable to those that have been conducted with young bilinguals in Canada (Heller, 1994, 1996, 1999) or Catalunya (Boix, 1993; Pujolar, 2000). However, it is through such research that we can develop a deeper understanding of the complex cultural and ideological pressures on young people's commitment to continued engagement with the Welsh language.

Despite the rich insights it affords into micro-interactional practices, ethnographic and discourse-analytic research in applied linguistics has often been overlooked by policymakers. Tollefson (1995) observed that "The focus on interaction in applied linguistics research has had the effect of removing language specialists from policy debates" (p. 3). Nevertheless, equally important is the focus on the interactional order of classrooms and playgrounds. It is by situating these local practices within the wider social and institutional order that we can gain the deepest insights into the processes of cultural and linguistic reproduction at work in bilingual settings such as those that we have examined in this chapter.

REFERENCES

Aitchison, J. W., & Carter, H. (2000). *Language, economy and society: The changing fortunes of the Welsh language in the twentieth century.* Cardiff: University of Wales Press.

Arnau, J. (1997). Immersion education in Catalonia. In J. Cummins & D. Corson (Eds.), *Bilingual education. Encyclopedia of language and education* (Vol. 5, pp. 297–303). Dordrecht, Netherlands: Kluwer Academic.

Baker, C. (1993). Bilingual education in Wales. In H. Baetens-Beardsmore (Ed.), *European models of bilingual education* (pp. 7–29). Clevedon, Avon, UK: Multilingual Matters.

Baker, C., & Jones, M. P. (1999). *Continuity in Welsh language education.* Cardiff: Welsh Language Board.

Baker, C., & Jones, M. P. (2000). Welsh language education: A strategy for revitalization. In C. H. Williams (Ed.), *Language revitalization: Policy and planning in Wales* (pp. 116–137). Cardiff: University of Wales Press.

Bellin, W. (1984). Welsh and English in Wales. In P. Trudgill (Ed.), *Language in the British Isles* (pp. 449–479). Cambridge, UK: Cambridge University Press.

Bellin, W., Farrell, S., Higgs, G., & White, S. (1999). The social context of Welsh medium bilingual education in anglicised areas. *Journal of Sociolinguistics, 3*(3), 173–193.

Boix, E. (1993). *Triar no és trair: Identitat i llengua en els joves de Barcelona.* [Choosing is not betraying: identity and language among the youth of Barcelona]. Barcelona: Edicions 62.

Bourdieu, P. (1977). L'économie des échanges linguistiques. *Langue française, 34,* 17–34.

Butt, P. A. (1975). *The Welsh question.* Cardiff: University of Wales Press.

Davies, J. (1999). *The Welsh language.* Cardiff: University of Wales Press.

Evans, W. G. (2000). The British state and Welsh language education 1914–1991. In G. H. Jenkins & M. Williams (Eds.), *Let's do our best for the ancient tongue: The Welsh language in the twentieth century* (pp. 343–369). Cardiff: University of Wales Press.

Garmendra, M. C., & Agote, C. (1997). Bilingual education in the Basque country. In J. Cummins & D. Corson (Eds.), *Bilingual education. Encyclopedia of language and education* (Vol. 5, pp. 99–108). Dordrecht, Netherlands: Kluwer Academic.

Golwg [View]. (2001). 'Ail-agor dadl iaith yr ysgolion Sir Gâr' [Re-opening the language debate in Carmarthensire]. May 3rd issue.

Gruffudd, H. (1996). *Y Gymraeg a Phobl Ifanc* [Welsh and Young People]. Swansea: University of Wales Swansea.

Gruffudd, H. (2000). Planning for the use of Welsh by young people. In C. H. Williams (Ed.), *Language revitalization: Policy and planning in Wales* (pp. 173–207). Cardiff: University of Wales Press.

Gumperz, J. J. (1982). *Discourse strategies.* Cambridge, UK: Cambridge University Press.

Heath, R. (2000). *A right, a duty or an economic advantage: Reasons for choosing Welsh-medium, post-16 education.* Paper presented at the British Educational Research Association Annual Conference, Cardiff, Wales.

Heller, M. (1994). *Crosswords: Language, education and ethnicity in French Ontario.* Berlin, Germany: Mouton de Gruyter.

Heller, M. (1996). Legitimate language in a multilingual school. *Linguistics and Education, 8*(2), 139–157.

Heller, M. (1999). *Linguistic minorities and modernity.* London: Longman.

Heller, M., & Martin-Jones, M. (Eds.). (2001). *Voices of authority: Education and linguistic difference.* Westport, CT: Ablex.

Jaffe, A. (2001). Authority and authenticity: Corsican discourse on bilingual education. In M. Heller & M. Martin-Jones (Eds.), *Voices of authority: Education and linguistic difference* (pp. 269–298). Westport, CT: Ablex.

Jones, D. V. (1997). Bilingual mathematics: Development and practice in Wales. *The Curriculum Journal, 8*(3), 393–410.

Jones, D. V. (2000). Bilingual talk and texts: Observations from mathematics lessons in Wales. *Welsh Journal of Education, 9*(2) 102–119.

Jones, H., & Williams, C. H. (2000). The statistical basis for Welsh language planning: Data, trends, patterns, processes. In C. H. Williams (Ed.), *Language revitalization: Policy and planning in Wales* (pp. 48–82). Cardiff: University of Wales Press.

Löffler, M. (2000). The Welsh language movement in the first half of the twentieth century: An exercise in quiet revolutions. In G. H. Jenkins & M. Williams (Eds.), *Let's do our best for the ancient tongue: The Welsh language in the twentieth century* (pp. 181–215). Cardiff: University of Wales Press.

Martin-Jones, M. (2000). Bilingual classroom interaction: A review of recent research. *Language Teaching, 33,* 1–9.

Martin-Jones, M., & Heller, M. (1996). Language and social reproduction in multilingual settings. *Linguistics and Education, 8*(1 & 2), 3–16, 127–137.

May, S. (2001). *Language and minority rights.* London: Longman.

National Assembly for Wales (NafW). (2001). *Schools in Wales: General statistics.* Cardiff: NAfW.

Phillips, D. (1998). *Trwy Dulliau Chwyldro.* [By revolutionary means]. Llandysul, Wales: Gomer Press.

Phillips, D. (2000). The history of the Welsh language society 1962–1998. In G. H. Jenkins & M. Williams (Eds.), *Let's do our best for the ancient tongue: The Welsh language in the twentieth century* (pp. 463–490). Cardiff: University of Wales Press.

Phillipson, R. (1992). *Linguistic imperialism.* Oxford, UK: Oxford University Press.

Pryce, W. T. R., & Williams, C. H. (1988). Sources and methods in the study of language areas: A case study of Wales. In C. H. Williams (Ed.), *Language in geographic context* (pp. 171–181). Clevedon, Avon, UK: Multilingual Matters.

Pujolar, J. (2000). *Gender, heteroglossia and power.* Berlin, Germany: Mouton de Gruyter.

Reynolds, D., Bellin, W., & ab Ieuan, R. (1998). *A competitive edge.* Cardiff: Institute of Welsh Affairs.

Roberts, D. T. (1998). *The language of the Blue Books.* Cardiff: University of Wales Press.

Sinclair, J., & Coulthard, M. (1975). *Towards an analysis of discourse.* Oxford, UK: Oxford University Press.

Tollefson, J. W. (1991). *Planning language, planning inequality: Language policy in the community.* London: Longman.

Tollefson, J. W. (Ed.). (1995). *Power and inequality in language education.* Cambridge, UK: Cambridge University Press.

Welsh Language Board. (1999). *Welsh medium and bilingual education in Wales: In perspective.* Cardiff: Welsh Language Board.

Welsh Language Board. (2000). Language revitalization: The role of the Welsh Language Board. In C. H. Williams (Ed.), *Language revitalization: The role of the Welsh Language Board in Wales* (pp. 83–115). Cardiff: University of Wales Press.

Welsh Office. (1985). *Statistics of education in Wales.* Cardiff: The Welsh Office.

Welsh Office. (1991). *Statistics of education in Wales.* Cardiff: The Welsh Office.

Welsh Office. (1995). *Statistics of education in Wales.* Cardiff: The Welsh Office.

Williams, C. (1995). *Cyfres datblygu dulliau addysgu.* [Developing teaching approaches series]. Bangor, Wales: Y Ganolfan Adnoddau.

Williams, C. H. (2000). On recognition, resolution and revitalization. In C. H. Williams (Ed.), *Language revitalization: Policy and planning in Wales* (pp. 1–47). Cardiff: University of Wales Press.

Williams, G. (1971). Language, literacy and nationality in Wales. *History, 56,* 1–16.

Williams, G., & Morris, D. (2000). *Language planning and language use: Welsh in a global age.* Cardiff: University of Wales Press.

ENDNOTES

1. *Welsh-medium schools* were defined in the Education Reform Act of 1988 as "those where more than half of the following subjects are taught wholly or partly in Welsh: (a) Religious Education; (b) the subjects other than English or Welsh which are Foundation Subjects in relation to the pupils at the school." In Welsh-medium schools, Welsh is a Core Subject, along with English, Maths, and Science, and every pupil between the ages of 5 and 16 years of age receives Welsh lessons. In schools that are not classified as "Welsh-medium," Welsh is taught as a Foundation Subject. From September, 1999, onward, this applied to all pupils between the ages of 5 and 16 years of age.

2. *Normalization* is a term originally coined by Catalan sociolinguists. It refers to the process of restoring a language to its former (or "normal") status as a language of public life within a particular polity.

3. The WJEC (*Cyd-Bwyllgor Addysg Cymru* or *CBAC*) was originally established in 1948, under the terms of the 1944 Education Act. It was set up as an association of all local education authorities in Wales.

4. Previous legislation, under the 1967 Welsh Language Act, had been limited in scope. It had stipulated that Welsh and English should have "equal validity" in legal proceedings, but its terms did not extend to other domains of public life. The focus on the language of law reflected the use of the law courts by the language activists of the 1950s and 1960s as a forum for claiming their language rights.

5. The Education Act of 1998 defined the Key Stages in education as follows:

Primary schools:	Key Stage 1	Ages 5–7	Years 1–2
	Key Stage 2	Ages 7–11	Years 3–6
Secondary schools:	Key Stage 3	Ages 11–14	Years 7–9
	Key Stage 4	Ages 14–16	Years 10–11

4

Dangerous Difference: A Critical–Historical Analysis of Language Education Policies in the United States

Teresa L. McCarty
University of Arizona

[U]nless the stream of [German] importation could be turned ... to other Colonies, ... they will so out number us, that all the advantages we have will not ... be able to preserve our language, and even our government will become precarious.

—U.S. statesman and inventor Benjamin Franklin, in a letter to a British member of Parliament, May 9, 1753 (cited in Crawford, 1992, p. 19).

No unity or community of feeling can be established among different peoples unless they are brought to speak the same language, and thus to become imbued with like ideas of duty. Deeming it for the very best interest of the Indian, both as an individual and as an embryo citizen, ... no school will be permitted on the reservation in which the English language is not exclusively taught.

—Commissioner of Indian Affairs J. D. C. Atkins, in his annual report of 1887 (cited in Crawford, 1992, pp. 50–51).

Gobernar es poblar translates "to govern is to populate".... Will the present majority peaceably hand over its political power to a group that is simply more fertile? ... As Whites see their power and control over their lives declining, will they simply go quietly into the night? Or will there be an explosion?

71

—John Tanton, cofounder of U.S. English and founder of the Federation for American Immigration Reform, in a memorandum to supporters, October 10, 1986 (cited in Crawford, 1995, p. 68).

As ideological constructs, language policies both reflect and (re)produce the distribution of power within the larger society. Language policies may be officially sanctioned, as in the 1887 dictate of Commissioner Atkins, just mentioned, or as exemplified a century later in the 1986 passage of California's Proposition 63, making English the state's official language. Language policies are often assumed to involve "government action or lack of it" regarding language statuses and uses (Ricento & Burnaby, 1998, p. 33). This definition, however, tends to reify official acts and formal state policies, and to obscure the complex human dynamics these policies represent. Here, I view language policy as a *sociocultural process*: that is, as modes of human interaction, negotiation, and production mediated by relations of power (see, e.g., Bourdieu, 1977; Levinson, Foley, & Holland, 1996; Wiley, 2000). From this perspective, language policy includes public and official acts and documents, but equally important, it constitutes and is constituted by the practices each of us engages in every day. "When we fight in support of a community-based language program," Pennycook (2001) writes, "when we allow or disallow the use of one language or another in our classrooms, when we choose which language to use in Congress, conversations, conferences, or curricula, we are making language policy" (p. 215). Holm (in press), and Parsons-Yazzie (1996/1997) provide a more specific and intimate example: When a bilingual Navajo child hears a request in Navajo from her parent and chooses to respond in English, that child is also responding to a wider discourse on language policies. At the same time, child and parent are negotiating the language policy of the home.

Schools are among the most dominating discursive sites in which both official and unofficial language policies are produced and legitimated. In this chapter, I offer a critical–historical analysis of these enactments in the education sphere. Grounded in critical pedagogy and a historical–structural approach to language planning (see, e.g., Bourdieu, 1977; Forester, 1985; Freire, 1970, 1993, 1998; Pennycook, 1999; Tollefson, 1991, 2002), this analysis assumes that medium-of-instruction policies are neither historically nor socially neutral. As Pennycook (2001) points out, they are not simply about "the educational efficiency of one code over another" (p. 195). Rather, choices about media of instruction, whether officially sanctioned or not, concern struggles for political and economic participation, democracy, and human rights. Expanding on an earlier analysis of Indigenous educational and linguistic rights (Lomawaima & McCarty, 2002; McCarty, 2002a), I argue that these struggles can be conceptualized as contests over what constitutes "safe" versus "dangerous" difference in human social life.[1] In these contestations, language becomes a proxy for social class and race.

For example, how do we explain the paradox of the value placed on foreign language instruction in U.S. schools, and the simultaneous devaluing of those same "foreign" languages among Indigenous and immigrant minorities? In Arizona, the state with the most restrictive antibilingual education policy to date, public school districts have been placed in the position of expunging non-English languages from English language learners (ELLs), while being simultaneously required to provide foreign language instruction as part of the core K–12 curriculum. Who are the intended recipients of these two different medium-of-instruction policies? Whose interests are being served by sorting language education in these ways? And, if we assume a federal commitment to eradicate Indigenous languages, as articulated by Commissioner Atkins in 1887, how do we explain the subsequent federally sponsored development and dissemination of Native language teaching materials? How do the 1968 Bilingual Education Act, the 1975 Indian Self-Determination and Educational Assistance Act, and the 1990/1992 Native American Languages Act square with widespread standardizing regimes focused on English (only) and scripted reading programs?

In the context of historically constituted power relations, these apparent policy contradictions can be seen as responses to larger political, socioeconomic, and demographic forces. When linguistic and cultural diversity have been viewed by dominant interests as instrumental, "safe," or nonthreatening—as was the case in the colonial United States, Benjamin Franklin's protestations notwithstanding—linguistic and cultural pluralism has been tolerated and even supported in official and unofficial ways (Heath, 1992). "Dangerous" difference—manifest, for instance, in the presence of enslaved Africans who were systematically denied access to English literacy, and more recently in the Ebonics controversy—is frequently associated with what Hill (2001) calls "language panics." The Ebonics controversy, in which the Oakland, California school board's recognition of the vernacular language of its African American students unleashed months of media furor, is one illustration of a "national language panic" (Hill, 2001, p. 250). One response to the controversy was the introduction of bills in the California legislature and the U.S. Congress disapproving the use of state or federal funds for Ebonics instruction, and requiring that any existing funds for such instruction be immediately shifted to the teaching of English (Chen, 2001; Hill, 2001). Language panics, Hill (2001) asserts, "are not really about language … they are about race" (p. 245). And, I argue, they are about social class, power, and control.

The United States provides an especially revelatory context for the analysis of these struggles over medium-of-instruction policies. As the most powerful country in the world in which English dominates as the national if not the official language, debates over the status and role of English have shaped educational practices for centuries. The United States also represents a colonial power with ongoing territorial interests. In Puerto Rico, language education policies continue to be hotly debated, and the schools, especially, have become "a battleground over Americanization" (Crawford, 1992, p. 11; see also Delgado Cintrón, 1994; García, Morín, & Rivera, 2001; Language Policy Task Force, 1992).

Finally, the United States is one of the most linguistically and culturally diverse countries in the world. At the end of the 20th century, "people of color made up 28% of the nation's population.... The [U.S. Bureau of the Census] predicts that their numbers will grow to 38% of the nation's population in 2024 and 47% in 2050" (Banks, 2001, p. ix). A significant proportion of this population are English language learners who speak over 150 different languages and who represent the "new immigration"—those who have come to the United States since 1965, when Congress abolished the national origins quota system (Qin-Hilliard, Feinauer, & Quiroz, 2001). Unlike earlier waves of immigration, which originated in Europe and were largely White, the "new immigrants" come primarily from Latin America, Southeast Asia, and the Caribbean (Qin-Hilliard et al., 2001; Suárez-Orozco, 2001). These demographic shifts are having a profound impact on U.S. schools. According to Suárez-Orozco (2001), immigrant children are "the fastest growing sector of the U.S. child population .... Nationwide, there are now over 3.5 million ELL youth enrolled in U.S. schools" (pp. 351–352).

Efficacious medium-of-instruction policies that build on this growing diversity, treating it as an individual and a collective resource (Ruiz, 1984), could not be more timely. Instead, we are witnessing another seeming paradox: Even as pressures mount for cultural and linguistic homogenization—reflected most visibly in English-only mandates and the growing standardization movement—a clear pattern of heightened social, economic, and educational stratification exists. Virtually every social indicator demonstrates a widening gap between those with and without access to economic and social capital. Indigenous and other minoritized students[2] experience the lowest rates of educational attainment, the lowest family incomes, and, particularly among Indigenous youth, the highest rates of depression and teen suicide (Garcia, 2002; Lomawaima & McCarty, 2002; Valdés, 2001). Suárez-Orozco (2001) notes further that, "Among immigrants today, the length of residence in the United States seems associated with *declining* health, school achievement, and aspirations" (p. 354). Acculturation, ostensibly a force for homogenization, appears to lead not to a more equitable distribution of resources and opportunity, but rather "to detrimental health, more ambivalent attitudes toward school, and lower grades" (Suárez-Orozco, 2001, p. 354).

A critical–historical analysis of medium-of-instruction policies sheds a revelatory light on these processes. In this chapter, I examine key episodes in the enactment of language education policies in the United States. This informs an examination of more recent developments, particularly anti-bilingual/anti-immigrant legislation and the "New Literacy Movement" (Gutiérrez, 2001), characterized by phonics-driven reading programs and a renewed emphasis on school "accountability" and testing. Although these developments illuminate the levers of power that have been clamped on difference deemed to be proscribed, or dangerous, they also reveal the windows of opportunity that have been levered open by minoritized groups in struggles for linguistic and educational self-determination.

This is not a comprehensive historical overview. For that, readers are referred to the classic analyses of Fishman (1966), Kloss (1977), and Ferguson and Heath (1981), and to the more recent work of Crawford (1992), González & Melis (2001a, 2001b), Piatt (1990), Ricento and Burnaby (1998), and Wiley (2000, 2002). However, I do cover a wide historical horizon, beginning with the first encounters between Native peoples and Europeans.

EXPEDIENT TOLERANCE

In the swirl of interests that engulfed the North American continent following the European invasion, multilingualism was both common and necessary, a tool of trade and intertribal communication among Native peoples, and of the diffusion of Christianity and European ideas. Goddard (1996) documents 62 language families and more than 300 distinct languages indigenous to North America—a remarkably rich diversity of peoples and mother tongues. Although less diverse, colonial languages also flourished, with Spanish, French, English, Dutch, German, and Russian being the most numerically significant. It is not surprising, then, that there also was widespread use of regional lingua francas, both among Indigenous speakers and between them and Europeans, as a means of practical communication for specific purposes (Silverstein, 1996, p. 117).

Beginning with Christopher Columbus' late 15th century voyage, and continuing in the 16th century with Ponce de Leon's colonization of Puerto Rico and Florida, and the subsequent expeditions of Cabeza de Vaca, Cortés, de Soto, Alarcón, and Oñate, "Spaniards held a virtual [colonial] monopoly over the southern half of this country for one entire century before the arrival of other Europeans" (Castellanos, 1992, p. 14). In his comprehensive treatment of the overlapping "cycles of conquest" in what is now the southwestern United States and northwestern Mexico, Spicer (1962) asserts that the ruling principle of the Spanish Catholic Church—"an obligation to civilize the barbarians"—"was never questioned as the *raison d'etre* of the Spanish conquest" (p. 281). Native life was to be reorganized around the missions, led by the Jesuits in the south (until their expulsion from New Spain by the King of Spain in 1767), and the Franciscans in the north. The fundamental change introduced by the missionaries "was summed up in the conception of 'reduction'"—that is, settlement in compact villages where Native people presumably would be more susceptible to social manipulation and ideological management (Spicer, 1962, p. 288). The indoctrination of children was a major focus of the missionaries' efforts, and in schools in or near the missions, they taught literacy and numeracy in Spanish (Spicer, 1962).

Instruction in Native languages also was fundamental to the Spanish program. Particularly among the Jesuits (less so for the Franciscans, at least in northwest New Spain), there was an emphasis on the missionaries' acquisition of Native languages. Indeed, according to Spicer, some Jesuit missionaries hesitated to teach Spanish because of its perceived destabilizing effects on Native people who gravitated to Spanish mining settlements in search of employment. "To distribute land to [Natives] ...to encourage Indians to mingle with the riffraff of the frontier settlements would ... break up the little kingdoms of God" (Spicer, 1962, p. 307).

Nearly all Indigenous languages of Sonora and Chihuahua were committed to writing by Spanish Jesuits. The oldest surviving Native North American grammar of Timucua, spoken in what is now Florida and Georgia, was completed by the Franciscan missionary Francisco Pareja (Goddard, 1996). Goddard (1996) writes that, "Many Timucuas, both men and women, learned to read and write using Pareja's books" (p. 18). And, as early as 1688, there is evidence of Native literacy in Apalachee, a Muskogean language spoken in what is now the Florida Gulf Coast (Goddard, 1996).

The policy of using Indigenous languages as media of instruction, and of developing Indigenous writing systems to create religious texts, continued with the English and French Jesuits in New England and New France. In 1663, working with Native speakers, Congregationalist minister John Eliot completed a translation of the Bible into Massachusett. Like other Puritan missionaries, Eliot deemed Native peoples to "have no principles ... nor wisdom of their own" (Eliot, 1651, cited in Szasz, 1988, p. 106). One of his chief projects was the Indian praying town, small, self-governing villages where Native children could be removed from the influences of family and tribal community, and instructed in Christianity and the "civilized" arts. Native languages were essential to the civilizing process, and in the 18th century, "Native literacy became widespread in the praying towns" (Goddard, 1996, p. 23).

German Moravian, Russian Orthodox, Dutch Reformed, Presbyterian, and Roman Catholic missionaries adopted similar practices. A primer in Delaware, an Eastern Algonquian language, was developed by Moravian missionary David Zeisberger and became "the first school book used in the state of Ohio" (Goddard, 1996, p. 23). Working with Cherokee speaker David Brown, Congregationalist missionary Daniel Buttrick produced a Cherokee spelling book in 1819 (Buttrick & Brown, 1819, cited in Goddard, 1996,

p. 31; see also Noley, 1979). This was displaced by Sequoyah's syllabary in 1821. In accordance with 19th century church policy, Russian Orthodox missionaries also developed alphabets, grammars, dictionaries, and primers in Aleut and Central Yup'ik (Goddard, 1996).

Missionaries were not alone in the instrumental value they attached to Indigenous languages and literacies. Thomas Jefferson recorded vocabularies of Unquachog and Unami, spoken in what is now Long Island and New Jersey. William Anderson, a member of Captain James Cook's 18th century maritime expeditions, compiled a Nootka vocabulary. Meriwether Lewis and William Clark collected linguistic data on their cross-country expedition, and numerous other European traders and invaders found it expedient to become knowledgeable of Indigenous languages (see, e.g., Goddard, 1996).

Thus, from the initial invasion through the early 1800s, there was a striking consistency in the formal and informal policies of Europeans toward Native languages and their speakers. These policies can be characterized as ones of expedient tolerance. Although the transmission of colonial languages was clearly a priority, this aim, and the larger ones of religious conversion and territorial usurpation, could only be achieved *through* knowledge and use of Native tongues.

Early colonial policies toward Native languages, however, cannot be decoupled from the larger colonizing agenda and its more diffuse and deadly impacts. Although estimates vary, prior to European encroachment, the Native North American population numbered in the tens of millions (Dobyns, 1983; see also Lomawaima, 1995, p. 332). Two centuries of contact and conflict with Europeans decimated that population, leaving fewer than 250,000 in 1890 (Adams, 1988, p. 3; Lomawaima, 1995, pp. 332–333). Native people often felt the impact of Europeans well before they saw a European. Western European crops, material culture, livestock, and disease spread more quickly than did the Europeans, transforming Indigenous sociopolitical systems and cultural practices. Corruption and brutality among both state and church officials was rampant (see, e.g., Spicer, 1962). Language policies were but one aspect of a much broader cultural transformation project carried out by several competing colonial powers—all intent on asserting dominion over Native lands and lives.

CALCULATED TOLERANCE

As missionaries and colonial civil authorities prosecuted their interests, "settlers from almost every northern and western European nation continued to arrive in the Americas" (Castellanos, 1992, p. 15). In 1664, 18 European languages, in addition to Indigenous Algic languages, were spoken by people of 20 nationalities in what is now Manhattan Island (Castellanos, 1992).

In much the same way that missionaries and traders found it advantageous to learn Indigenous languages, statesmen and other colonists in the emerging republic placed an instrumental value on the use and coexistence of multiple colonial languages. Among the founding leaders of the new republic there was an ideological commitment to democracy, and an explicit rejection, at least with regard to White Europeans, of any appearance of aristocratic coercion (Heath, 1992). Silverstein (1996) also notes that at this time, many European languages were only emerging as "standardized, written vehicles and communicative emblems of crowns, of nation-states, and of aggressive colonial enterprises" (p. 117). In other words, there were "no colonial language policies or programs to build upon" (Heath, 1992, p. 20). There also seems to have been a pragmatic recognition of the value of multiple languages for diffusing the ideals of the new government: "[I]f leaders recognized the potential of plural languages to spread the ideas of the new government, the citizens would become capable of helping legitimate the new government" (Heath, 1992, p. 24). And, it was recognized that the spread of English might be more readily achieved without coercion, as English became associated with liberty (Heath, 1992, p. 24). Heath (1992) characterizes this as a dual ideology of universalism—the notion that the ideals of political liberty are universal—and pragmatism (see also Crawford, 1992, p. 9). Between 1780 and 1820:

> The national elite recognized the plural nature of American society …. During this period … [d]iversification in language choice, change, and use not only prevailed, but was purposefully left unrestrained by leaders' repeated failure to provide a national language academy. (Heath, 1992, pp. 30–31)

The case of German in the emerging republic is of particular interest. Wiley (1998) notes that German was then "in an analogous position to that of Spanish in the United States today" (p. 215). But German enjoyed a much more elevated status than Spanish ever has in the U.S. For example, the Continental Congress published extracts of many of its documents in German (Piatt, 1990). During this time there were significant regional concentrations of Germans and, in the early 19th century, German immigration increased. By the 1830s, there were 100,000 Germans in New York alone (Wiley, 1998).

Not surprisingly, in areas with large concentrations of Germans, German was used as a medium of instruction. In 1840, the first German public school was established. According to Crawford (1995), during this period "no uniform language policy prevailed" (p. 23)—at least with regard to native speakers of European languages.[3] Bilingual education, Crawford (1995) maintains, "was likely to be accepted in areas where language-minority groups had influence and to be rejected where they had none" (p. 23).

It was not until the latter part of the 19th century that state legislatures began to pass measures intended to suppress non-English colonial languages. In the case of German, this was largely in reaction to German Catholic schools "as tools for the Holy Roman subversion" (Wiley, 1998, p. 218; see also Crawford, 1995, pp. 24–25). Still, at the turn of the 20th century, more than a half-million German students were being schooled in their mother tongue (Crawford, 1995).

The U.S. entry into World War I brought on a full-fledged language panic. German Americans were suspected of sabotaging food supplies, and newly created state councils of defense took the use of German in schools, churches, and newspapers as a sign of disloyalty. Wiley (2002) reports that Germans were beaten, tarred and feathered, and otherwise threatened. German book-burnings were common, both by xenophobic mobs and German Americans desperately trying to demonstrate their patriotism. Thousands of Germans were fined for "language violations" (Wiley, 1998, p. 223).

During this period, several states passed legislation banning instruction in languages other than English, focusing especially on the primary grades "to make foreign languages inaccessible during those ages when children would have the best opportunity for acquiring them" (Wiley, 2002, p. 232). It was in this context that, in May of 1920, a teacher in Hamilton, Nebraska was charged and convicted under Nebraska law for using a German Bible to teach reading. The teacher, a Mr. Meyer, appealed to the state supreme court, arguing that his 14th amendment rights to due process had been violated. When the state court upheld the conviction, Meyer appealed to the U.S. Supreme Court. What is important for present purposes is that in overturning the Nebraska court's ruling, the U.S. Supreme Court recognized the constitutional right to speak one's mother tongue. (For greater detail on the 1923 Meyer v. Nebraska case, see, e.g., Piatt, 1990.)

Meyer v. Nebraska is significant in another sense, for it was the first U.S. Supreme Court decision in which language rights were contested. That the Supreme Court found in favor of Meyer is a positive sign for the protection of language rights, as is the fact that *Meyer v. Nebraska* has never been overturned. That the case was brought at all, however, suggests a deeper subtext. It is not coincidental that during the same period, 20 states enacted legislation establishing Americanization programs "to insure that all immigrants would learn English" (Piatt, 1990, p. 17). Large manufacturing companies, including Ford Motor Company and International Harvester, offered English classes for employees. In 1921, Congress introduced national immigration quotas, and in 1924, the National Origin Act was passed, limiting immigration to 150,000 Europeans per year, placing quotas on immigrants from other nations, and prohibiting immigration from Japan (Piatt, 1990, p. 18).

In the industrializing United States, linguistic and cultural tolerance was giving way to nativism, and difference was becoming dangerous and proscribed.

THE CIVILIZING PROJECT

Following the American revolution, the new federal government turned its attention to pacifying and "civilizing" Native peoples, "so that they would live on small farms and, therefore, make available their hunting grounds to White settlers" (Spring, 1996, p. 12). Toward this end, Congress passed the 1819 Civilization Fund Act to support the work of missionaries on the frontier. Education and civilization were synonymous, as illustrated by this co-terminous statement to Congress by the House Committee on Indian Affairs:

> Put into the hands of [Indian] children the primer and the hoe, and they will naturally ... take hold of the plow; and as their minds become enlightened and expand, the Bible will be their book, and they will grow up in habits of morality and industry, ... and become useful members of society. (cited in Adams, 1988, p. 2)

Throughout the 19th century, the campaign for Indian removal and containment continued through a policy of military aggression, removal to reservations, and formal schooling. Toward the end of the century, as treaty-making ended, the federal government looked increasingly to schooling as the solution to the "Indian problem." "There is something whimsical in planting schoolhouses where no man [sic] can read," a missionary to the Lakota reflected at the time. "It is a remedy for barbarism we think ... and so we give the dose" (cited in Adams, 1988, p. 3). Unlike earlier missionary efforts, the goal was now complete annihilation of Indigenous languages and lifeways. In the words of the same missionary: "Uncle Sam is like a man setting a charge of powder. The school is the slow match. He lights it and ... in time it will blow up the old life, and of its shattered pieces will make good citizens" (cited in Adams, 1988, p. 3).

In 1887, Congress initiated a two-fisted policy designed to "blow up the old life." The General Allotment or Dawes Act provided for dividing reservation lands into 160-acre family plots, with the "surplus" to be sold to Whites. The effect of the Allotment Act was to dispossess tribes of millions more acres of their land. At the same time, the federal government declared a policy of compulsory school attendance for Indian children, with threats of imprisonment for parents who failed to comply. Adams (1988) characterizes the federal goal as "education for citizenship focused on [English] language instruction and political socialization" (p. 8). English-only policies were "largely instrumental," Adams maintains, with the real objective being "the Indian's political socialization" (Adams, 1988, p. 9).

The chief instruments of this plan were the boarding schools. "Schools ... could not only civilize," Adams (1988) points out, "they could civilize quickly" (p. 12). Over the next century, on- and off-reservation boarding schools proliferated as sites where Indian children could be isolated for years at a time, until their deculturation and re-ethnification were complete. The boarding school experience has been well documented (see, e.g., Ellis, 1996; Horne & McBeth, 1998; Lomawaima, 1993, 1994, 1996; McCarty, 2002b; Trennert, 1988), and I will not repeat that here. What is of interest for present purposes are the shifts in educational policy that have attended federal efforts to discern what constitute "safe" or allowable practices, versus those that are so dangerously different that they must be neutralized (Lomawaima & McCarty, 2002).

For part of the 20th century, the boarding schools remained the bedrock of the government's assimilation campaign (Ellis, 1996, p. 20). Prohibitions against speaking Indigenous languages were strictly enforced. "There is not an Indian pupil ... who is permitted to study any other language than our own," Commissioner of Indian Affairs Atkins affirmed in 1887, articulating a policy that would remain in effect well into the 20th century (Crawford, 1992, p. 49). Stories abound of students having their mouths "washed" with yellow bar or lye soap, or of standing for hours holding stacks of books over their heads as punishment for speaking the Native language (McCarty, 2002b, p. 45).

Coupled with an English-only curriculum was a program of military drill, harsh discipline, and training in the manual trades—all aimed at preparing Indian people as a working class, "amenable to federal control" (Lomawaima, 1995, p. 332). Textbooks included such titles as *Baking Dictionary* (Rhodes, 1953a), *Shoe Repairing Dictionary* (Rhodes, 1953b), *Please Fill the Tank* (Benton & Kinsland, 1953), *Be a Good Waitress* (Payne, Wallace, & Shorten, 1953), and *I Am a Good Citizen* (Williamson, 1954).

The abuses of the boarding schools eventually came under public scrutiny, prompting Secretary of the Interior Hubert Work to commission an independent survey of school conditions. In 1928, the study's director, Lewis Meriam, issued his team's report, a scathing indictment of federally controlled Indian education (Meriam et al., 1928). Over the next few decades, the Bureau of Indian Affairs (BIA) loosened its stranglehold over the use of Indigenous languages in schools, and in the context of the progressive education movement, authorized the development of some Native-language teaching materials. Under Commissioner of Indian Affairs John Collier, who served President Franklin D. Roosevelt from 1933 to 1945, the Indian New Deal included tribal economic development, self-government, and "civil and cultural freedom" for tribes (Szasz, 1974, p. 41). Although the Collier-era reforms represented a decided break with the past, they did not radically alter the status quo. Newly authorized tribal governments were patterned after the U.S. constitution, with BIA oversight. And newly created day schools—intended in theory to be schools from which children would return to their families at the end of the day— were in practice little more than local boarding schools. Although the edifices had changed, the ideologies held by BIA school personnel were not so easily modified (see, e.g., Szasz, 1974, pp. 71–72). "'We weren't allowed to talk Navajo,' one day school graduate recalls, '[a]nd our visitation from our parents was very limited—maybe 5 or 10 minutes, that was it" (McCarty, 2002b, p. 49).

Through the 19th and part of the 20th centuries, federal Indian education policy was one of almost zero tolerance for linguistic and cultural difference. The underlying agenda was the complete subjugation of Indian people and the confiscation of their lands. This agenda was justified by a civilization-savagery Protestant ideology (Adams, 1988; Spring, 1996). Although John Collier and his successors instigated important reforms, including the introduction of bilingual instruction at selected locales, the assimilationist goals and ideology of racial superiority were never threatened. As late as 1953, BIA Education Director Willard Beatty—an architect, with Collier, of New Deal reforms—wrote that Indian education required "a recognition that the richest future for Indians ... lies in a mastery of the material culture of the dominant race" (1953, pp. 10–11).

SELF-DETERMINATION OR MASKED COLONIZATION?

The government's assimilationist agenda was not simply received by its intended targets. "Formal education did change my behaviors and attitudes," boarding school graduate Galena Sells Dick writes. "At the same time, I maintained a strong belief in my language and culture. Looking back, ... this foundation led me to become a bilingual teacher in my own community" (Dick, 1998, p. 24).

One unintended outcome of the boarding school system was the nurturing of an alliance of Native people from diverse tribes who grew up together in the schools, and who shared the sentiments espoused by Galena Dick, just mentioned (see, e.g, Horne & McBeth, 1998; Lomawaima, 1994). In the context of the Civil Rights Movement and liberal-Democratic reforms, these experiences and sentiments found expression in a growing movement for Indigenous self-determination. Perhaps more than any other episode in the history of American education, the struggle for self-determination lays bare the fault lines between "safe" and "dangerous" difference.

In 1970, President Richard M. Nixon delivered a historic message to Congress, proclaiming "every Indian community wishing to do so should be able to control its own Indian schools" (American Indian Policy Review Commission [AIPRC], 1976, p. 111). Nixon's address inaugurated a policy of Indigenous self-determination. This policy, however, did not emanate from sudden federal enlightenment. Just months before, the Senate Subcommittee on Indian Education, chaired by Robert Kennedy and, after his assassination, by his brother Edward Kennedy, had released a report on a 2-year Congressional investigation that condemned federal Indian education policy as "one of coercive assimilation" (U.S. Office of Education, 1969, p. 21). Moreover, in 1966, the Navajo community of Rough Rock, Arizona, had established the first Indian school to have its own governing board, and to teach in the Native language (McCarty, 2002b; Roessel, 1977). Other Indian communities were poised to follow suit.

These developments had been foreshadowed in the strong support for education of Presidents John F. Kennedy and Lyndon B. Johnson. In 1954, *Brown v. Topeka, Kansas Board of Education* reversed a century-and-a-half of legal doctrine upholding "separate but equal" racial segregation sanctified in *Plessy v. Ferguson* in 1886, and in 1964, Congress passed both the Civil Rights Act and the Economic Opportunity Act, which, respectively, provided legal protection from discrimination and authorized community development programs for the poor. A spirit of innovation and emancipation characterized the field of education (Crawford, 1995, p. 12). In 1968, Congress passed the Bilingual Education Act (authorized as Title VII of the 1965 Elementary and Secondary Education Act [ESEA]), calling for new and imaginative programs that used children's native language while they learned English. In a reversal of past policies, the Bureau of Indian Affairs embraced bilingual education as one of the most promising approaches for educating Indigenous students (Bauer, 1970, p. 223).

For a time, state interests and those of Indigenous and other minoritized communities seemed fortuitously aligned. In 1972, Congress passed the Indian Education Act (initially Title IV of the ESEA)—the first federal legislation to support Indigenous bilingual/bicultural materials development and teacher preparation—and in 1975, the Indian Self-Determination and Educational Assistance Act (P.L. 93–638) was passed, codifying the procedures for Indian tribes and communities to run their own schools. Together with the Bilingual Education Act, this legislation laid the legislative and financial framework for placing American Indian education under local control (McCarty, 1997, p. 46).

By 1978, there were 34 American Indian community-controlled schools. Supported by Title IV, Title VII, and P.L. 93–638, Indigenous communities across the nation were producing a corps of bilingual teachers, a corpus of Native-language teaching materials, and evidence of substantial student benefits (AIPRC, 1976, p. 265). The policy paradigm had shifted.

But the liberatory goals of Native educators have not gone uncontested by the federal bureaucracy, and many have been curtailed or turned back. When its funding was reauthorized in 1974, the Bilingual Education Act took on an explicitly remedial emphasis. In subsequent years, the trend has been toward transitional bilingual education as well as alternative approaches (such as English immersion programs) that do not include bilingual instruction at all. (See the discussion of "English for the Children" statutes below. See also Grinberg and Saavedra [2000] for an insightful critique of the processes through which the Bilingual Education Act has been subverted from its original emancipatory goals, to a new form of minority docilization.)

Furthermore, the exercise of Indigenous self-determination has been undermined by the very legislation ostensibly designed to promote it. From the beginning, Indian community-controlled schools have operated under a constant cloud of financial insecurity. Delays in contract negotiations between Indigenous school boards and the BIA were notorious (see, e.g., AIPRC, 1976). "The system we operate under would defeat the President of General Motors," Rough Rock School Director Ethelou Yazzie stated in federal testimony. "It is a political game in which the community or school that refuses to lie down and die wins just enough to stand up for the next punch" (AIPRC, 1976, p. 311). "We are made to feel like the proverbial stepchild," the Coalition of Indian Controlled School Boards pointed out in federal testimony; "too much time and effort goes into securing funds rather than focusing on the educational needs of our children" (AIPRC, 1976, p. xii). Other critics have charged that achieving self-determination under P.L. 93–638 was "like trying to climb a greased pole" (Senese, 1986, p. 153).

The 1988 passage of P.L. 100–297, which provided a forward-funding system for Indian community-controlled schools, has been touted by federal officials as a cure for these problems and a boost to Indian self-determination (see DeConcini, in White House Conference on Indian Education, 1992, p. 6). Participating in these forward-funding arrangements, however, requires schools to meet standards determined not by local school boards, but by national accrediting organizations. Thus, Native American schools have been plunged into the treacherous waters of English-only standards, accountability, and high-stakes testing. In this scenario, there is little room for instruction that incorporates local languages and knowledge.

In 1974, Richard Nixon's Commissioner of Indian Affairs pledged that, "From any angle you ... look at the Bureau's education program today—and increasingly so in the future—you will see emblazoned on the school walls: Indian control" (AIPRC, 1976, p. 119). That federal rhetoric was and is tethered to a bureaucracy that cannot shake loose its colonial moorings. The fact that Native people have managed to survive in this system and to carve out places of difference, such as community-controlled schools, is testimony to their ingenuity, perseverance, and genuine belief in self-education as an inherent human right. Two hundred years after the first federal forays into American Indian education, that fundamental right is still under assault.

DANGEROUS DIVERSITY

As these battles have continued in American Indian and Alaska Native education, a wider struggle for linguistic human rights and educational self-determination has gained momentum across the United States. Indeed, as Fishman (1991, 1994, 2001) and Skutnabb-Kangas and Phillipson (1994) demonstrate, the struggle is international in scope (see also Phillipson, 2000; Skutnabb-Kangas, 2000; Tollefson, 2002). In the United States, this struggle has centered on moves to make English the nation's official language, and to outlaw bilingual education in public schools.

The English-Only movement had its official beginnings in 1981, when Senator S. I. Hayakawa introduced an amendment to the U.S. constitution that would make English the nation's official language. Two years later, Hayakawa and John Tanton, a physician who had earlier founded the Federation for American Immigration Reform (FAIR), started U.S. English, a group determined to stop what it called "the mindless drift toward a bilingual society" (Crawford, 1995, p. 65).

Between 1981 and 1995, 14 Official English bills were introduced in Congress (Chen, 2001, pp. 61–62). To date, none has been approved. Although still working at the national level, English-Only supporters have taken their message—and their dollars—to the state level. In 1986, with financial support from U.S. English, California—the state with the fastest growing "minority majority," primarily Latinos—declared English the state's official language. Within 2 years, nine additional states adopted official English statutes (Piatt, 1990, p. 22; for more on the English-Only movement, see Adams & Brink 1990; Crawford, 1992; Fishman, 1988; González & Melis, 2001a, 2001b). How is it that citizens feel compelled to safeguard a language that, without official safeguards, has become the most power-linked language in the world?

If we look closely at the recent history of immigration to the United States, we see certain striking parallels. In 1965, following proposals by President Kennedy, Congress abolished national origin quotas on immigration. As indicated earlier in this chapter, the vast majority of recent immigrants have come from Latin America, the Caribbean, and Southeast Asia. As the racial and ethnic background of newly arrived immigrants has shifted, Congress and some states (e.g., California) have imposed tighter immigration laws. In 1986—the same year as California's official language referendum—Congress passed the Immigration Reform and Control Act, the first legislation to impose sanctions on employers who hire undocumented workers, and to require English proficiency as a condition of permanent residence and citizenship (Piatt, 1990, p. 20).

Difference in the United States has taken on not only new languages, but new colors. In an increasingly conservative and nativist sociopolitical environment, the new colors of diversity are perceived by many in the dominant White mainstream as dangerous indeed.

REPRODUCING THE GREAT DIVIDE

With the passage of twin English-for-the-Children statutes in California (1998) and Arizona (2000), the movement to officialize English has been taken to the classroom. Initiated and financed by California software millionaire Ron Unz, both statutes require public schools to replace multi-year bilingual education programs with 1-year English immersion for English language learners. In California, Proposition 227 was followed by the adoption of an English-Only school accountability program (Gutiérrez et al., 2002). In Arizona, exceptions to the statute may be granted if parents request a waiver, subject to approval by the school superintendent and "under guidelines established by ... the local governing body and ... state board of education" (A.R.S. Title 15, Chapter 7, Article 3.1, Section 15–753). The waiver requires that parents provide "written documentation of no less than 250 words," demonstrating their child's "special needs." This document must then be placed in the child's permanent file.

Arizona's Proposition 203 makes clear that its authors understand perfectly the distinction between safe and dangerous. In Section 15–753, B.1, parental waivers are unproblematic for children who already know English and score at or above grade level on standardized tests—that is, enrichment bilingual and foreign language instruction is not to be denied to middle- and upper-class (White) students. On the other hand, non-English-speaking children—those who already possess native fluency in the languages their middle- and upper-class peers will acquire less well through enrichment and foreign language programs—are constructed in the statute as deficient, abnormal, and underachieving. Worse, they are permanently ensnared in this construction, as the documentation of it—*penned in their parents' hands*—will follow them for the remainder of their school careers. The hegemonic entrapment could not be more complete.

There is nothing neutral or impartial about these media-of-instruction policies. Furthermore, they are not disconnected from more widespread standardizing regimes and scripted reading programs. The latter constitute what Gutiérrez (2001) calls the New Literacy Movement: "reductive literacy practices [that] are bolstered by English-only legislation" (p. 565). In school districts across the country, phonics-based reading programs have become the panacea for "dismal test scores, high student mobility, and the growing demographic of English language learners" (Gutiérrez, 2001, p. 565). Affluent and middle-class White students elude these pedagogies by virtue of their social position and access to private and gifted education (see, e.g., Gee, in press). Those most disadvantaged by these pedagogies, Lankshear (1998) points out, "are those *already* most marginal within educational, economic, and social life" (p. 368).

Elsewhere I argue that these dynamics represent a 21st century "Great Divide" (McCarty, in press). Great Divide arguments can be traced to the distinction first made by Goody and Watt (1963) between oral and written language and, by extension, between those with and without literacy (Collins, 1995). It is not far from this distinction to related claims for single, standard, or "pure" forms of language and literacy. When these claims intersect with ideologies of meritocracy and privilege—as they inevitably do —the result is the naturalization of existing power hierarchies, "whereby deviations from the norms are defined as deficiencies and disabilities" (Collins, 1995, p. 83).

Great Divide ideologies are implicit and explicit in current U.S. media of instruction policies, and they are constructing two kinds of people: those with and without access to opportunity and resources. Despite the calls of conservative politicians to "leave no child behind"—codified in Federal education policy under President George W. Bush—an unconscionable number of English language learners, students of color, and working-class children are, in fact, being left behind (see, e.g., Cummins, in press). When we examine the policies underwriting English for the Children and the New Literacy Movement, we must ask whether that is not exactly what those policies are intended to do.

CONCLUDING THOUGHTS

This analysis would be incomplete without highlighting real possibilities for positive change. For example, in the summer of 1988, Native American educators from throughout the United States came together to draft the resolution that would become the 1990/1992 Native American Languages Act. NALA is the only federal legislation that explicitly vows to protect and promote Indigenous/minoritized languages. It might be argued that, given more than two centuries of federally sponsored linguicidal policies and the attendant decline of Native languages,[4] NALA is a relatively innocuous and symbolic act. Nevertheless, this legislation has spurred some of the boldest efforts in heritage language recovery to date (see, e.g., Hinton & Hale, 2001; McCarty, Watahomigie, & Yamamoto, 1999). These initiatives, and similar ones among other minoritized communities, are fundamental to cultural survival and self-determination.

There is no question, however, that the United States is in the midst of a national language panic, where language has become a proxy for social class and race (Hill, 2001). Spanish speakers, in particular, have been singled out as the targets of national language hysteria. The horrific events of September 11, 2001 have exacerbated these xenophobic trends, placing Arabic speakers—indeed, all those who "look Middle Eastern" (see, e.g., Noonan, 2001)—in great jeopardy as well. In the current sociopolitical environment, racial and linguistic profiling, antibilingual measures, and the New Literacy Movement can be seen as all of the same cloth. Enacted in official decrees, in government rhetoric and media disinformation, and informally in everyday practice, these policies serve to discipline minoritized groups, reminding them "that they can be defined as illegitimate members of the larger population" (González, 2001, p. xxviii).

Can these truly dangerous forces be resisted and transformed? During his first year as head of the bureau of education in Sao Paulo, Paulo Freire (1993) observed that education "is not a lever for the transformation of society, but ... it *could* be" (p. 48; emphasis added). Medium-of-instruction policies are at the heart of the challenge—and the possibilities—of what education *could* be. Although these policies can be instruments of linguistic and cultural imperialism, they also can be tools for strengthening the rich diversity that is the nation's heritage and its future. This vision of education has the power to lead the United States out of the either–or politics and pedagogies of English-for-the-Children and the New Literacy Movement, toward a more democratic, just, and equitable educational system for all.

REFERENCES

Adams, D. W. (1988). Fundamental considerations: The deep meaning of Native American schooling, 1880–1900. *Harvard Educational Review, 58,* 1–28.

Adams, K. L., & Brink, D. T. (1990). *Perspectives on Official English: The campaign for English as the official language of the USA.* Berlin and New York: Mouton de Gruyter.

American Indian Policy Review Commission (1976). *Report on Indian education.* Washington, DC: U.S. Government Printing Office.

Banks, J. A. (2001). Series foreword. In G. Valdés (Ed.), *Learning and not learning English in school: Latino students in American schools* (pp. ix–xiii). New York and London: Teachers College Press.

Bauer, E. (1970). Bilingual education in BIA schools. *TESOL Quarterly, 4,* 223–229.

Beatty, W. W. (1953). *Education for culture change.* Chilocco, OK: Chilocco School Press.

Benton, N. A., & Kinsland, J. E. (1953). *Please fill the tank.* Ogden, UT: Defense Printing Service, U.S. Department of the Interior, Bureau of Indian Affairs.

Bourdieu, P. (1977). The economics of linguistic exchanges. *Social Science Information, 16,* 645–668.

Castellanos, D. (1992). A polyglot nation. In J. Crawford (Ed.), *Language loyalties: A source book on the Official English controversy* (pp. 13–19). Chicago and London: University of Chicago Press.

Chen, E. (2001). Statement on the civil liberties implications of Official English legislation before the United States Senate Committee on Governmental Affairs, December 6, 1995. In R. D. González & I. Melis (Eds.), *Language ideologies: Critical perspectives on the Official English movement, Vol. 2: History, theory, and policy* (pp. 30–62). Urbana, IL, and Mahwah, NJ: National Council of Teachers of English and Lawrence Erlbaum Associates.

Collins, J. (1995). Literacy and literacies. *Annual Review of Anthropology, 34,* 75–93.

Crawford, J. (Ed.). (1992). *Language loyalties: A source book on the Official English controversy.* Chicago and London: University of Chicago Press.

Crawford, J. (1995). *Bilingual education: History, politics, theory, and practice* (3rd ed.). Los Angeles, CA: Bilingual Educational Services, Inc.

Cummins, J. (in press). Can schools effectively challenge coercive power relations in the wider society? In T. L. McCarty (Ed.), *Language, literacy, and power in schooling.* Mahwah, NJ: Lawrence Erlbaum Associates.

Delgado Cintrón, C. (1994). *El debate legislativo sobre las leyes del idioma en Puerto Rico.* San Juan: Editorial de la Revista del Colegio de Abogados de Puerto Rico.

Dick, G. S. (1998). I maintained a strong belief in my language and culture: A Navajo language autobiography. *International Journal of the Sociology of Language, 132,* 23–25.

Dobyns, H. F. (1983). *Their number become thinned.* Knoxville: University of Tennessee Press.

Ellis, C. (1996). *To change them forever: Indian education at the Rainy Mountain Boarding School, 1893–1920.* Norman and London: University of Oklahoma Press.

Ferguson, C. A., & Heath, S. B. (1981). *Language in the USA.* Cambridge, UK: Cambridge University Press.

Fishman, J. A. (Ed.). (1966). *Language loyalty in the United States.* The Hague, Netherlands: Mouton.

Fishman, J. A. (1988). "English only": Its ghosts, myths, and dangers. *International Journal of the Sociology of Language, 74,* 125–140.

Fishman, J. A. (1991). *Reversing language shift.* Clevedon, UK: Multilingual Matters Ltd.

Fishman, J. A. (1994). On the limits of ethnolinguistic democracy. In T. Skutnabb-Kangas & R. Phillipson (Eds.), *Linguistic human rights: Overcoming linguistic discrimination* (pp. 49–61). Berlin and New York: Mouton de Gruyter.

Fishman, J. A. (Ed.). (2001). *Can threatened languages be saved? Reversing language shift, revisited: A 21st century perspective.* Clevedon, UK: Multilingual Matters Ltd.

Forester, J. (1985). *Critical theory and public life.* Cambridge, MA: MIT Press.

Freire, P. (1970). *Pedagogy of the oppressed.* New York: Seabury Press.

Freire, P. (1993). *Pedagogy of the city.* New York: Continuum.

Freire, P. (1998). *Pedagogy of freedom.* Oxford, UK: Rowman and Littlefield.

Garcia, E. (2002). Bilingualism and schooling in the United States. *International Journal of the Sociology of Language, 155/156,* 197–204.

García, O., Morín, J. L., & Rivera, K. (2001). How threatened is the Spanish of New York Puerto Ricans? In J. A. Fishman (Ed.), *Can threatened languages be saved? Reversing language shift, revisited: A 21st century perspective* (pp. 44–73). Clevedon, UK: Multilingual Matters Ltd.

Gee, J. P. (in press). Literacies, schools, and kinds of people in the New Capitalism. In T. L. McCarty (Ed.), *Language, literacy, and power in schooling.* Mahwah, NJ: Lawrence Erlbaum Associates.

Goddard, I. (1996). The description of the Native languages of North America before Boas. In W. C. Sturtevant (Gen. Ed.) & I. Goodard (Vol. Ed.), *Handbook of North American Indians, Vol. 17: Languages* (pp. 17–42). Washington, DC: Smithsonian Institution.

González, R. D. (2001). Introduction. In R. D. González & I. Melis (Eds.), *Language ideologies: Critical perspectives on the Official English movement, Vol. 2: History, theory, and policy* (pp. xxv–liii). Urbana, IL and Mahwah, NJ: National Council of Teachers of English and Lawrence Erlbaum Associates.

González, R. D., & Melis, I. (2001a). *Language ideologies: Critical perspectives on the Official English movement, Vol. 1: Education and the social implications of official language.* Urbana, IL and Mahwah, NJ: National Council of Teachers of English and Lawrence Erlbaum Associates.

González, R. D., & Melis, I. (2001b). *Language ideologies: Critical perspectives on the Official English movement, Vol. 2: History, theory, and policy.* Urbana, IL and Mahwah, NJ: National Council of Teachers of English and Lawrence Erlbaum Associates.

Goody, J., & Watt, I. (1963). The consequences of literacy. *Comparative Studies of Social History, 5,* 305–326, 332–345.

Grinberg, J., & Saavedra, E. (2000). The constitution of bilingual/ESL education as a disciplinary practice: Genealogical explorations. *Review of Educational Research, 70,* 419–441.

Gutiérrez, K. D. (2001). What's new in the English language arts: Challenging policies and practices, *¿y qué? Language Arts, 78,* 564–569.

Gutiérrez, K. D., Asato, J., Moll, L. C., Olson, K., Horng, E. L., Ruiz, R., Garcia, E., & McCarty, T. L. (2002). "Sounding American": The consequences of new reforms on English language learners. *Reading Research Quarterly, 37,* 328–343.

Heath, S. B. (1992). Why no official tongue? In J. Crawford (Ed.), *Language loyalties: A source book on the Official English controversy* (pp. 20–31). Chicago and London: University of Chicago Press.

Hill, J. (2001). The racializing function of language panics. In R. D. González & I. Melis (Eds.), *Language ideologies: Critical perspectives on the Official English movement, Vol. 2: History, theory, and policy* (pp. 245–267). Urbana, IL and Mahwah, NJ: National Council of Teachers of English and Lawrence Erlbaum Associates.

Hinton, L., & Hale, K. (Eds.). (2001). *The green book of language revitalization in practice.* San Diego, CA: Academic Press.

Holm, W. (in press). The goodness of bilingual education for Native American students. In T. L. McCarty & O. Zepeda (Eds.), *One voice, many voices: Recreating Indigenous language communities.* Tucson: American Indian Language Development Institute, University of Arizona.

Horne, E., & McBeth, S. (1998). *Essie's story: The life and legacy of a Shoshone teacher.* Lincoln and London: University of Nebraska Press.

Kloss, H. (1977). *The American bilingual tradition.* Rowley, MA: Newbury House.

Krauss, M. (1998). The condition of Native North American languages: The need for realistic assessment and action. *International Journal of the Sociology of Language, 132,* 9–21.

Language Policy Task Force. (1992). English and colonialism in Puerto Rico. In J. Crawford (Ed.), *Language loyalties: A source book on the Official English controversy* (pp. 63–71). Chicago and London: University of Chicago Press.

Lankshear, C. (1998). Meanings of literacy in contemporary educational reform proposals. *Educational Theory, 48,* 351–372.

Levinson, B. A., Foley, D. E., & Holland, D. C. (Eds.). (1996). *The cultural production of the educated person: Critical ethnographies of schooling and local practice.* Albany: State University of New York Press.

Lomawaima, K. T. (1993). Domesticity in the federal Indian schools: The power of authority over mind and body. *American Ethnologist, 20,* 1–14.

Lomawaima, K. T. (1994). *They called it Prairie Light: The story of Chilocco Indian School.* Lincoln and London: University of Nebraska Press.

Lomawaima, K. T. (1995). Educating Native Americans. In J. A. Banks & C. A. M. Banks (Eds.), *Handbook of research on multicultural education* (pp. 331–347). New York: Macmillan.

Lomawaima, K. T. (Ed.). (1996). Special Issue on Indian boarding schools. *Journal of American Indian Education, 35* (entire volume).

Lomawaima, K. T., & McCarty, T. L. (2002). When tribal sovereignty challenges democracy: American Indian education and the democratic ideal. *American Educational Research Journal, 39,* 279–305.

McCarty, T. L. (1997). American Indian, Alaska Native, and Native Hawaiian bilingual education. In J. Cummins & D. Corson (Eds.), *Encyclopedia of language and education, Vol. 5: Bilingual education* (pp. 45–56). Dordrecht, Netherlands: Kluwer Academic Publishers.

McCarty, T. L. (2002a). Between possibility and constraint: Indigenous language education, planning, and policy in the United States. In J. W. Tollefson (Ed.), *Language policies in education: Critical issues* (pp. 285–307). Mahwah, NJ: Lawrence Erlbaum Associates.

McCarty, T. L. (2002b). *A place to be Navajo: Rough Rock and the struggle for self-determination in Indigenous schooling.* Mahwah, NJ: Lawrence Erlbaum Associates.

McCarty, T. L. (in press). Introduction: Resisting the "great divide." In T. L. McCarty (Ed.), *Language, literacy, and power in schooling.* Mahwah, NJ: Lawrence Erlbaum Associates.

McCarty, T. L., Watahomigie, L. J., & Yamamoto, A. Y. (Guest Eds.). (1999). Reversing language shift in Indigenous America: Collaborations and views from the field [Theme Issue]. *Practicing Anthropology, 21,* 2–47.

Meriam, L., Brown, R. A., Cloud, H. R., Dale, E. E., Duke, E., Edwards, H. R., McKenzie, F. A., Mark, M. L., Ryan, W. C., Jr., & Spillman, W. J. (1928). *The problem of Indian administration.* Baltimore, MD: The Johns Hopkins Press.

Noley, G. (1979). Choctaw bilingual and bicultural education in the 19th century. In American Indian Studies Center (Ed.), *Multicultural education and the American Indian* (pp. 25–39). Los Angeles: American Indian Studies Center, University of California, Los Angeles.

Noonan, P. (2001, October 19). Profiles encouraged. *Opinion Journal.* Retrieved October 22, 2001, http://www.opinionjournal.com/columnists/pnoonan/?id=95001349

Nover, S. M. (1995). Politics and language: American sign language and English. In C. Lucas (Ed.), *Sociolinguistics in deaf communities* (pp. 109–163). Washington, DC: Gallaudet University Press.

Parsons-Yazzie, E. (1996/1997). Nihałchini dayist'í̜ǫ nahalin. *Journal of Navajo Education, 14,* 60–67.

Payne, N. A., Wallace, L., & Shorten, K. S. (1953). *Be a good waitress.* Brigham City, UT: Materials Preparation Department, Intermountain School.

Pennycook, A. (1999). Introduction: Critical approaches to TESOL. *TESOL Quarterly, 33,* 329–348.

Pennycook, A. (2001). Lessons from colonial language policies. In R. D. González & I. Melis (Eds.), *Language ideologies: Critical perspectives on the Official English movement, Vol. 2: History, theory, and policy* (pp. 198–220). Urbana, IL and Mahwah, NJ: National Council of Teachers of English and Lawrence Erlbaum Associates.

Phillipson, R. (Ed.). (2000). *Rights to language: Equity, power, and education.* Mahwah, NJ: Lawrence Erlbaum Associates.

Piatt, B. (1990) *¿Only English? Law and language policy in the United States.* Albuquerque: University of New Mexico Press.

Qin-Hilliard, D. B., Feinauer, E., & Quiroz, B. (2001). Introduction. *Harvard Educational Review, 71,* v–ix.

Rhodes, J. (1953a). *Baking dictionary.* Brigham City, UT: Materials Preparation Department, Intermountain School.

Rhodes, J. (1953b). *Shoe repairing dictionary.* Brigham City, UT: Materials Preparation Department, Intermountain Indian School.

Ricento, T., & Burnaby, B. (1998). *Language and politics in the United States and Canada: Myths and realities.* Mahwah, NJ: Lawrence Erlbaum Associates.

Roessel, R. A., Jr. (1977). *Navajo education in action: The Rough Rock Demonstration School.* Chinle, AZ: Navajo Curriculum Center Press.

Ruiz, R. (1984). Orientations in language planning. *NABE Journal, 8,* 15–34.

Senese, G. (1986). Self-determination and American Indian education: An illusion of control. *Educational Theory, 36,* 153–164.

Silverstein, M. (1996). Dynamics of linguistic contact. In W. C. Sturtevant (Gen. Ed.) & I. Goodard (Vol. Ed.), *Handbook of North American Indians, Vol. 17: Languages* (pp. 117–136). Washington, DC: Smithsonian Institution.

Skutnabb-Kangas, T. (2000). *Linguistic genocide in education–or worldwide diversity and human rights?* Mahwah, NJ: Lawrence Erlbaum Associates.

Skutnabb-Kangas, T., & Phillipson, R. (Eds.). with Rannut, M. (1994). *Linguistic human rights: Overcoming linguistic discrimination.* Berlin and New York: Mouton de Gruyter.

Smith, H. L. (1998). Literacy and instruction in African American communities: Shall we overcome? In B. Pérez, with T. L. McCarty et al. (Eds.), *Sociocultural contexts of language and literacy* (pp. 189–222). Mahwah, NJ: Lawrence Erlbaum Associates.

Spicer, E. (1962). *Cycles of conquest: The impact of Spain, Mexico, and the United States on the Indians of the Southwest, 1533–1960.* Tucson: University of Arizona Press.

Spring, J. (1996). *The cultural transformation of a Native American family and its tribe 1763–1995: A basket of apples.* Mahwah, NJ: Lawrence Erlbaum Associates.

Suárez-Orozco, M. (2001). Globalization, immigration, and education: The research agenda. *Harvard Educational Review, 71,* 345–365.

Szasz, M. (1974). *Education and the American Indian: The road to self-determination.* Albuquerque: University of New Mexico Press.

Szasz, M. (1988). *Indian education in the American colonies, 1607–1783.* Albuquerque: University of New Mexico Press.

Tollefson, J. W. (1991). *Planning language, planning inequality: Language policy in the community.* London: Longman.

Tollefson, J. W. (Ed.) (2002). *Language policies in education: Critical issues.* Mahwah, NJ: Lawrence Erlbaum Associates.

Trennert, R. A., Jr. (1988). *The Phoenix Indian School: Forced assimilation in Arizona, 1891–1935*. Norman and London: University of Oklahoma Press.

U.S. Office of Education. (1969). *Indian education: A national tragedy—a national challenge*. Washington, DC: U.S. Government Printing Office.

Valdés, G. (2001). *Learning and not learning English: Latino students in American schools*. New York and London: Teachers College Press.

White House Conference on Indian Education. (1992). *The final report of the White House Conference on Indian Education* (Vols. 1 & 2). Washington, DC: Author.

Wiley, T. G. (1998). The imposition of World War I era English-only policies and the fate of German in North America. In T. Ricento & B. Burnaby (Eds.), *Language and politics in the United States and Canada: Myths and realities* (pp. 211–241). Mahwah, NJ: Lawrence Erlbaum Associates.

Wiley, T. G. (2000). Continuity and change in the function of language ideologies in the United States. In T. Ricento (Ed.), *Ideology, politics, and language policies: Focus on English*. Amsterdam, Netherlands: John Benjamins.

Wiley, T. G. (2002). Accessing language rights in education: A brief history of the U.S. context. In J. W. Tollefson (Ed.), *Language policies in education: Critical issues* (pp. 39–64). Mahwah, NJ: Lawrence Erlbaum Associates.

Williamson, V. (1954). *I am a good citizen*. Ogden, UT: Defense Printing Service, Department of the Interior, Bureau of Indian Affairs.

ENDNOTES

1. I am indebted to my colleague, K. Tsianina Lomawaima, for first pointing out to me the policy implications of "safe" versus "dangerous" difference in American Indian education (Lomawaima & McCarty, 2002).

2. I prefer the term *minoritized* to *minority*, as the latter term can be stigmatizing and is often numerically inaccurate. Minoritized more accurately conveys the power relations by which certain groups are socially, economically, and politically marginalized. It also implies human agency and the power to effect positive change.

3. The notable exceptions were federal policies toward American Indians, state policies toward enslaved Africans, and policies toward deaf students. With the passage of the Civilization Fund Act in 1819, federal policy became increasingly oriented toward the eradication of Indigenous languages. At the same historical moment, "Every Southern state except Tennessee had laws expressly forbidding instruction for African Americans" (Smith, 1998, p. 191). And, throughout much of the 19th and 20th centuries, audism and oral methods emphasizing speech competency over the use and development of American Sign Language have been the rule in schools serving deaf students (Nover, 1995).

4. According to Krauss (1998), there are now 175 Indigenous languages still spoken in the United States, only 20 of which are being naturally acquired by children.

II

Language
in Post-Colonial States

5

Medium of Instruction in Hong Kong: One Country, Two Systems, Whose Language?

Amy B. M. Tsui
The University of Hong Kong

Hong Kong was under British colonial rule for more than 150 years, having been colonized by the British in 1842 as a result of the Opium War. In 1997, after a lengthy negotiation with the British Government that began in 1984, China resumed its sovereignty over Hong Kong, and on 1st of July, Hong Kong became a Special Administrative Region (SAR) of China.

Hong Kong has a population of over 7 million. About 96% of the population are Chinese, 2% are Filipinos, and 2% are other nationalities, including Indonesian, American, Canadian, Thai, Indian, British, Australian, Japanese, and Nepalese (see Tsui & Bunton, 2000). According to a sociolinguistic survey conducted in 1993, 81.6% of the population speaks Cantonese as their mother tongue and 91.9% are able to speak Cantonese. Only 1.3% are native speakers of English. In recent years, the number of Cantonese speakers has increased. According to the 1996 By-Census, 88.7% of the population indicated that Cantonese is the usual language spoken (see Bacon-Shone & Bolton, 1998, p. 73, 75). For social communication between Cantonese speakers and speakers of other Chinese dialects (for example, immigrants from the People's Republic of China), Cantonese is also the lingua franca. Since 1997, there has been an increase in the use of Putonghua, especially for communication between business people and government officials from the People's Republic of China. Putonghua has also become a subject in most primary and secondary schools.

Despite the fact that the overwhelming majority of the population speaks Cantonese—and reads and writes Modern Standard Chinese—English was the sole official language until 1974, when Chinese (that is, Cantonese for the spoken language and Modern Standard Chinese for the written language) was recognized as an official language after considerable public pressure. Nevertheless, English remained the primary official language until shortly before the hand-over back to China.

MEDIUM-OF-INSTRUCTION POLICY

In Hong Kong, there are about 450,000 primary students and roughly the same number of secondary students. Chinese (Cantonese for the spoken form and Modern Standard Chinese for the written form) is the medium of instruction for the majority of primary schools. Before the change of sovereignty in 1997, English was the medium of instruction for the overwhelming majority of secondary schools. Prior to the implementation of the mandatory mother-tongue education policy in 1998 (according to figures provided by the Hong Kong Government Education Department), about 94% of the students were studying in English-medium secondary schools,[1] whereas only 6% were studying in Chinese-medium schools. The figures for primary students were almost the exact reverse (93% studying in Chinese and 7% studying in English; see Education Department, 1995–1997).

Mandatory Mother-Tongue Education

Under the British regime, the choice of medium of instruction had been left very much in the hands of the schools, despite the fact that educational consultancy reports had repeatedly recommended mandating mother-tongue education. In 1990, the Education Commission, a government advisory body on educational policy, recommended in its fourth report (referred to as the *Education Commission Report No. 4* [hereafter, *ECR 4*]), that mother-tongue education should be used as the medium of instruction in the majority of secondary schools from Secondary One (Grade 7) to Secondary Three (Grade 9) (Education Commission, 1990). Schools that wanted to adopt English as a medium of instruction (hereafter EMI) had to seek approval from the Education Department (the equivalent of the Ministry of Education). The government laid down three criteria that schools needed to satisfy before they would be granted permission to use English as the medium of instruction (see the following section for details about the criteria). A vetting committee was also set up to consider applications from schools. Unlike past consultation reports, this document actually stated a time line for implementation over a period of 8 years. In the first few years, schools were to be *encouraged* to adopt Chinese as a medium of instruction (hereafter CMI). However, by 1998, schools would be given so-called *firm guidance* on which medium they should adopt. Out of a total of 421 government and government-subsidized secondary schools, 124 schools applied to use English as the medium of instruction. One hundred schools were considered to have satisfied the criteria and were granted approval, while 24 schools were disallowed. Among these 24 schools, 20 appealed against the decision. An independent Appeals Committee was set up to handle the appeals, and a further 14 schools were subsequently granted approval. Consequently, a total of 114 schools were permitted to adopt EMI.

Reactions From the Community

This change in medium-of-instruction (hereafter MOI) policy aroused strong emotional reactions from every sector of the community. Schools saw the new policy as being socially divisive, and taking away their autonomy. A survey conducted by the Hong Kong Subsidized School Council in 1999 showed that 66% of school principals disagreed with the policy. And many of the CMI schools were resentful that they had seemingly become second-class schools and their students, second-class students. In early 1999, questionnaires administered by the Chinese as a Medium-of-instruction Support Center (CMI Centre) at The University of Hong Kong to all CMI schools (307 in total) showed that out of 152 school administrators who responded, 52.7% indicated that their schools had suffered a reduced intake of better ability students, and 32% indicated that the academic standards of their student intake had declined. Parents who could not get their children into EMI schools saw the policy as jeopardizing their children's future. The business sector objected vehemently, and warned that this would lead to a decline in English standards and hence would compromise the competitiveness of Hong Kong as an international city.

Four years after the implementation of the controversial policy, there is plenty of evidence that students have actually benefited from learning in their mother tongue. Surveys conducted by the CMI Centre at The University of Hong Kong in 1999 and 2002 showed that learning through the mother tongue has had a positive effect on students' academic performance, motivation, and self-confidence. For example, the survey conducted in 2002 on 287 CMI schools showed that 65% of the respondents (174 schools) agreed that students showed improvement in their academic performance; 60% agreed that students took more initiative in asking questions and engaging in discussions in class; and 65% agreed that students became more self-confident. Marsh, Hau, and Kong (2000) conducted a longitudinal study of 12,784 students' achievements in Chinese, English, geography, history, mathematics, and science from Secondary One to Three (Grades 7 to 9) after the implementation of the new policy. The findings showed that whereas EMI had a positive effect on students' English proficiency, and a slightly negative effect on their achievements in mathematics, it had, in the words of the researchers, "incredibly" negative effects on achievement in geography, history, and science. These negative effects were consistent throughout all 3 years, and affected students of all levels of ability.

Studies of teaching and learning in CMI and EMI classrooms (in content subjects, such as history and science) also show that there were qualitative differences in teacher–student interaction: in terms of the types of questions asked and the responses elicited; the opportunities that students were afforded to engage in collaborative construction of knowledge; and the precision of the language used by the teacher and the students (which in turn had important effects on the precision of the concepts taught; see Marton & Tsui, in press; Ng, Tsui, & Marton, 2001).

Despite such evidence, criticism of mother-tongue education has not abated, and there is no sign that the policy is gaining greater acceptance in the community. A very recent survey conducted by the Chinese University of Hong Kong showed that among 805 adults surveyed—although 50% of them supported mother-tongue education, and 64.3% agreed that learning in the mother tongue would be more effective—only 12.9% intended to send their children to CMI schools, whereas 53.5% intended to send their children to EMI schools (Ming Pao Daily, 6 September, 2002). Critics have frequently listed the enforcement of the policy as one of the failures of the SAR government, alongside other failures such as its ill-conceived housing policy, which led to the collapse of the property market, and its inability to revive the economy (see Lui & Chiu, 2000).

The Chief Executive of the Hong Kong SAR, Tung Chi Wah, reiterated on a number of occasions—including in his policy speeches—the commitment of the Hong Kong SAR Government to mother-tongue education. Yet, at the same time, conflicting messages have emanated from top government officials and influential members of its advisory bodies. For example, when the policy met with strong objections, the former Chief Secretary, Anson Chan, made public her views about the importance of maintaining the standard of English in Hong Kong. And when Anthony Leung, the current Financial Secretary, took his former position as Chairman of the Education Commission in 1999, one of the first pronouncements he was reported by the press to have made was that the policy would be reviewed after his first year in office. These conflicting messages created a great deal of uncertainty and anxiety in schools about the government's commitment to the MOI policy. The current Chief Secretary, Donald Tsang (who succeeded Anson Chan), was reported by the press to have advocated using English in meetings in the government as a way of getting the civil servants to "brush up" on their

English. Arthur Lee, the newly appointed Secretary of the Education and Manpower Bureau in the Chief Executive's newly formed cabinet (who assumed office in August, 2002), was quick to voice his opinion that the MOI policy should be more flexible. This immediately generated speculation among schools that the policy would be changed.

To justify the change in MOI policy, both the colonial government as well as the Hong Kong SAR government put forward strong educational arguments and research evidence. Both denied that the change in MOI policy had anything to do with the change of sovereignty and that it was purely motivated by their concern for the educational benefits of the students. The questions that this chapter raises and attempts to address are: Was the change in MOI policy really just motivated by an educational agenda? If so, why is it that in more than 150 years of colonial rule, despite the fact that educational consultants had recommended time and time again that mother-tongue education should be adopted (and even made mandatory) because it is the best medium for learning, the colonial government failed to take their recommendations on board, and left the choice of MOI to schools and parents? A change in sovereignty is often accompanied by a change in language policy. The establishment of a national language and using it as a medium of instruction are important means of nation building, as the history of former colonies shows. It is perfectly legitimate for the new MOI policy to have been motivated by the political agenda of nation building. But why did the SAR government deny this motivation? Why is it that 5 years after its implementation, there is still so much controversy, not least within the Hong Kong SAR government itself?

The conflicting messages sent to the public by government officials—wittingly or unwittingly—suggest that the issue is indeed very complex. There are a number of forces that have shaped the formulation and the implementation of the policy since 1998, as the Chinese government conducts the unprecedented social and political experiment of "one country, two systems" in Hong Kong. This chapter is an attempt to explore these forces.

EDUCATIONAL AGENDA
FOR MEDIUM-OF-INSTRUCTION POLICY

From the official documents issued by the colonial and the Hong Kong SAR governments (and their public rhetoric), the mandatory implementation of mother-tongue education was based entirely on educational grounds. The *Medium-of-instruction Guidance* issued to schools by the Education Department outlined the educational benefits of mother-tongue teaching as follows:

> With the use of Chinese as MOI lifting language barriers in the study of most subjects, students will be better able to understand what is taught, analyze

problems, express views, develop an enquiring mind and cultivate critical thinking. Mother-tongue teaching thus leads to better cognitive and academic development. (Education Department, September 1997, p. 3)

The government laid down three criteria that schools using EMI must meet. The first criterion pertained to students' academic ability. No less than 85% of the Secondary One (Grade 7) students in schools adopting EMI must belong to the top 40% to 50% of the internal school assessment in English and Chinese.[2] The second criterion had to do with teachers' English language ability. Teachers of all subjects, except Chinese, in EMI schools must be able to conduct lessons effectively in English. The English proficiency of the teachers is to be certified by the principal of the school applying for EMI status. The third criterion is that the school has in place programs and strategies to help Secondary One (Grade 7) students to switch from learning through Chinese to learning through English.

The criteria used for vetting applications from schools were based on several research studies, some of which were conducted in the mid-1980s. The first criterion was based mainly on a study by Brimer et al. (1985) on the effectiveness of different language media (including English only, Chinese only, and a mixture of English and Chinese) on learning in Anglo–Chinese schools.[3] The results of these studies showed that only about 30% of the students with top English proficiency could perform effectively when the text and the medium were in English. They also showed that another 30% or so had serious difficulties coping with English-medium but would be able to work effectively in Chinese medium. The remaining students fell somewhere in between. The effects of different media of instruction were more significant in heavily language-dependent subjects like history but less significant in subjects such as science (see also Johnson, Chan, Lee, & Ho, 1985; Ip & Chan, 1985). These studies further showed that more and more Cantonese was used for instruction in English-medium schools, with teachers resorting to Cantonese to explain complex concepts, for example. Cantonese or mixed code[4] was also found to be more effective in promoting classroom interaction. These studies suggest that in order for students to benefit from English-medium instruction, their English proficiency must have reached a threshold level. Otherwise, their academic achievement would suffer badly.

The requirement that students need to be proficient in Chinese as well, in order to benefit from English-medium education, was based on the concept of *Common Underlying Language Proficiency* propounded by Cummins and Swain (1986), and supported by a series of research studies that they conducted. According to their findings, skills acquired through a first language can be transferred to a second language, and students who are proficient in their mother tongue are better learners of a second language. Hence good performance in Chinese, and in learning through Chinese, can be said to predict a high ability to cope with learning through English. Indeed, in the study by Brimer et al. (1985), Chinese proficiency was strongly correlated with proficiency in English.

The second criterion was based on findings from classroom observations that many teachers, especially science and mathematics teachers, had difficulties teaching entirely through English because of their own inadequate command of English. Furthermore, their use of mixed code in teaching had adverse effects on students' English proficiency. The third criterion was based on observations made by researchers that there is a gap between the students' English proficiency and the demands of the secondary curriculum on their English. Consequently teachers have to resort to Cantonese, especially when they are dealing with complex concepts. To bridge the gap, researchers proposed that assistance should be given to enable students to switch from Chinese medium to English medium in the form of a "bridging course" (Johnson & Swain, 1994). In addition to the studies just discussed, there were a number of research studies that reached a similar conclusion (e.g., see Ho, 1986; Siu, 1979; Siu & Mak, 1992). There is little doubt that the new MOI policy and the vetting criteria were supported by educational research evidence.

The previous discussion seems to suggest that the decision made by both governments to mandate the adoption of mother-tongue education in schools was indeed driven by an educational agenda, as had been assured. In denying the political motivation behind the change in MOI policy, both governments argued that the policy had already been laid down in 1990, and that it was sheer coincidence that the implementation date should fall after the change of sovereignty and not before. However, it must be pointed out that the debate over the MOI policy in Hong Kong schools had been going on for more than a century, and—as previously mentioned—educational consultants in the colonial regime had recommended, time and again, on educational grounds, that the mother tongue should be used as the medium of instruction. Despite this, the colonial government had always used the demand for English by parents, and the need to maintain a high standard of English for the economic development of Hong Kong as reasons for not taking the recommendation on board. This seems to suggest that the colonial government placed social and economic agendas over and above the educational agenda. What was it, then, that caused the colonial government to reverse its priorities on the eve of the hand-over, despite unprecedented objections from parents and schools, as well as from the business sector? A brief review of the history of the MOI policy in Hong Kong shows how unconvincing the arguments of both governments were in presenting the educational agenda as the only motivation for policy change.

MEDIUM-OF-INSTRUCTION POLICY
IN THE COLONIAL REGIME

For nearly 150 years, educators (both local and overseas) have advocated using Chinese as a medium of instruction in schools in Hong Kong. As far back as the 1860s, Frederick Stewart (an influential figure in the early education development of Hong Kong, who was the first Inspector of Government schools and subsequently the Chairman of the Education Commission) pointed out that learning through a foreign language would adversely affect the quality of learning, and that having a good foundation in the mother tongue was necessary for the acquisition of another tongue. He cautioned that there should not be any attempt to "denationalize" the young people of Hong Kong (see Tsui, 1996; Tsui, Shum, Wong, Tse, & Ki, 1999). However, his views were not accepted by the then Governor, Hennessy, who decided that from the point of view of the government, the provision of English education should be the primary objective, and the provision of vernacular education should be left to private and voluntary bodies. The aim, as blatantly stated by E.R. Belilios, a member of the Education Commission, was to anglicize the Chinese so that they could act as intermediaries between the colonial government and the locals (see Pennycook, 1998).

A century later, in 1963, R. Marsh and J. Sampson, appointed by the government to examine the education needs of Hong Kong, remarked that using English as a medium of instruction imposed a very heavy burden on students, and that there should be more Chinese-medium schools in which English was taught as a second language (see Marsh & Sampson, 1963). Although the government agreed that many pupils in Anglo–Chinese schools were unable to benefit fully from English-medium education because of the difficulty of studying through the medium of a second language, it was reluctant to adopt Marsh and Sampson's recommendation. This, according to the government, was due to "marked parental preference for Anglo-Chinese secondary education", and the fact that "the English language is an important medium of international communication and a knowledge of it has undoubted commercial value in Hong Kong" (Hong Kong Government, 1965, p. 83). In other words, the government presented parental preference and the economic development of Hong Kong as its top priorities. In the subsequent White Paper on education in 1965 (a policy document), the whole issue of the medium of instruction was not even mentioned in the main text of the Report.

About a decade later—after primary education was made compulsory in 1971, causing a subsequent expansion in secondary education—the issue was revisited. The government published a consultation paper on education (referred to as a Green Paper), in which it was proposed yet again that Chinese should be used as the language of instruction at junior secondary level, and that English should be learnt only as a subject (Hong Kong Government, 1973, p. 6). This proposal was very similar to the new MOI policy put forward in 1998. However, once again, the subsequent White Paper on Education Policy published in 1974 did not adopt the recommendation made in the Green Paper, and the same arguments about parental concern and Hong Kong's economic development were put forward as justification for not doing so. However, instead of merely dropping the recommendation, the White Paper left the choice of MOI to individual schools, and in 1974, for the first time, the public school leaving examination, the Hong Kong School Certificate Examination, could be taken by the students in English or Chinese.

The change in the government's position with regard to MOI is not surprising if we consider the wider sociopolitical context at the time. Until the 1970s, the British had maintained an old-fashioned colonial style of government in which they saw themselves as colonizers and the Hong Kong people the colonized. Their educational policy was very much guided by the need to produce an English speaking Chinese elite who could act as the intermediary between the colonizer and the colonized. This style of government generated much resentment that culminated in a minor social disturbance in 1966 and a riot in 1967. The riot, in particular, alerted the government to the fact that it needed to strengthen the legitimacy of its colonial rule. To this end, it carried out a number of reforms without, however, making major changes in the institutional structure. One of the major reforms was to provide more channels for social participation (see Lui & Chiu, 2000). One important channel was public consultation, which later evolved into the setting up of advisory committees that included lay members (see Cheng & Wong, 1997). Vocal critics of the government were appointed to these committees, and some of their views were incorporated in the consultation documents, although it was carefully ensured that these critics were in the minority. The public was also consulted and their views were partly incorporated. The Education Green Paper in 1973 was one such consultation document, and therefore the 1974 White Paper partly incorporated the views of these critics and the public. At the time, strong views were expressed by teachers and university academics against the use of English as a medium of learning on the ground that it had detrimental effects on students' cognitive development (see for example, Cheng, Shek, Tse, & Wong, 1973). It is in this context that schools were given the flexibility to adopt Chinese or English as the medium of instruction. In the meantime, China had begun to play a more prominent role in international politics due to its "ping-pong diplomacy" and the fact that it became a member of the United Nations in 1972, both of which had a strong impact on the people of Hong Kong. During the 1970s, there was an increasingly strong awareness of the Hong Kong people's Chinese identity, and an increasing demand for the recognition of Chinese as one of the official languages. Thousands of demonstrators took to the streets for this cause. And in 1974, under mounting public pressure, Chinese was established as an official language.

Given the social and political sentiments at the time, it would not have been possible for the government to continue to ignore an educational agenda, which had become increasingly emotionally charged. To ensure political stability and to legitimize its colonial rule, the government ameliorated the situation by shifting the choice of MOI to the schools and by allowing more flexibility in the choice of MOI at subject level, while at the same time continuing to uphold the social and economic agenda. The government, however, was well aware of the fact that this flexibility would not lead to any fundamental changes for three main reasons: English was still the only *functioning* official language; a good command of English was still the most important requirement for joining the civil service; and the most prestigious university was English medium. The supposition was indeed correct. Although the number of Chinese-medium schools increased from 79 to 114, it was outnumbered by the number of English-medium schools, which increased from 89 to 229.

Eight years after the publication of the White Paper in 1974 (Hong Kong Government, 1974), the then governor, McLehose, as part of his reform program, brought in a panel of overseas educationists, headed by Llwellyn, to conduct a comprehensive review of education in Hong Kong. One major observation that they made was the "lamentable" situation in education in which students from non-English speaking Chinese families had to learn in English, a language that they had not mastered and in which they could not express themselves. The consequence of this, the panel observed, was that students had to resort to rote learning and regurgitation. The panel proposed that the mother tongue was the best medium for teaching and learning because it "reflects the soul and culture of a people" (Llewellyn, Kirst, & Roeloffs, 1982, p. 25). In view of the likely objection from parents, it proposed a compromise between adopting mother tongue for junior secondary education and making English medium available to only a selected number of schools. Early years of compulsory education, that is, from Primary One to Primary six, were to be provided through the mother tongue, and there would be a gradual progression to a genuinely bilingual program with half of the subjects taught in English and half in Chinese by Secondary Three (i.e., Grade 9).

However, the first report of the Education Commission, *ECR No. 1*, published 2 years after the Llewellyn Report, largely maintained the status quo by leaving the choice of the medium of instruction to individual schools, with extra resources given to CMI schools to strengthen English teaching (Education Commission, 1984). To justify maintaining the status quo, the

Report once again cited the need for Hong Kong to maintain a high level of English proficiency in order to retain its position as a leading international financial center. The Report also argued against mandating Chinese as the medium of teaching and learning by stating that "education should allow the greatest possible development for students having regard to their different needs and aptitudes" (p. 45). Instead, it proposed that schools should not be labeled according to their medium of instruction (that is, Anglo–Chinese school for English medium and Chinese Middle school for Chinese medium). Indication of which language was used for completion of the public school leaving examination was also removed. This proposal was at best cosmetic, for it did little to change the fact that the majority of the schools were still EMI, and the minority CMI, and that the parents were fully aware of which schools used which medium.

Paradoxically, at the same time as the government was rejecting recommendations made by its own educational consultants, it had commissioned academics to conduct research on MOI (such as the one conducted by Brimer et al. [1985] at the University of Hong Kong). These research studies, as mentioned before, all showed that using the mother tongue was far superior to using English as a medium for learning. Given such clear evidence, Brimer et al. argued that it would be unjustifiable to leave the choice of the medium of instruction to schools and parents. Unfortunately, this recommendation had little impact on policy at the time, and the number of CMI schools continued to drop.

In 1990, as mentioned previously, the Education Commission, in its *ECR No. 4*, again revisited the MOI issue and recommended that mother-tongue education be mandated. A time line was laid down for implementation in order to allow time for schools to prepare for the transition. Although the Report mentioned the importance of English in maintaining the status of Hong Kong as an international business, financial, and trading center, it argued that the interests of the students should come first: "In catering for the needs of our economy, we believe that the interests of the majority of our students should not be sacrificed" (Education Commission, 1990, p. 102). This recommendation was made at a time when there was an outcry from the business sector about the declining English standards in Hong Kong. The business sector was so concerned about this issue that the big enterprises (known locally as the big "Hongs")—led by the largest and politically most influential bank in Hong Kong at the time, the Hong Kong and Shanghai Bank—launched the Language Campaign to improve English standards in schools, and committed resources in the millions to the cause. The change in MOI policy therefore stood in stark contrast to the call for improvement in English standards at primary and secondary levels (see Tsui, 1996).

The Report also mentioned parental objection to MOI, which had previously been used as a reason for not mandating Chinese medium in schools, but which this time was not seen as an insurmountable problem. The Report argued that the increasing use of Chinese in government and law, the localization of the civil service, and the strengthening of the Chinese identity as 1997 approached would all serve to change the views of the parents.

The fact that the proposed change in MOI policy gave an educational agenda top priority must be interpreted in the wider political context. The Joint Declaration was signed in 1984, at which point the future of Hong Kong became clear. There was no illusion that colonial rule would be extended beyond 1997.[5] The colonial government started to prepare for a "noble retreat" from Hong Kong by taking measures to localize top government officials, enforce widespread bilingual communication in the government, introduce direct election in the Legislative Council, and institute other changes. The new MOI policy was very much part of the plan for the retreat in which the educational benefit of the children of Hong Kong was presented as being of utmost importance. However, the strategic timing of the policy ensured that the challenge of implementing a highly sensitive and emotionally charged policy would be faced by the Hong Kong SAR Government, rather than the colonial government.

This brief summary of the more than 150-year history of the MOI policy in Hong Kong fully demonstrates that its formulation had always been motivated by a political agenda, no matter whether the policy was to maintain the status quo or to introduce a drastic change. This is true for the colonial government as well as for the SAR government. Yet, not once in the policy papers did the political motivation come to the fore. When the political agenda and the educational agenda were in conflict, the latter had always been sacrificed. It was only when both agendas converged that educational considerations were attended to. However, this is not to suggest that the political agenda was the only force at work. Quite the contrary, it is precisely because there were often other forces at work, notably social and economic forces, that the government was able to put forward different agendas to the public to defend its policy at different times.

MEDIUM OF INSTRUCTION IN THE POST-COLONIAL ERA

With China's resumption of sovereignty over Hong Kong, the Chinese language, being the national language, should enjoy a much higher status. The people of Hong Kong should have a stronger awareness of Chinese identity. The adoption of Chinese as the medium of instruction in the majority of the schools should enhance the status of the Chinese language, as well as strengthen the national identity of Hong Kong people and their patriotic sentiments. Consequently, the community should be less resistant to this policy (see Education Commission, 1990). However, as pointed out earlier in this chapter, this has not proved to be the case. Whereas most former colonies have been eager to establish their national identity upon decolonization (see Gill, chap. 7, this volume), this does not seem to have happened in Hong Kong. The reasons for this are complex, but at the risk of over-simplification, I propose that there are at least two major reasons. One is pragmatic and the other is political, but they are intertwined, as we see in the following section.

National Identity and Pragmatism

In most cases, when a colony has gained its independence, the first and foremost task has been to raise the status of its own language (although the language of the former colonizer might be retained as one of the official languages). A national language is a symbol of national identity and unity. And it would not have been surprising if, after more than 150 years of colonial rule, the people of Hong Kong had been glad to see English relegated to secondary importance, compared to Chinese. Yet, what happened was quite the contrary. There was a great deal of nervousness—especially within the business sector—that English would be neglected after 1997. The chief executive of one of the biggest banks in Hong Kong voiced his concern at an international conference to celebrate the handover in 1997 as follows:

> If Hong Kong is to remain the great economic success that it is in the competitive global economy, it is vital for its voice to be heard and its products to be promoted. A good command of English is essential for that, especially among the territory's leaders. (Au, 1998, p. 180)

The business sector is not only keen to maintain Hong Kong's competitiveness in the international market, it is also very keen that Hong Kong should not become just another city in China. One of the greatest advantages that Hong Kong has over other cities in China is the English proficiency of its people. Since the 1970s, Hong Kong has grown from a largely monolingual community to a bilingual community. According to two sociolinguistic surveys conducted in 1983 and 1993, the percentage of people who indicated that they could speak English rose from 43.3% to 65.8%. And schooling was found to be the vehicle for bringing this about (see Bacon-Shone & Bolton, 1998).

Most people in Hong Kong see English not as the language of colonization but as the language of international commerce. Many see mother-tongue education as a sign of the narrow nationalism that suggests that even the act of learning a language other than the mother tongue means that one is no longer truly Chinese (see Matthews, 2001). A local political commentator, Frank Ching, wrote,

Hong Kong has already [since 1997] become much less international. To a large extent, that is the result of the Tung administration's actions, asking people to identify with China, forcing parents to accept Chinese as the medium of instruction for their children and increasingly using Chinese rather than English in the government. (Ching, 1998)

English is seen as a commodity that everybody desires. The business tycoons see it as an important means of maintaining the competitive edge of the city's business status, and parents see it as the golden passport to a successful future for their children.

National and Cultural Identity

In the previous section, I have outlined the resistance to mother-tongue education as motivated by pragmatic concerns. Underlying this resistance, there is perhaps something more profound than sheer pragmatism, connected with the cultural identity of Hong Kong people that is at odds with the national identity symbolized by mother-tongue education.

Since the 1970s, Hong Kong has developed its own identity. This was brought about by a conscious attempt on the part of the colonial government after the riot in 1967 to inculcate a sense of belonging among the Hong Kong people. At the time, a number of measures were taken, such as holding the annual Hong Kong Festival and designating the bauhinia as the flower of Hong Kong. The terms *Hong Kong people* or *Hongkongese* were coined at the time. In addition, Hong Kong people have established a sense of pride in themselves because of the rapid economic development of Hong Kong that has set it apart from China and has placed the city on the international map.

Studies conducted on the Hong Kong people's sense of identity show the following interesting findings (see Table 5.1).

TABLE 5.1
SURVEYS OF NATIONAL AND CULTURAL IDENTITY

	1986 *(Lau & Kuan, 1988)*	*1996* *(Fung, 1996)*	*1998* *(Yuen, 1998)*
Hongkongese (Hong Kong people)	59%	35%	40%
Hong Kong Chinese		28%	
Chinese	36%	30%	20.6%
Chinese in HK			16%
HK people in China			23%

As Table 5.1 demonstrates, various categories are used to describe the identity of the people of Hong Kong, which indicates the complexity of the issue. We can see from Table 5.1 that in all three studies of national and cultural identity in Hong Kong, less than 40% of all respondents considered themselves simply "Chinese". The majority of the respondents considered their primary identity to be Hongkongese or people of Hong Kong rather than Chinese.

Matthews (2001) conducted 45 interviews of younger university educated members of the Hong Kong middle class to find out how the change in sovereignty had affected their cultural identity. He found that there were two ways in which his interviewees insisted on distinguishing themselves from mainland Chinese: first, Hong Kong's exposure to the world (their international outlook) compared with China's isolation; and second, Hong Kong's wealth as opposed to China's poverty. In addition to these two distinctions, Hong Kong people have also accepted western values, such as public morality, equality, democracy, and freedom of press and speech. These values are shared particularly by middle-class professionals, whose numbers have grown considerably in the last 20 years. These are values that Hong Kong people have felt were lacking in China.

Hong Kong people therefore are ambivalent toward the change of sovereignty. Although some of them are glad that they are no longer colonized, there is a strong resistance to identifying themselves with the Chinese government. The urge to preserve a separate Hong Kong identity can be seen from the efforts made to preserve the use of Cantonese in oral communication in education, government, and administration. For example, there was intense discussion about whether Cantonese or Putonghua should be used when the Chief Executive and his officials swore their oath on 1 July 1997, and whether Cantonese or Putonghua should be used by the Chief Executive to deliver his first policy speech in October, 1997. Although it was generally accepted that Putonghua should be used in the oath-taking ceremony because it marked the resumption of Chinese sovereignty over Hong Kong, there was a strong feeling in the community that the policy speech should be in Cantonese, the language of Hong Kong.

Cantonese, one could say, has been taken as symbolic of the preservation of "two systems" in the "one country, two systems" principle. As Pierson (1998) observes, "Cantonese could have … a symbolic value … Cantonese might … become the symbol of freedom, democracy and independence" (p. 107). The debate over whether Putonghua instead of Cantonese should be used as the medium of instruction in CMI schools has been going on ever since the hand-over. Both educational and economic arguments have been put forward by people with opposing views. Underlying the debate is probably the political agenda of how far Hong Kong should or could retain its own identity and autonomy.

Given the strong desire of the Hong Kong people to maintain their own identity, it is not surprising that the mandatory mother-tongue education policy, which is a crucial part of the unification with the mainland, has been resisted so strongly by every sector in the community, particularly by the business sector and by middle-class parents.

ONE COUNTRY, TWO SYSTEMS: WHOSE LANGUAGE?

The Chief Executive of the Hong Kong SAR Government is caught in a dilemma. On the one hand, he was appointed by the Chinese Central Government, and it is part of his mission to "revive" a sense of Chinese identity in Hong Kong people and to instill a sense of national pride. To achieve this goal, he has reiterated the message "We are Chinese, and we are proud to be Chinese" on many occasions, including in his policy speech. Tung has tried to revive traditional Chinese cultural values, which are essentially Confucian, and to emphasize "trust, love and respect for our family and elders ... a belief in order and stability; an emphasis on obligations to the community rather than rights of the individual" (Yeung, 1996; SCMP, cited in Matthews, 2001, p. 296). He called on teachers to raise the ethnic and national consciousness of the young people of Hong Kong. In his policy speech in 2000, he pointed out that the history of Hong Kong is intertwined with the history of China, and called on young people to learn about the history of their own country. He said, "Our young students have much to learn about the history of our country. They should find out more about our great cultural heritage" (Tung, 2000, p. 27). Implementing mother-tongue education is therefore very much part of this social and political project. In his 1998 policy speech, he devoted a whole section to medium of instruction, and assured the public that his government remained "fully committed to the promotion of mother-tongue education," and would "adhere to the principles behind this initiative" (pp. 34–33).

On the other hand, the Tung government is also a probusiness government. The number of senior business executives and entrepreneurs who have been appointed to head government advisory committees is higher than ever. The voice of the business sector comes through loud and strong in all areas of government policy, not least in education and language policy.

In his 1998 policy speech (which took place at a time when mother-tongue education had been implemented for only 1 month and had provoked a strong negative reaction from the community), Tung promised that he would conduct a review of the policy in 3 years' time. It is now 5 years since the implementation, but no review has yet been conducted. The future of this new policy can probably be gleaned from the fact that in the first three policy speeches, that is, 1997–1999, Tung reiterated his commitment to mother-tongue education. However, there was no longer any mention of mother-tongue education in his policy speeches in 2000 and 2001. Instead, in his 2001 policy speech, he mentioned the importance of maintaining English standards in an international city such as Hong Kong, and outlined the measures that his government has already taken and intends to take to achieve this goal.

The task ahead for the Hong Kong SAR government is an onerous one. The government has to fulfill its mission of making Hong Kong part of "one country" by strengthening the national identity of its people, by raising their awareness of Chinese history, and by inculcating Chinese values and traditions. Yet on the other hand, it has to fulfill its mission of maintaining "two systems," which requires Hong Kong to operate with financial, legal, administrative, educational, and political systems that are different from China. This necessarily entails a set of moral values and principles that are typically western. But in whose language should this unprecedented social and political experiment be conducted? In English, in Cantonese, or in Putonghua? Or in all three? It is clear from the conflicting messages emanating from top government officials that this is a complex issue that the members of the Hong Kong SAR government, after 6 years in office, still have not been able to resolve amongst themselves.

CONCLUDING REMARKS

It has been pointed out by many language policy studies that language policy is never simply an educational issue. It must be understood in the broader social and political context (e.g., Pennycook, 2002; Tollefson, 2002). Central to decisions on language policy is the choice of the medium of instruction, as this determines who will participate in power and wealth.

The history of the medium-of-instruction policy in Hong Kong under the colonial regime and the implementation of the new medium-of-instruction policy in the post-colonial era richly demonstrate that medium-of-instruction policies are shaped by an interaction between political, social, and economic forces. However, among these agendas, it is always the political agenda that takes priority. Other agendas, be they social, economic, or educational, come to the fore only if they converge with the political agenda. Yet it is always these agendas that will be used as public justification for policy making.

REFERENCES

Au, A. (1998). Language standards and proficiency (An Employer's View Point). In B. Asker (Ed.), *Building Hong Kong on education* (pp. 179–183). Hong Kong: Longman.
Bacon-Shone, J., & Bolton, K. (1998). Charting multilingualism: Language censuses and language surveys in Hong Kong. In M. Pennington (Ed.), *Language in Hong Kong at century's end* (pp. 43–90). Hong Kong: Hong Kong University Press.

Brimer, A., Cheng, W., Ip, B., Johnson, K., Lam, R., Lee, P., Leung, J., Sweeting, A., & Tong, S. M. (1985). *The effects of the medium of instruction on the achievement of Form 2 students in Hong Kong secondary schools.* Hong Kong: Educational Research Establishment, Education Department, Hong Kong Government and Faculty of Education, Hong Kong University.

Cheng, N. L., Shek, K. C., Tse, K. K., & Wong, S. L. (1973). *At what cost?: Instruction through the English-medium in HK schools / a report for the public.* Hong Kong: Shum Shing.

Cheng, K. M., & Wong, S. Y. (1997). Empowerment of the powerless through the politics of the apolitical: Teacher professionalisation in Hong Kong. In B. J. Biddle, T. Good, & I. Goodson (Eds.), *International handbook of teachers and teaching* (pp. 411–436). Dordrecht: Kluwer.

Ching, F. (1998, October 22). Tung: A disappointing speech. *Far Eastern Economic Review.*

Cummins, J., & Swain, M. (1986). *Bilingualism in education.* London: Longman.

Education Commission. (1984). *Education Commission Report No. 1,* Hong Kong: Government Printer.

Education Commission. (1990). *Education Commission Report No. 4,* Hong Kong: Government Printer.

Education Department. (1995–1997). *Annual summary / Enrolment survey.* Hong Kong: Government Printer.

Education Department. (1997). *Medium of instruction guidance for secondary schools.* Hong Kong: Hong Kong Government.

Fung, W. K. (1996, February 17). Public softens stance on hand-over but rights fears remain. *South China Morning Post.*

Ho, K. K. (1986). The effect of written language in Chinese or English on Form 1 social studies achievement. *Education Research Journal, 1,* 16–21.

Hong Kong Government. (1965). *Education policy.* Hong Kong: Government Printer.

Hong Kong Government. (1973). *Report of the Board of Education on the proposed expansion of secondary school education in Hong Kong over the next decade. (Green Paper).* Hong Kong: Government Printer.

Hong Kong Government. (1974). *Secondary education in Hong Kong during the next decade (White Paper).* Hong Kong: Government Printer.

Ip, B., & Chan, G. (1985). *Studies on the modes of language of instruction at junior secondary levels in Anglo-Chinese schools.* Hong Kong: Educational Research Establishment, Education Department, Hong Kong Government.

Johnson, K., & Swain, M. (1994). From core to content: Bridging the L2 proficiency gap in late immersion. *Language and Education 8*(4), 211–229.

Johnson, R., Chan, R. M., Lee, L., & Ho, J. (1985). *An investigation of the effectiveness of various language modes of presentation, spoken and written in Form III in Hong Kong Anglo-Chinese secondary schools.* Hong Kong: Hong Kong Government, Education Department.

Lau, S. K., & Kuan, H. C. (1988). *The ethos of the Hong Kong Chinese.* Hong Kong: Chinese University Press.

Llewellyn, J., Kirst, M., & Roeloffs, K. (1982). *A perspective on education in Hong Kong.* Hong Kong: Government Printer.

Lui, T. L., & Chiu, S. W. K. (2000). Introduction—Changing political opportunities and the shaping of collective action: Social movements in Hong Kong. In S. W. K. Chiu & T. L. Lui (Eds.), *The dynamics of social movements in Hong Kong* (pp. 1–20). Hong Kong: Hong Kong University Press.

Marsh, H. W., Hau, K. T., & Kong, C. K. (2000). Late immersion and language instruction (English vs. Chinese) in Hong Kong high schools: Achievement growth in language and non-language subjects. *Harvard Educational Review, 70*(3), 302–346.

Marsh, R., & Sampson, J. (1963). *Report of Education Commission.* Hong Kong: Government Printer.

Marton, F., & Tsui, A. B. M. (in press). *Classroom Discourse and the Space of Learning.* Mahwah, NJ: Lawrence Erlbaum Associates.

Matthews, G. (2001). Cultural identity and consumption in post-colonial Hong Kong. In G. Matthews & T. L. Lui (Eds.), *Consuming Hong Kong* (pp. 287–318). Hong Kong: Hong Kong University Press.

Ng, D., Tsui, A. B. M., & Marton, F. (2001). Two faces of the reed relay. In D. Watkins & J. Biggs (Eds.), *The Chinese teacher* (pp. 135–160). Hong Kong and Melbourne, Australia: CERC and ACER.

Pennycook, A. (1998). *English and the discourses of colonialism.* London: Routledge.

Pennycook, A. (2002). Language policy and docile bodies: Hong Kong and governmentality. In J. Tollefson (Ed.), *Language policies in education: Critical issues* (pp. 91–110). Mahwah, NJ: Lawrence Erlbaum Associates.

Pierson, H. (1998). Societal Accomodation to English and Putonghua in Cantonese-speaking Hong Kong. In M. Pennington (Ed.), *Language in Hong Kong at century's end* (pp. 91–112). Hong Kong: Hong Kong University Press.

Siu, P. K. (1979). *The final report on the effects of the medium of instruction on student cognitive development and academic achievement.* Hong Kong: School of Education, Chinese University of Hong Kong.

Siu, P. K., & Mak, S. Y. (1992). The relationship between the medium of instruction and the teaching activities in junior secondary classrooms. *Hong Kong Education Research Journal 20*(2), 101–111.

Tollefson, J. (2002). Introduction: Critical issues in language policy. In J. Tollefson (Ed.), *Language policies in education: Critical issues* (pp. 3–16). Mahwah, NJ: Lawrence Erlbaum Associates.

Tsui, A. B. M. (1996). English in Asian bilingual education: From hatred to harmony—A response. *Journal of Multilingual and Multicultural Development, 17*(2–4), 241–247.

Tsui, A. B. M., Shum, M. S. K., Wong, C. K., Tse, S. K., & Ki, W. W. (1999). Which agenda?—Medium of instruction policy in post-1997 Hong Kong. *Language, Culture and Curriculum, 12*(3), 196–214.

Tsui, A. B. M., & Bunton, D. (2000). Discourse and attitudes of English teachers in Hong Kong. *World Englishes, 19*(3), 287–304.

Tung, C. H. (2000, October 11). *Serving the community sharing common goals,* Address by the Chief Executive The Honourable Tung Chee Hwa at the Legislative Council meeting.

Yeung, C. (1996, October 27). A need to keep local virtues. *South China Morning Post.*

Yuen, H. M. (1998, October 9). Who are Hongkongese? *Apple Daily,* p. H3.

ENDNOTES

1. The figures provided, however, are misleading. Ever since the late 1970s (when 9-year compulsory education was introduced), many teachers in the so-called English medium schools actually used mixed code (a mixture of Cantonese and English) as the spoken medium of instruction, while retaining English as the written medium in teaching and assessment. This will be discussed in further detail later.

2. The internal school assessments take place in Primary Five and Six. In order to ensure comparability across all schools, the internal assessment results are scaled by an academic aptitude test (AAT), which was administered to Primary Six pupils each year until 2001, when the test was abolished.

3. Prior to 1984, Hong Kong secondary schools were named according to their medium of instruction (i.e., Anglo–Chinese schools and Chinese Middle schools; the former used English and the latter used Chinese as a medium of instruction). In 1984, this distinction in name was removed, and all schools were called secondary schools. However, the distinction in the teaching medium still exists.

4. Mixed code refers to intra- and intersentential switching between English and Cantonese.

5. A delegation led by Sir S.Y. Chung lobbied the British Government to extend its colonial rule beyond 1997 (Tsui et al., 1999).

6

Medium-of-Instruction Policy in Singapore

Anne Pakir
National University of Singapore

Among the world's many multiethnic countries, the island-nation and city-state Republic of Singapore offers a unique case study of a successful program of bilingualism and language management. Founded in 1819 by the British, Singapore gained internal independence in 1959, briefly became part of the Federation of Malaysia (1963–1965), and has been a sovereign nation since 1965. Its per capita income today ranks among the highest in the world. Singapore is a country where language planning and its impact on medium-of-instruction policies are of paramount importance. It represents an impressive case of a well-planned and effectively implemented language-policy program.

Since independence in 1965, this small multilingual country, with approximately 4 million people in 226 square miles, has negotiated carefully its language policy and the attendant-sensitive choice of a language for the medium of instruction in its state educational system. The result today is a uniquely defined English-knowing bilingualism (Pakir, 1992), arising from the school system and measured by proficiency in English and one other official language of the country. In a global, knowledge-based economy, where the future of English as the world's dominant language is assured for at least the first half of the 21st century (Graddol, 1997), English is the first school language and the main medium of instruction in all national schools. At the same time, the ethnic mother tongues (which are "determined on the basis of ethnicity," see Gopinathan, 1997, p. 47) are considered to be of paramount importance to the pupils in the Singapore school system for "understanding their cultural heritage" (Singapore Fact Sheet Series, http://www.mita.gov.sg).

The high level of achievement in English-knowing bilingualism is no mean feat for a country which has a population that is 77% Chinese, 15% Malay, 7% Indian, and 1% "Other" (an official label that includes the Eurasians, a small but influential community). Besides being one of the four official languages of the country, English was deemed politically neutral for the three main ethnic groups, and therefore was selected as the working language of the country. It was also recognised very early in the days of independence that English was a language of wider communication and the language of multinational corporations (MNCs) and industrialists who were investing in Asia. The mid-1960s to the mid-1970s was a period of making Singapore attractive to MNCs, and the policy of English-knowing bilingualism supported this goal.

The commitment to a multilingual state and a bilingual school system with English as its foundation is clear. In addition, the overall language policy of equal treatment for the three major groups in the country has been supported by the bilingual education policy that recognizes and emphasizes the importance of the three other official languages: Malay (also the national language), Chinese (Mandarin), and Tamil. In 1987, English became the main medium of instruction and the first school language (abbreviated to "EL1" in the national school system). The other official languages are taught in schools as second school languages: Malay (ML2), Tamil (TL2), and Chinese (CL2). Pupils are expected to select their second school language on the basis of their ethnic classification. Mandarin, which is the second school language for Chinese pupils, is mainly offered as CL2, although high achievers are also given the opportunity to take Chinese at the first language level ("Higher Chinese") along with English as a first language. The official ethnic languages are supported, promoted, and taught as second school languages, wherein language and literacy skills, as well as moral values rather than content instruction, are emphasized.

Language policy changes, arising from national and international socioeconomic developments in the last half of the 20th century, have had a direct impact on pedagogical issues. These have been discussed in several publications. For example, Pakir (1994a) analyses the role and impact of language planning in education in Singapore from 1959 to 1989. Gopinathan (1998) examines the relationship between politics and pedagogy from 1979 to 1997. Gopinathan, Pakir, Ho, and Saravanan (1994, 1998) present an update of the sociocultural, linguistic, and educational aspects of language in Singapore, including analysis of individual communities (Chinese, Malay, and Indian) and their ethnic mother tongues vis-à-vis

English. Tan (1998) analyses the language-planning processes in Singapore within a power and ideology framework. Other relevant studies dealing with the processes of language policymaking and management and their impact on language education in Singapore include Gopinathan (1980, 1988), Gupta (1994), Kuo and Jernudd (1994), and Pakir (1991a, 1993a, 1994b, 1995a, 1995b, 1998b, 2000a, 2000b, 2001a).

The current discussion of medium of instruction in Singapore revolves around the question of what more can be done to facilitate higher achievements in bilingualism and biliteracy and how instruction in the students' ascribed ethnic mother tongues can be used to help them understand their cultural heritage. Although this question focuses primarily on the educational agenda of providing effective language- and cultural-heritage lessons as well as subject content instruction and language skills, medium-of-instruction policies also raise important political questions: With English as the main medium of instruction, can it still be considered a neutral language, or does it benefit particular ethnic and linguistic groups or socioeconomic groups that had earlier turned to English as a predominant language in their lives? What language policy best fulfils the need for interethnic communication?

The aim of this chapter is to elucidate the complex cultural, economic, political, and social agendas that underpin the evolving educational decisions on medium-of-instruction policies, and highlight some of the resulting tensions. The analysis begins with basic information about education in Singapore and the country's educational agenda. The chapter then describes the successful language-management system that has evolved and been fine-tuned over the years. The pedagogical aspects of the policy are examined, as well as key political and sociocultural issues that have arisen against the backdrop of an emergent hegemony of English in Singapore.

DICTUM FOR EDUCATIONAL EXCELLENCE

The principal act of balancing the macro- and micro-aspects of language development in Singapore is best observed in the highly centralized education system. For a country without natural resources except human beings, the economic agenda is clear: a highly skilled and well educated labor force, one that is additionally expected to be flexible and adaptable for the 21st century. The driving philosophy has always been "educational excellence," built on the five pillars of (a) literacy (including biliteracy), (b) numeracy, (c) bilingualism (in English and one other official language), (d) physical education (and general well-being), and (e) moral education (for the transmission of culturally based values).

Half a million pupils ranging from 6 years old (entry point) to 18 years old (exit point for those attempting pre-university courses) are taught in

195 primary schools, 4 full schools (primary and secondary), 148 secondary schools (including 18 autonomous schools and eight independent schools), 2 centralized pre-university institutes, and 14 junior colleges (see Singapore Fact Sheet Series, http://www.mita.gov.sg). Almost 60% of these students go on to higher levels of education, either in the four polytechnics or the three universities in the country, with a substantial number proceeding overseas for further study.

English is officially the first school language (EL1) and, except for 10 Special Assistance Programme (SAP) schools where Chinese (Mandarin) is also offered as a first school language (CL1), the majority of the 363 schools in Singapore offer Chinese as a Second Language (CL2), Malay as a Second Language (ML2) and Tamil as a Second Language (TL2). Children of North Indian descent are given the opportunity to have language instruction in their ethnic mother tongues (Punjabi, Hindi, Gujerati, Urdu, and Bengali) as a second school language and can offer these for examination at the 'O' levels (a nationwide examination for 16-year-olds).

The early stages of providing trilingual and then bilingual streams of education from the 1950s were outgrowths of the post-colonial experience, when different media of education were made available to the different ethnic groups, based on the platform of multilingualism with equal treatment for the four official languages of the country. In the early years of independence, English became increasingly important and widely accepted as the working language of the country. It was made the main medium of instruction for all state schools in 1987.

It is now official policy that all children in Singapore schools become bilingual and biliterate in English and one other official language (Malay, Mandarin, or Tamil). An English-knowing bilingual in the Singapore context is one who has been schooled in the state system and has had exposure to English simultaneously for language and subject content instruction (Pakir, 1991b). High levels of bilingual attainment are expected and achieved by students who are in the independent schools, the autonomous schools, and the Special Assistance Programme schools. These students, who also generally do well in science, mathematics, and humanities, usually enter the most prestigious junior colleges and gain admission into the universities. Perceived slow learners, who find it difficult to cope with both content instruction as well as language skills, are given generous assistance with support programmes offered after school hours. This group includes those who are disadvantaged in language skills, having come from non-school-language home environments (for example, the dialects of Chinese [Hokkien, Teochew, Cantonese, Hainanese, etc.]) or other languages, such as Telegu or Malayalam.

Since the country became a sovereign nation, three distinct phases of education have been identified: a survival-driven period (1965–1978), an efficiency-driven period (1979–1991) and an ability-driven period (1992–present). Each of these phases has coincided with the political and sociocultural changes taking place at home and abroad. After the tumultuous early years, when the survival of the country was at stake, there followed a period of revamping the educational system to increase efficiency and to reflect the growing importance of Singapore's role in the international business arena. One major goal during this period was to reduce the attrition rate in schools by separating the students into those who could benefit from both bilingualism and biliteracy and those who could only manage monolingual literacy (i.e., English reading and writing skills, but only basic competence in reading and writing the second school language). The goal of reducing attrition has been achieved with significant success. The current phase aims to nurture talent and to develop human potential to the fullest, with the motto of "thinking schools, learning nation." Critical and creative thinking, the fullest utilisation of information technology, and national education to "strengthen the development of social cohesion, instinct for survival and confidence in the future" (see Singapore Fact Sheet Series, http://www.mita.gov.sg) are the key goals of the current phase. The major aim is that of continuous learning for a knowledge-based economy.

Throughout these phases, the pedagogical issues have always focused on the following: (a) assessing bilingual attainment and its use for admission to higher levels of education, (b) creating standards and norms for the first school language (English), which is a second language for most of the students, (c) improving the teaching of the second school languages, such as Mandarin, (d) encouraging community representation, specifically allowing minority Indian languages other than Tamil in the school system, (e) examining exogenous influences on and encouraging indigenisation of the curriculum, and (f) evolving new pedagogies based on Asian cultural scripts. For each of these issues, there has been debate, discussion, and external and internal reviews to fine-tune the educational system so that it matched societal and parental expectations.

The questions that need to be addressed in the discussions and debates on these issues pertained to whether slow learners are handicapped because the main medium of instruction is English and they are expected to also perform well in the second school language; whether those who come from homes where English is the predominant language (23% of the Singaporean population) are advantaged, having come into the school system with more than basic language skills; and whether students are spending too much curriculum time and after-school hours polishing their language skills at the expense of content subjects, and failing to achieve their potential for learning.

LANGUAGE SHIFT

As a result of the implementation of the language policy just outlined, two language shifts are currently taking place in Singapore: a primary one to English (for the entire multilingual population) and a secondary one to Mandarin (for the majority ethnic group). Interestingly, they are marked by two significant current public campaigns, the Speak Mandarin Campaign (SMC, launched as far back as September 1979) and the Speak Good English Movement (S-GEM, launched recently in April 2000). Table 6.1 of the Census of Population taken for 1980, 1990, and 2000 indicates clearly that language shifts have taken place among the multilingual citizens of Singapore.

By the 1990s, it was clear that English was gaining in terms of more speakers using it as the predominant household language. The nature of the language shift to English as a primary language in the country has been analysed by Gupta (1994, 1998) from a sociohistorical perspective, Kuo and Jernudd (1994) from a sociological perspective, Pakir (1994c, 1998a) from an educational perspective, and Baetens-Beardsmore (1998) from a cultural perspective. The following trends have been confirmed in one of the series of Advance Data Releases of the Census of Population, 2000 (Leow, 2001): a rise in multilanguage literacy; higher literacy in English; increased use of English and Mandarin at home, along with continued use of the vernacular languages as the most common varieties spoken at home by the three main ethnic groups; English emerging as the home language of the young among all three main ethnic groups; increased use of English among the better-educated; and a positive correlation between socioeconomic status and the use of English at home. There is also a generation gap between older multilingual

TABLE 6.1
RESIDENT POPULATION AGED 5 YEARS AND OVER,
BY LANGUAGE MOST FREQUENTLY SPOKEN AT HOME

LANGUAGE	1980	1990	2000
English	11.6	18.8	23.0
Mandarin	10.2	23.7	35.0
Chinese dialects	59.5	39.6	23.8
Malay	13.9	14.3	14.1
Tamil	3.1	2.9	3.2
Others	1.7	0.8	0.9

Sources: Census of Population, 1980, 1990, 2000. Singapore: Department of Statistics.

speakers with relatively low levels of literacy and younger individuals who are bilingual and biliterate in two official languages of the country.

A major consequence of the language shift is that English proficiency levels reflect socioeconomic status, education, and professional background. The higher literacy and language-proficiency levels of the younger population have been the result of constant attention to better and more effective language-skills transmission for both English and the other languages taught in the schools. Improvements in the teaching of the second school languages have included progressive measures, more for the majority Chinese population (Mandarin) and for the general English-learning multilingual population (English), and rather less for Tamil and Malay. Mandarin for Chinese school children has seen educational measures such as the introduction of Hanyu Pinyin and simplified Chinese characters and the development of new Chinese instructional materials incorporating "a reform in CL learning methodology in Singapore" (Ang, 1998, p. 342).

The majority of Tamil-speaking children learn Tamil as a school language, but it remains very much a classroom language (for an exposition of language shift among the Tamils, see Saravanan, 1998). As language shifts are normally toward the languages of greatest utility, the lack of economic use for Tamil has made much of the younger population shift to English as their predominant language. No amount of innovative teaching methods or inspired teaching will be able to counterbalance the pragmatic forces that prevail in favor of English.

Malay, the country's national language as enshrined in the constitution, has kept its mother-tongue status among its approximately 500,000 speakers relatively well, and Malay results in the school system have been predictably and uniformly good. However, the bilingual policy has impacted on the Malay language, which is the lingua franca of the Riau archipelago (extending from Indonesia, Malaysia, and to the Philippines). As a result of the bilingual policy of English and the mother tongue (the mother tongue being an ethnically ascribed one), most children do not learn a second school language that is not their ethnic mother tongue. The apparent lack of choice has resulted in the dwindling numbers of Chinese-knowing and Tamil-knowing Malays (cf. the Malaysian situation, where Malay children learn Chinese as a second or third language in the national-type primary school system; see Kamsiah & Bibi, 1998).

One of the thrusts toward excellence in education has involved taking note of exogenous influences and gaining the confidence to indigenise the curriculum (Ho, 1998). Although the global spread of English has stimulated research devoted to the teaching of English, theory and practice about English language teaching have largely emanated from British and North American scholarship, often accepted wholesale, without reference to the context of situation or even the worldliness of English (cf. Pennycook,

1994). Recent scholarship has been sensitised to the one-sidedness of the English language teaching enterprise (e.g., see Canagarajah, 1999; Chew, 1999; Phillipson, 1992). For example, Seidlhofer (2000) makes the argument that English as lingua franca should be taken as seriously as English as mother tongue in terms of research endeavours. In Singapore, the curricular changes to the English language syllabus every 10 years take into account the needs of a local population accustomed to exposure to the world at large via the internet and other international links. Singapore's teaching materials and textbooks (besides the English language ones) are now being used and modelled on by other countries in the region. Similar to this thrust of localisation and indigenisation is the attempt to evaluate the pedagogies based on non-Asian cultural scripts, and to write a script that is relevant and important to the population.

Paradoxically, for a country that invests heavily in bilingualism and language management, Singapore seems linguistically insecure, perhaps in part because the standards for its languages are derived from elsewhere: Malay standards follow those set by Indonesia, Malaysia, and Brunei; English standards implicitly come from Britain; and Mandarin follows Beijing's standards. Yet Singapore has done remarkably well in pursuing its goal of educational excellence. In tandem with the rising standards of education and a higher quality workforce, the per capita income for Singaporeans has risen to among the highest in the world.

CURRENT ISSUES IN THE LANGUAGE POLICY OF SINGAPORE

Rapid change in Singapore's plural society, in transition from a colonial outpost to an important economic and technological power in Southeast Asia, has been catalysed by the careful selection of English as the instrument to achieve socioeconomic transformation. However, on the national level, the development of English as a principal language in Singapore raises continuing issues: its impact on identity and the transmission of values, language maintenance and shift patterns, equity and meritocracy, and linguistic norms.

Identity and the Transmission of Values

Singapore's relationship with English has been and continues to be unique. English is a global language as well as a local language, helping Singapore in its international outlook as well as its intranational interaction. In a paradoxical way, English is made to carry the nation's voice in a land of many multilingual Asian voices. A uniquely Singaporean identity is being crafted in English, but with Asian imagery and imagination. Paradoxically, English is considered a linguistic heritage from British colonial times, but not a heritage language. It is the working language of the country, and although almost one quarter of its population use it as the predominant household language, it does not merit designation as a mother tongue (only the ethnicity-linked official languages are referred to as "mother tongues"). Of utmost concern are the educational implications of giving premier status to English as a co-official language in competition with the Asian official languages.

A major paradox is that English has emerged as the only contender for the supra link language to express a uniquely Singaporean identity, yet it is at the same time perceived to be the channel for avant garde, pseudo-westernised behaviours as opposed to conservative beliefs and practices grounded in and transmitted via the ethnic languages. Thus, there arises the tension of ethnic identity (based on ethnic-linked cultural values expressed in Chinese, Malay, Tamil, or other ethnicity-linked languages in Singapore) versus a national identity (based on a supra-ethnic value of social cohesiveness in a multicultural context, and expressed in English). A secondary tension to be urgently resolved is that of making the population forward-thinking, forward-moving, and ultramodern for the 21st century while trying to make it at the same time continue in conservative and traditionalist customs and mores. A recent debate in the country has been over how to balance the needs of the "Cosmopolitans" (mainly English-educated movers and shakers who generate the country's wealth) and the "Heartlanders" (the mainly vernacular-speaking core of workers). The issue has been of concern at the highest levels of government, seen in Prime Minister Goh Chok Tong's comment,

> The challenge is for us to get the heartlanders to understand what the cosmopolitans contribute to Singapore's and their own well-being, [and] to get the cosmopolitans to feel an obligation and sense of duty to the heartlanders … if the cosmopolitans and the heartlanders cease to identify with each other, our society will fall apart. (cited in Rubdy, 2001, p. 352)

Singapore's current search for foreign talent has also been at the forefront of the public consciousness, especially in the "coffee shop talk" of those who come from the heartland of public housing estates (comprising 80% of residential dwellings) and who carry the social norms that provide social ballast and stability in the country.

Language Maintenance and Shift

A great deal of effort has been put into continuing official encouragement and support for (Asian) languages other than English; thus, the natural drift toward English as a dominant household language is carefully monitored. Singapore's management of its medium-of-instruction policy involves an educational programme where knowing how to read and write in one's ethnic mother tongue is emphasised as equally important for heritage purposes, and building cultural ties. Clearly, multilingualism and multiculturalism are a given in Singapore, and the official policy is to support the official languages of the country in the school system. The principal dilemma here is that of maintaining high standards of proficiency in English while ensuring that students become biliterate and bilingual. With the increasing use of English as a home and community language in Singapore, a process of "invisible planning" has begun to take place in the two major settings for the young: the home and the school, and the interface between the two (see Pakir, 1994c). The question is whether the shift to English and Mandarin will disrupt this careful balance between the value and use of the language varieties.

Equity and Meritocracy

In terms of equity and equality (see Tan, 1998), an outstanding unresolved problem is the official "mother tongue" for the Eurasians. By linguistic definition, English is the mother tongue for these "Others" who speak only English at home and at school, while learning a true second language in the school. However, English has not been accorded "mother-tongue" status in Singapore because of the unique evolution of the label and what it designates. Furthermore, along with the speakers of the North Indian languages (Punjabi, Urdu, Bengali, Hindi, and Gujerati), Eurasians are often confronted with the dilemma of choosing a second school language that will not disadvantage them against the main ethnic groups.

For the 10 Special Assistance Programme (SAP) schools, which were originally Chinese-medium schools, the status of English as the main medium of instruction deepens the debate over whether a truly Chinese education can be fully realized. On the other hand, a developing concern among the non-Chinese is the creation of a new English–Chinese knowing bilingual elite class, schooled in these special and selective SAP programmes that cater to the brightest and the best bilinguals in English and Chinese (see James, 1998).

For the Malays (and some Indian Muslims), Madrasah schools in Singapore are valued for promoting religious education, and the trend of sending children to these schools is continuing. The concern here is whether the Malays can maintain their culture and at the same time not be deprived of their opportunities to gain access to higher education and employment, and to participate effectively in public life as well as in economic activities.

Linguistic Norms

Within the national school system, the question of standards and norms for English (Pakir 1993b, 1997, 1998a) is a stark reality because the first school language (English) is but a second language for most of the students (about 70%). There is also the constant attention to proficiency in English (Standard English) while ensuring that students become biliterate and bilingual. The complexity arising from this tension has important educational implications. Languages in contact phenomena have given rise to Creole-like features of a new lingua franca in Singapore—Singapore Colloquial English (Singlish) in place of Bazaar Malay, which had been the lingua franca for interethnic communication. Educators in Singapore face the constant struggle of promoting Standard English (taught in schools) and disparaging Singlish (a form of nonstandard English prevalent in Singapore society). The debate continues regarding the varieties of English and educational models, and whether there is the necessity to distinguish between proficiency in English and proficiency in Standard English (Gupta, 1998).

In tandem with the resolute approach to language planning in Singapore, the Speak Good English Movement (S-GEM), launched in April 2000, promotes the use of Standard English among Singaporeans. Rubdy (2001) examines the movement as an example of language management through manufacturing and obtaining social consent on language issues for the greater good of the country (see Tan, 1995). In the globalized era, the preference for a variety of English that has greatest utility in the marketplace is great. Although Singlish does create feelings of rapport, solidarity, and familiarity, it would—if it represented the dominant variety in Singapore—disadvantage a population that needs an internationally viable form of English for its survival. Standard English, although it is reserved for formal domains and carries with it a sense of distance and propriety, must be mastered before children leave school, equipping them with the best chances of gaining employment.

On the educational scene, a model such as the expanding triangles of English expression for all Singapore school children (Pakir, 1991c) has been suggested.

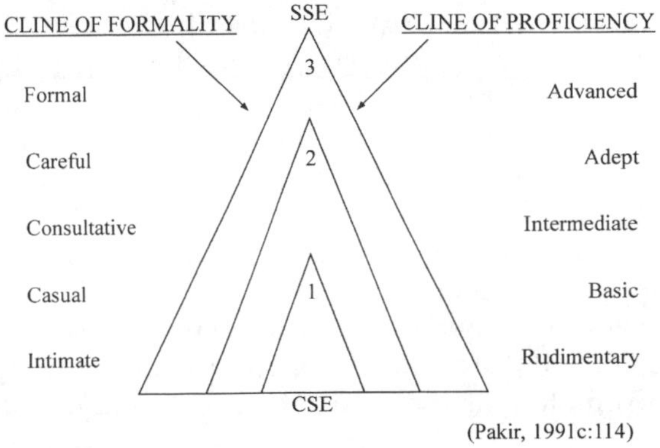

(Pakir, 1991c:114)

FIG. 6.1. Expanding Triangles of English.

A triangle is formed by a Colloquial Singapore English (CSE) base line, a cline of proficiency and another cline of formality. Standard Singapore English (SSE) is at the apex. Users of English with the highest levels of education are located at the top ends of both the cline of formality and of proficiency. Having control of the largest triangle of English expression, they are capable of both the Standard (SSE) and the Colloquial (CSE) forms of English, and are adept register users, moving with fluidity along the whole range of the formality cline. Those with lower levels of proficiency, most often coming from the lower socioeconomic strata of society and having lower levels of education, are found to have the smallest triangle of English expression. They are typically restricted in their movement along the formality cline, and have rudimentary to intermediate proficiencies in English. The model suggests that the ultimate achievement would be to have all Singaporean English-knowing bilinguals command large triangles of English expression representing the maximum potential for English use. Singaporeans would all be able then to switch from one (colloquial, uniquely Singaporean) variety to the other (formal, internationally intelligible) variety, depending on the domains and spheres of use.

CONCLUSION

This chapter has examined the delicate balance that has been achieved between the educational agenda and other underlying sociocultural and political agendas in Singapore. It has outlined important historical, political, and ideological factors that have contributed to the ascendancy of English in the nation-state, at the expense of other languages (including Mandarin, Malay, and Tamil). The primary shift to English (for a large part of the Singaporean population) and the secondary shift to Mandarin from other Chinese dialects (by Chinese Singaporeans, who make up 77% of the population) are giving rise to new challenges of linguistic and cultural management of diversity, and pedagogical developments unique to Singapore. The thrust of this chapter has been to explore the distribution and management of value and use among languages in the multilingual speakers' linguistic repertoire, and patterns of language change that may lead to socioeconomic inequality and eventually impact Singapore's developing national identity.

Many observers of language in education find it fascinating that a former Crown Colony of Britain has accorded premier status to English and is willing to promote it as the medium of instruction in all its schools.

However, the argument for national appropriation of a language that empowers its users is strong, especially in this nation that is known for its "pragmatic multilingualism" (Kuo & Jernudd, 1994, p. 76).

In a "quest for the best of all possible worlds" for societal bilingualism (Fishman, 1977, p. 331), Singapore has developed and fine-tuned sensitive language policies, obtained social consensus for an acceptable bilingual education policy, and is now in the process of debating what it wants to do with its English-knowing bilingual and biliterate population (see Pakir, 2001a). The age differentials in the patterns of home-language use confirm that young children are using English more than older youths and adults. The Census of Population 2000 also confirms the trend of increasing use of English as well as Mandarin. Will a new cosmopolitan class (comprising mainly elite English-Mandarin bilinguals and imported foreign talent) dominate the socioeconomic scene? Can English (and which variety?) be used to bridge the gap between the cosmopolitans and the heartlanders?

In this post-colonial nation, the educational agenda of using the most effective medium for education is driven by a pragmatism born of necessity. Language issues, although sensitive, are not clouded by the political agenda of nation building, as national identity and cohesiveness are worked out through all four official languages. Political stability is achieved by balancing the interests of different ethnic groups and rests on the rise of the English-knowing bilingual community. The success of language management in Singapore is a result of the sociopolitical and socioeconomic forces at work in the community that clarify for most Singaporeans the value of English as the medium of instruction for a small country, with people as its only resource.

Singapore represents one of what I have termed *ascendant English-knowing bilingual communities for a globalized world* (Pakir, 2001b), set to meet the challenges of the 21st century, including new work patterns and network information and management. An ascendant English-knowing bilingual community has emerged in Singapore from the educational agenda of using English as the main medium of instruction, following a consistently pursued bilingual education policy, and supplementing the official language policy. What this community does, with whom, and in which languages, will determine Singapore's future survival as a sovereign nation with a first world economy.

ACKNOWLEDGMENT

This chapter was completed during the author's sabbatical leave (2001–2002), supported by the National University of Singapore. I am grateful to the University of Sydney (Australia) and the Institute of Southeast Asian Studies (Singapore), for their hospitality. I owe much to John Gibbons of the Department of Linguistics and Richard B. Baldauf of the Language Centre at the University of Sydney, and to the editors of this volume for their helpful comments on this article.

REFERENCES

Ang, B. C. (1998). The teaching of the Chinese language in Singapore. In S. Gopinathan, A. Pakir, W. K. Ho, & V. Saravanan (Eds.), *Language, society and education in Singapore: Issues and trends* (pp. 335–352). Singapore: Times Academic Press.

Baetens-Beardsmore, H. (1998). Language shift and cultural implications in Singapore. In S. Gopinathan, A Pakir, W. K. Ho, & V. Saravanan (Eds.), *Language, society and education in Singapore: Issues and trends* (pp. 85–98). Singapore: Times Academic Press.

Canagarajah, S. (1999). *Resisting linguistic imperialism in English teaching.* Oxford, UK: Oxford University Press.

Chew, P. G. L. (1999). Linguistic imperialism, globalism and the English language. In D. Graddol & U. H. Meinhof (Eds.), *English in a changing world. AILA Review,* 13, 37–47.

Fishman, J. A. (1977). English in the context of international societal bilingualism. In J. A. Fishman, R. L. Cooper, & A. W. Conrad (Eds.), *The spread of English* (pp. 329–336). Rowley, MA: Newbury.

Gopinathan, S. (1980). Language policy in education: A Singapore perspective. In E. A. Afrendras & E. C. Y. Kuo (Eds.), *Language and society in Singapore* (pp. 175–202). Singapore: Singapore University Press.

Gopinathan, S. (1988). Bilingualism and bilingual education in Singapore. In C. B. Paulston (Ed.), *International handbook of bilingualism and bilingual education* (pp. 391–404). Westport, CT: Greenwood Press.

Gopinathan, S. (1997). Education and development in Singapore. In J. Tan, S. Gopinathan, & W. K. Ho (Eds.), *Education in Singapore: A book of readings* (pp. 33–53). Singapore: Prentice Hall.

Gopinathan, S. (1998). Language policy changes 1979–1997: Politics and pedagogy. In S. Gopinathan, A. Pakir, W. K. Ho, & V. Saravanan (Eds.), *Language, society and education in Singapore: Issues and trends* (pp. 19–44). Singapore: Times Academic Press.

Gopinathan, S., Pakir, A., Ho, W. K., & Saravanan, V. (Eds.). (1994). *Language, society and education in Singapore: Issues and trends* (1st ed.). Singapore: Times Academic Press.

Gopinathan, S., Pakir, A., Ho, W. K., & Saravanan, V. (Eds.). (1998). *Language, society and education in Singapore: Issues and trends* (2nd Rev. ed.). Singapore: Times Academic Press.

Graddol, D. (1997). *The future of English? A guide to forecasting the popularity of the English language in the 21st century.* London: British Council.

Gupta, A. F. (1994). *The step-tongue: Children's English in Singapore.* Clevedon, UK: Multilingual Matters.

Gupta, A. F. (1998). A framework for the analysis of Singapore English. In S. Gopinathan, A. Pakir, W. K. Ho, & V. Saravanan (Eds.), *Language, society and education in Singapore: Issues and trends* (pp. 119–132). Singapore: Times Academic Press.

Ho, W. K. (1998). The English language curriculum in perspective: Exogenous influences and indigenisation. In S. Gopinathan, A. Pakir, W. K. Ho, & V. Saravanan (Eds.), *Language, society and education in Singapore: Issues and trends* (pp. 221–244). Singapore: Times Academic Press.

James, J. (1998). Linguistic realities and pedagogical practices in Singapore: Another perspective. In S. Gopinathan, A. Pakir, W. K. Ho, & V. Saravanan (Eds.), *Language, society and education in Singapore: Issues and trends* (pp. 99–116). Singapore: Times Academic Press.

Kamsiah, A., & Bibi, J. M. A. (1998). Malay language issues and trends. In S. Gopinathan, A. Pakir, W. K. Ho, & V. Saravanan (Eds.), *Language, society and education in Singapore: Issues and trends* (pp.179–190). Singapore: Times Academic Press.

Khoo, C. K. (1981). *Singapore census of population 1980: Languages spoken at home.* Statistical Release 8. Singapore: Department of Statistics,

Kuo, E. C. Y., & Jernudd, B. H. (1994). Balancing macro- and micro-sociolinguistic perspectives in language management: The case of Singapore. In T. Kandiah & J. Kwan-Terry (Eds.), *English and language planning: A Southeast Asian contribution* (pp. 70–91). Singapore: Times Academic Press.

Lau, K. E. (1993). *Singapore census of population 1990: Literacy, languages spoken and education.* Statistical Release 3. Singapore: Department of Statistics.

Leow, B. G. (2001). *Singapore census of population, 2000. Education, language and religion.* Statistical Release 2. Singapore: Department of Statistics.

Pakir, A. (1991a). Bilingualism in Singapore: Tradition and change among the Chinese. *Journal of the Institute for Asian Studies, 18,* 117–145. Tokyo: The Institute for Asian Studies, Asia University.

Pakir, A. (1991b). The range and depth of English-knowing bilinguals in Singapore. *World Englishes, 10*(2), 167–179.

Pakir, A. (1991c). The status of English and the question of "standard" in Singapore: A sociolinguistic perspective. In M. L. Tickoo (Ed.), *Languages and standards: Issues, attitudes, case studies* (Anthology Series 26, pp. 109–130). Singapore: SEAMEO Regional Language Centre.

Pakir, A. (1992). English-knowing bilingualism in Singapore. In K. C. Ban, A. Pakir, & C. K. Tong (Eds.), *Imagining Singapore* (pp. 234–262). Singapore: Times Academic Press.

Pakir, A. (1993a). Two tongue tied: Bilingualism in Singapore. *Journal of Multilingual and Multicultural Development, 14*(1 & 2), 73–90.

Pakir, A. (Ed.). (1993b). *The English language in Singapore: Standards and norms.* Singapore: UniPress.

Pakir, A. (1994a). The role of language planning in education in Singapore. In A. Hassan (Comp.) *Language planning in Southeast Asia* (pp. 151–175). Kuala Lumpur: Dewan Bahasa dan Pustaka, Ministry of Education.

Pakir, A. (1994b). Educational linguistics: Looking to the East. In J. E. Alatis (Ed.), *GURT 1994: Educational linguistics, cross-cultural communication and global interdependence* (pp. 371–383). Washington DC: Georgetown University Press.

Pakir, A. (1994c). Education and invisible language planning: The case of English in Singapore. In T. Kandiah & J. Kwan-Terry (Eds.), *English language planning: A Southeast Asian contribution* (pp. 158–181). Singapore: Centre for Advanced Studies and Times Academic Press.

Pakir, A. (1995a). Beginning at the end: "Bilingual education for all" in Singapore and teacher education. In J. E. Alatis, C. A. Straehle, B. Gallenberger, & M. Ronkin (Eds.), *GURT 1995: Linguistics and the education of language teachers: Ethnolinguistic, psycholinguistic, and sociolinguistic aspects* (pp.112–131). Washington DC: Georgetown University Press.

Pakir, A. (1995b). Expanding triangles of English expression in Singapore: Implications for teaching. In S. C. Teng & M. L. Ho (Eds.), *The English language in Singapore: Implications for teaching* (pp.1–13). Singapore: Singapore Association for Applied Linguistics.

Pakir, A. (1997). Standards and codification for World Englishes. In L. E. Smith & M. L. Forman (Eds.), *World Englishes 2000 (Literary studies East and West, 14)*, (pp. 169–181). Honolulu: University of Hawaii Press.

Pakir, A. (1998a). English in Singapore: The codification of conflicting norms. In S. Gopinathan, A. Pakir, W. K. Ho, & V. Saravanan (Eds.), *Language, society and education in Singapore: Issues and trends* (pp. 65–84). Singapore: Times Academic Press.

Pakir, A. (1998b). Innovative second language education in Southeast Asia. In D. Corson & R. Tucker (Eds.), *Second language education, encyclopedia of language and education, 4* (pp. 221–230). Dordrecht, The Netherlands: Kluwer Academic Publishers.

Pakir, A. (2000a). Singapore. In W. K. Ho & R. Wong (Eds.), *Language policies and language education: The impact in East Asian countries in the next decade* (pp. 259–284). Singapore: Times Academic Press.

Pakir, A. (2000b). The development of English as a "glocal" language: New concerns in the old saga of language teaching. In W. K. Ho & C. Ward (Eds.), *Language in the global context: Implications for the language classroom* (Anthology Series 41, pp.14–31). Singapore: SEAMEO Regional Language Centre.

Pakir, A. (2001a). Bilingual education with English as an official language: Sociocultural implications. In J. E. Alatis & A. H. Tan (Eds.), *GURT 1999: Language in our time – Bilingual education and official English, ebonics and standard English, immigration and the Unz initiative* (pp. 341–349). Washington, DC: Georgetown University Press.

Pakir, A. (2001b, October 8–11). *Which English? The nativization of English and the negotiations of language choice in Southeast Asia.* Keynote paper presented at the international conference, Anglophone Cultures in Southeast Asia: Appropriations, Continuities, Contexts. Hong Kong: Chinese University of Hong Kong.

Pennycook, A. D. (1994). *The cultural politics of English as an international language.* London: Longman.

Phillipson, R. (1992). *Linguistic imperialism.* Oxford, UK: Oxford University Press.

Rubdy, R. (2001). Creative destruction: Singapore's Speak Good English Movement. *World Englishes, 20*(3), 341–356.

Saravanan, V. (1998). Language maintenance and language shift in the Tamil-English community. In S. Gopinathan, A. Pakir, W. K. Ho, & V. Saravanan (Eds.), *Language, society and education in Singapore: Issues and trends* (pp. 155–178). Singapore: Times Academic Press.

Seidlhofer, B. (2000). Mind the gap: English as a mother tongue vs. English as a lingua franca. *Views, 9*(1), 51–68.

Singapore Fact Sheet Series. "Education." (2001). Singapore: Ministry of Information and the Arts, Publicity and Programmes Division. (See also http://www.mita.gov.sg)

Tan, S. H. (1995). The manufacturing of social consent: The dynamics of language planning in Singapore. *Working papers in language, literature and theatre.* Singapore: Department of English Language and Literature, National University of Singapore.

Tan, S. H. (1998). Theoretical ideals and ideologized reality in language planning. In S. Gopinathan, A. Pakir, W. K. Ho, & V. Saravanan (Eds.), *Language, society and education in Singapore: Issues and trends* (pp. 45–64). Singapore: Times Academic Press.

7

Medium-of-Instruction Policy in Higher Education in Malaysia: Nationalism Versus Internationalization

Saran Kaur Gill
Universiti Kebangsaan Malaysia

Since attaining independence from British rule, Malaysia, a multiracial and multicultural nation, has been working toward building a strong sense of identity and unity. After 45 years of nation building, Malaysians of all ethnic origins, particularly groups whose ancestors were immigrants and who have been in the country for three to five generations, regard Malaysia as their home. Matters regarding the nation are of equal concern to indigenous Malays and those of immigrant ancestry, such as the Chinese and Indians who came to the country for economic reasons.

One of the ways of achieving a sense of national identity and unity in this multiracial nation was through the implementation of a new language policy. Thus, Bahasa Malaysia was established as the official language and the medium of instruction. The English language, which played a dominant official role prior to independence, was gradually relegated to the status of a second language. At the same time as these changes were made to the language policy, Malaysia had to face the challenges presented by globalization and internationalization, which require its people to be competent in English. The demands of both national interest and internationalization place Malaysia at a linguistic crossroads. In addition, Malaysia's multi-ethnic population presents particularly complex challenges.

In this multifarious context, the linguistic complexities are most clearly manifested in higher education, due to the nation's need for graduates who are fluent in both Bahasa Malaysia and English. The Malaysian government is keen to ensure the development of intellectual human resources able to communicate effectively in national and international contexts and to contribute to the successful development of an industrialized nation. It is the aim of this chapter to unravel the linguistic complexities in this challenging context by focusing on the medium-of-instruction policy in higher education institutions in Malaysia.

This chapter begins by tracing the development of nationalism through language policy in post-independence Malaysia. This section provides the context for examining the current medium-of-instruction policy in both public and private institutions of higher learning. The implications of the adoption of conflicting language policies for the nation are discussed. To further widen the context, this chapter draws on the experiences of other countries that have also had to deal with national interests and the demands of internationalization. The chapter ends with recommendations for a nation that needs to consider both national and international interests in attaining the goal of becoming an industrialized nation by the year 2020.

NATIONALISM AND LANGUAGE POLICY IN POST-INDEPENDENCE MALAYSIA

When colonies have gained independence, building up their own national identity is always a top priority. Having a national language is often important for enhancing feelings of nationalism and unity. As Fasold points out, "Language, together with culture, religion and history, is a major component of nationalism" (Fasold, 1987, p. 3). Many colonized countries, on attaining independence, reacted against the language of the colonial powers and adopted the language of the indigenous people as the national language. This process is emphasized by Fasold (1987):

> For a nationality which has just acquired its own geographical territory, the last language it would want as a national symbol would be the language of the state that had denied it territorial control. (p. 5)

After gaining independence, Malaysia instituted Malay, the language of the indigenous people, the Malays, as the national language to replace English. In the immediate post-independence period, the national language was referred to as Malay, but gradually, in order to build up a sense of national identity across all ethnic groups, the language was referred to as Bahasa Malaysia. (Henceforth in this chapter, it will be referred to as Bahasa

Malaysia.) For example, Tengku Abdul Rahman, the first Prime Minister of Malaysia, made the following pronouncement:

> It is only right that as a developing nation we should want to have a language of our own. If the national language is not introduced our country will be devoid of a unified character and personality—as I could put it, a nation without a soul and without a life. (Wong & Hong, 1975, p. 79)

There were various reasons why Bahasa Malaysia was chosen as the national language. First, it was the language of the indigenous ethnic group, the Malays, who formed the majority of the population. (Malays constituted 49.78% of the total population. The other ethnic groups were the Chinese, who made up 37.1%, and the Indians, who made up 11.0% of the population.) Second, Bahasa Malaysia had always been the main language for interethnic communication, even before independence. The third reason was that Bahasa Malaysia had been for centuries the language of administration in the Malay states, and the means of communication between kingdoms in the Malay archipelago (Asmah, 1979, 1987).

To add force to the argument for using Bahasa Malaysia as a tool for developing national identity and unity during the post-independence period, slogans articulated strong messages with regard to the role of Bahasa Malaysia. "Bahasa jiwa Bangsa" ("Bahasa Malaysia is the soul of the people") was one of the many messages.

Multi-Ethnicity and Medium-of-Instruction Policy

With Bahasa Malaysia established as the language of nationalism, it was also necessary to make decisions about the language of government and education. This was a difficult process because the people involved were ethnically as well as linguistically heterogeneous.

Prior to independence, most of the schools in urban areas were English-medium. English-medium schools offered students ample opportunities for further education, employment in the civil service and access to scholarships. These schools received generous funding from the government. Because they were situated in the urban areas, where few Malays lived, the majority of the student population was non-Malay, in fact, mostly Chinese. Thus, economic and academic achievements came to be associated with ethnic groups from the urban areas, and the majority of the Malays, located mainly in the rural areas, did not benefit from these opportunities.

To address this situation, in the landmark recommendation of the Razak Education Commission in 1956, the government implemented the National Education Policy, which stipulated Bahasa Malaysia as the main medium of instruction in schools. The rationale for the policy was spelled out clearly in the report as follows:

We believe further that the ultimate objective of educational policy in this country must be to bring together the children of all races under a national educational system in which the national language is the main medium of instruction, though we recognize that the progress towards this goal cannot be rushed and must be gradual. (Awang, 1994, p. 21)

The aim of this policy was to remove the identification of a particular ethnic group with school achievement and reduce the inequality of opportunity among ethnic groups.

The institution of Bahasa Malaysia as the official language and the medium of instruction was an important move toward altering the privileged status that English had long enjoyed. If English had been retained as the joint official language with Bahasa Malaysia, it would have been difficult for the latter to establish itself as the official language of administration and the language of education. One reason was that when the policy change was first introduced, the non-Malays held partisan views that were biased toward English, the language of prestige and opportunity. In fact, with the change in policy, there was an exodus of middle-class, non-Malays from the country because of the fear that Bahasa Malaysia would not be able to succeed as the language of education and the national language of the country, and that as a result of the policy change, Malaysians would no longer be competitive (Gill, 2000).

Any measure of change naturally brings along with it feelings of anxiety. However, unless these national language policy measures had been taken, there would not have been the impetus necessary for the people to learn Bahasa Malaysia and use it for official purposes. For this, English had to be moved out of the dominant position. People were encouraged to assimilate and acquire the national language by being provided with professional and economic opportunities, such as job recruitments, study grants, and bonuses.

The Changing Status of English

English was seen as a language of prestige and was also the language of the British Empire. This, together with the international economic and technological strength of the English language, threatened the establishment and the development of the Malay language. Therefore, for Bahasa Malaysia to retain its prominence and status in the country, English had to be relegated to a less dominant role and measures to boost the status of Bahasa Malaysia had to be taken, as outlined previously.

Although English was to become a less important language, it still remained an official language for 10 years before it became a second language. From being the medium of instruction in schools, it became a compulsory school subject that students needed to take but not to pass

(Asmah, 1997). In other words, there was no drastic severing of English from the various domains.

The transition from English to Bahasa Malaysia as the main medium of instruction began in 1958, starting from primary level. By 1983, the transition at university level had been achieved. The transition throughout all levels of education took 26 years to complete, and it was done gradually and pragmatically. This extended time frame provided for more efficient language planning, as well as the development of a corpus to allow Bahasa Malaysia to cope with science and technology (Asmah, 1979).

Having traced the post-independence journey of the implementation of Bahasa Malaysia as the national and official language, and the relegation of the status of English, I now focus on the changes in the medium-of-instruction policy in higher institutions. I examine the lessons from the past and discuss whether further changes are needed if Malaysia is to become a regional center of education.

HIGHER EDUCATION IN MALAYSIA

Tertiary education is the major means of meeting human-resource needs if Malaysia is to achieve its vision of becoming an industrialized nation, according to the Education Development Plan (2001–2010) ("Blueprint for the Future," 2001, pp. 1–2). In Malaysia, higher education is made up of both public and private institutions of higher learning, whose origins may be different, but which face similar challenges in the 21st century.

Public Institutions of Higher Education

In Malaysia, public institutions of higher education have the social responsibility of developing human resources needed for industry and the nation, and improving the socioeconomic status of the general population. For this reason, the government provides generous funding for the development of public universities. There are 14 public universities in Malaysia, which were founded from the 1970s through the 1990s. They include the more established institutions, such as Universiti Sains Malaysia (the science university), University Putra Malaysia (the agricultural university, formerly known as Universiti Pertanian Malaysia), and Universiti Teknologi Malaysia (the university of technology). In the 1990s, to provide more opportunities for students in different parts of the country to receive higher education, new public universities were set up in the north of Malaysia, such as Universiti Utara Malaysia, and in East Malaysia, such as Universiti Malaysia Sarawak and Universiti Malaysia Sabah.

One of the main roles of the public universities is to help achieve the objectives of the National Economic Policy and ensure that there are sufficient opportunities for human-resource development among the Malays. The National Economic Policy was designed to minimize the disparity between the economic achievements of the various ethnic groups in the country. The main objective was to ensure that the Malays achieved 30% of the economic share of the nation. Thus, ethnic quotas were instituted as part of the entry requirements to the public universities. Ethnic quotas were also instituted in the selection of programs of study to ensure that a sufficient number belonging to certain ethnic groups were provided with opportunities to take critical degrees, for example, in the fields of medicine, technology, and engineering.

In the year 2002, the quota system for entrance to the public universities was substituted by a system of meritocracy. Datuk Seri Dr. Mahathir Mohamad, the Prime Minister, declared that meritocracy would send a strong message to the Malays that they needed to obtain excellent results to get places in the public universities (Mohamad, 2002b, p. 1).

Private Institutions of Higher Education

Besides public universities, there are a number of private universities and institutions of higher learning in Malaysia. In recent years, there has been a rapid expansion in the private provision of higher learning and a diversification in the mode of higher education. This rapid expansion is due to two factors: first, the Asian economic crisis; and second, the need to increase the number of knowledge workers in order to meet with Malaysia's aspirations to become an industrialized nation.

The Asian economic crisis of the late 1990s resulted in a tremendous increase in the outflow of currency, to a total of RM 2 to 3 billion annually. Therefore, there was a need to encourage Malaysian students to study locally so that educational expenditures in foreign currency could be reduced. In addition, it was also necessary to attract foreign students whose tuition fees would increase the amount of foreign currency coming into the country. Both moves would help to ensure a reduction in the country's outflow of foreign currency, which was essential for financial and economic strength and stability (Tan, 2002; Yahya, 2001).

The need to increase the number of knowledge workers is based on the government's awareness of the new demands of globalization and the shift from an information-based to a knowledge-based society. This means that the country needs to produce skilled human resources and knowledge workers who are "much more knowledgeable, technologically capable and advanced, versatile and adaptable in this electronic era of the borderless world" (MAPCO, 2001, November, p. 8). The rapid expansion in private provision of higher learning is to enable Malaysia to keep pace with developments in the field of information technology, as well as to ensure the nation's international competitiveness.

The two factors just discussed led to urgent moves by the government to allow the private sector to participate in the provision of tertiary education. The Ministry of Education pushed through legislation to position Malaysia as a regional education hub. In order to achieve this goal, foreign universities were allowed to set up offshore branches in Malaysia and local colleges could develop educational partnerships with foreign universities to provide higher education. At the same time, corporations were given the mandate to establish private universities (Ministry of Education, http://www.moe.gov.my/educ3.htm). This resulted in a binary system in Malaysian private higher education, comprising 10 private universities and 616 private colleges (Tan, 2002).

The private colleges have adopted a transnational model of education through twinning programs in which they have established strong links with universities from Australia, the United States, and Britain. Students are thus able to study in degree programs that require 1 year locally and 2 years abroad, or 2 years locally and 1 year abroad, depending on the agreements worked out between institutions.

The private universities, all of which were established after 1998–1999 when the economic crisis set in, range from engineering universities set up by the three public utility corporations (Telekoms, the National Telecommunications Company; Tenaga Nasional, the National Electricity Board; and Petronas, the National Petroleum Company), to three branch campuses of foreign universities: Monash University and Curtin University from Australia, and Nottingham University from the United Kingdom (Tan, 2002).

Student enrolment at private higher education institutions for the period 1999–2000 was 203,391, increasing to 232,069, by May, 2001. Enrolment at public universities was 167,507 in 1999–2000. This shift reflects the increasing demand for places in private higher education institutions as opposed to public universities (MAPCO, 2001, November).

MEDIUM OF INSTRUCTION IN INSTITUTIONS OF HIGHER EDUCATION IN MALAYSIA

Nationalism and Medium of Instruction in Public Institutions of Higher Education

The University of Malaya, the oldest university in Malaysia, was established in the 1960s with English as the medium of instruction. However, once the wheels of the National Education Act had been set in motion in the school system, it was necessary for this university to take steps to convert the medium of instruction to Bahasa Malaysia. This change was to ensure that the university was ready to accept the first batch of students educated in the Bahasa Malaysia-medium schools. The conversion took place in

1965, beginning with two parallel streams: the Bahasa Malaysia medium for arts subjects and the English medium for science and technology subjects. Gradually, the bilingual system became a completely monolingual system, using only Bahasa Malaysia.

The process of changing the medium of instruction in higher institutions was conducted in a pragmatic manner. The bilingual system was used as an interim measure to allow time for academic staff, especially non-Malays, to develop their competence in the delivery of content knowledge in Bahasa Malaysia. However, this was not a viable long-term system due to the demand from the majority of the population to have Bahasa Malaysia take over completely as the medium of instruction. A bilingual approach in the national system of education would have created bifurcation in the education system and would have sabotaged the adoption of Bahasa Malaysia as the sole medium of instruction.

Because of the nationalistic fervor at the time, the total conversion of the University of Malaya into Bahasa Malaysia-medium was considered too slow by the Malay public. As a result, in late 1967, Malay intellectuals in Kuala Lumpur urged the government to establish a university that used only the national language as the medium of instruction. In response to this demand, the Universiti Kebangsaan Malaysia (National University of Malaysia) was set up in 1970. All universities established from then onward were required to use Bahasa Malaysia as the medium of instruction, in keeping with the National Education Policy. By 1983, all subjects, including the sciences, were taught in Bahasa Malaysia in all public universities.

Linguistic Challenges Facing Public Institutions of Higher Education

The ultimate test of whether a language can be used effectively as a medium of instruction, especially in the field of science and technology, is whether it has a corpus that is able to express and disseminate knowledge. Bahasa Malaysia is not traditionally associated with science and technology, and therefore it faced new challenges when used as a medium of instruction (Asmah, 1994). To tackle this problem, Dewan Bahasa dan Pustaka, an agency set up by the government to promote the use of Bahasa Malaysia for academic and technological purposes, has over the years, and with the help of language experts and academics, come up with a corpus of linguistic terms in the field of science and technology. This process has helped tremendously in facilitating the use of Bahasa Malaysia as the medium of instruction in tertiary institutions (Gonzalez, 1994). Efforts have also been made to translate academic books into Bahasa Malaysia. Despite all of this, however, the translators could not keep up with the pace of publications in science and technology, which are mostly in English.

Thus, in order to keep up with new developments, especially in the field of science and technology, undergraduates have to be competent in English. Unfortunately, undergraduates educated in the Bahasa Malaysia medium have difficulties understanding academic texts in English. In fact, Asmah (1987, p. 16) attributes this "linguistic deficit" in English to the adoption of Bahasa Malaysia as the main medium of instruction. As far back as the late 1980s, Asmah voiced the anxiety shared by employers, language experts and academics (Gill, 1993, 1999, 1999/2000):

> There has been a feeling among Malaysians, including the top leaders, that there has been a drop in the attainment level of proficiency in English among Malaysians. This impression has proven to be a fact supported by performance in schools, colleges and universities. It has now become an uphill task for students in the universities to refer to texts written in English, let alone discourse on their academic subjects in the language. In the public sector, there has been a general decry of the fact that the government officials of today are no longer efficient in handling tasks in English compared to their predecessors. (Asmah, 1987, p. 16)

When a language is no longer used as a medium for academic discourse, the students' mastery of the language cannot be expected to attain the level that it did when it was used as a medium of instruction (Wong & James, 2000).

It is this linguistic situation that the government has been worried about. Maintaining English as the means of international communication will become difficult because of the decreasing number of people who are able to utilize it as such. In an interview with a *Far Eastern Economic Review* correspondent, then Malaysian Deputy Education Minister, Fong Chan Oon, said,

> we have been worried about the decline of English for some time … . The Government's chief concern is that declining standards of English could hinder Malaysia's progress towards achieving developed nation status. (Vatikiotis, 1991, p. 28)

Consequently, the government had to look at matters pragmatically and make drastic changes in language policies.

Reinstating English as a Medium of Instruction

In 1993, 10 years after conversion to the Bahasa Malaysia medium of instruction was completed, the Malaysian government made a controversial move to allow the use of English in science, engineering, and medical courses in universities and colleges. This move was considered by the government to be essential for the economic and technological development of the nation. However, many Malay intellectuals found this move to be unwarranted and disconcerting. The viewpoints of both camps are discussed further in this chapter.

Datuk Seri Dr. Mahathir Mohamad, the Prime Minister of Malaysia, outlined the reasons for reinstating English as the medium of instruction in higher institutions as follows:

Competence in English is necessary:

1. for Malaysia to remain competitive at an international level,
2. to prevent the efficiency and capability of our people from being lower than those in other countries,
3. because the pace of translation cannot keep up with the generation of knowledge and information in the field of science and technology (Mohamad, 1993, December 28, p. 2).

In support of reinstating English as the medium of instruction in higher education, the former Deputy Prime Minister, Anwar Ibrahim, said:

> [This move] will not de-emphasize the importance and position of Bahasa Malaysia as the National Language. Instead the move would enhance the position of Bahasa Malaysia as the language of communication and knowledge. … This decision should not erode our confidence in Bahasa Malaysia as our national language and medium of communication. Through Dewan Bahasa dan Pustaka (DBP), government agencies and the education system, the Government will continue to strengthen the use of Bahasa Malaysia. (Ibrahim, 1993, December 31, p. 7)

Malaysians were advised by the Deputy Prime Minister not to allow their sentiments to cloud a rational view of the issue. The government's argument was that if Malaysians did not support the change in linguistic policy, then they would lose in the international race in the fields of industry, science, and technology (Ibrahim, 1993, December 31).

Political groups, even the opposition political parties, lauded the government's decision. Karpal Singh, a leader of the Democratic Action Party, one of the nation's major opposition parties, summarized the responses from many members of society as follows:

> Bahasa Malaysia has been given pride of place as the national language. The time has come to give English significant priority. It will be in the national interest to do so. In fact, the national interest demands it. (Singh, 1993, December 29, p. 3)

This move was naturally a matter of great concern to the Malay intellectuals. They held the same concerns as they had during the post-independence period, when nationalism was promoted by establishing Bahasa Malaysia as the official language and the medium of instruction. In response to this change in language policy, the Congress of Malay Intellectuals submitted a memorandum to the government, which stated the following resolutions:

1. to reject any move to introduce English as a medium of instruction for science and technological subjects;
2. to encourage the use of foreign languages, including English, which help in the acquisition and mastery of knowledge;
3. to emphasize the fact that Malay has been the medium of instruction for about 20 years and has not faced any problems that necessitate a change in the language policy, especially regarding the use of Malay as the language for imparting knowledge and instruction (Cendekiawan Melayu puas hati, 1994, January 8).

In response to this memorandum, Datuk Seri Dr Mahathir Mohamad reiterated the government's decision to allow English to be used as the medium of instruction for science and technological subjects in institutions of higher learning, but emphasized that this would not compromise the status of Bahasa Malaysia (Ramayah & Menon, 1994, January 9).

One of the main reasons for Datuk Seri Dr. Mahathir Mohamad's determination to drastically change the language policy was that it was necessary from a pragmatic point of view. He declared:

> We need to do it. It is the Government's opinion that once we have become a successful race, our language by itself will gain the respect of others. On the other hand, a race, which is not successful, will not be able to gain the respect for its language even though they hold strongly to it. (Mohamad, 1993, December 28, p. 2)

Because Malaysia needs to move quickly in its efforts to acquire the competencies needed to compete globally, and the ability to communicate effectively in an international lingua franca is essential, the Malaysian Cabinet felt that this change in linguistic policy was a measure that had to be taken.

However, the Malaysian Cabinet's decision did not have the support of the majority of the public universities. Malay intellectuals are a strong and cohesive group with social as well as political clout. They fought hard and succeeded in maintaining the status quo (i.e., retaining the use of Bahasa Malaysia as the language for science and technology in institutions of higher learning).

There is little doubt that the Malay intellectuals have won a political victory in protecting the national language policy for which they have worked so hard. But the political victory was not won at their expense, because they already possess competency in the English language. This situation is similar to Gonzalez's description of the elite in other post-colonial situations:

the elite will either support the status quo or support the national language movement full-scale to identify themselves with current nationalistic trends, all the while secure in their mastery of the second code for themselves and their children. (Gonzalez, 1994, p. 101)

Unfortunately, it is the students of public institutions of higher learning, educated in the Bahasa Malaysia medium of instruction, who are losing out in this linguistic battle. These students may manage to obtain their degrees based on lecture notes in Bahasa Malaysia and manuals that have been written in Bahasa Malaysia. However, it is becoming increasingly difficult for them to read widely in their own field in English, a capability that is central to university education. Students may pass their examinations but they face great obstacles in crossing the bridge between university and industry. Their inadequate command of English will be an even greater obstacle in this age of global competition, where English is the common working language in much of the world.

This is not the only problem facing higher education in Malaysia. As a result of education budget cuts in many parts of the world, public universities in countries such as the United Kingdom, the United States, Australia, Canada, Germany, and France have been forced to compete for funds and student enrollment in the international market (Altbach, 1991; Wagner & Schnitzer, 1991). Malaysia would not be able to compete with these universities if Bahasa Malaysia was the sole medium of instruction. In order to attract international students, Malaysia has opened its doors to a model of transnational education with collaborative links with foreign institutions of higher learning, a move that itself necessitates a change in language policy.

Medium of Instruction in Private Institutions of Higher Education

The Education Act, which was first implemented in 1960, contains a principal law that regulates education in Malaysia at all levels. It lays down an education policy that affirms the role of the national language as the medium of instruction and provides a common curriculum and common public examinations for schools (Sri Nusa, 1996). The Act was amended in 1995 to further reinforce the position of Bahasa Malaysia as the national language. This amendment requires the use of Bahasa Malaysia as a medium of instruction to be extended from public education institutions to all educational institutions in the private sector (Tan, 2002, p. 94).

Despite the Education Act, the reality in the private education sector is that English is used as the medium of instruction. There was no enforcement of the national language act in the private sector because the government realized that for the educational sector to flourish, freedom to select the medium of instruction had to be given. Furthermore, the private educational sector was largely driven by funding from corporations and wealthy individuals, and was not dependent on financial support from the government. Therefore the enforcement of this educational act would not have been welcomed by the private education industry.

In order to provide private institutions of higher learning with the freedom to use English as the medium of instruction, the government had to ensure that it was implemented via educational legislation. Therefore, in 1996, the Education Act 1996 and the 1996 Private Higher Education Institutions Act were introduced. The former approved the use of English as a medium of instruction for technical areas in postsecondary courses, and the latter allowed for the use of English in courses that were provided through twinning arrangements with overseas institutions as well as offshore campuses. To ensure that Bahasa Malaysia did not become sidelined by English, the legislation stipulates that the national language is a compulsory subject in the private educational institutions:

> Where the main medium of instruction in an educational institution is other than the national language, the national language shall be taught as a compulsory subject in the educational institution. (Laws of Malaysia, Education Act 1996, p. 23)

Therefore, despite the strong feelings of traditional nationalism still found in certain quarters, the positioning of the English language in Malaysia has come almost full circle, back to the status that it previously enjoyed, equal to the national language, Bahasa Malaysia.

IMPLICATIONS OF BIFURCATION IN INSTITUTIONS OF HIGHER EDUCATION

As a result of the liberalization of higher education policies, two streams of higher education have emerged: public universities where undergraduates study in Bahasa Malaysia, and private institutions of higher learning where instruction is in English. The bifurcation has serious social and political consequences. First, private universities are more expensive than public universities, which are heavily subsidized by the government. This means that students enrolled in private universities are usually from middle-class families, whereas those from working-class families can only afford to enroll in public universities. Second, the majority of the students in the public universities are Malays, whereas the majority of the students in private universities are Chinese. As a result, undergraduates are divided not only along socioeconomic lines but also along ethnic lines.

Compared with their counterparts in private universities, graduates of public universities are disadvantaged when seeking employment in the private sector because of their weaker English competence, although they are doing well in the government sector where Bahasa Malaysia is largely used. The linguistic disadvantage facing graduates from public universities manifests itself in the large numbers (approximately 44,000) who are not able to obtain jobs in the private sector. Datuk Mustapha Mohamed, the executive director of the government sponsored National Economic Action Council, articulates the reasons for this problem when he says:

> This is basically a Malay problem as 94% of those registered with the Government are [Malays] (Chinese constitute 3.7% and Indians 1.6%). It has to do with the courses taken, and ... also their poor performances in, and command of, the English language. (Mohamed, 2002c, March 14, pp. 1 & 12)

Professor K. S. Jomo, of the University of Malaya, who is also a leading political economist, laments the situation in which graduates from public universities have become victims of the universities' adherence to nationalistic language policies:

> Ironically, the main victims of the slide have turned out to be the Malay students. They are the ones being punished when it's time to enter the job market. Non-Malays are basically trilingual and tend to cope slightly better: it is a tremendous disadvantage for the Malays. (Tan, 1994, January 2, p. 8)

LESSONS FROM OTHER COUNTRIES

It would be useful at this juncture to consider recent developments in countries that have held onto a policy of using only their national language with just as much fervor as the Malays (e.g., France, which has strongly safeguarded the use of French for official purposes, and Japan, which developed as an industrialized nation in the Japanese language). These countries have recently had to adopt more realistic measures to both ensure that their undergraduates are competent in English, and to attract international students to their tertiary level programs, by using English as the medium of instruction in some subjects and institutions. In a memorandum to the Ministry of Education, the Malaysian Association of Private Colleges (MAPCO) made the following observations:

> In Japan, Germany and France, where they have been using their own languages for many years in their education systems, they are now using English as a medium of instruction after realizing that it is important to be proficient in this language if they are to compete effectively in the global arena. (MAPCO, 2001, November, p. 18)

In China, as the country prepares to participate fully in the World Trade Organization (WTO), universities and colleges have been instructed to use English as the main teaching medium for selected professional subjects, including information technology, biotechnology, new-material technology, finance, foreign trade, economics, and law. This change was affirmed in a circular from the Education Ministry in China, which said that 5% to 10% of the universities' total courses must be taught in a bilingual manner in 3 years' time. These instructions came after Premier Zhu Rongji made the following statement in June 2001, at one of the premier business schools in China (the Qinghua University Economics and Management School): "I hope all the classes will be taught in English. I don't worship foreign languages, but we need to exchange our ideas with the rest of the world" (China varsities [sic] to teach in English, 2001, September 20).

Even Indonesia, the country that was a role model for Malaysia in its own language planning stages, is pragmatically relaxing its control over mother-tongue medium of instruction in favor of English, in order to attract international students. Recently, a medical degree from Padjadjaran University in Bandung was advertised in the Malaysian papers as a program that is conducted fully in the English language (Medical Degree, 2001, August 14).

Europe is a continent where multilingualism is widespread. Recently, a lead article in *Business Week* titled "The Great English Divide" discussed the fact that in Europe, speaking the lingua franca separates the haves from the have-nots. The people of Europe can no longer get by just speaking and communicating in their respective mother tongues. This is particularly so with greater cross-border collaborations and the expansion of the European Union. A European Commission report makes the following statement:

> While English is fast becoming a prerequisite for landing a good job in Europe, only 41% of the people on the Continent speak it—and only 29% speak it well enough to carry on a conversation. The result is an English gap, one that divides Europe's haves from its have-nots. In the 19th and 20th centuries, Europeans brought peasants into the workforce by teaching them to read and write the national language. These days the equivalent challenge is to master Europe's international language. Those that fail—countries, companies and individuals alike—risk falling far behind. (The Great English Divide, 2001, August 13, p. 36)

CONCLUSION: NATIONALISM AND INTERNATIONALIZATION

What is the way forward for Malaysia? For the sake of national identity, the country can hold steadfast to existing language policies. But if this takes place, the school system will not give undergraduates full opportunities to master the English language. Thus, if public universities do not change their medium-of-instruction policy, they will deprive their undergraduates of the opportunity to acquire skills that would enable them to be competitive on the global scene. Furthermore, Malaysia will not be able to realize its aspiration of becoming a fully industrialized nation.

A drastic change in language policy can only be brought about by political will. The Prime Minister of Malaysia recently declared that science and mathematics subjects will be taught in English not only at tertiary levels but also during the first year of schooling (Mohamad, 2002a, p. 1).

After months of speculation over the issue, the Education Minister, Tan Sri Musa Mohamad, announced the details of implementation approved by the cabinet. He said that the teaching of science and mathematics will be taught in English in Standard One (which is the first year at primary level), Form One (which is the first year at secondary level) and Lower Six (which is equivalent to the first year of the "0-levels") next year (2003) and eventually to be introduced at all other levels (see report by Chok Suat Ling, 2002, July 12, p. 1).

Unlike in 1993, when the same pronouncement was issued, resistance to the change of policy this time has been minimal. Public universities seem to have adopted a more pragmatic stance. This pragmatic attitude may help reduce ethnic tension and enable all Malaysians to keep up with the rapid advances in technology. It will also help to realize the country's aspirations of becoming an industrialized nation by 2020.

REFERENCES

Altbach, P. G. (1991). Impact and adjustment: Foreign students in comparative perspective. *Higher Education, 21,* 305–323.

Asmah, H. O. (1979). *Language planning for unity and efficiency.* Kuala Lumpur: University Malaya Press.

Asmah, H. O. (1987, September 6–8). *English in Malaysia: A typology of its status and role.* Paper presented at Seminar on Language Planning in Multilingual Settings: The Role of English. National University of Singapore.

Asmah, H. O. (1994). Nationalism and exoglossia: The case of English in Malaysia. In H. Abdullah (Ed.), *Language planning in Southeast Asia* (pp. 66–85). Kuala Lumpur: Dewan Bahasa dan Pustaka and Ministry of Education.

Asmah, H. O. (1997). From imperialism to Malaysianisation: A discussion of the path taken by English towards becoming a Malaysian language. In M. S. Halimah & K. S. Ng (Eds.), *English is an Asian language: The Malaysian context* (pp. 12–21). Kuala Lumpur: Association of Modern Languages, Malaysia and The Macquarie Library Pty. Ltd.

Awang, H. S. (1994). Multiple dimensions for policy and pedagogical considerations in English language education in Malaysia. In S. K. Gill et al. (Eds.), *Proceedings of the International English Language Education Conference: National and international challenges and responses.* (pp. 20–30). Bangi: Language Centre, Universiti Kebangsaan Malaysia.

Blueprint for the future (2001, November/December). *Education Quarterly, 19,* 1–2.

Cendekiawan Melayu puas hati [Malay intellectuals satisfied]. (1994, January 8). News report translated from *Utusan Malaysia.*

China varsities [sic] to teach in English. (2001, September 20). Reported in the *South China Morning Post* cited in Web pages of The Straits Times Interactive, http://straitstimes.asia1.com.sg/home.

Chok Suat Ling. (2002, July 21). English at three levels next year. *New Sunday Times*, 1.

Fasold, R. (1987). *The sociolinguistics of society.* Oxford: Blackwell.

Gill, S. K. (1993). Standards and pedagogical norms for teaching English in Malaysia. *World Englishes, 12*(2), 223–238.

Gill, S. K. (1999). Standards and emerging linguistic realities in the Malaysian workplace (Symposium on Standards, Codification and World Englishes). In S. K. Gill & A. Pakir (Eds.), *World Englishes, 18*(2), 215–231.

Gill, S. K. (1999/2000, Winter). Voices and choices: Concerns of linguists, advertisers and society. *Asian Englishes, 2*(2) 36–58.

Gill, S. K. (2000, Winter). The past, present, and future of English as a global/international language: Issues and concerns in the Malaysian context. *Asian Englishes, 3*(2), 98–126.

Gonzalez, A. (1994). English and education in the Association of Southeast Asian Nations (ASEAN) region: Past, present and future. In T. Kandiah & J. Kwan-Terry (Eds.), *English and language planning: A Southeast Asian contribution* (pp.106–123). Singapore: Times Academic Press.

The Great English Divide. (2001, August 13). *Business Week*, 36–40.

Ibrahim, A. (1993, December 31). Assurance on position of national language. *New Straits Times*, 7.

Laws of Malaysia: Act 550, Education Act. (1996). Kuala Lumpur, Malaysia: Malaysia National Publishers.

MAPCO (Malaysian Association of Private Colleges) Memorandum to the Ministry of Education. (2001, November). *Responding to the challenges of globalisation and liberalisation on the current education system: Private sector perspective.*

Medical Degree. (2001, August 14). *The Malay Mail.* Padjadjaran University.

Ministry of Education, Malaysia. http://www.moe.gov.my/educ3.htm.

Mohamad, M. (1993, December 28). English to be medium of instruction in some subjects. *New Straits Times*, 2.

Mohamad, M. (2002a, May 11). Maths, science to be in English. *New Straits Times*, 1.

Mohamad, M. (2002b, May 20). System of meritocracy. *New Straits Times*, 1.

Mohamed, M. (2002c, March 14). NEAC: Institutions must ensure graduates are employable. *New Straits Times*, 1 and 2.

Ramayah, J., & Menon, V. (1994, January 9). Bahasa policy stays. *New Sunday Times*, 1.

Singh, K. (1993, December 29). Report on decision on using English lauded. *New Straits Times*, 3.

Sri Nusa, A. T. (1996). *How to make Malaysia a centre of excellence for private higher education in the context of the Education Act 1995.* Paper presented by Deputy Director-General of Private Education Department, Ministry of Education, Malaysia, at Seminar on Private Higher Education in Malaysia, Kuala Lumpur.

Tan, A. M. (2002). *Malaysian private higher education: Globalisation, privatisation, transformation and marketplaces.* London: ASEAN Academic Press.

Tan, J. (1994, January 2). Fears over status of Bahasa rekindled. *New Straits Times*, 8.

Vatikiotis, M. (1991, December 12). Purity and perception. *Far Eastern Economic Review*, 28–30.

Wagner, A., & Schnitzer, K. (1991). Programmes and policies for foreign students and students abroad: The search for effective approaches in a new global setting. *Higher Education, 21,* 275–288.

Wong, H. K., & Hong, E. T. (1975). *Education in Malaysia* (2nd ed.). Kuala Lumpur, Malaysia: Heinemann Educational Books (Asia).

Wong, R. Y. L., & James, J. E. (2000). Malaysia. In W. K. Ho & R. Y. L. Wong (Eds.), *Language policies and language education: The impact in East Asian countries in the next decade* (pp. 209–227). Singapore: Times Academic Press.

Yahya I. (2001, March 29–30). *Rejuvenating the education system: The challenges and the prospects.* Paper presented at National Conference on Education in the New Millennium: Challenges and Responses. Asian Strategy and Leadership Institute.

8

Rural Students and the Philippine Bilingual Education Program on the Island of Leyte

Iluminado Nical
Leyte Institute of Technology

Jerzy J. Smolicz
Margaret J. Secombe
University of Adelaide

Under the impact of economic, political, and cultural globalisation, it could be expected that the world will become increasingly homogeneous, with a convergence of cultures. Paradoxically, however, through weakening the authority and appeal of the nation-state (Eisenstadt, 2001), globalization has generated forces that counteract at least some of its homogenizing effects. As various aspects of control slip out of its grasp, the state faces the rising demands of its local, regional, and other minority groups, which are gaining confidence and demanding their place in the sun (Grant, 1997; Safran, 1995; Smolicz, 1998). With voices of protest against linguistic assimilation rising from a great variety of indigenous minorities around the world (Skutnabb-Kangas & Phillipson, 1994, 1998), regional linguistic groups have been particularly self-assertive in Catalonia, the Basque country, Quebec, Flanders, Sri Lanka, and elsewhere. Yet in the chorus of demands for language rights regarding the teaching of home languages in the school and their use as languages of instruction, the voices of Philippine linguistic communities other than Tagalog have been noticeably silent (Smolicz, 1986).

THE LANGUAGE CONTEXT OF THE PHILIPPINES

In Asia, there has been a traditional recognition of multilingualism that many European states lack. This does not mean that Asia has been free of strife or attempts at state-induced linguistic homogenization, in part due to the unfortunate importation of the outdated European model of a monolingual nation-state (Tombiah, 1996). In the Philippines, a belief in the need for one national language as a symbol of national independence has largely prevailed, as the country has come to terms with its heritage of domination by two former colonial tongues—Spanish (now almost phased out of existence) and English (used as virtually the sole medium in many domains, including higher education and scientific training in the schools). In their efforts to establish one of the indigenous languages, labeled *Filipino*, as the "national" language, the authorities appear to have placed the emphasis almost entirely on the use of Filipino and English. Indeed, in the current implementation of the national bilingual education policy, these two languages are the official media of instruction in schools. The other languages of the Philippines (spoken daily by almost two thirds of the population) are largely ignored in medium-of- instruction policies.

The lack of confidence among speakers of the various Filipino regional languages in the maturity of their home tongues, as reported in our earlier study of non-Tagalog speakers (Smolicz & Nical, 1997), is understandable in view of over three centuries of subordination to colonial tongues. The present policy of achieving "filipinization" through the imposition of Filipino/Tagalog as the only national language and the exclusion of other Filipino languages from the schools is yet another factor contributing to this diffidence. Yet the current worldwide upsurge of historic non-state languages indicates that such a lack of confidence in the maturity of one's native tongue is unlikely to last forever. If the Philippine authorities feel impelled to follow the widely contested European tradition, in which each state should possess a single national language, it is only a matter of time before similar notions are adopted by the non-Tagalog provinces of the Philippines. This has already occurred in the Islamic region of the Southern Philippines, where the population, with its distinct cultures and religion, has been in long standing rebellion against government authority, and has already been successful in winning a special status for Arabic, as well as a degree of local autonomy.

The danger point is reached when minority groups are placed under such heavy pressure by the dominant group that they lose faith in its intentions and feel so insecure in the common state that separation is perceived to be the only alternative to the ultimate demise of their linguistic and cultural heritage. In the rather somnolent linguistic scene in the Philippines, such a scenario may seem unlikely; little dissatisfaction with the current vernacular-Filipino diglossia is expressed, and the relationship between Filipino and the vernacular is overshadowed by the prestige of English as the language of higher education, business, and globalization (Smolicz, Nical, & Secombe, 2001). The study reported in this chapter probes the extent of the apparent linguistic quiescence among Filipinos in non-Tagalog regions of the country by investigating how the exclusion of the home regional languages from education is perceived by those most closely involved with it. The focus is on young people from provincial rural backgrounds, as well as their parents and their teachers, who were asked about their perceptions of current bilingual education policies. Specifically, the project examines language proficiency, language activation, and language attitudes toward the two languages of instruction at school and respondents' regional home language. Of particular interest was identification of any possible changes in literacy levels across generations, given that at least some of the parents would have had a modicum of literacy instruction in their home language during their early schooling, prior to the 1974 bilingual education reforms. The responses also provided a useful comparison with those of young people and their parents from provincial urban contexts who participated in an earlier study on the same language issues (Smolicz & Nical, 1997).

This study is designed to fill the gap caused by the paucity of research on patterns of linguistic usage among non-Tagalog speakers, particularly in rural areas, and the consequent lack of understanding about the educational outcomes and linguistic consequences for students who have been obliged to do their school study in languages other than the ones they use at home. By locating the research on the island of Leyte, with two clearly delineated linguistic communities far removed from metropolitan Manila, it was hoped to gain insight into the differential perceptions of school language policy and the degree to which the local languages are being maintained. The data gathered in the study can only be fully understood and interpreted if placed in the context of the country's multilingual heritage, the push for a national language, and the Bilingual Education Program (BEP), in which the two languages of instruction are Filipino and English.

MULTILINGUAL HERITAGE AND PUSH FOR A NATIONAL LANGUAGE

Throughout its history, the Philippines has been a country of cultural and linguistic complexity, with a heritage that includes the infusion of a variety of cultures on the Indo-Malay base (Zialcita, 1995). The multi-ethnic population speaks more than 80 major and minor languages and many dialectical variants, mainly belonging to the Austronesian family. Although they constitute separate languages, in that they are not mutually intelligible and have many subordinate dialects, they are clearly related to one another and regarded as belonging to the "Philippine type" (Gonzales, 1998, p. 493).

The indigenous Filipino cultural stream had been infiltrated by other peoples long before the country was conquered by Spain in the 16th century. In the South, Islamic influences had begun to spread, bringing with them Arabic and Persian influence. During the three centuries of rule by Spain, Spanish became established as the language of government and the small ruling elite. The Spanish colonizers showed much more preoccupation with the inculcation of Christianity than with the imposition of Spanish (De la Costa, 1961) and, in fact, limited education at higher levels to Spaniards alone until 1863. Even then, it was only the elite that adopted Spanish over the latter half of the 19th century.

With the imposition of American rule came the promulgation of compulsory education in English for all Filipinos. Individuals who successfully learned English enjoyed rewards that included career opportunities, government service, and participation in politics. Although the American English language initiatives were initially directed mainly against Spanish, they were almost equally hostile to the indigenous languages of the country, with penalties imposed on pupils using their home languages on the school premises (Manhit, 1980, 1981). Throughout the period of American rule, indigenous languages were excluded from schools and universities and most forms of public life. Yet they continued to thrive in the homes and hearts of the people until just before the Second World War, when the emerging demand for political independence was paralleled by a movement for the recognition of the right of Filipinos to their own national language(s).

One of the main obstacles on this path arose out of the country's linguistic mosaic in which some 10 major languages were able to claim songs, poetry, and a body of prose to their credit, and some half a dozen could be viewed as serious contenders for more than purely local status (Tenazas & Ramas, 1974; Yap, 1990). Among the latter, the two strongest contenders for national status were Cebuano and Tagalog. Cebuano, which at the time of the 1960 census still had the greatest number of mother-tongue speakers (about one fourth of the population), was widely spoken south of Manila in the Visayas, where it functioned as a lingua franca for the whole region. Tagalog, on the other hand, was the language of the capital, Manila, and further developed in the literary and political spheres, as well as being known to the greatest number of Filipinos, many of whom used it as a second language. By 1970, Tagalog had also overtaken Cebuano as the most commonly used first (or home) language.

Despite the pressure for recognition of the country's indigenous languages throughout the period of the American occupation, much hesitation surrounded the moves to establish just one national language. The initial opposition to Tagalog, renamed Pilipino to advance its cause, was "so fierce that there was a danger that a foreign language like English might be adopted as the Philippine national language" (Bautista, 1981, p. 6). In order to forestall such a possibility, the linguists and educators who were committed to Pilipino resorted to a compromise commitment to develop a fusion of all the Philippine languages, which would give rise to a multibased national language to be called Filipino. In subsequent years a supposedly "enriched" and intellectualized version of Tagalog/Pilipino was adopted under the label of Filipino (Gonzales, 1996, p. 230), assuming the role of both a national and official language, alongside English and (until 1986) Spanish.

In general, the adoption of the Tagalog-based compromise was interpreted by native Tagalog speakers as an inevitable outcome, whereas most of the elite members of other language groups were eventually reconciled to accepting such a compromise, provided that English remained dominant in government, universities and business life. Those who supported the adoption of Filipino often pointed to the negative impact of English on Philippine society (Sibayan, 1994). The imposition of English by the colonial regimes in Asia and Africa, it was claimed, had led to colonized people internalizing the norms and ideology of the colonizers and becoming alienated from their own linguistic and cultural heritages (Phillipson, 1992). In the context of the Philippines, the time spent learning English meant not only that the learning of indigenous languages was neglected, but also that the children from rural non-elite masses found it difficult to reach adequate standards in other subjects, because these were being studied in what to them was a foreign language (Constantino, 1982).

THE BILINGUAL EDUCATION PROGRAM

The struggle between the advocates of English and Filipino was resolved in 1974 through the adoption of the Bilingual Education Program, which aimed to develop a nation competent in both English and Filipino (Manuel, 1974). This effectively extinguished any initial literacy education in the regional languages, which had been used during the previous two decades as media of instruction at Grades 1 and 2 in non-Tagalog parts of the country. The decision to exclude languages other than English and Filipino from the schools was carried out in spite of evidence of the advantages gained by children beginning their schooling in their mother tongue. An early study carried out in the Iloilo province, for example, involved experimental classes taught in the regional language (Hiligaynon) in the first two primary grades, with a shift to English as a medium of instruction delayed until Grade 3. The educational progress of students, which was followed from Grade 1 to 6, was then compared with the outcome for the control group where English was the language of instruction from Grade 1. The results showed that children who were taught in their home regional language became literate in it and mastered the content of the curriculum without ultimately any negative impact on their ability to learn English in the higher grades (Isidro, cited by Nical, 2000, p. 147). Such findings are in agreement with subsequent international research (Cummins, 1984; Cummins & Swain, 1986; Skutnabb-Kangas, 1984; Skutnabb-Kangas & Cummins, 1988), but at the time of the implementation of the BEP, these findings were disregarded in favor of the push for Tagalog/Filipino, carried out in the name of the monolingual nation-state ideal.

Despite difficulties in its implementation over the next decade, the BEP was reaffirmed in the democratic transformation that succeeded the Marcos regime. The 1987 guidelines of the Department of Education, Culture and Sports (reprinted in Sutaria, Guerrero, & Castano, 1989) stated that English and Filipino were to be taught in all grades of elementary and secondary schools. Filipino was to be the medium of instruction in Social Studies/Social Science, Character Education, Work Education, Health Education, and Physical Education; English was to be the medium of instruction in all other areas, in particular, Science and Mathematics. A provision in relation to the Muslim regions of the country was added, whereby "Arabic was to be used in areas where it was necessary." Some allowance continued to be made for schools to use the local non-Tagalog "vernacular" or regional language of the area "as auxiliary to the media of instruction, but only when necessary to facilitate the understanding of concepts being taught in English, F(P)ilipino or Arabic" (Quisumbing, 1989, p. 300).

In the ministerial guidelines, no support was provided for the actual teaching of Philippine languages other than Tagalog/Filipino as subjects in their own right. According to Sibayan (1994):

> If the speakers of the Philippine major languages [other than Tagalog] would like to have their native language as a medium of instruction in the early grades...they should be willing to provide financial support for the program ... The Filipino who reads and writes in Filipino will have no difficulty in reading and writing in his own language if necessary. (p. 80)

Yet the Minister of Education acknowledged the difference between Tagalog-speaking students, for whom the "national language education actually starts from childhood and continues throughout life, [with] the school serving to reinforce and refine such language education," and the non-Tagalog speaking students. Rather than encouraging the latter to become literate first in their home languages, Minister Quisumbing (1989) reassured them that "compensatory education has been set up for the purpose of equalizing competence in Filipino among Tagalog and non-Tagalog groups through the development of appropriate teaching materials, the offering of special language teachers, the offering of special classes and the establishment of incentives for teachers of Filipino for acquiring minimum standards of language proficiency" (p. 314). The implication that the students' home languages, if other than Tagalog, were a handicap that must be ameliorated by compensatory programs recalls the assimilationist policies toward migrant children in the United States and Australia (Clyne, 1991; Smolicz, 1995).

The fact that bilingual education appears to have been accepted without much turbulence since the 1980s would suggest that at least the more influential sections of the population have been able to accommodate themselves to its demands. In upper- and middle-class homes throughout the country, English is often used, so that children have a background knowledge of the language when they start school at age 6, or even earlier when they have their formal introduction to English in a fee-paying preschool. Private schools have often been able to increase the time allocated to English without incurring much trouble with those responsible for monitoring the ministerial directives.

Voices of dissent against what is perceived as Tagalog/Filipino nationalism have taken two main forms, one championing indigenous languages and the other English. Probably the most provocative has been a statement coming from a former Governor of Cebu, who declared his full support for Filipino, provided this label referred to Cebuano. Instances have also been recorded in Cebu of the Philippine national anthem being sung in Cebuano, a move supported by the Cebu provincial government (Nical, 2000, p. 24). At the other end of the non-Tagalog spectrum of opinion, fear of what was perceived as the downgrading of English has caused some elite Ilocano-speaking public figures to attack the Bilingual Education Policy (although such fears were misplaced, according to Gonzales [1996, p. 42]). Our previous study revealed significant differences in the way various speech communities evaluated the two languages of instruction, with some communities (such as Ilocano) favoring Filipino and others (like Cebuano) English (Smolicz & Nical, 1997).

Bilingual education remains a controversial, if often understated, issue in the Philippines. Reports of the failure of the bilingual policy appear in the press with reference to the perceived decline in the standard of English in the schools. This is usually attributed to the time allocated to Filipino and the influence of Filipino linguistic structures on English usage. The learning of Mathematics and Science is said to have become more difficult, as these subjects are taught in a language that is not fully comprehensible to the students. The Congressional Commission on Education (1991) expressed concern about the decline of educational standards in the country as a whole, when it bluntly stated, "Our elementary and high schools are failing to teach the competence the average citizen needs to become responsible, productive and self-fulfilling" (p. xii).

Public criticism, however, rarely focuses on the impact of the present Bilingual Education Program on native speakers of non-Tagalog languages, especially those from areas of rural poverty or low socio-economic status. With little or no English or Tagalog within their home setting, they face a double linguistic barrier to learning, which inevitably affects their school performance, so that only the most able and dedicated can hope to advance to and successfully complete their higher education studies (Gonzales, 1998; Smolicz, 1986).

THE RESPONDENTS IN THE PRESENT STUDY

In order to explain the impact of the Bilingual Education Program on non-Tagalog speakers in rural communities, we studied two non-Tagalog linguistic communities, Cebuano and Waray, in rural districts of the island of Leyte. The study focused on senior secondary students whose home backgrounds provided them with little or no direct initiation into English and for whom Filipino was not the everyday home language.

This rural-based study was designed to extend our previous research on senior high school students drawn from largely middle-class non-Tagalog backgrounds and attending schools in provincial urban centers. These students represented some of the relatively privileged sections of the school population in that they had already been successful at school in the face of the linguistic barrier of learning in two languages other than their home tongue (Smolicz & Nical, 1997; Smolicz, Nical, & Secombe, 2001). The Cebuano respondents, for example, were drawn from the city of Cebu, a major metropolis and the political center of the Cebuano speech communities in the Visayas. In contrast, the present study includes Cebuano respondents living along the western coastline of Leyte, specifically, final (fourth) year high school students from schools located in small towns ("poblaciones"). These schools draw their clientele from rural municipalities with an average population of 25,000, scattered over a wide area of the countryside, and made up of smaller units or "barangays." Most of the parents are small farmers, with a sprinkling of small business people.

Following elementary schooling that covers Grades 1 through 6 (beginning at age 6), the 4-year state secondary school provides a college-preparatory curriculum designed to offer an avenue to either state-supported universities and colleges or their private counterparts, whether sectarian or nonsectarian. In all of these tertiary institutions, English is the sole medium of instruction, except where the Filipino language is taken as a subject. For this reason, the more prosperous rural parents generally prefer to have their children educated in the larger urban centers, an alternative requiring significant expenditures for commuting and/or boarding that only a few rural people can afford.

Despite their rural background, our 4th-year student respondents could not, however, be regarded as the poorest of the rural population, because a large number of students leave school during the secondary years (and some even at the elementary stage), when their labor is required at home (mostly on farms) or in paid employment needed to sustain the welfare of the families, many of which are below the poverty line. Students such as our respondents, who had reached the final secondary grade at the age of 16, had some hope of reaching tertiary education. Only a proportion of them, however, were likely to fulfill that goal, due to the expense of meeting the fees charged by private colleges, or the necessary boarding and/or transport outlays in free institutions. Rural students who do enroll at a university are frequently the first ones to drop out, not only because of financial difficulties, but because of their failure to cope with the demands of college work in which success depends on high levels of communicative competence in English. For most rural students, such levels of competence are beyond their reach; neither the home nor the community nor the school provides sufficient opportunity to learn English. In a Bilingual Education Program geared toward making Filipino a nationally used language, exposure to English is limited solely to the study of Science, Mathematics, and English as a subject.

METHODOLOGY

The aim of this study is to examine the students', parents', and teachers' perceived speaking proficiency and literacy skills, their language activation, and their attitudes toward the three languages (regional language, Filipino, and English). In this way, the study investigates the effect of the Bilingual Education Program some 30 years after it was first imposed on the non-Tagalog speaking areas and thereby eliminated regional languages as media of instruction in all grades of schooling.

The study replicated the research instruments adopted in our earlier investigations, but involved larger groups of respondents and included the teachers of the students, as well as their parents. Another innovative feature was that its scope was limited to the island of Leyte and its two linguistic communities, Waray and Cebuano, geographically separated by a mountain range running across the island.

The student respondents, numbering almost 1,000, were drawn from 28 randomly selected public (state-supported) schools, 10 of which were located in the Cebuano speaking region, where they constituted more than half the total number of schools in that area. The other 18 were in the Waray speaking community. Also asked to complete the questionnaire were the students' parents and teachers, providing almost 2,000 participants in all. The percentage distribution of the three respondent groups in the two language communities is given in Table 8.1 below.

Because research assistants personally administered the questionnaires to the students and the teachers in the classrooms and waited until they were completed, the retrieval rate for these groups was very high (95%), with only a very few refusing to participate. In the case of the parents, however, the questionnaires had to be sent home through the students; the retrieval rate for this group was 73%.

The language proficiency data were coded on a 5-point scale, where "excellent" was assigned the numerical value of 5; "very good" 4, "good" 3, "fair" 2, and "poor" 1, in relation to speaking, reading, and writing (termed *communication activities*) in each language. A 5-point scale was also adopted to numerically code the responses to questions on the activation of the languages in the three communication activities, using 1 for "never," 2 for "seldom," 3 for "sometimes," 4 for "often," and 5 for "always." Language activation was further investigated by ascertaining the frequency with which the students spoke the languages with different interlocutors in the various domains of their lives, such as family, friends, teachers, and market vendors. In addition, attitudes toward the languages were explored by asking respondents to agree or disagree with statements about each language and specifically about their use in the school context. In order to analyze these data statistically, the numerical value of 3 was assigned to the positive responses, 2 to uncertain, and 1 to those that were negative.

The questionnaire data were analyzed through the calculation of the mean for each set of respondents (students, teachers, and parents), and for the two language communities, as presented in Tables 8.2 through 8.4. Across the rows, combined mean scores were calculated as the mean of the

TABLE 8.1
Respondents to Research Questionnaire

	Waray		Cebuano		Total	
	N	%	N	%	N	%
Students	584	60	388	40	972	100
Teachers	152	63	91	37	243	100
Parents	415	58	297	42	712	100
Total	1,151	60	776	40	1,927	100

total number of respondents in each language group. Down the columns, the combined mean for each language skill or attitude was the mean for the total number of respondents from both language groups in each set (students/parents/teachers). The mean scores for each set of respondents, for the two communities and for the interaction of these two factors were all subjected to an analysis of variance based on the calculation of F and t ratios, in order to determine whether any of the differences between the various groupings were statistically significant. The computer-based SPSS program was employed for the analysis.

RESULTS

Proficiency in the Languages

In relation to proficiency in their respective regional languages, Waray and Cebuano, respondents from all groups claimed to be generally at the very good level in speaking, with the Waray respondents having significantly higher scores than the Cebuano (see Table 8.2).

Proficiency in reading and writing the regional language was at a relatively lower level than speaking, although it was still reported as "good" to "very good." Teachers proved to be the most proficient group in reading, followed by parents, and then students, with the Cebuano respondents being significantly better than the Waray. For writing in Cebuano and Waray, the parent group in both linguistic communities had significantly higher scores than the teachers and the students, with the Waray parents having the highest mean and the Waray students the lowest.

The pattern of proficiency in Filipino was the same for all three communication activities. Although all the scores for both linguistic communities and all the sets of respondents fell within the "good " to "very good" range, the student means were significantly higher than those of the teachers and parents. Moreover, the scores for all the Waray sets of respondents were significantly above the Cebuano, with Warray students the highest.

In the case of communication in English, the means from the different sets of respondents tended to converge at the "good" level, somewhat below the means reported for the other two languages. For all three communication activities, however, teachers had significantly higher means than the students, with the parental group being the lowest. The lowest proficiency mean for both the parent and student respondents was in the speaking of English. There were no significant differences between the two linguistic communities.

Language Activation

The trends revealed in the means for language activation (given in Table 8.3) were similar to those for proficiency. For all sets of respondents and lan-

TABLE 8.2
**Mean Values Indicating the Proficiency of Three Sets of Respondents
in Two Linguistic Communities***

Communication activities	Sets of respondents			Combined
by type of community	Students	Parents	Teachers	mean
Regional Language				
Speaking				
Waray	4.05	4.14	4.05	**4.09***
Cebuano	3.98	3.87	3.87	3.92
Mcombined	4.02	4.03	3.98	
Reading				
Waray	3.49	3.71	3.64	3.59
Cebuano	3.65	3.63	**3.85***	**3.68**
Mcombined	3.56	3.68	**3.72**	
Writing				
Waray	3.38	**3.68***	3.49	3.51
Cebuano	3.58	3.62	3.53	3.60
Mcombined	3.46	**3.66**	3.50	
Filipino				
Speaking				
Waray	**3.82***	3.58	3.52	**3.69**
Cebuano	3.65	3.15	3.21	3.40
Mcombined	**3.75**	3.40	3.40	
Reading				
Waray	**3.95***	3.67	**3.79**	3.83
Cebuano	3.87	3.37	3.67	3.65
Mcombined	**3.92**	3.54	3.74	
Writing				
Waray	**3.79***	3.53	3.52	3.59
Cebuano	3.72	3.21	3.36	3.47
Mcombined	**3.76**	3.40	3.46	
English				
Speaking				
Waray	3.02	2.78	3.22	3.98
Cebuano	3.04	2.81	3.30	2.98

Communication activities by type of community	Sets of respondents			Combined mean
	Students	Parents	Teachers	
Mcombined	3.03	2.79	**3.31**	
Reading				
Waray	3.53	3.18	3.73	3.49
Cebuano	3.46	3.18	3.67	3.35
Mcombined	3.50	3.14	**3.71**	
Writing				
Waray	3.19	2.9	3.35	3.11
Cebuano	3.23	2.96	3.24	3.13
Mcombined	3.20	2.93	**3.31**	

*Means are based on following scores: 5 = excellent, 4 = very good, 3 = good, 2 = fair, 1 = poor. The bold figures represent the highest statistically significant means, with * indicating statistically significant interaction between scores for the sets of respondents and the linguistic communities. The combined means were calculated as the mean of the total number of respondents in the relevant cells.

guage communities, the language most frequently used ("often" to "always") for the purpose of speaking was Waray or Cebuano.

The means for student and parent respondents were significantly higher than that for teachers, with Cebuano students having the highest mean. The frequency of reading and writing these regional languages was notably lower, in the "seldom" to "sometimes" range for students and teachers (the latter scoring lowest), but significantly higher (at the "sometimes" to "often" level) for the parents. In relation to Filipino, all scores were in the "sometimes" to "often" range, with students claiming significantly higher usage than parents and teachers. In addition, all the Waray respondents had means significantly above those of their Cebuano counterparts. In contrast, for English, the respondents with the significantly highest means for all three communication activities were both the Waray and Cebuano teachers, who reported reading and writing English "often," followed by students and then parents. The lowest levels of usage were for the speaking of English, particularly among the parents.

Insights into what the scores meant in everyday life could be gained from responses to questions on domains of activation for the speaking of each language, which are discussed later in qualitative terms. These data revealed that the regional language, whether Waray or Cebuano, was the language predominantly spoken by all sets of respondents with parents, brothers and sisters, relatives, and friends, but not to the total exclusion of either Filipino or English. In dealings with interlocutors outside the immediate family, such as salespeople, market vendors, office people, and school

TABLE 8.3
Mean Values Indicating the Language Activation of Three Sets
of Respondents in Two Linguistic Communities*

Communication activities	Sets of respondents			Combined
by type of community	Students	Parents	Teachers	mean
Regional Languages				
Speaking				
Waray	4.46	4.58	4.10	4.46
Cebuano	**4.65***	4.53	4.08	4.53
Mcombined	**4.56**	**4.56**	4.09	
Reading				
Waray	2.99	3.73	2.73	3.22
Cebuano	3.16	3.74	2.80	3.35
Mcombined	3.08	**3.74**	2.76	
Writing				
Waray	2.90	3.66	2.88	3.17
Cebuano	2.98	3.78	2.96	3.29
Mcombined	2.94	**3.72**	2.91	
Filipino				
Speaking				
Waray	3.55	3.49	3.30	**3.50**
Cebuano	3.35	3.34	3.27	3.34
Mcombined	**3.45**	3.43	3.28	
Reading				
Waray	4.11	3.81	3.49	**3.92**
Cebuano	3.92	3.44	3.44	3.67
Mcombined	**4.04**	3.66	3.47	
Writing				
Waray	4.06	3.63	3.44	**3.72**
Cebuano	3.87	3.32	3.11	3.56
Mcombined	**3.96**	3.48	3.32	
English				
Speaking				
Waray	3.07	2.70	3.42	2.93
Cebuano	2.86	2.65	3.47	2.85

| Communication activities | Sets of respondents | | | Combined |
by type of community	Students	Parents	Teachers	mean
Mcombined	2.96	2.68	**3.44**	
Reading				
Waray	3.89	3.41	4.17	**3.74**
Cebuano	3.72	3.04	3.98	3.48
Mcombined	3.82	3.26	**4.04**	
Writing				
Waray	3.76	3.03	4.10	3.54
Cebuano	3.72	2.89	3.98	3.42
Mcombined	3.74	2.97	**4.05**	

*Means are based on the following scores: 5 = always (in the sense of all the time), 4 = often, 3 = sometimes, 2 = seldom, 1 = never. The bold figures represent the highest statistically significant means, with * indicating statistically significant interaction between scores for the sets of respondents and the linguistic communities. The combined means were calculated as the mean of the total number of respondents in the relevant cells.

teachers, the most common pattern for all groups of respondents was regional language "often," with Filipino and English being employed "sometimes," or "seldom" in the case of English with market vendors.

In particular, both sets of parents claimed that they spoke the regional language "always" (in the sense of "all the time") in the family context, with Filipino being incorporated "sometimes" and English only "seldom." The Cebuano student respondents also claimed to use their regional language all the time in family contexts. Among both student groups, English was "seldom" spoken to parents. Elsewhere in the family and in contacts with fellow students and salespersons, both Waray and Cebuano students used all three languages in the pattern of regional language "often," and the two languages of school instruction "sometimes." At school, however, in communication with teachers, the students indicated that they used all three languages "often." Regional languages were used even in communication with teachers, although to a greater extent among the Cebuano than the Waray student respondents.

Some variations in the pattern just discussed were apparent among the teachers. In the formal domains of school instruction, teachers indicated that they most often spoke English to supervisors, students, office people, and visitors, with Filipino and Cebuano or Waray used "sometimes." The Waray teachers also claimed to use Filipino "often" with students. In less formal contacts in the school domain, or where it seemed most appropriate, such as with parents of students, colleagues, and co-teachers, both the Cebuano and Waray teachers claimed to use their regional language "often," and the other two languages "sometimes." However, Waray teachers tended to make greater use of Filipino and English, whereas the Cebuano teachers more frequently employed their own regional language.

Language Attitudes

The mean scores for language attitudes (see Table 8.4) showed that all of respondents were more positive to English and Filipino than to their regional language. This held both for attitudes to the languages per se and attitudes to their use in school. However, there were significant differences among the various sets of respondents and between the two language communities.

The greatest consensus was evident in relation to English. The respondents most positive to the language itself were the teachers, followed by the students and parents. Although the Cebuano teachers had the highest mean, the Waray respondents, as a whole, had significantly higher means than the Cebuano. English as a language in schools, however, elicited a high level of support from all categories of respondents in both communities.

In relation to Filipino, greater variance was evident across the groupings. The mean of the student group for Filipino both as a language and for school use was significantly higher than those of the parents and the teachers. The support for Filipino was significantly higher among the Waray respondents than among the Cebuano. Cebuano teachers revealed the lowest level of support for Filipino, and Waray students the highest.

Generally, the lowest attitude means recorded by all respondents were for the regional languages. However, parental means for Cebuano and Waray as languages were significantly above those for students and teachers. In addition, the Cebuano respondents were significantly higher than the Waray, the highest mean reported being for Cebuano parents. Attitudes to the regional languages in the school context reversed the trends in that student respondents reported the most positive attitudes, and the Waray means were significantly higher than the Cebuano.

DISCUSSION

The proficiency and activation data from the rural respondents on the island of Leyte confirm one of the key findings from earlier studies (Gonzales, 1996, 1998; Gonzales & Bautista, 1986; Smolicz & Nical, 1997) in that all the respondents were trilingual and activated all three languages in the communication activities of their everyday lives. Overall, the pattern of spoken language activation showed that no one language was being used exclusively, but that all three were being activated with varying frequency

TABLE 8.4
Mean Values Indicating the Attitudes to Languages among Three Sets of Respondents in Two Linguistic Communities*

Languages as Seen by the Respondents	Sets of respondents			Combined mean
	Students	Parents	Teachers	
Regional languages				
As a language				
Waray	2.07	2.14	2.04	2.09
Cebuano	2.16	2.32	2.10	**2.21**
Mcombined	2.10	**2.22**	2.06	
As used in school				
Waray	1.99	1.76	1.60	**1.85**
Cebuano	1.88	1.78	1.45	1.79
Mcombined	**1.95**	1.77	1.55	
Filipino				
As a language				
Waray	2.77	2.65	2.63	**2.71**
Cebuano	2.69	2.53	2.50	2.61
Mcombined	**2.74**	2.60	**2.74**	
As used in school				
Waray	2.31	2.28	2.20	**2.28**
Cebuano	2.24	2.23	2.03	2.21
Mcombined	**2.28**	2.26	2.14	
English				
As a language				
Waray	2.75	2.62	2.83	**2.72**
Cebuano	2.62	2.51	**2.84***	2.61
Mcombined	2.70	2.58	**2.83**	
As used in school				
Waray	2.40	2.36	2.30	2.38
Cebuano	2.35	2.33	2.32	2.34
Mcombined	2.38	2.35	2.31	

*Means are based on following scores : 3 = positive, 2 = unsure, 1 = negative.
The bold figures represent the highest statistically significant means, with * indicating statistically significant interaction between scores for the sets of respondents and the linguistic communities. The combined means were calculated as the mean of the total number of respondents in the relevant cells.

in different domains. Even in the school, where Filipino and English were the official languages of instruction, the regional languages were not excluded from use in informal interaction with leaders and fellow students, although students and their parents claimed to speak their regional language more often than the teachers.

The present rural study, when taken in conjunction with the earlier results from the corresponding urban investigation, provides insights into language patterns on the island of Leyte. These can be analyzed along three dimensions, which bring into focus *generational*, *linguistic community* and *rural-urban* distinctions.

The *generational dimension* highlights the different patterns of literacy usage and proficiency among students on the one hand, and their parents and teachers on the other. The parents' higher activation of Cebuano and Waray for reading and writing no doubt reflects, at least in part, the fact that some of them were taught to read and write in their mother tongue in the first 2 years of primary school, an advantage that has been denied to those from the younger generation. The teachers' low literacy usage in the regional language could be linked to their professional obligation to limit school instruction to Filipino and English. Low activation of regional language literacy did not necessarily translate into lack of proficiency, because both teachers and parents significantly exceeded students in home language literacy, with teachers showing significantly higher scores in reading and the parents in writing.

Although the Bilingual Education Program would seem so far to have had little negative influence on the use of regional languages for oral communication in everyday life, particularly in the home domain, there is evidence of a negative effect emerging in relation to attitudes. The parents in both communities were significantly more positive to their regional language than the students and teachers. Even more noteworthy were the low-attitude means for regional languages in school, indicating that respondents generally were unsure of the relevance and/or appropriateness of these languages in formal education. The student respondents, however, were significantly less negative to regional languages in the school context than were the other sets of respondents.

The effects of the BEP, with its emphasis on Filipino literacy, can best be observed in the way students who had been brought up under the program displayed significantly higher scores in both activation and proficiency for Filipino. The results obtained for English, however, showed that the students' gains in Filipino literacy had not been matched in English. Although parents were, not surprisingly, the least skillful in English activation and proficiency, the students' scores were quite mediocre and well below those reported by their teachers. In fact, it is clear that teachers were most comfortable in employing English, and their scores for English activation and proficiency were significantly higher than the other respondents in all three communication activities.

In summary, the generational analysis was valuable in the way it demonstrated the longer-term outcomes of the BEP, with parents relying on their regional language literacy to the greatest extent, while showing significantly lower proficiency scores in both Filipino and English. Although students had benefited from the BEP in relation to literacy skills in Filipino, their lower levels of proficiency and activation in English are a danger signal for their tertiary aspirations, because all university instruction is in English. Teachers, however, because of their tertiary studies in English and their obligation to employ English together with Filipino as a language of instruction in the schools, exhibited high proficiency and activation of English.

The *linguistic community* dimension provided further insights by taking into account the differences in usage, skills, and outlook between the two linguistic communities sharing the island of Leyte. Although the language activation means for speaking the regional languages were highest, those for reading and writing Filipino were highest. This suggests that Filipino is used for communication in a wider range of areas compared to regional languages and English, and that it has become in practice the national lingua franca. The significantly higher proficiency and activation in Filipino reported by the students would suggest that the BEP could take much of the credit for this development. However, sets of data for students, teachers, and parents each showed an important divergence between the Cebuano and Waray communities in the activation and proficiency in Filipino. Waray respondents achieved significantly higher scores in Filipino than Cebuano in every respondent category in all three communication activities, with those in language activation and proficiency being statistically significant. This result was in agreement with the well-known Cebuano antipathy to Filipino as the enforced national language, and in accord with the finding from our previous study, in which the Cebuano respondents came from the city of Cebu. The fact that this result was replicated for the Cebuano respondents of Leyte, which lies at the periphery of the Cebuano linguistic community in the Visayas, can be taken as indicative of the latent tensions that underlie the ostensibly peaceful acceptance of the BEP, which in its current form discriminates against regional languages.

These results reflect the general Cebuano belief that there is no need for Filipino, when they can rely on English in conjunction with their own native tongue, which (unlike Waray) has its own rich literary heritage. Indeed, our Cebuano respondents have access to more literary materials than are available for the Warays. A similar trend was evident in the attitudinal scores, which demonstrated that the Cebuano respondents were less positive toward Filipino, both as a language and in the school context, than their Waray counterparts. Although differing from the Cebuanos in their more sympathetic acceptance of Filipino, the Waray respondents shared the positive sentiments of the Cebuanos toward English. This consensus was particularly evident in the case of Cebuano and Waray teachers, whose scores for both activation and proficiency in English were significantly higher than those reported by the other sets of respondents.

The third dimension relates to the *rural–urban* comparison of language patterns among rural students and parents in this study with their urban counterparts in our previous study (which did not include any teachers). Speaking the regional language had the highest mean frequency for both rural and urban respondents, but the rural students, and particularly their parents, showed greater activation of regional language literacy than their urban counterparts. In all communication activities, rural students and parents indicated higher literacy activation and proficiency in Filipino.

The situation was reversed in the case of English, which was the language of lowest activation and proficiency levels among the rural respondents. Although the student means were higher than those of the parents, especially in relation to speaking and writing, the school would appear to have been much more effective in developing rural students' proficiency and activation in Filipino than in English, reflecting the lack of domains outside the school in rural areas where English could be activated. It is also noteworthy that English usage among rural teachers was less extensive than that claimed by urban parents and students. For these reasons, it is hardly surprising that rural students and their parents showed even lower means for the proficiency and activation of English, confirming the observation that the rural poor suffer the greatest disadvantage under the current BEP, a deprivation that is not shared by their middle-class, urban counterparts. It should also be noted that lower proficiency and fewer opportunities for activation did not lead to negative attitudes toward English. The attitude means for English were higher for all sets of respondents in both rural linguistic communities than those reported for the other two languages.

There was no difference between rural and urban students in terms of generational comparisons, with parents out-performing the students in regional language literacy, and students ahead of parents in Filipino literacy. The same trend prevailed for English literacy among rural respondents, but urban Waray parents showed a higher score in reading and writing English than the students, in relation to both activation and proficiency. This result may reflect the drilling in English in schools under the American rule and in the early post-independence period, prior to BEP in the Waray region, when the local language had a more slender literary base than Cebuano.

CONCLUSION

Different countries have responded in different ways to their linguistic diversity, ranging from support for multiculturalism to policies that attempt to eliminate the languages of non-dominant groups. For many years, the Philippines has been following a Tagalog/Filipino assimilation policy in education, under the umbrella of the ex-colonial and globally dominant language, English. The research reported in this chapter shows, however, that the regional languages of the Philippines other than Tagalog/Filipino continue to be maintained among students in their family, local community, and regional settings. Although there have not been pressing signs of dissent or vociferous demands for changing the current policies, varying degrees of discontent were evident in our research, with a potential for more vigorous requests for linguistic equity in the future. In view of the world trend toward increasing minority demands for cultural and linguistic recognition, it may be salutary for the Philippines to learn from the example of countries seeking to foster multilingualism alongside a national language.

In Spain since the 1980s, for example, regional languages have been adopted in educational systems within their respective territories (Conversi, 1997; Lecours, 2001). However, as regional boundaries do not coincide with linguistic ones, students with the same home language may face different school policies. For example, Huguet and Llurda (2001) compared the Catalan language in a province on the Catalan side of the border, where it enjoys official language status together with Spanish and where it is used in public contexts, with its position in Eastern Aragon, where Catalan is used at the family level but is progressively substituted by Spanish in other settings. The study revealed that Aragon-based students who attended Catalan classes after school hours showed more positive attitudes toward Catalan than those who did not, and at levels comparable to students in Catalonia. Moreover, the attitudes of those learning Catalan in Aragon were as favorable to Spanish as of those of the non-attending group. Thus, the students who showed the most positive attitudes toward both languages were those living in Aragon and attending Catalan classes. In other words, students' study of the regional language did not detract from the status of the national language.

The Spanish study shows the crucial role of school not only in language learning per se but also in shaping speakers' attitudes and self-awareness (cf. Baker, 1988). As Baker (1992) notes: "Through the formal or hidden curriculum and through extra-curricular activities, a school may produce more or less positive attitudes and may change attitudes" (p. 243). Although the interplay of family, community and school is a complex one (Smolicz, Secombe, & Hudson, 2001), and thus comparisons across contexts are difficult, the situation in Spain suggests that a clearly defined language policy that protects regional languages need not detract from the status and activation of the national language. Should the Philippines face rising demands for language rights in education for speakers of Cebuano, Waray, and other minority languages, this lesson may provide the basis for a new bilingual education policy for the country.

REFERENCES

Baker, C. (1988). *Key issues in bilingualism and bilingual education.* Clevedon, UK: Multilingual Matters.

Baker, C. (1992). *Attitudes and language.* Clevedon, UK: Multilingual Matters.

Bautista, M. L. S. (1981). An explanatory note: Round-table conference on Philippine national language development. In A. Gonzales & M. L. S. Bautista (Eds.), *Aspects of language planning and development in the Philippines.* Manila: Linguistic Society of the Philippines.

Clyne, M. (1991). *Community languages: The Australian experience.* Cambridge, UK: Cambridge University Press.

Congressional Commission on Education. (1991). *Making education work.* Manila/Quezon City: Congress of the Republic of the Philippines.

Constantino, R. (1982). *The miseducation of the Filipino.* Manila: Philippines Foundation for Nationalist Studies.

Conversi, D. (1997). *The Basques, the Catalans and Spain.* London: Hurst.

Cummins, J. (1984). *Bilingualism and special education: Issues in assessment and pedagogy.* Clevedon, UK: Multilingual Matters.

Cummins, J., & Swain, M. (1986). *Bilingualism in education.* New York: Longman.

De la Costa, H. (1961). *The Jesuits of the Philippines.* Cambridge, MA: Harvard University Press.

Eisenstadt, S. N. (2001). The vision of modern and contemporary society. In E. Ben-Rafael & Y. Sternberg (Eds.), *Identity, culture and globalization* (pp. 25-48). Leiden, The Netherlands: Brill.

Gonzales, A. (1996). Language and nationalism in the Philippines: An update. In M. L. S. Bautista (Ed.), *Readings in Philippine linguistics* (pp. 228-239). Manila : De La Salle University Press.

Gonzales, A. (1998). The language planning situation in the Philippines. *Journal of Multilingual and Multicultural Development, 19,* 487-525.

Gonzales, A., & Bautista, M. L. S. (1986). *Language surveys in the Philippines* (1966-1984). Manila: De La Salle University Press.

Grant, N. (1997). Democracy and cultural pluralism: Towards the 21st century. In R. J. Watts & J. J. Smolicz (Eds.), *Cultural democracy and ethnic pluralism: Multicultural and multilingual policies in education* (pp. 25 –50). Frankfurt am Main, Germany: Peter Lang.

Huguet, A., & Llurda, E. (2001). Language attitudes of Spanish children in two Catalan/Spanish bilingual communities. *International Journal of Bilingual Education and Bilingualism, 4*(4), 267-282.

Lecours, A. (2001). Regionalism, cultural diversity and the state in Spain. *Journal of Multilingual and Multicultural Development, 22*(3), 210-226.

Manhit, B. J. (1980). The case for reading: a socio-political perspective. *Education Quarterly, 26*(4), 32-41.

Manhit, B. J. (1981). Alternatives for functional literacy: a socio-pyschophilosophical perspective. *Education Quarterly, 27*(4), 1-25.

Manuel, J. L. (1974). Department of Education and Culture, Department Order No. 25, s. 1974, Implementing guidelines for the policy on bilingual education. Reprinted in M.C. Sutaria, J. S. Guerrero, & P. M. Castano (1989) (Eds.), *Philippine education: Vision and perspectives* (pp. 350-352). Manila: National Bookstore Inc.

Nical, I. (2000). Language usage and language attitudes among education consumers: *The experience of Filipinos in Australia and in three communities in the Philippines.* Unpublished doctoral dissertation, University of Adelaide, Adelaide, Australia.

Phillipson, R. (1992). *Linguistic imperialism.* Oxford, UK: Oxford University Press.

Quisumbing, L. (1989). The DECS bilingual education policy. In M. C. Sutaria, J. S. Guerrero, & P. M. Castano (Eds.), *Philippine education: Vision and perspectives* (pp. 309-315). Manila: National Book Store Inc.

Safran, W. (1995). Nations, ethnic groups, states and policies: A preface to an agenda. *Nationalism and Ethnic Policies, 1,* 1-10.

Sibayan, B. P. (1994). Philippine language problems. In J. E. Acujia (Ed.), *The language issue in education* (pp. 47-86). Manila: Congressional Oversight Committee in Education, Congress of the Republic of Philippines.

Skutnabb-Kangas, T. (1984). *Bilingualism or not: The education of minorities.* Clevedon, UK: Multilingual Matters.

Skutnabb-Kangas, T., & Cummins, J. (Eds.). (1988). *Minority education: From shame to struggle.* Clevedon, UK: Multilingual Matters.

Skutnabb-Kangas, T., & Phillipson, R. (Eds.). (1994). *Linguistic human rights: Overcoming linguistic discrimination.* Berlin & New York: Mouton de Gruyter.

Skutnabb-Kangas, T., & Phillipson, R. (1998). Language in human rights. *Gazette: The International Journal for Communication Studies, 60*(1), 27-46.

Smolicz, J. J. (1986). Multilingual policy in the Philippines. In B. Spolsky (Ed.), *Languages and education in multilingual settings* (pp. 97-116). Clevedon, UK: Multilingual Matters.

Smolicz, J. J. (1995). Language - A bridge or a barrier? Languages and education in Australia from an international perspective. *Multilingua: A Journal of Cross-Cultural and Interlanguage Communication, 14*(2), 151-182.

Smolicz, J. J. (1998). Nation-states and globalization from a multicultural perspective. *Nationalism and Ethnic Politics, 4*(4), 1-18.

Smolicz, J. J., & Nical, I. C. (1997). Exporting the European idea of a national language: Some educational implications for the use of English and indigenous languages in the Philippines. *International Review of Education, 4,* 5-6, 1-21.

Smolicz, J. J., Nical, I., & Secombe, M. J. (2001). English as the medium of instruction for science and its effects on the languages of the Philippines. In U. Ammon (Ed.), *The Dominance of English as a language of science: Effects on other languages and language communities* (pp. 205-226). Berlin: Mouton de Gruyter.

Smolicz, J. J., Secombe, M. J., & Hudson, D. (2001). Family collectivism and minority languages as core values of culture among ethnic groups in Australia. *Journal of Multilingual and Multicultural Development, 22*(2), 152–172.

Sutaria, M. C., Guerrero, J. S., & Castano, P. M. (Eds.). (1989). Appendix, *Philippine education: Vision and perspectives.* Manila: National Book Store Inc.

Tenazas, R. C. P., & Ramas, L. L. (1974). A map of the better-known cultural minorities of the Philippines. *Philippine Quarterly of Culture and Society, 2,* 1-3.

Tombiah, S. J. (1996). The nation-state in crisis and the rise of ethnonationalism. In E.
    N. McAllister (Ed.), *The politics of difference* (pp. 124-143). Chicago: The Univer-
    sity of Chicago Press.
Yap, F. A. (1990). *A comparative study of the Philippine lexicons*. Manila: Institute of
    Philippine Languages, Department of Education, Culture and Sports.
Zialcita, F. N. (1995). State formation, colonialism and national identity in Vietnam
    and the Philippines. *Philippine Quarterly of Culture and Society, 23*, 72-117.

9

Medium of Power: The Question of English in Education in India

E. Annamalai
Central Institute of Indian Languages

With about 200 languages, India is not just demographically multilingual, but also functionally multilingual, with many languages used in different domains. The question of English in India is about its place in relation to other languages within this functional multilingualism. There are two official languages, Hindi and English, at the federal level and 15 additional ones at the state level. In one state, Nagaland, English is the official language and in other states the use of English for official purposes continued after Independence in varying degrees while the local Indian language took its place gradually. Newspapers and magazines are published in over 90 languages; radio programs broadcast in over 70 languages; and television programs and movies made in 13 languages. English is one of the languages used in all of these contexts. Publications in English, and their readership, have increased since Independence. The share of English newspapers in the total circulation of newspapers in all languages, for example, was 22% in 1981, which was an increase of 15% from the circulation in 1971 (Annamalai, 1994). Readership in English continues to increase.

In the crucial domain of education, 33 languages, including English, are used as the media of instruction. Forty-one languages, including English, are made available for study in the school curriculum (NCERT, 1999).[1] The three languages students must learn in schools come from these 41 languages and they are taught as a first, second, or third language, in the curricular sense of

177

number of years taught and competence level to be achieved. The first language in most cases is the mother tongue (which may be a minor or a minority language different from the majority or the official language of the state) or the regional language (which is the majority language of the state and generally is its official language). The second language is English and the third language is Hindi (where it is not the regional language).[2] English is the only language taught in all states as a first, second or third language and it is taught in the largest number of schools (see Table 9.1).

It is difficult to estimate the number of students learning English, but the percentage of students who will have some proficiency in English after schooling can be roughly estimated. Those who had completed their education with 10 years of schooling made up 11% of the population, according to the figures in the National Family Health Survey in 1992 to 1993 (Probe Team, 1999, p. 9). These students must have learnt English for at least 5 or 6 years, besides Hindi and another Indian language. The 6% of the population who continue their education beyond secondary school, according to this survey, carry on the study of English in college (2 years of junior college, and, for some, another 3 years at undergraduate college and professional college). However, by the end of college, the average student acquires more passive competence in English than productive competence.

TABLE 9.1
Percentages of Schools that Teach English in India

	Primary (classes 1 to 4/5)	Middle (classes 4/5 to 8)	Secondary (classes 9 to 10)
English as a first language	2.91%	4.25%	6.57%
English as a second language	21.65%*	55.05%	54.12%
English as a third language	6.58%*	38.02%	35.79%
Total for English	30.40%	97.32%	96.48%

*The percentage figures given in the Survey (NCERT, 1999) for teaching English in primary classes as a second language (60.33%) and a third language (69.67%) are erroneous. The figures provided in Table 9.1 for these two categories are calculated from information given in other parts in the Survey. The percentages for other categories in the Table are as given in the Survey, although they are marginally different from the figures I calculated.

THE SOCIAL CONTEXT

The elite of the society, who make up 6% of the population and who continue their education beyond secondary school, come to have power and wealth disproportionate to their numbers. Decision-makers in the government (other than some elected legislators and ministers in general) and opinion-makers in the society are drawn from this segment. The interests of these elite play a central role in the decisions made about the medium of education, and in advocating English as the preferred medium. One claim made by this segment of the population to legitimize the role of English in education is that English is not an alien language.

English, to be sure, has been indigenized functionally, pragmatically and grammatically in India. It is used in creative literature and publications of economic and academic value for dissemination of information. It is used in high-level business and industrial sectors. It is not just a language for international communication but also for intranational communication among educated Indians. Although the use of English is a colonial legacy, it has been accepted and developed after Independence, like many other Western institutions left behind by the British. It is considered to have the advantage of being ethnically neutral, as it is a second language to all and does not bestow natural advantage to any linguistic group. But it is not class neutral. It is the language of the elite, as just mentioned. The debate about the medium of English in education must be interpreted in this social context. A historical sketch of English in education during the colonial period is given below to show the continuity of the issues in the medium of education debate.

THE HISTORICAL CONTEXT

The question of medium of education was a matter for public debate during the colonial period in India. The colonial government, in the initial period (from 1757 when the Mughal ruler was defeated in Bengal by the forces of the East India Company), did not consider education or other areas of social development to be its responsibility. It was not until the Crown renewed the charter of the East India Company in 1831 that it began to recognize its educational responsibility. The considerations that led to the change in the Company's role in education were evangelical: to give the local population "useful knowledge and ... religious and moral improvement" (as stated in the British cabinet resolution on the subject). They were also political: to make the local population "more English than Hindus" (as stated in the minutes of Macaulay, described later; Annamalai, 2001, pp. 91–93). The evangelical and political purposes were not unrelated; they in fact reinforced each other. Both aimed at producing consenting subjects. The "useful knowledge" to be imparted was defined as the European knowledge of science and the perception of the nature of society as derived from the Enlightenment. The "moral improvement" was the acquisition of European values and world view derived from Christian theology. The central question was which language should be used as the medium through which "useful knowledge" and "moral improvement" would be imparted to the subjects, with minimal fiscal and political cost.

There were three positions taken by the British and Indian public leaders, on ideological and practical grounds, in relation to the strategy of achieving these twin goals and getting as large a proportion of the population as possible to accept them. The first position was that English-medium education would be made available, with government support, selectively to the upper segment of the Indian population, who in turn, as teachers, would impart European knowledge and values to the masses through the medium of vernaculars, in schools established through nongovernmental initiatives. This was known as the *Anglicist position*. This, it was argued, would keep the government's expenses on English education low and limit the number of English-educated subjects seeking employment in the government, thus preventing the political disquiet that would arise from failure to obtain employment. The second position was that European knowledge and values would be transferred by translating English texts to the classical languages of India, primarily Sanskrit and Persian, which were the media used by the traditional elite controlling conventional education. Those who learned the new knowledge and values through the classical languages would in turn impart them to the masses through the vernaculars. This was called the *Orientalist position*. This position, it was believed, would co-opt the traditional elite and would not challenge the existing power structure in education. Both positions were based on a theory called *Downward Filtration* of knowledge and values to the masses. They differed, however, in those they considered to be the agents of this downward filtration. The third position was that European knowledge and values would be taught directly to the masses through the medium of the vernaculars irrespective of the cost to the government. However, this was a minority position in terms of the political and administrative support it received.

The Anglicist position won the debate in 1835, when the Governor General William Bentinck, based on the minutes of Thomas Macaulay, Chairman of the Committee on Public Instruction, made the decision that government funds would be available only for English education. English was favored as an "obvious means of assimilating" the ruled with the rulers, as expressed by Charles Grant, whose treatise on India (published in 1792 under the title "Observations on the state of the society among the Asiatic subjects of Great Britain, particularly with respect to morals, and the means of improving it') had a lasting influence on the education policy of the colonial government (Annamalai, 2001, p. 91, 96). The medium and content of education became an instrument for the control of minds and the assimilation of behavior. Thus, the question of medium of instruction became an integral part of the principle and purpose of governing.

THE ECONOMIC CONTEXT

The charter of the East India Company, renewed in 1833, provided a major economic impetus to English education. It allowed the recruitment of Indians for the civil service in the colonial government, in order to offset the rising administrative cost of governing India. A certain degree of proficiency in English was made a prerequisite for employment in the government, and education through the medium of English was considered an effective means of attaining that degree of proficiency. The Anglicist policy of using the medium of English to provide education came into force 2 years later to fulfill this need of the government. Clerical employment in the government and in new industries, and positions in professions like law, medicine, accounting, and teaching, obtained through English-medium education, created a new urban elite among Indians. This new elite became part of the ruling class, and the nexus between the foreign rulers and the general population. They also gained access to power, wealth, and status. The colonial association of English with power, wealth, and status, and the association of proficiency in English with its use as medium of education, continue to hold to date. Similarly, the dissemination of European knowledge and values through an English-educated elite to the rest of the population continues to take place. Although "European knowledge and values" has now been rephrased as "scientific knowledge" and "modern values," the controlling role of English in their dissemination and the elitism English created through education remain the same in the post-colonial period.

It should be noted, however, that in reality the upper-caste Indians pursuing English education detached moral improvement from its theological overtone even during the colonial period, and were interested in acquiring the knowledge useful for material well being. For the local population, education has always appeared as a means of economic advancement, whatever the moral goal set in the curriculum. Furthermore, English education contributed to political awareness and nationalistic aspirations, and facilitated political communication among the educated in different regions of the country. These economic and political outcomes were contrary to the goal of assimilation of the ideology and acceptance of the legitimacy of the colonial government by the local population, although assimilation in the sense of co-opting the native elite into the government and to the ideology of European Enlightenment was successful. English education, besides opening avenues of employment in the government and in professional spheres, also opened entry to university education to Indians from 1857 onward, when the first three universities were established. The requirement of proficiency in English as a condition for admission into universities increased the demand for English-medium education in schools. Contrary to the policy of containing the spread of English to the masses, English, not just the content in it, moved downward.

The downward spread of English-medium education was also accelerated by the missionary schools, which had the primary goal of bringing about the "moral improvement" of the masses.[3] These schools started by using vernaculars as the media of education in order to take the gospel directly and intimately to the people. However, school officials soon realized that to attract upper-caste students, who would have influence on the masses, the schools should provide English-medium education. This change of policy concerning the medium of education has become so entrenched that the convent schools, which were historically run by Christian missionaries, are now synonymous with English-medium schools, whether they are run by missionaries or private agencies. The schools established by native civic leaders and associations, which were an alternative to the missionary schools and the colonial government schools, also provided English-medium education so that their students would not be deprived of the economic advantages that English offered. In this way, English, which had also become more or less the universal medium of education at secondary and tertiary levels in the second half of the 19th century, continued its dominant position for well over 50 years.

CHANGE IN MEDIUM OF INSTRUCTION IN THE COLONIAL PERIOD

At the turn of the 20th century and under the leadership of Gandhi, the independence movement changed from a native elitist movement of the English educated demanding greater share in power and wealth, to a mass movement of political freedom and social reconstruction. This change forced the colonial government to initiate political reform and introduce a political system called *diarchy*, in which the legislative and executive powers were shared by Indian political parties and the British. The Indian political parties were given the education portfolio. As a result of their initiatives, major Indian languages were introduced as the alternative media of education at secondary level from 1921. Textbooks and technical terms were created in Indian languages so that they could be used as the media of secondary education. By 1937, 51% of secondary schools in Madras Presidency offered an Indian language as the medium of instruction (Nurullah & Naik, 1951, p. 650). Despite the change in the political climate, not every school opted for using an Indian language as the medium of education.

This was in part due to the fact that English-medium education continued to provide students with better educational and economic opportunities, because the medium of education at college level and the medium of business and government administration remained English.

Despite the partial change in medium of instruction from English to Indian languages during the later part of the colonial period, the political objective of the British remained the same: to prevent social unrest by controlling access to English and consequently to government positions; and to engineer social consent for colonial rule by shaping the popular mind with European knowledge and values. Education, whether offered through English or Indian languages, had the same instrumental role in achieving this objective. This objective could be clearly seen as early as the dispatch from Charles Wood, President of the Board of Control of the East India Company, to the British Crown in 1854, which said, "We look therefore to the English language and to the vernacular languages of India together as the media for the diffusion of European knowledge" (Bhatt & Aggarwal, 1977, p. 8). In fact, echoes of this policy can be heard in other British colonies as well. In Hong Kong, for example, the report of a Committee on education to the Hong Kong government in 1902 stated as follows:

> The Committee are fully alive to the extreme importance of spreading the English language among the Chinese ... but they maintain that the spread of knowledge is no less essential. Their opinion [is] that a knowledge of English has not always proved sufficient in itself to ensure a feeling of good will towards the Empire ... It is essential that Western knowledge should be a compulsory subject in every Standard [in the vernacular schools]. (*Report of the Committee on Education, The Hong Kong Government Gazette*, 11 April, 1902, p. 499, 501, cited in Pennycook, 1998, pp. 115–116)

POST-COLONIAL POLICY

The political objective of imparting knowledge and skills to the population that serve the interests of the ruling elite has not changed in post-colonial India. Knowledge and skills, as defined by the ruling class, that are needed to sustain a vast, centralized bureaucracy, a capital intensive, urban-based industrial economy[4] and a huge, technologically modern military establishment are imparted through English in higher levels of education. These skills and knowledge are expected to percolate down to schools and beyond through Indian languages, a process similar to the colonial government's policy of Downward Filtration. This policy helps the English educated elite to maintain their control over the society, because those who control knowledge available in English come to control the society, and because their input is considered essential for nation building.

The policy of using English as the medium in higher education also increased the demand for English-medium instruction at lower levels of education. English-medium education became available in the largest number of states and union territories: In 1990, out of the 28 states and seven Union Territories,[5] English-medium education was available in more than 30 at each of the three levels, viz., primary, middle, and secondary. However, the percentage of English-medium schools in the total number of schools at primary and middle levels is small—around 10%, most of which are in urban areas. The Indian language-medium schools make up 91.62% at primary level and 88.64% at middle level (NCERT, 1999). Although English-medium schools, by and large, are attended by urban middle- and upper-class students who belong to the influential and vocal segments of the society, it should be noted that the class-based preference for English-medium schools is changing, and they are now demanded by the urban poor and rural parents alike.

There has also been, however, a counter position in the debate surrounding medium of education, both during the Independence movement and after Independence (Shah, 1968). Advocates of education for students from diverse social backgrounds, universal quality education, and the use of Indian languages as a symbol of national pride have called for Indian languages to be the media of education. This position has become the public platform of all political parties, as well as the accepted policy of the governments at the state and federal levels. Schools run or financed by the government, therefore, provide Indian language-medium of instruction. However, the preference for English-medium education by parents has led to a discrepancy between the legislated policy and the implementation of that policy.

A brief description of the official actions toward formulating a policy of medium of education will be helpful in understanding the source of this dissonance. At the time of Independence in 1947, the medium of education was an important issue in the program of national development, as were the medium of administration and the medium of law. In all these domains, the consensus was that English would be replaced by Indian languages at the federal level and the state level. The only difference was the time frame for the implementation of the new policy. The Constitution did not prescribe any time frame for the change in medium of education, as it did in administration and in law. Various education committees and commissions were constituted by the government of India immediately before and after Independence, to study and make recommendations on education policy at specific levels, including medium of education at those levels. Their reports were submitted to the government or to the parliament for approval. All of these committees and commissions were chaired by eminent educationists, who recommended switching from English to Indian languages as media of instruction. The Secondary Education (Mudaliar) Commission (1953) re-iterated the pre-Independence recommendations of the Wardha (Zakir Hussain) Committee (1937) and the Committee of the Central Advisory Board of Education (1937), which stated that "the mother tongue or the regional language should generally be the medium of instruction throughout the secondary stage" (Bhatt & Aggarwal, 1977, p. 152). At the tertiary level of education, the Conference of Vice Chancellors of Universities (1948) suggested a time limit of 5 years to begin the gradual replacement of English as the medium of education. This was diluted in the following year in the recommendation of the University Education (Radhakrishnan) Commission, which changed the specific time frame to "as early as practicable" (Bhatt & Aggarwal, 1977, p. 117). The Indian Education (Kothari) Commission (1968), which conducted a comprehensive study of the Indian education system, did not prescribe a time frame for switching to Indian languages as media of education at tertiary level, but the Parliamentary Committee that examined the Commission's report for the government fixed a 5-year time limit. Nevertheless, the National Policy on Education, which is a statutory document on which educational planning is based, as approved by the parliament and promulgated by the government in 1976, did not mention any time frame. It said instead that

> the regional languages are already in use as media of education at primary and secondary levels. *Urgent steps* should be taken to adopt them as media of education at the university level. (Bhatt & Aggarwal, 1977, p. 312; emphasis added)

A new policy on education formulated by the government in 1986 reiterated the earlier policy with regard to the medium of education. This policy has been in operation since then.

IMPLEMENTATION OF POLICY

Three features of implementation of the medium-of-education policy must be noted in the post-Independence history of education policy. First, there is no commitment to an absolute time frame for changing the medium of instruction from English to Indian languages at the tertiary level. Such nonspecific phrases as *generally*, *as early as practicable*, and *urgent steps* have absolved the governments of accountability in implementing the policy. The primary reason for not specifying a time frame for changing the medium of instruction was the belief that the change should wait until the Indian languages were ready to be used for this purpose. To achieve this goal, it was argued, Indian languages must acquire the requisite technical terms to encode modern scientific knowledge. Materials, textbooks, and reference books in Indian languages must be produced and teachers must be linguistically equipped in these languages (native or learned) to teach academic subjects (especially science) at higher levels. Therefore the implementation of the policy was contingent on the availability of language resources, and not government action.

Second, the change in the medium-of-education policy actually involved the use of major Indian languages, called regional languages, at the level of the states, and not the use of Hindi. After Independence, the country was reorganized linguistically into states, each with one Indian language as the regional language.[6] There are 12 regional languages, which are the official languages of the states and generally their majority language. States were given the option in the Constitution to choose Hindi or the regional language as the medium of education in place of English. However, all states chose their own regional languages (except Nagaland, which has no local language as the majority language). The medium-of-education policy debate, consequently, was in the domain of states and was centered on a state level choice between English and regional languages, not a nationwide choice between English and Hindi. Unlike the domains of public administration and courts, there was no national level implementation program (as different from policy) for changing the medium from English to Indian languages in the domain of education.

Third, because education is a policy area in which states can legislate as well as the national parliament, there are differences in the extent to which individual states implement the policy and the flexibility that they exercise in relation to medium of education. Some states do not allow English-medium education in schools run or funded by the government; some allow parallel streams of English medium and Indian language medium in schools funded by the government. One state, Nagaland, has only English medium in all its schools from class one. Some states allow the use of more than one language as the medium of instruction, including their official language, in the same school or in different schools. The additional medium may be the minority language of the state, Hindi or English. English may be allowed as the minority mother tongue of the community of the descendants of mixed parentage (of Indians and Europeans), called *Anglo-Indians*. The percentage of schools that have more than one language as parallel media is 7.21% at primary level, 12.49% at upper primary level, 13.34% at secondary level, and 17.40% at higher secondary level. The percentage of schools using more than one medium increases at higher levels and in urban areas (NCERT, 1999).

An important point to be noted in the policy implementation, besides the variation in the use of Indian languages across levels of education and across states, is the dilution of the policy by the government to satisfy conflicting political interests. More specifically, the interests of the entrenched elite of bureaucrats and professionals, who want to retain the positions of power they gained through English, are in opposition to the interests of the emerging elite in the fields of language, literature, and culture, who want to empower their regional languages as well as themselves. Compromises in the policy are made to reconcile the conflicting interests of these two elites. The policy is compromised by allowing alternative sources of schooling, for example, the schools of the Central Board of Education, private schools such as the Matriculation schools in the state of Tamilnadu (about 5% of the schools in that state), and educational institutions established by minorities under a constitutional provision of safeguard for preservation of diversity (about 5% of the schools in Tamilnadu; Probe Team, 1999, p. 102). These schools adopt English as the medium of instruction for different reasons, such as serving people who need to move from state to state, providing re-source-rich education to fee-paying parents and curbing the dominance of the majority language by the minority in a state. In addition, exceptions are made by the government for English medium due to the political pressure from individual schools that have been privately established. A common strategy is for an entrepreneur to start a fee-collecting school without being accredited by the State Board of Education, so that the school will have the freedom to adopt English-medium education, and subsequently, after a few years, to bring parental and political pressure for accreditation on the government when the students have to take the public examination admin-istered by the Board. At that point, the argument is that it is important for the school to be accredited because the students' future is at stake. Despite the fact that there is no guarantee that these schools will be accredited, par-ents are willing to take the risk and pay fees for English-medium education.

LEGAL CHALLENGES TO INDIAN LANGUAGE MEDIUM OF INSTRUCTION

The policy of making the Indian language-medium of instruction obligatory has been challenged legally by various interest groups. One legal challenge concerns the constitutional right of minorities to establish educational insti-tutions. The courts have interpreted this right to include choice of medium of education, which could be English (Annamalai, 1998). A further legal chal-lenge is based on the right to education, which, it has been argued, should in-clude the student's right to have education in a medium of his or her choice, including English. The High Court of Tamilnadu ruled recently in favor of the Association of Matriculation schools and others to provide English-me-dium education, and quashed an order of the government of Tamilnadu mandating all primary schools in the state to change to Tamil medium within a stipulated period. The court based its ruling not only on an International Covenant on educational rights, to which India is a signatory, but also on pro-cedural lapses on the part of the government of Tamilnadu and the commis-sion it appointed to make recommendations on the medium of education.

The procedural lapses are symbolic of the casual attitude of the government toward the question of changing the medium of instruction. The court ruling in fact helped the government to retain English-medium education while maintaining the posture of favoring Tamil-medium education by the executive order. The executive orders by the government to give preferential treatment to the graduates of Indian language-medium education in the selection for admission to professional colleges and jobs in the government have been ruled by courts as discriminatory and therefore unconstitutional. Unlike positive discrimination for the socially disadvantaged, which is enshrined in the Constitution, preferential treatment in favor of graduates of Indian language-medium schools in admission to higher education and in government jobs is viewed legally as an incentive to individuals, and not as a corrective measure to ensure social justice.

MEDIUM OF EDUCATION AND SOCIAL INEQUALITY

Contributing to the government's ambivalence about the implementation of the new policy on the medium of education is the strong demand for English-medium instruction from parents. The opposition to changing the medium of education from English at the university level, which percolates down to the school level, is based on the presumption that learning through an Indian language will disadvantage students because they will not be able to access modern knowledge, which is mostly encoded in English. Furthermore, it is argued that this disadvantage will then hinder their efforts to seek educational and economic opportunities in developed English-speaking countries. This presumed disadvantage, it must be noted, is a problem only for those who are able to obtain postsecondary education; they constitute less than 6% of the entire population. The percentage of the population that finishes college education and progresses to graduate and professional studies in India and abroad is much smaller.

The majority of the population will be disadvantaged by English-medium education if the interests of this tiny, but vocal section of the population are given disproportionate importance. Forced to learn by rote through a language in which they are not fluent, the majority of the students receive poor education, with inadequate understanding of the subjects. Thus, the medium of instruction becomes a further cause of failure in school. The advantage of English medium in higher education and employment is a mirage for those students whose command of English is poor at the end. The often cited success stories of Indian students who get into professional, managerial, and academic positions nationally and internationally because of their mastery of both English and subject knowledge are misleading. These highly successful students are most likely to have studied through English medium in well funded schools. They are also likely to have come from families that have used English as a second language for at least one preceding generation and to have had exposure to English through reading materials and conversations at home. These students already have a solid cultural and linguistic foundation in English; their education merely supplements this advantage. They are also a small minority of the student population and are by no means representative. A much larger proportion of the student population is made up of first-generation learners from poor families, who do not have access to the same kind of support at home as their middle-class counterparts. Thus, a social advantage for the minority of students has been misleadingly projected as the advantage of English-medium education.

Another argument in favor of English-medium education stems from the fear of depriving students and teachers of the opportunity for moving to educational institutions in other parts of the country. However, this fear is largely unfounded, as the numbers of students and teachers who move across linguistic regions again constitute a small minority. Moreover, this argument has little relevance because, in practice, preference is given to local candidates in student admission and faculty appointment, except in those educational institutions fully financed by the central government.

Yet another argument maintains that the change in medium of education should wait until knowledge available in English has been translated into Indian languages and the necessary new technical terms and scientific discourse styles have been developed in them. This means that Indian languages must become like English before they can replace it as the medium of education. The interminable problem with this argument is that given the current rate of knowledge growth, it is impossible to determine when one will be able to decide that the Indian languages have "caught up with" English. Furthermore, the development of a language takes place through use, not prior to use, and it is a fallacy to argue that the language must be developed before it is put to use.

The arguments supporting English-medium education have wide currency, in spite of their lack of universal application to the society at large. This is in part because of the social power of those who put forward these arguments and their ability to camouflage their vested interests as national interest, and also because of the imagined appeal of the wealth, power, and status that people have been led to believe English will bring them irrespective of other social barriers.

The opposition to the use of regional languages as a medium of education at the primary level of education is of a different nature. One source of opposition is from the linguistic minorities, whose children would benefit pedagogically from using the mother tongue as the medium of initial education. However, instead of demanding initial education through the mother tongue, even these groups advocate English-medium education in order to achieve the political purpose of containing the power of the regional language, as mentioned earlier. English-medium, in their view, will nullify the advantage that the speakers of the regional languages have over them; it will even give a competitive edge to the students speaking minority languages.

Another source of opposition is from the emerging middle class in semi-urban and rural areas, which sees English as the ladder to further their power, wealth, and status to be on par with those enjoyed by the urban middle and upper classes. The preference of the urban middle class has ipso facto become the preference for the rural and urban poor aspiring to become a member of that class.

Thus, contrary to the claim that schooling is a means of leveling social differences, a two language system of education in schools, one with English-medium for the select few and another with Indian language medium for the masses, perpetuates social inequality and creates social tension. This system also creates two cultures in terms of world view and social attitude (Krishna Kumar, 1996). The built-in ambivalence in the policy on the medium of education leads to this inequality (Tollefson, 1991). This educational inequality is reinforced by the prevalence of English as the prestigious medium in science colleges and the sole medium in professional colleges and by the job market, which favors students from English-medium schools (because of their higher English proficiency and the better resourced education that they have received). Students in arts and humanities in college, who opt for Indian language medium, are in general poor economically and scholastically (Shanmugan & Pandian, n.d.).

The divide in medium of instruction also perpetuates an unequal linguistic dichotomy in terms of language ideology. From the time of colonial rule, English has been projected as the vehicle for the ideas of the European Enlightenment—a language of rationality and progress—and hence the vehicle for modernity. The Indian languages, on the other hand, are portrayed as vehicles for tradition and as instruments that fulfill emotional needs and maintain cultural values and practices. This ideological divide between material progress and cultural roots preempts the possibility for speakers of Indian languages to become modern and progressive without switching their tongue.

MEDIUM OF EDUCATION AND EDUCATIONAL PRIORITY

For the reasons just described, neither English medium for all nor English medium for a few is a desirable policy option. This leaves the option of Indian language medium for all. This policy option, however, is subverted, as we have seen in the preceding discussion.

One solution to reduce the negative impact of English-medium education, which has been tried out in selective settings, is to adopt a bilingual medium of instruction. For example, in central schools, science subjects are taught through English and other subjects through Hindi, irrespective of the mother tongue of the students. This means that literacy skills are not taught in the students' home language. This model has been fairly successful in terms of students' bilingual competence and subject knowledge. However, it would be presumptuous to say that the positive result is due to the complementary use of two languages as the medium of education, because the students going through bilingual medium schooling are mainly from urban middle-class families (Annamalai, 1980) and these schools are well funded.[7] These students would have been successful academically and linguistically even if the media were solely English. Other successful models of bilingual instruction with local variations in private schools, such as Sardar Patel Vidyalaya in Delhi, have a similar bias in the socioeconomic background of their students. It is doubtful whether this model can be widely adopted in the state schools with the bilingual medium of English and a regional language, because most of their students are from poor socioeconomic background with no adequate English language support at home. Moreover, the bilingual model that associates Indian languages with "soft," (i.e., nonscience) subjects will have adverse effects on the development of Indian languages as vehicles of scientific knowledge. The ideological conflict—between empowering people with English and empowering them with their native languages by using the latter in domains of power such as science and technology—must be taken into consideration when making decisions on medium of education.

The solution to the problems of education through the medium of English is to teach English effectively while imparting education through the medium of Indian languages. It would be far more effective to change the popular perception that using English as the medium of education is the most effective way to acquire English competence. To effect this change, it would be necessary to demonstrate that proficiency in English could be achieved by teaching it as a second language.

Many pedagogical strategies have been suggested to improve the teaching of English in India. One demand from parents is to start teaching English at an earlier age, on the assumption that increasing the hours of instruction will lead to better learning. Their preference is to start English teaching in the first grade. The strategy of "catching them young" with regard to learning English also finds political support. For example, the state of West Bengal, which is governed by the communist party, has changed its policy to start English teaching from the first grade instead of beginning it at postprimary level.

However, starting English language teaching early is no solution for a number of reasons. First, there is no definitive research evidence to support the assumption that earlier is better. There is actually evidence against giving early formal instruction of a second language to children from a disadvantaged background. Lightbown and Spada (1993) point out that for children deprived of a literacy environment at home, emphasis on the development of literacy in the mother tongue at school is highly beneficial. Swain, Lapkin, Rowel, and Hart (1990) show the positive role of mother-tongue literacy in learning another language.

Second, primary school teachers in India do not have college educations and generally do not come from families exposed to English at home. Their lack of training in second-language teaching methods for children and their limited proficiency in the target language lead to poor quality teaching and hence undermine the goal of starting English teaching at primary level. Providing training in English language teaching to all primary teachers would be very costly because of the large number of primary schools involved: 570,455 primary schools in the country, of which 89% are in rural areas. The human and financial resources needed for such a task are enormous, even with the use of modern technology and the help of international aid.

A more realistic approach would be to focus effort and resources on improving the quality of English teaching at middle and secondary levels. The number of teachers at these levels is about 300,000, much less than the number of primary teachers, and they are graduates with college-level English. There is infrastructure available for in-service training in the educational research and training institutions at national and regional levels that focus specifically on English teaching, as well as in the resource centers in selected districts that provide additional materials and guidance for English teachers.

From the point of view of skill development for nation building, the resource implications of enhancing the teaching of English must be considered in the context of educational priority. One third of all children in the 6 to 14 years-of-age group were out of school in 1991, and two thirds of all adults did not complete middle school (8 years of schooling), which is the constitutionally mandated level of education to be achieved universally (Probe Team, 1999). These people who do not attend school, or drop out of school before they attain a reasonable level of literacy, contribute to illiteracy in the country. Keeping them in school and giving them literacy skills in their mother tongue or a regional language must take priority in India over teaching English skills from Grade one.

REFERENCES

Anand, C. L. (1971). *The study of the effect of socioeconomic environment and medium of instruction on the mental abilities and academic achievement of children in Mysore State.* Unpublished doctoral dissertation, University of Mysore, Mysore.

Annamalai, E. (Ed.). (1980). *Bilingualism and school achievement.* Mysore: Central Institute of Indian Languages.

Annamalai, E. (1994). English in India: Unplanned development. In T. Kandiah & J. Kwan-Terry (Eds.), *English and language planning: A Southeast Asian contribution.* Singapore: Times Academic Press.

Annamalai, E. (1998). Language choice in education: Conflict resolution in Indian courts. *Language Science, 20*(1), 29–43.

Annamalai, E. (2001). The colonial language in multilingualism and the process of modernization. In E. Annamalai, *Managing multilingualism in India: Political and linguistic manifestations.* New Delhi: Sage

Bhatt, B. T., & Aggarwal, J. C. (1977). *Educational documents in India (1813–1977).* New Delhi: Arya Book Depot.

Chaturvedi, M. G., & Singh, S. (1981). *Third all India educational survey: Languages and media of instruction in Indian schools.* New Delhi: National Council for Educational Training and Research.

Krishna Kumar. (1996). Two Worlds. In Krishna Kumar (Ed.), *Learning from conflict.* Hyderabad, India: Orient Longman.

Lightbown, P. M., & Spada, N. (1993). *How languages are learned.* Oxford, UK: Oxford University Press.

NCERT. (1999). *Sixth all India educational survey: Main report.* New Delhi: National Council for Educational Research and Training.

Nurullah, S., & Naik, J. P. (1951). *A history of education in India (during the British Period)* (2nd ed.). Bombay: Macmillan.

Pennycook, A. (1998). *English and the discourses of colonialism.* London: Routledge.

Probe Team, The. (1999). *Public report on basic education in India.* New Delhi: Oxford University Press

Shah, A. B. (Ed.). (1968). *The great debate.* Bombay: Lalvani Publishing House.

Shanmugan, M., & Pandian, S. V. (n.d.). *College education through Tamil.* Madurai: Muthu Padippagam.

Srivastava, A. K., & Ramasamy, K. (1988). *Effects of medium of instruction: An Indian experience in bilingual education.* Mysore: Central Institute of Indian Languages.

Swain, M., Lapkin, S., Rowel, N., & Hart, D. (1990). The role of mother tongue literacy in third language learning. *Language, Culture, and Curriculum, 3*(1).

Tollefson, J. W. (1991). *Planning language, planning inequality.* London: Longman.

Tsui, A. B. M. (1996). English in Asian bilingual education: From hatred to harmony: A response. *Journal of Multilingualism and Multilingual Development, 17*(2), 241–247.

ENDNOTES

1. The languages used as medium are 14 less than the 47 languages reported in the Fourth All India Educational Survey of 1970 (Chaturvedi & Singh, 1981). The languages taught in schools are 17 less than the 58 reported in that survey. These reductions are noteworthy in the context of the increase in the curricular time for teaching English, although this increase is not the cause for the reduction in the number of languages taught or used as a medium of instruction.

2. The states where Hindi is the regional language teach another Indian language as the third language. One state and one union territory do not teach Hindi and the government schools in them teach only two languages.

3. The same charter of 1813, which gave the responsibility for education to the colonial government, allowed Christian missionaries to do evangelical work and start schools. The government schools did not teach religion.

4. Tsui (1996) shows that the economic policy of retaining the preeminent place of Hong Kong in international trade and financial services promotes indirectly English-medium education, hence defeating, not unexpectedly, the educational policy favoring Chinese-medium education.

5. Union Territories, unlike the States, are under greater financial control of the Union government. They are small territories, often a city or a historical residue from the making of states on linguistic basis.

6. During the colonial period, there were principalities ruled by kings and provinces created for the administrative convenience of the British. The provinces of the Indian Union were not linguistic and cultural units until after Independence. The linguistic states formed after Independence promoted the use of their majority languages for roles of power, including use as media of education.

7. For the effect on academic achievement of the intersecting variables of socioeconomic background and medium of instruction in state schools, see Anand (1971); for the effect of intelligence and other variables in addition to socioeconomic background, see Srivastava and Ramasamy (1988).

10

Medium of Instruction in Post-Colonial Africa

Hassana Alidou
Alliant International University

Political independence does not necessarily lead to educational or economic independence. Four decades after most sub-Saharan African countries gained their political independence from Western powers, the goal of formulating and implementing an effective language policy for education and other development sectors remains sadly unfulfilled. This situation persists despite research findings related to effective medium of instruction that indicate, in the case of Africa, the retention of colonial language policies in education contributes significantly to ineffective communication and lack of student participation in classroom activities. Moreover, it explains to a large extent the low academic achievement of African students at every level of the educational systems (Alidou, 1997; Bokamba, 1984).

In an attempt to address the medium-of-instruction issue, ministries of education in the early 1970s created a few experimental bilingual schools using indigenous languages (hereafter "national languages") along with the official colonial languages as media of instruction for at least the first 3 years of schooling. Only Tanzania and Ethiopia have generalized the use of national languages in entire primary school systems, with the implementation of comprehensive and extensive use of national languages throughout their formal educational systems. In the majority of African countries, however, the use of national languages as media of instruction or in bilingual education has become a long-term educational experiment, with very little hope of expanding them to wider contexts, despite the positive outcomes revealed by most evaluative reports related to these experiments (Mahamane, 1986).

Since 1990, however, the Francophone countries Burkina Faso, Mali, and Niger have embarked on a bilingual education revitalization program with the technical and financial support of a few international donors to African education. For the last 15 years, I have worked in these countries as a language-education consultant for several international organizations. In this capacity, I have been involved directly in the formulation and implementation of language-education policy at both macro and micro levels. Therefore, I provide here an active participant's and researcher's analysis of the current issues affecting the use of African languages as media of instruction along with English, French, Spanish and Portuguese.

The purpose of this chapter is to critically review medium-of-instruction policies in sub-Saharan African countries since the 1990 Jomtien "Declaration of Education for All by 2000". I specifically identify and analyze certain political, economic, and pedagogical issues surrounding the medium-of-instruction debate in sub-Saharan Africa. Based on my own experience as an international education consultant for several development agencies and as a bilingual education teacher, I argue that three main sets of factors—economic, political, and pedagogical—trigger the problem of medium of instruction in African schools. Economic factors include the retention of textbook markets for Western publishing companies. Political factors include African elites' reluctance to implement a language policy that may reduce the gap between two unequal social classes—a tiny privileged minority of educated Africans who have access to political and economic power and the underclass of noneducated masses deprived of economic and political resources. Pedagogical factors include inadequate preparation of school personnel in bilingual education, ongoing corpus planning (the codification of African languages), and the need to develop qualified human resources in publishing educational materials in African languages. Finally, I address the question of whether African languages must be standardized before they can be used as media of instruction in African schools.

CULTURAL POLICIES AND THE POLITICAL ECONOMY OF COLONIZATION

An adequate assessment of the medium-of-instruction problem in Africa necessitates a critical review of colonization. Therefore, I provide in this section a sociohistorical account of colonial language policies. I describe how African children were educated, particularly how they learned their culture and language prior to colonization, and I describe how children were initiated into the world of work.

Prior to colonization, each ethnolinguistic group in Africa used its own language for children's education. There was no debate about medium of instruction, as such education was linguistically and culturally context-ualized in order to respond to the needs of the population. In Hausaland of Niger and Nigeria, for example, the Hausa language was used both for intragroup communication among the different Hausa people and for all types of initiation activities. Children were socialized and initiated in their mother tongue, Hausa. Because the majority of Hausa became Muslim prior to colonization, they also used Arabic for religious education. The main goal of education provided in the Makaranta (religious schools) was reading koranic verses and learning how to pray. Makaranta students who were able to develop advanced literacy skills in Arabic used their newly ac-quired skills to write in their mother tongue. That is, they used the Arabic alphabet to write in Hausa through transliteration. Such practice is referred to as *Ajami*. This type of transliteration was also popular among other West African ethnic groups, such as the Fulani, who speak Fulfulde, and the Mende people, who speak Mende. Bledsoe and Robey (1993) report that Mende people currently use Ajami for personal correspondence and record keeping. In addition to basic literacy, a literate society developed in North-ern Nigeria with the creation of the Islamic library by Usman Dan Fodio in the great city of Kano. Dan Fodio also translated Greek mathematics into Hausa using Ajami. Unfortunately, his intellectual and educational efforts were destroyed by the British colonial administration when there was Mus-lim resistance to colonization.

The use of literacy for children's education also existed within the Tuareg culture. The Tuareg, living in Mali, Mauritania, and Niger, and speaking Tamajeq, have their own writing system—Tifinagh—that they use for intragroup communication as well as for passing on their traditions. Generally, mothers are the main users of Tifinagh; they teach children how to read and write Tamajeq using Tifinagh.

As these examples suggest, prior to colonization, the different ethno-linguistic groups in Africa did not have a medium-of-instruction problem. Each group used its own language to educate its children, essentially mak-ing education linguistically and culturally responsive within each tribal or ethnic setting. In other words, education was "naturally intertwined with the life of a person and community, and [it was] therefore impossible to think of it as an isolated system" (Tedla, 1995, p. 116). In each community, parents identified appropriate socialization and initiation strategies that they used to introduce their children into adulthood. For indigenous edu-cation purposes, no child attended a "classroom" where the language of in-struction was foreign. Thus, I argue (as did Tedla [1995]) that the medium-of-instruction problem emerged in the late 1800s with the intro-duction of Western education in Africa.

Africa

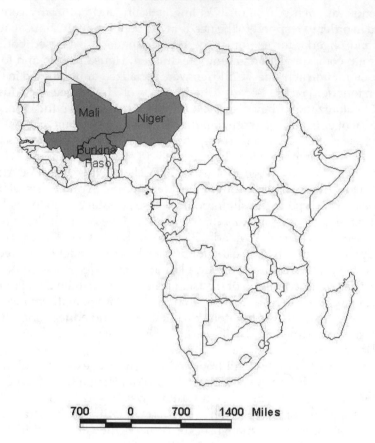

FIG. 10.1.   Map created by Lynn M. Burlbaw using ArcView GIS 3.2.

During the colonial era (1885–1958; see July, 1970), new forms of education were introduced. Formal education was initiated by colonial administrators and Christian missionaries who accompanied them. Children from different ethnolinguistic groups who might or might not speak the same language were put together in order to receive basic education in the colonial languages—French, English, Spanish, and Portuguese. All colonizing forces had cultural and economic reasons for developing formal education in Africa. French colonial administrators were particularly straightforward in stating their goals. For instance, a former French Governor-General of West Africa stated:

We must train indigenous cadres to become our auxiliaries in every area, and assure ourselves of a meticulously chosen elite. We must also educate the masses, to bring them closer to us and transform their way of living ... From the economic viewpoint, we must train the producers and consumers of tomorrow. (Governor-General Brevie of French West Africa, quoted in Moumoni, 1998, pp. 42–43)

As this quote suggests, colonial education policy was not aimed at developing an educational system that was culturally and economically responsive to the needs of the African population. Rather, colonial schools were created to serve European economic and political interests. The use of European languages and European-based curricula were necessary conditions for this endeavor. For the first time, children from various ethnic and linguistic communities were forced into common classrooms. Because children often did not speak the same language, colonial school administrators were forced to identify a common language for instruction. Providing basic education to each child speaking the same language was not economically viable, nor did it serve the imperialist goals of the colonizers. Therefore, in each European colony, the colonial language became either the exclusive or dominant language of instruction.

With regard to African languages, two types of policies developed in colonial schools. In former British colonies, African languages and English were used transitionally as media of instruction. English became the dominant language of instruction in 4th grade and the sole language of instruction in secondary schools. Such a policy was in line with the British policy of indirect rule in its former colonies (Wolf, 2001). The French colonial administration implemented more hegemonic language and cultural policies in its African territories by strictly excluding the use of African languages and Arabic in schools. Literacy through the use of Ajami, Tifinagh, or any other writing system was strictly prohibited by the decree of May 10, 1924, regulating French colonial schools (Alidou, 1997). Article 64 of the decree clearly defines the French medium-of-instruction policy in colonial schools: "French will be the sole language in schools. Teachers are forbidden to use local languages with their students."

In order to "civilize" and assimilate African students into French culture, the schools required children to learn the French language. Coercive measures included physical punishment and public shaming of children who spoke their mother tongue in the schoolyard or their own neighborhood. Upward mobility in school and access to jobs in the colonial administration were strictly tied to mastery of French. The impact of colonial language policies on children is well described by Ngugi wa Thiong'o (1986), who laments that "the language of an African child's formal education was foreign. The language of the books he read was foreign. Thought in him took the visible form of a foreign language" (p. 17).

Of course the use of coercive measures did not turn all Africans into European people, nor did it promote mass literacy and education. On the contrary, colonial education throughout Africa was very selective and male oriented. (Most of those who attended schools were males, the majority from royal families.) Thus, colonial education not only contributed to gender problems that persist today, but it also deepened existing social inequalities within African societies. Mateene (1980) argues that colonial education created a new type of social division, based on the mastery of the colonial language. This social division was:

> a linguistic division which has been based on the fact that one group knows better the colonial language, has got access to an education considered better, whereas the other group in fact the majority, only knows the national African languages, which by government decision, give it no right of access to useful and valuable education, and consequently condemn it to remain always an ignorant class, dominated and with inferiority complex. (p. 18)

Calvet (1974) suggests that cultural and linguistic domination are closely related to the development of a significant market for the colonizers. He argues: "In all cases where a language has been imposed, there is the fact that the community speaking that language had imposed itself before, imposing at the same time, its market" (as cited and translated by Mateene, 1980, p. 60). Indeed, colonial schools opened a huge textbook market for the British and French textbook industries. An evaluation of textbooks used during both the colonial and post-colonial eras in countries such as Burkina Faso, Mali, Niger, and Senegal indicates that major publishing companies based in France, including EDICEF, Hachette, and Nathan, produced most of the books used in African schools (Alidou-Ngame, 2000). For instance, the reader *Mamadou et Bineta*, first published by EDICEF in 1950, is regularly reedited and used in African schools to the present. In a recent study of the economics of publishing educational materials in Francophone Africa, Bgoya et al. (1997) state:

> It is, however, important to emphasize the fact that textbook publishing was controlled by government from pedagogical point of view, not from that of manufacture. Editorial functions and production were carried out in France by French publishers, under commission or through tendering. The Dakar-based Nouvelles Editions Africaines (NEA) was owned by the governments of Senegal, Ivory Coast and Togo and by the French publishing firms EDICEF, Arman Colin, Nathan, Présence Africaine and Le Seuil in a 60/40 percent share holding. They published books for almost all the Francophone countries in West Africa ... This was possible because the education systems in those countries were the same and were patterned on the French system. (p. 31)

French and British publishing companies, such as EDICEF and Heinemann, continue to hold a monopoly on the textbook market in Africa, due to restrictive regulations imposed by the World Bank and international development agencies that finance African education. Indeed, a study conducted by donors to African education indicates clearly that little has changed since the end of colonization (Alidou-Ngame, 2000). European publishing companies continue to dominate the textbook industry and colonial languages remain the dominant languages of education. Some French publishing companies have hired African curriculum specialists to produce manuscripts, but the books they produce do not take into consideration the cultural and linguistic backgrounds of African children. In contrast, textbooks produced entirely by the curriculum units of national ministries of education are increasingly responsive as they take into account children's cultural and socio-economic backgrounds.

Thus, France, Great Britain, Spain, and Portugal benefited financially and culturally from the imposition of their languages as media of instruction and administration in their respective colonies. At the end of colonization, very few African languages were used for the education of the masses. Moreover, because few Africans had access to colonial education, colonial languages were acquired by only a tiny minority of the African population. As Mateene (1985) notes:

> The knowledge and practice of a colonial language have never reached more than a quarter of the population. So much so, that the majority of this population continues to live by their diverse languages and are not really affected by the linguistic unification of a colonial nature. (p. 61)

POST-COLONIAL EDUCATION AND LANGUAGE POLICIES

The creation of post-colonial multilingual and multiethnic states with few people speaking the colonial languages posed serious language-planning and language-policy problems. Whereas during the colonial era, linguistic imposition was unilateral, in the post-colonial era, language choice for education and administration required a more democratic dialogue among the multiethnic African elites who replaced colonial administrators. Thus, in the post-colonial period, the medium-of-instruction debate became a highly political issue.

When Africans took over political control of their countries, they quickly realized they could not easily replace colonial education systems and language policies. In independent, multilingual African countries, the retention of colonial languages as official languages of government ironically became the most practical and politically correct choice. Avoidance of ethnic war was the main reason for the retention of colonial languages. Mazrui (1975) argued that nation building and the detribalization of African governments depend on the use of the colonial language. Therefore in the post-colonial era, European languages were viewed as neutral means of communication for the linguistically diverse citizens of the newly independent states. (For a more extensive discussion of post-colonial language policies, see Bokamba [1984].)

An additional problem in the post-colonial period is the lack of corpus planning (including orthography) for many African languages. Because African languages were prevented from being elevated to official status, none of the African languages were considered to be qualified for use in international communication, including science and technology. For example, with regard to the retention of French as the official language of former French colonies, Senghor, the former President of Senegal, argued that access to universal civilization and a common language are possible only through the use of French language: "To access modern and universal civilization, African nations need a common language. None of the African languages can fulfill this role: French can and it must become a unifying factor" (author's translation of Painchaud, 1972, p. 30, cited in Alidou, 1997, p. 30).

In summary, several forces favored the retention of French, English, Portuguese, and Spanish as dominant languages of education: widespread multilingualism, limited corpus planning for African languages, and the need for languages of wider communication that could allow Africans to engage with the international world.

The retention of European languages as the dominant media of instruction has had a serious negative impact on African education in general, and primary school students' academic performance in particular. In Francophone countries, French is spoken by less than 20% of the urban population and less than 10% of the rural population, yet French remains the exclusive language of instruction in mainstream classrooms. The mismatch between school language and children's home language poses serious language learning and literacy development problems for most students. A recent evaluation conducted by UNESCO in Burkina Faso and Mali raises serious questions about students' mastery of French (UNESCO, 2000). Indeed, sub-Saharan African countries that have maintained colonial languages in education continue to be among the poorest, most illiterate, and most poorly educated countries in the world (UNESCO, 2000). Countries such as Burkina Faso, Mali, and Niger face both access- and quality-of-education issues, with more than 70% illiteracy among the adult population and only 30% of school-aged children with access to basic education. Those children who attend school face serious educational problems due to their lack of mastery of the medium of instruction. For example, the dropout rate between fifth and sixth grade is more than 30% of all students. In addition, there is a high rate of class repetition. According to UNESCO's annual evaluations, more than 35% of all students repeat a class or two before they finish the 6 years of compulsory education (UNESCO, 2000).

In 2000, UNESCO through its assessment unit, the Southern Africa Consortium for Monitoring Educational Quality (SACMEQ), conducted a study of students' achievement in several African countries. The results of this study indicate that in both Anglophone and Francophone countries, students are still struggling with the language of instruction (UNESCO, 2000). UNESCO's experts report very poor student performance all over Africa. With regard to student performance on tests taken in English in Nigeria, for example, they report:

> In Nigeria when researchers administered cognitive tests of literacy, numeracy and life skills to fourth graders as part of the Monitoring Learning Achievement project, the results were described as generally poor. The mean percentage of scores was 32% in numeracy, 25% in literacy and 33% in life skills. In one test item pupils were instructed to copy a five-line passage into a given space. Only 8% of them were able to do so accurately, and 40% were unable to copy a single word or punctuation mark. (UNESCO, 2000, p. 34)

Similar results are reported in Senegal, where tests were administered in French. The experts raise serious concern:

> It becomes a problem if a relatively large proportion of pupils fall into the category of under-achievers. Such pupils may be at risk of being unable to pursue lifelong learning or to integrate effectively into society and the world of work. (UNESCO, 2000, p. 38)

To address such problems, in 1990, UNESCO, the World Bank, and the European Community sponsored the World Conference on Education for All in Jomtien, Thailand. Most developed and developing countries were represented. All governments and development agency representatives at the meeting recognized that educational provision is qualitatively and quantitatively inadequate in sub-Saharan Africa. The conference highlighted the need in Africa to develop quality education that is socially equitable and culturally relevant. The promotion of African languages as media of instruction was announced as one of the best strategies for promoting effective learning in formal basic education.

The 10-year action plan developed after Jomtien by the national ministries of education anticipated the expansion of the use of national languages in all elementary schools in these countries. Unfortunately, since 1990, little public debate has focused on popular reaction to the use of national languages for formal basic education. Since Jomtien, African governments have held only two major conferences on language policy in education and development (in Cape Town, South Africa, and Accra, Ghana). These gatherings were academic and political in nature, reemphasizing the need to invest in the development and use of African languages. Unfortunately, at the national level, most policymakers are reluctant to implement a new medium-of-instruction policy. Therefore, bilingual schools in sub-Saharan African remain merely experimental projects.

In spite of the fact that the World Bank calls for the promotion of quality education in Africa and recognizes the value of children's mother tongue for attaining this goal, World Bank-funded projects in Africa do not specifically include budgets for bilingual schools. In countries such as Burkina Faso, the government does not include salaries for bilingual teachers in its national budget. In effect, poor populations are required to take on this financial responsibility in order for their children (the majority of whom are girls) to have access to formal basic education. Such a burden is not put on parents whose children attend publicly financed schools where French is the exclusive means of education.

As an international education consultant, I have had several formal and informal discussions with European development agencies and World Bank education program coordinators and consultants for Burkina Faso, Mali, and Niger. During these discussions, I have explicitly asked questions about the World Bank's language-in-education policy in Francophone countries. Invariably, the Bank's educational experts have justified their institution's lack of financial support for bilingual education in Francophone Africa as a careful consideration of the implications of such policies for French cultural and language policy in its former colonies. The French government, they suggest, opposes expanding the use of national languages in its former colonies. As the main sponsor of African development programs at the World Bank, France will not support funding for programs that promote the comprehensive use of African languages in schools. As a Representative of the Burkina Faso Ministry of Education stated at a UNESCO conference held in April 2000 in Dakar, Senegal: "If African governments can finance for themselves this specific aspect of their education, we can move forward with this linguistic question" (personal communication, April, 2000).

Mazrui (2000) helps us understand the Bank's position. Mazrui points out that the World Bank's policies are similar to British and French colonial and post-colonial development policies. He notes that the Bank's loans to African countries are always linked to a package of conditions requiring the countries to import textbooks from Western countries, particularly France, England, and Canada. Such policies, he argues, have contributed significantly to the weakening of local publishing companies. World Bank loans have also secured the predominance of French and English languages as media of instruction in African schools. Thus, Mazrui clarifies the Bank's

> preference for Euro-languages which create and maintain social divisions serving an economy dominated primarily by foreign economic interest and, secondarily, by small aspiring African bourgeoisie ... As leading institutional representatives of international capitalism, the World Bank and the IMF naturally have a vested interest in this interplay between linguistics and economics. (p. 55)

Thus, there has been little change in medium of instruction since the colonial era. Indeed, an evaluation of colonial, post-colonial, and post-Jomtien language use in African elementary schools reveals little difference from one country to another or from one period to another. In Francophone Africa, experimental bilingual schools remain marginalized schools. In Anglophone Africa, post-colonial language policy continues to require only transitional use of national languages in the first 3 years of elementary education.

Experimental Bilingual Schools: Hopes and Limitations

After Jomtien, Niger, Burkina Faso, and Mali renewed their interest in revitalizing experimental bilingual schools originally initiated in the mid-1970s and early 1980s. In Niger, the national assembly passed a law recognizing all 10 languages as national languages and media of instruction. It also looked for international funding to reinvigorate its "Ecoles Expérimentales." In Mali, the government created "les écoles de la pédagogie convergente" and in Burkina Faso, the government and UNICEF created "les écoles satellites" in rural areas. The main purpose of these experimental bilingual schools was to promote the use of children's mother tongues as media of instruction in the first 3 years of elementary education. In these schools, French is taught as a subject and is introduced in the 4th grade as the main language of instruction.

In spite of the World Bank's continuing reluctance to embark on a program of comprehensive bilingual education in Africa, ministries of education since 1990 have sustained some momentum in favor of African languages. In Burkina Faso, Mali, and Niger, experimental bilingual schools have been revitalized. Intensive corpus planning and specific pedagogical projects have moved these countries closer to the use of national languages for formal education. Moreover, the national ministries of education have won the support of a few international funding and technical agencies. Burkina Faso, Mali, and Niger have developed a close partnership with the German Foundation for International Development (DSE) in order to remedy the lack of quality textbooks in national languages. I have served as the Academic Director of the professional development projects initiated by DSE in these three countries. My involvement has provided me an opportunity to observe and analyze how national and international organizations deal with the issue of the medium of instruction, both at the macropolicy level and at the grass-roots level. Therefore, the following discussion on experimental bilingual education in Francophone Africa is mainly an insider's account of the situation.

In Burkina Faso, Mali, and Niger, the respective governments have identified in each country a few regional languages to serve as media of instruction in the experimental bilingual schools. These languages are generally lingua francas and, as such, they are spoken fluently by children who have them either as a native language or a second language. Thus, the national languages used in the experimental schools are not necessarily the first languages (or mother tongues) of all the students. But in multilingual settings, there are always a few languages that emerge as a means of wider communication, and are reasonable choices for media of instruction. In Niger for example, Hausa and Zarma are used in two bilingual schools in Niamey, the capital city. The adoption of these two languages is justified by the fact that they have become equally used as lingua franca in Niamey (originally populated by Zarma people). The bilingual school that uses Hausa and French as media of instruction is located in Lazaret, a neighborhood populated predominantly by Hausa speakers. (Hausa is spoken as a native tongue by 52% of Niger's population, and 82% of all people in Niger speak Hausa.) The bilingual school using Zarma and French is located in Gamkalle, a neighborhood predominantly inhabited by Zarma speakers.

Thus, in Niger, the ministry of education has carefully taken into account the sociolinguistic characteristics of the capital city before selecting the national languages that can serve as media of instruction in the bilingual schools. In addition, there is wide agreement from the community about the choice of these languages as media of instruction. As a result, the government's decision is a sound one, both pedagogically and politically. By carefully considering the sociolinguistic profile of the population before selecting a language of instruction, ministries of education can avoid policies that cause resentment on the part of the population that does not identify with the language and the culture it represents.

These schools are supported by joint DSE-ministries of education projects in Francophone countries that seek to train language curriculum-development specialists and to produce culturally relevant language arts textbooks in national languages for 1st, 2nd, and 3rd grades. Since the implementation of these regional projects in 1994, the following ongoing issues have required attention: (a) the availability of qualified bilingual school teachers and curriculum specialists; (b) corpus planning, specifically the codification of African languages; (c) quality of education and materials published in national languages.

Availability of Qualified Bilingual Teachers and Curriculum Specialists.
Two key factors affecting the quality of education are the availability of qualified teachers and provision of relevant educational materials, particularly textbooks in the classrooms. These issues are pervasive in both French-based and bilingual schools. In bilingual schools in Africa, there is indeed a critical need for educational materials, but most of all for qualified bilingual teachers who are fluent in the national language(s) and the countries' official language (English or French). The teacher-training schools do

not include in their core curriculum a specialization in bilingual education. Therefore the majority of teachers in experimental classrooms are either regular classroom teachers who volunteer to teach in the bilingual programs or they are graduates of secondary schools who are recruited and provided with 2 to 3 months of training for teaching in the bilingual schools. Both categories of teachers are unfamiliar with teaching in two languages and they are often more literate in French than in the national language that serves as first language in the classroom. Yet oral proficiency and competency in a language does not necessarily translate into reading and writing proficiency. For this reason, most teachers I have observed in the bilingual schools need significant in-service training with regard to national language transcription, orthography, reading and writing. It is only in demonstration schools that I have found teachers with high proficiency and competency in national languages. Often these teachers believe politically in the use of national languages as media of instruction and they have extensive experience in literacy activities in national languages.

In Francophone countries, all bilingual education teachers are recruited among regular classroom teachers trained for teaching exclusively in French. (The only exception is Burkina Faso, where graduates of secondary schools are hired and sent to teach with 2 months' training in teaching in national languages.) These teachers receive very limited training in teaching in national languages. For example, in order to become familiar with writing in national languages, they receive 2 months of intensive training in national language orthography, teaching in national languages and general pedagogy. These trainings occur mainly when ministries of education receive financial support from international donors such as UNICEF, the German Technical Cooperation Agency (GTZ), the German Foundation for International Development (DSE), or United States Agency for International Development (USAID). Due to the limited availability of funds, often pedagogical units from ministries of basic education can offer only 1 to 3 months of training for bilingual teachers. Teachers often leave these sessions without having mastered national language alphabets, orthographies, or methods of teaching in national languages.

Since 1997, GTZ has developed in Niger a 9-year project whose aim is three-fold: bilingual teacher training, production of educational materials, and creation of a literate environment in national languages. This project contributes to the reinforcement of in-service teachers and it also organizes the 3 months of initial training for the new teachers. However, the GTZ project is not closely integrated into the ministry of basic education training program. It maintains an independent status, and the project managers identify the main training activities. Because the GTZ project is sufficiently funded, I believe it could have a greater impact on the provision of qualified bilingual teachers if its activities were better integrated into the ministry of education teacher training programs. I suggest that such projects should be located in the teacher-training schools, so that the project's technical experts can participate more actively in the design and implementation of an initial bilingual teacher training program and the production of relevant educational materials in both national languages and French. Such a strategy can better affect the quality of bilingual education in Niger. It can also help in producing annually a significant number of bilingual teachers who can serve in all primary schools in Niger. Moreover, such a strategy makes the project and its outcomes (namely human resource development in bilingual education) more sustainable for the ministry of education. Ultimately, this strategy can contribute more effectively to the generalization of bilingual education throughout the primary school system.

This critique of the status of GTZ project can be directed to most international development projects found in Africa. Their independent status and their limited integration to national development and training priorities render them less effective; they have very limited and unsustainable effects. Such a situation contributes to the weakening of the support for bilingual education. Opponents of bilingual education in Africa have often complained about the lack of cost-effectiveness of these projects. I argue that their integration into national development programs could guarantee more positive outcomes and sustainability, and they could be cost effective in the long run.

Among Anglophone countries, Nigeria developed, with financial support from the Ford Foundation, the Ife Primary Education Research Project from 1970 to 1978. The aim of this project was three-fold: training of bilingual curriculum specialists, production of relevant educational materials in Nigerian languages and English as a second language, and systematic initial and in-service training for all bilingual classroom teachers. (The successful outcomes of the project were reported by Fafunwa, Macauley, and Sokoya [1989].) Unfortunately, the activities of the project ended when funding from the Ford Foundation ended. One would think that government educational agencies and also private organizations would take over and provide financial support for a project that has produced very successful bilingual students. However, this was not the case. Professor Fafunwa and his colleagues from The University of Ife were forced to reduce their activities with regard to teacher training and curriculum development for mother-tongue education. In light of the Ife project, I believe that reforming teacher-training programs so that they include a field of specialization for bilingual education could help solve the problem of shortage of qualified bilingual teachers in Sub-Saharan Africa and reliance on foreign funds to provide adequate initial training and continuous professional development for teachers. I also agree with Bamgbose (2000):

> [R]esults from experiments and projects tending to support alternatives to current practices are often not given the necessary backing and follow-up, and proposals to the same effect are often ignored. The major reason for this is

that it is extremely difficult to break away from existing practices in which imported official languages are the dominant media of instruction. Even when there is an overwhelming case for changing to an African language, such is the force of dominance that there is a great resistance to change. (p. 3)

Overall, the lack of financial resources and refusal of hesitant elites to promote African languages as media of instruction render the issue of bilingual education and training of bilingual teachers daunting tasks in sub-Saharan Africa.

Corpus Planning. Bilingual schools have been justified in North America and elsewhere by scientific evidence of the positive influence of mother-tongue literacy on child psychological and linguistic development and the dependency of second-language acquisition on the development of children's mother tongues (Cummins, 1979, 1981). Such arguments apply in contexts where both the dominant language and minority language have long traditions of literacy, such as in the case of English and Spanish in the United States. This is not the case with African languages. Most are in the process of acquiring an official orthography and few publications are available in these languages. The development of literate culture and the availability of meaningful linguistic input (both oral and written) are necessary conditions for the effectiveness of mother-tongue education and the transferability of literacy skills from African languages into European languages used in experimental bilingual schools. In the case of Africa, the lack of literate environments in the national languages constitutes a serious barrier, preventing African children from developing adequate literacy skills in the national languages. For this reason, studies conducted in African bilingual schools do not produce strong evidence for linguistic interdependence or transferability of literacy skills from first language to the second language (as Cummins has found in North American contexts [1979]). Rather, the development of a literate environment and literate culture using national languages must take place. Once this condition is met, the use of national languages as media of instruction can aid the development of effective literacy in these languages, and children will be able to use literacy skills developed in the national languages to acquire the dominant language of school (French, English, Spanish, or Portuguese). Effective literacy can also be cultivated in rural communities by creating libraries that serve not only the schools, but the whole community. The promotion of a literate culture and environment can facilitate the development of literacy in national languages.

The lack of adequate financial resources and political will often make impossible the creation of coordinated educational and linguistic programs. However, policymakers and education specialists should always consider research-based findings in addressing their educational problems. It is in light of this consideration that I identify the factors that can influence the development of adequate bilingual basic education programs in sub-Saharan Africa. Thus, a condition for the development of effective bilingual schools in Africa is a coordinated effort in corpus planning among linguists, writers, and local publishing companies. Linguists should work intensively on the codification and standardization of African languages; writers should promote and produce all types of literary work in these languages; and the private local publishing companies must invest in the production of these materials. The development of a literate environment depends on availability of books, creation of libraries for community use, and above all, the promotion of African languages as the media of formal and nonformal communication in local, national and regional administration (government) and the private sector.

Often governments and the international community have argued that the development of standardized languages must be completed before bilingual education in Africa is possible. Yet, clearly in post-colonial Africa extreme poverty and dependency on foreign aid seriously slow down the effort of corpus planners. Therefore, to argue that bilingual schools can be developed only when there are full orthographies, grammars, and dictionaries for all the national languages is simply, as Ouane puts it, "une stratégie de retardement"—a strategy of delay. In other words, requiring standardization before using the national languages in education is a delaying tactic that has maintained the power position of colonial languages, while little effort is devoted to the development of African languages. I believe that linguists, teachers, curriculum developers, and textbook publishers should work together to further the use of African languages in education. For instance, the ministry of education in Burkina Faso is not waiting for all languages to be described before it develops bilingual schools. Instead, it invites diverse groups of experts to work together to improve existing materials and to produce new materials and teacher-training programs. The governments of Mali and Niger have adopted the same strategy, with the support of funding from technical agencies such as the German Foundation for International Development, the Danish development agency (DANIDA), and SNV, a Dutch development agency. Interestingly, there are no French or British government development agencies or nongovernment organizations supporting the bilingual education initiative in Mali, Niger, or Burkina Faso.

Policymakers argue that it is too expensive to develop national languages. I argue that African countries have invested too much in European education over the last 40 years. African governments spend more than 30% of the national budget on education. Yet, in all of the sub-Saharan countries, more than 70% of the population remains illiterate and uneducated. The economic and social cost of continued exclusive investment in European languages is unbearable. The retention of colonial medium-of-instruction policies in most African educational systems has prevented African children and adults from having an education that positively affects their lives. Due to the lack of adequate basic education and literacy, Africans are negatively impacted by preventable diseases, such as malaria and HIV/AIDS. Most of the health information is available in the official languages, which the majority of the populations do not speak, and thus they cannot read crucial health information. Moreover, social and gender inequalities persist, worsened by high poverty and scarcity of national resources that trigger intense competition among people.

Thus, I argue that African governments should not wait until all African languages are well described before they promote such languages as media of instruction in formal basic education and adult literacy. Indeed, the promotion of African languages as media of instruction will influence the production not only of textbooks but other types of literary production, which in turn will facilitate the development of a literate culture in these languages. In this context, national publishing companies will develop interest and will encourage writers to produce reading materials in these languages. This is the only way African languages can become marketable nationally and regionally.

Quality of education and materials published in national languages. The promotion of quality education relies on educators' understanding of the sociopolitical context of education. Therefore, professional training for teachers, linguists, and curriculum developers involved in the bilingual schools should be based on critical pedagogy and multicultural education as philosophical and theoretical bases. Indeed, teachers and curriculum developers must become aware that the promotion of quality education in Africa depends on critical knowledge about power and how it is constructed in society. They must understand how current language policies, patterns of language use, and curriculum content perpetuate social inequality and injustice in African societies. They must understand that as teachers and curriculum developers they have the power to promote practices that undermine hegemonic ideologies through their use of language and their selection of culturally relevant curriculum content.

Unfortunately, diversity is not considered in African school curricula, and African countries face serious problems in managing diversity, as demonstrated by the recurrent ethnic wars facing the continent. Teachers and curriculum developers for bilingual education should have training in critical multicultural education in order to be able to effectively address issues of diversity facing their communities. The curriculum of professional development training must include topics such as gender and social inequality in education, peace education, and global education.

The materials produced in national languages must be of high quality linguistically, culturally, and pedagogically. My evaluation of textbooks currently used in experimental bilingual schools finds that most are merely translations of textbooks originally produced in French or English. As a result, the curriculum content taught in national languages is similar to the curriculum content taught in French and English, and education in the national languages fails to solve the problem of textbook irrelevance in mainstream African education. Thus, translated books used in experimental bilingual schools promote hegemonic Western values that undermine African languages and cultures. In most textbooks, African cultures and languages are exclusively associated with imagined archaic traditions, whereas French and English are associated with modernism and technological advancement. Such representation of African languages and cultures in textbooks for experimental bilingual schools must be challenged. Textbooks in national languages should be conceived from a critical pedagogical perspective, based on the need to challenge Western and African elite hegemony. Such an approach, however, must not prevent textbook producers from considering that African societies are dynamic and include elements of authenticity and modernity. Moreover, they should consider that African education seeks to develop global learners and workers who are globally competitive. This complexity should be reflected in the textbooks produced in national languages

The production of culturally relevant textbooks depends on the training of qualified human resources for bilingual education. Teachers and curriculum developers must learn how to write in their own languages. During my classroom observations, I have noticed that many teachers have not mastered official orthographies in the national languages. A similar problem is encountered during the workshops I facilitate for textbook developers and curriculum specialists who produce educational materials. Intensive training must be regularly conducted in order to help teachers, textbook writers, and curriculum developers master the transcription of their own languages. This training must include not only academic exercises, but also significant opportunities for writing in one's own language.

CONCLUSION

In the colonial period, the medium-of-instruction problem was created by colonial powers that imposed for economic and cultural reasons their own languages as media of instruction in the territories that they occupied. In the post-colonial era, the search for effective solutions to medium-of-instruction problems in Africa is constrained by the desire among African elites to maintain their social status and power based on mastery of official languages, and by the economic power of Western international development agencies to determine African development policies.

It is crucial that analyses of medium of instruction and bilingual education in Africa include sociohistorical, economic, cultural, and pedagogical

III

Managing and Exploiting Language Conflict

11

Language Policy
in Post-Apartheid South Africa

Vic Webb
University of Pretoria

South Africa has a population of 43 million (1996 census) with about 80 languages (Department of Arts, Culture, Science and Technology [DACST], 1996). The main languages are the Bantu languages: Ndebele, Swazi, Xhosa and Zulu, which belong to the Nguni sub-family; Pedi, Tswana, and Sotho, which belong to the Sotho subfamily; and two that belong to neither— Tsonga and Venda. Also widely spoken are Afrikaans (an "Africanised Dutch") and English. Each of these languages includes numerous varieties. In addition, there are a number of European languages, Asian languages, religious languages, and urban mixed varieties (Fanakalo, and an urban youth vernacular Flaaitaal/Tsotsitaal/Iscamtho), as well as several African languages spoken by immigrants from neighbouring countries.

The South African Constitution of 1996 (Government of the RSA, 1996) declares that 11 languages will be used for official functions in the country. These 11 official languages include the two official languages of the apartheid era (Afrikaans and English) and the nine major Bantu languages of the country. The Constitution prescribes parity of esteem and equitable treatment for all 11 official languages, includes linguistic human rights as a cornerstone of public life, prohibits discrimination, commits the government to the promotion of all other languages commonly used by communities (including sign language, religious languages, and the country's first languages—Khoi, Nama, and San), and gives explicit recognition to the princi-

217

ple of linguistic diversity. Together, these constitutional stipulations express a philosophy of political pluralism.

The post-apartheid government has had to perform enormous tasks since the statutory establishment of democracy in 1994. These tasks include developing and implementing nonracist policies for all sectors of public life, restructuring all governmental institutions into non-racist institutions, transforming the civil service into a demographically more representative entity without engendering conflict or seriously impairing service delivery, providing equal educational and employment opportunities and equal health and social security services, providing housing and land for formerly dispossessed citizens, establishing democracy, and combating racism and sexism. It is thus unrealistic to expect that the government could have fully implemented the constitutional language stipulations in the years since their inception. Specifically, medium-of-instruction policy has only been partially spelled out.

This chapter discusses language-policy development and implementation in post-apartheid, democratic South Africa within a strategic planning approach. The following issues are examined: the country's language planning framework, language policy development, the language political realities in which policy implementation must occur, and language-in-education policy development, with particular attention to medium-of-instruction policy.

THE FRAMEWORK FOR LANGUAGE
PLANNING IN SOUTH AFRICA

The development of a comprehensive language policy for South Africa must occur within the macrocontext of the national ideals set for the country, the government's macro-economic policies, and the language stipulations contained in the Constitution. Each of these is briefly summarized below.

The Country's National Ideals

The vision of what the country wants to become is expressed in the national ideals accepted by the political leaders during the debates on the democratisation of South Africa in the period 1992 to 1993. These ideals include: (a) establishing democracy; (b) promoting equality and human rights; (c) developing national unity and promoting mutual tolerance and respect among the different cultural, linguistic, religious, racial, and sociopolitical groups; (d) developing the people of the country; (e) administering the country effectively; (f) implementing affirmative action; and (7) retaining the country's cultural diversity. A comprehensive language policy and plan of implementation for South Africa is expected to give expression to these visions and values.

Macro-Economic Policies

The second major context within which language policy formulation must occur is the Reconstruction and Development Programme (the RDP). The RDP is a strategy for the development of the country's human, natural and financial resources. It is designed to play a concrete role in the life of the citizens of the country, in the sense of creating employment opportunities, operationalising citizenship, breaking down social barriers, and instilling tolerance and respect. The RDP entails coordinating public programmes into a coherent and purposeful whole, meeting the aspirations of the citizens and encouraging their direct participation in government institutions and programmes, and recognising that national development cannot occur in an unstable society.

In February 1996, the government outlined a new economic strategy, the Growth and Development Strategy. According to Ryan (1996), this programme aims to "eradicate poverty, remove wealth disparities between people, de-emphasise racial ownership, foster rapid economic expansion and, in the process, cement social and political peace" (p. 3). These goals are to be achieved by "massive investment in education and training, job creation, competitiveness in international markets, and the development of a system designed to draw the poorest members of society into the economic mainstream" (p. 3). The current macro-economic policy of the government, which contains similar objectives, is called GEAR: growth, employment, and redistribution. Even a superficial consideration of the RDP, the Growth and Development Strategy, and GEAR will indicate that language needs to be given a central role in the realisation of these programmes, particularly in education for employment. Indeed, all language policies must be explicitly directed at facilitating the realisation of these macro-economic policies.

The Constitutional Language Stipulations

The 1996 constitutional language stipulations summarized at the beginning of this chapter provide a clear expression of the national ideals that the political leadership of South Africa wants to achieve. As such, they can be described as the "mission statement" of the government with regard to language—a description of the broad goals the government has set for itself.

Chapter 2 of the Constitution contains a Bill of Rights that guarantees equality (by prohibiting discrimination on grounds such as race, gender, ethnic or social origin, sexual orientation, disability, age, religion, belief, culture, and language); equal educational opportunities (with everyone having the right to receive education in the official language or languages of individual choice in public educational institutions where that education is reasonably practical); and the right to form cultural, religious, and linguistic communities (ensuring that persons who belong to a cultural, religious, or linguistic community may not be denied the right to enjoy their culture, practice their religion, and use their language, nor the right to form, join, and maintain cultural, religious, and linguistic associations and other organs of civil society).

Criticisms of the Constitutional Language Stipulations

These language stipulations are a significant improvement on the language policies of the apartheid regime. They acknowledge the need to centralise the major communities in the country, that is, to make them part of the mainstream of public life through the recognition of their languages, and they establish principles that are basic to both the democratisation of the country and its social transformation. However, these stipulations do not constitute a language policy and are at most a description of the long-term goals that the government has set for itself. The key question is thus whether these stipulations can be transformed into a meaningful and comprehensive national language policy that will facilitate the effective reconstruction and transformation of the national society, within the context of the national ideals and macro-economic policies. This issue is discussed in the following section.

A frequently expressed criticism of the constitution, generally from uninformed quarters, is that an 11-language decision is impossible to implement, because the necessary human and material resources are not available to realise such an ambitious goal. However, two features of the stipulations make it clear that the writers of the constitution did not have such a literal interpretation in mind. First, the stipulations implicitly work with the notion of functional differentiation as expressed in subsection (3) (a) of the stipulations: "The national government and provincial governments may use *any particular* official languages for the purposes of government" (emphasis added). Second, the stipulations bind both the national and the provincial governments to use *at least two* official languages. The government is thus not bound to using all 11 languages for all official functions in all domains of public life.

A more serious criticism of the language stipulations is that they contain a number of clauses that may allow the government to avoid the full and meaningful implementation of any future policy. These conditions, often called "escape clauses," include the provision that policies should take "into account usage, practicality, expense, regional circumstances, and the balance of the needs and preferences of the population" (section 6[3][a] of the Constitution, p. 4; see Webb, 1999). These conditions qualify the government's commitment to policy implementation, and could even be used to undermine the language stipulations.

The constitutional language stipulations have been critically analysed by du Plessis (1999), Strydom and Pretorius (1999), and Webb (2002b). Strydom and Pretorius criticise the constitutional language directives for (a) lack of clear guidance; (b) confusion between the principles espoused (parity of esteem, equity, language promotion) and practicality (the qualifying clauses), in particular whether priority is to be given to principle or practice; and (c) the lack of follow-up measures to clearly explicate the purpose of the directives and provide a substantial basis for their implementation, thus giving them credibility (Strydom & Pretorius, 1999). Du Plessis (1999) takes a similar position, questioning the government's commitment to developing and implementing official multilingualism, suggesting that it has adopted "a laissez-faire approach regarding language matters" (p. 18), and adding that this stance was taken in order "not to enter into a debate on the unassailable position of English as the language of liberation" (p. 18).

In fairness, these criticisms must be seen within the context of the fact that there are far more urgent tasks to perform from the government's perspective, as well as that it is inordinately difficult to transform the language politics of a country. It is unrealistic to expect major changes in the language politics of South Africa in the short period since the end of apartheid.

To summarize: The constitutional language stipulations, read in the context of the national ideals and the macro-economic policies of the government, present language planners in South Africa with two major challenges—to devise a comprehensive national language policy that will guide the country to linguistic transformation, and to produce a fully fledged, realistic, and cost-effective plan of implementation.

LANGUAGE POLICY DEVELOPMENT

The 1994 decision to recognise 11 official languages at the national level came as a surprise to persons interested in the politics of language; most observers expected English to be selected as the sole official language. The decision to recognise 11 languages was a result of the need for political compromise between the two sides negotiating about the democratisation of the country—the African National Congress (ANC) and the governing National Party. These two sides were driven by opposing interests. The National Party was concerned about its white Afrikaans support, whereas the ANC viewed Afrikaans as the symbol of apartheid. As a result, they had opposing language policy views: The National Party preferred a continuation of the existing language policy (Afrikaans and English as co-official languages, with the Bantu languages as regional official languages) and the

ANC preferred English as sole official language. The only way out of this impasse was, seemingly, the selection of Afrikaans and English along with all the indigenous languages of the country as official languages. Thus, the choice of 11 official languages was not a rational sociolinguistic decision, but a political one aimed at bringing about a political settlement.

Following the acceptance of an interim constitution in 1994 (which was followed in 1996 by the final constitution), a series of workshops was held on the language issue, leading in 1995 to the appointment of a language plan task group (called Langtag) by the government. This committee was instructed to describe a framework within which a future comprehensive national language policy could be developed. The committee obtained the direct participation through a network of subcommittees of about 50 language specialists (linguists, language planners, and language practitioners such as translators, interpreters, lexicographers, and terminologists), and dealt with language equity, language development, language as an economic resource, language in education, literacy, language in the public service, heritage languages, sign languages, augmentative communication systems, and language services (in particular translation, interpretation, and term-creation). In the course of its work, workshops were held across the country, and the pre-final version of the report was debated at a national conference lasting 2 days. The final report was presented to the government in August, 1996, and accepted by the cabinet soon afterward.

Following the completion of the Langtag report, the task of language policy development was taken further by the Department of Arts, Culture, Science and Technology, the department that is formally responsible for language-service provision and language planning. Since 1997, this department has been developing a draft language policy and plan, and has presented its proposals at a number of workshops. At the end of March, 2000, DACST arranged a workshop during which the committee tasked to prepare a comprehensive national language policy for South Africa presented its proposal. The proposal was accepted and subsequently formulated as the South African Languages Bill (Beukes, 2000; Department of Arts, Culture, Science and Technology, 2000). The draft bill was revised in June 2001, following a query from the cabinet about likely costs.

The South African Languages Bill

The draft bill begins with a list of its strategic goals, which are:

- To facilitate individual empowerment and national development;
- To develop and promote the Bantu languages;

- To provide a regulatory framework for the effective management of the official languages as languages of the public service;
- To facilitate economic development via the promotion of multi-lingualism;
- To enhance the learning of the South African languages;
- To develop the capacity of the country's languages, especially in the context of technologisation.

The revised draft bill is expected to be presented to the cabinet for consideration during the 2003 parliamentary session. Acceptance by the cabinet and parliament, however, is unlikely to lead to immediate and full implementation at all three levels of government and in all state departments. In fact, effective policy implementation could take several years, depending on the political commitment of the heads of state departments, and given national and provincial budgetary constraints.

The bill proposes the following policy decisions:

- The national government will use not less than four languages for official work.
- These languages will be selected from each of four categories of official languages on a rotational basis, namely: the Nguni languages (Ndebele, Swazi, Xhosa, and Zulu); the Sotho languages (Pedi, Sotho, and Tswana); Venda and Tsonga/Shangaan; and Afrikaans and English.

(The logic in the categorisation is clear in the case of the first two groups of languages, which are members of the same subfamilies. Venda and Tsonga/Shangaan are grouped together because they do not belong to the two former subfamilies, and Afrikaans and English are grouped together because most coloured, Indian, and white South Africans know both, albeit to different degrees.)

- Government at provincial and local levels, as well as institutions that perform public functions, will be subject to the policy provisions of the bill.
- The policy will be applicable to legislative, executive, and judicial functions.
- Language units will be established for each department of the national government and each province, to implement and monitor policy implementation, to conduct language surveys and audits in order to assess existing language policies and practices, and to inform the public about the policy.
- Regulations concerning a language code of conduct for public officials will be produced.

The bill also proposes a plan of implementation (what has to be done, by whom, for whom, and when) for selected core activities, such as the establishment of language units, the development of a language code of conduct, and language audits. An important facet in the preparation of the bill is, of course, the question of costs, and cost estimation has been undertaken for selected state departments.

The proposed bill is obviously not offered as a policy for specific state institutions. At most it provides a framework within which further policy development must take place. Each state department (at whatever level) will need to determine its own specific policy and plan of implementation on the basis of the functions it has to perform and the types and levels of communication in which it needs to be engaged in fulfilling its functions.

The bill is clearly an expression of the spirit of the constitutional language stipulations, and is thus moving toward their implementation. However, since 1994, official language practice has gradually become more and more monolingual, with English being used almost exclusively as the official public language, and with little indication that state institutions are contemplating any meaningful implementation of the multilingualism prescribed by the constitution. It will thus become increasingly difficult to change the direction in which the country is moving as regards official language practice. There have been signs, however, that institutions at both local and provincial levels, as well as state departments, have begun processes directed at language-policy development. If these processes actually gain momentum (albeit under legal pressure), it is possible that language planning in South Africa may become a meaningful event.

THE REALITIES OF SOUTH AFRICA'S
LANGUAGE POLITICS

Strategic language-policy development and implementation cannot, of course, occur in a vacuum. They need direct reference to the relevant external and internal environments.

The External Global Environment

The major external environment is globalisation, particularly the powerful controlling and normalising role of the United States, the United Kingdom, and Europe, economically, politically, and through the media. In addition, the demands of the so-called "new economy" and the "knowledge era" also impact on language-policy development in South Africa. As a report of the South African National Committee for Higher Education pointed out, these developments are characterised by the extensive use of computer technology, participatory forms of work organisation (team work), and more educated labour (in particular multiskilling and the "continuous deployment of new knowledge"; National Committee for Higher Education, 1996, p. 53). According to the report, these changes call "for training in broad, generic and transferable skills enabling workers at all levels to deal flexibly with varied problems, tasks, and new technologies" (p. 53). The work place is increasingly becoming knowledge driven and knowledge dependent, and training institutions therefore must produce "learning individuals" equipped with knowledge and skills that will enable them to learn how to handle new and unpredictable developments and problems (p. 61). As the report states: "(K)nowledge and the pursuit of knowledge have become key factors shaping the structures and dynamics of daily life" (p. 66). It is clear that if South Africa is to become competitive, training programmes must produce "learning individuals" who possess a highly developed knowledge base and high levels of transferable skills. Education has an enormous task, and language policy practice must not serve as an obstacle.

The Internal Environment

The internal environment for strategic language planning includes the language-related problems in the country (that is, problems in which language plays an important role), the language political environment, and language problems (that is, language-specific problems, such as standardisation).

Language-Related Problems.   Language-related problems are non-linguistic problems in which language plays some causal role (for instance, problems with educational, economic, political, and social development; see Webb [2002b]; Webb & Kembo-Sure [2000]). In South Africa, these problems include the following: (a) the educational underdevelopment of many South Africans, which is a direct consequence of Apartheid education; (b) uncompetitive performance in the workplace, low productivity, and generally unfair economic conditions, in particular poverty, the skewed distribution of wealth, and restricted occupational opportunities, which are all partly due to inadequate educational development; (c) inadequate political participation (partly due to the fact that the main language of political discourse is English) and the continuance of linguistic discrimination and intergroup conflict; (d) cultural alienation and the possible threat to the country's rich diversity, through ethnolinguistic shift and cultural assimilation to the Western world. As Webb (1996, 2002b) and Webb and Kembo-Sure (2000) show, language plays a fundamental role in each of these problems. Thus, language planning in the country must propose policies and strategies that will address the role of language in their resolution.

One crucial problem is low rates of educational development in many areas of the country (see FIG. 11.1).

As indicated in the Race Relations Survey for 1999–2000 (South African Institute of Race Relations, 2000, pp. 107–133), the literacy rate in 1999–2000 for the country as a whole was 64% (51% in the Limpopo Province); the country-wide pass-rate for Grade 12 was 49% (35% for the Limpopo Province); the percentage of secondary school graduates admitted to university study was 13% (7% in the Limpopo Province); and 26% of all teachers were underqualified.

Information supplied in Strauss and Burger (2000, pp. 7–8) on literacy and numeracy, obtained in an all-African survey in 1999, also supports this observation. According to their report, 54% of the learners in KwaZulu/Natal scored less than 50% in a literacy task, and 89.27% scored less than 50% in the numeracy task. In the Limpopo Province, the respective percentages were 71.35% and 94.66%. Although the situation is slightly more positive in more urbanised provinces (e.g., in Gauteng 37.27% scored less than 50% on the literacy task and 80.86% scored below 50% in numer-

PROVINCES OF SOUTH AFRICA

FIG. 11.1.   Political map of South Africa.

acy), literacy and numeracy rates among South Africa's learners are extremely disturbing.

Implicit in these findings is that the inadequate educational development is situated mainly in the black South African communities (understandably so, given the effect of apartheid). This is apparent from the following information supplied by the former Department of Education and Training (DET), which was responsible for the schools for black learners (commonly called "Bantu education") before 1994: (a) Of the 5 million persons older than 4 years of age who had no formal education in 1994, 3.5 million (70%) were black. (b) Of the professionally unqualified teachers in 1992, only 0.01% were white, whereas 99.9% were black.

In summary, South Africa has a long way to go educationally if it is to develop a well-educated population, which is an essential requirement if the country is to grow economically and become competitive in the global market.

The Language Political Environment.   Table 11.1 contains the numbers of speakers of the main South African languages, according to the 1996

TABLE 11.1
First-Language Speakers of the 11 Official Languages in Numerical Order, in Numbers and as Percentage of Population

	1996 Census			
Languages	Speaker numbers (home language	Percentage	Estimated knowledge as second language, in millions	Pansalb, 2001. (N = 2, 160)
1. Zulu	9 200 144	22.9	24.2	23.8
2. Xhosa	7 196 118	17.9	18	16.3
3. Afrikaans	5 811 547	14.4	16.5	16.5
4. Pedi	3 695 846	9.2	12.6	7.7
5. English	3 457 467	8.6	18.5	8.7
6. Tswana	3 301 774	8.2	11.3	9.5
7. Sesotho	3 104 197	7.7	10.5	6.8
8. Tsonga	1 756 105	4.4	4.7	3.2
9. Swazi	1 013 193	2.5	3.4	3.3
10. Venda	876 409	2.2	2.5	1.8
11. Ndebele	586 961	1.5	2.2	1.2

Sources: 1996 Census; Pansalb, 2001.

Census. Because national censuses may have involved estimates, particularly in rural areas, Table 11.1 also includes related information obtained from a survey commissioned by the Pan South African Language Board (Pansalb) from an independent research consultancy firm, Mark Data (Pty.). This survey was based on a sample of 2,160 South Africans 16 years of age and older, drawn from all social categories, rural and urban. The fieldwork was conducted in the language preferred by the respondents (Pan South African Languages Board, 2001).

Besides the main South African languages, Portuguese is reportedly spoken by 57,080 persons, German (11,740), Greek (16,780), Dutch (11,740), Italian (16,600), French (6,340), Hindi (25,900), Urdu (13,280), Gujarati (25,120), Telegu (4,000), and Tamil (24,720).

Table 11.1 indicates the widespread multilingualism of South Africa. Indeed, the majority of black South Africans are functionally highly multilingual (and probably know about four languages each), with the rest of the population bilingual (that is, they know Afrikaans and English).

The main South African languages are deeply embedded in the political history of the country. Colonialism and apartheid have meant that the languages have all acquired sociopolitical meanings, with English currently highly prestigious, Afrikaans generally stigmatised, and the Bantu languages largely without economic or educational value. The languages have thus developed asymmetric power relations: although the main Bantu languages are numerically in the majority, they are, along with Afrikaans, "minority languages" in terms of power and prestige. In contrast, English, although numerically a smaller language, is politically, economically, and educationally dominant, and is by far the preferred language of the public media, with a very high status. In the South African context, English is the major language, with Afrikaans lower on the power hierarchy, and the Bantu languages effectively marginalized. English has possibly become a vehicle for the struggle for power among the different social groups.

Little empirical information is available on attitudes toward the Bantu languages. Research underway in a small-scale survey (300 respondents) in two black residential areas in the Pretoria area, Atteridgeville and Mamelodi (Strydom, 2002), provides the following findings:

1. About 40% of the residents of these two areas (mainly speakers of Pedi, Tswana, and Zulu) regard English as important to know (compared to about 25% for Pedi, less than 9% for Tswana, and none for Afrikaans).
2. The preference for English (and the underestimation of the Bantu languages) is particularly marked among younger respondents with secondary and tertiary education.

3. English is regarded as the most valuable language for getting a job (94% of the respondents), with Afrikaans in second place (74%), and the Bantu languages scoring between 38% and 49%.
4. English is regarded as the language that will help one earn respect from others (87% of the respondents), followed by Pedi (76%), Tswana (62%), Zulu (59%), and Afrikaans (49%).

Several observations from local language politics can be made about these findings: (a) the strong position of English, especially among younger and more educated respondents; (b) the poor position of Afrikaans in the two communities, except for the work domain; and (c) the relatively strong position of the Bantu languages (especially Pedi), suggesting the possible emergence of sociolinguistic awareness (which is unexpected, considering the role of the Bantu languages in the policies of apartheid). Given the main home languages of the two residential areas (Pedi, Tswana, and Zulu), the strong position of English is striking, clearly indicating the continued asymmetric power relations among the languages of the area.

Asymmetric power relationships are also reflected in the prevalence of code-switching/code-mixing in South Africa, with switches/mixing mostly in the direction of English (but occasionally also toward Afrikaans and Zulu). Similarly supportive of English is the prevalence of informal diglossia, with English increasingly performing the high functions and becoming the language of the black middle class. The pattern of diglossia may imply that the former race-based inequality is being replaced by a class- and maybe even a language-based inequality.

An important feature of the language situation in South Africa is the fact that most of the major languages have been maintained, and have not exhibited significant signs of language shift. This was even clear in the time of apartheid, when there was little language shift in the case of the Bantu languages, despite the language policies of that time. This is also made clear by the Pansalb report (Pansalb, 2001, p. 4), which compared respondents' current home language with the main home language of their childhood. For example, 93% of the respondents who identified themselves as Afrikaans-speaking in 2000 used Afrikaans as their main home language during their childhood; 90% of the respondents who identified themselves as English-speaking in 2000 used English as their main home language during their childhood; and 96% of the respondents who identified themselves as Zulu-speaking in 2000 used Zulu as their main home language during their childhood. By comparison, (only) 82% of the respondents who identified themselves as Tsonga-speaking in 2000 used Tsonga as their main home language during their childhood. In general, therefore, the main languages of the country can be said to possess a reasonable degree of ethnolinguistic vitality. This view is supported by the Pansalb finding that the respondents were generally satisfied with the way in which their languages were treated in public contexts (2001). The respondents who expressed dissatisfaction with the way in which their home languages were treated were the "better educated and more affluent urbanites" (p. 11). In a sign of support for multilingualism, 61% of the respondents favoured a policy of developing disadvantaged languages, particularly in the case of speakers of Afrikaans, Sotho, Swazi, and Venda.

The high status of English and the strong preference for its use in public domains, including educational institutions, makes it necessary from a language-planning perspective to consider the levels of proficiency in English among black South Africans. The general impression one gets from moving around South Africa engaging in informal conversation in English is that many black South Africans know English well enough for basic interpersonal communication in urban areas. English speakers can get by in English on city streets asking for directions, negotiating parking, and directing inquiries at reception desks in post offices, municipal offices, and government departments. However, the English proficiency of black South Africans is generally not adequate for the purposes of formal learning (what Cummins [1979] refers to as "cognitive academic language proficiency"). Teachers of black learners in colleges for vocational education and training, for example, report that learners' generally do not comprehend technical, business, or academic concepts in English, very seldom participate in classroom discussions, and perform poorly in assessment tasks.

Macdonald (1989) shows that former DET primary school learners had an average English vocabulary of 300 to 700 words after the 4th grade, whereas textbooks for the 5th grade required a vocabulary of 3000 words. A large-scale survey conducted in 1996 (1,898 former DET learners in 20 rural schools in the Western Cape, the Eastern Cape, KwaZulu/Natal, the Free State, the Northern Cape, and Gauteng) and undertaken for an organisation called READ showed that most rural learners (of whom there are more than 5.6 million in the country) had inadequate reading and writing skills: (a) Only 33.6% of the Grade 5 learners were found to possess "average" reading skills, with 38.5% of the Grade 6 learners and 45.5% of the Grade 7 learners; (b) only 7.5% of the Grade 5 learners were found to possess "average" writing skills, with 12.6% of the Grade 6 learners and 19.3% of the Grade 7 learners (Le Roux & Schollar, 1996, pp. 12–13).

Similarly, van Rensburg (2000) reports that tests performed by consultants on the literacy and communication skills of 5,924 urban tertiary learners (who had English L2 as medium of instruction) indicate that less than 50% of the these learners had adequate English literacy skills, and, furthermore, that these skills declined from 51% in 1990 to 28% in 1994, and 22% in 1997. Webb (2000, 2002a) provides further information on the language issue at the tertiary level.

For many black South Africans, their proficiency in English is also inadequate for formal, but noneducational contexts. For instance, the Pansalb survey (2001) found that 49% of their respondents often did not understand or seldom understood speeches in English. This lack of English language proficiency rose to 60% among speakers of Tswana, Ndebele, and Venda, and among less educated respondents, respondents in rural areas, and respondents in semiskilled or unskilled communities. The lack of English comprehension skill is also apparent in informal contexts. Respondents rated their ability to follow a story on radio or television in English as follows: Sotho: 28%, Tswana: 14%, Pedi: 19%, Swazi: 27%, Ndebele: 3%, Xhosa: 24%, Zulu: 32%, Venda: 0%, and Tsonga: 24%.

Language Problems.   Two key language problems in South Africa that a comprehensive language policy must address are the asymmetric power relations among the official languages of the country and the low social prestige of the Bantu languages. It will be necessary to limit the role of English in public life and to effect positive language attitudes to the Bantu languages. Additional problems include standardising the Bantu languages and developing their functional capacity so that they can become effective instruments of educational, economic, political, and social development. For language standardisation, planning tasks include engineering the general acceptance of the present standard varieties (i.e., bridging the gap between traditional dialects, mixed urban varieties, and the standard), and adapting these standards into fully fledged languages of learning and workplace performance (see Calteaux, 1996; Nfila, 2002).

Given South Africa's political past, during which language was used as an instrument of statutory division, there remains a degree of hesitancy about giving linguistic diversity a positive role in the reconstruction and development of the country. However, as Kubchandani (1984) and Granville (1998, p. 259) point out, the recognition and support for diversity is important in the development of social security, a sense of self-worth, people's ability to "read the world," and their ability to act flexibly and innovatively in the globalised economy. Provided that the relationship between different languages and different language varieties is not seen as oppositional but as complementary, recognition and positive support for diversity at all levels is likely to ease potential ethnolinguistic tension and to increase opportunities to gain access to higher education and employment, as well as meaningful participation in public life.

LANGUAGE-IN-EDUCATION POLICY DEVELOPMENT

Language-in-education policy affects South Africa's 26,937 publicly supported schools, enrolling 12,026,661 learners, of whom 11.3% speak Afrikaans as a first language, 5.7% English, 20.3% Xhosa, 24.6% Zulu, 2% Ndebele, 10.3% Pedi, 7.4% Sotho, 7% Tswana, 4.9% Tsonga, 3.3% Swazi, 2.8% Venda, and 0.4% other languages (Department of Education, 1997, p. 60). Of all public schools, 72% are uniracial and the rest multiracial.

The Current Policy on Medium of Instruction

The national language-in-education policy of South Africa is collectively described in the South African constitution (1996) and a Department of Education language-in-education policy document. (See also Republic of South Africa, 1996; South African Schools Act of 1996.) The South African constitution (Section 29, section 2) provides the gist of the policy:

> Everyone has the right to receive education in the official language or languages of their choice in public educational institutions where that education is reasonably practicable. In order to ensure the effective access to, and implementation of this right, the state must consider all reasonable educational alternatives including single medium institutions, taking into account (a) equity (b) practicability and (c) the need to redress the results of past racially discriminatory laws and practices.

The Department of Education's language-in-education policy encourages the principle of *additive* multilingualism, but allows the governing body of each public school to determine the school's medium of instruction. The policy does not recommend any specific model, but does suggest that two such models are considered practical: the use of a first language as medium of instruction (with the requirement that an additional language also be studied), and a "structured bilingual approach" (presumably, initial instruction through the L1, with a gradual transition to English).

The policy document expresses quite a strong position on multilingualism. Besides describing multilingualism and multiculturalism as assets, it obligates schools to promote multilingualism by requiring that they stipulate how they will implement it, suggesting that they (a) use more than one medium of instruction and/or (b) offer additional languages as fully fledged subjects, and/or (c) apply special immersion- or language-maintenance programmes (particularly in cases where learners' home languages are not used as media of instruction). In practice, however, there is little evidence that the additive approach is being put into effect.

The language-in-education policy clearly follows a democratic approach. However, given the uneven political playing field in the country and the serious language-based problems in education, a more comprehensive directive on how governing bodies should go about developing their language policies is necessary.

Medium of Instruction: Practice in Schools

Department of Education information on schools' choice of medium of instruction for 1996 shows that 11% of all schools selected Afrikaans (whose speakers constitute 11.3% of the school population), 51% selected English (5.7% of the school population) and 37% selected a Bantu language (83% of the school population; Department of Education, 1997, p. 58.) The relationship between home language and the selected medium of instruction is clearly skewed in favour of English, especially regarding black learners (see Tables 11.2 and 11.3).

As Table 11.2 shows, the only language community in which the medium of instruction correlates to some degree with the number of home-language speakers is Afrikaans. English is positively skewed (selected by 66% of the Gauteng learners as medium of instruction, yet the home language of only 13%), with the Bantu languages all in a negatively skewed relationship between home language and choice as medium of instruction. (For example, Pedi is selected by only 2% of Gauteng learners as medium of instruction, yet is spoken as home language by 8% of the learners).

Table 11.3 summarises responses in the Pansalb survey to the following questions: (a) For subjects other than language, what is the language of tuition? (b) Do your teachers use other languages as well?

TABLE 11.2
Comparison of Home Language (HL) of Pupils with Choice of First Medium of Instruction (MoI) in all Schools in Four Provinces, as Percentages in 1997

Province (and total no. of pupils)		Afrikaans	English	Pedi	Tswana	Zulu
Gauteng	HL	17.5	13	8.3	8.9	20
(1.45M.)	MoI	19	66	2	2.5	8.5
KwaZulu/Natal	HL	1.2	10.6	-	-	85
(2.7M.)	MoI	1.6	64.3			34
Limpopo Province	HL[a]	2.6	0.4	56.7	1.5	0.8
(1.8M)	MoI	1.6	50.8	32.8	0.5	0.6
Western Cape	HL	60.1	19.6	-	0.06	-
(0.91M.)	MoI	66	28		-	

[a] Home language according to the 1991 census.
Source: Education Ministry Information Service, Personal communication.

TABLE 11.3
Overall Distribution of Language Use in the Educational Setting
in 2000 (in percentages)

	Home language	Medium of instruction	Informal secondary language of tuition
Afrikaans	17	16	33
English	9	80	29
Tswana	10	2	14
Pedi	8	0	7
Xhosa	16	2	28
Zulu	24	6	21

Source: Pansalb, 2001, p. 9.

As Table 11.3 suggests, the official medium-of-instruction policy often does not reflect actual practice. In most schools, teachers code-switch between English and a Bantu language, even, apparently, to the extent of using mainly the home languages of learners in classrooms. Ngcobo (2001), for example, reports a significant degree of code-switching in content subjects in KwaZulu/Natal schools, with 52.8% of the teachers reporting using Zulu alongside English. However, because all formal assessment is conducted in English, it is doubtful whether code-switching will solve the problem of educational performance.

An interesting aspect of medium-of-instruction policy in South Africa is that South Africans who are not involved in policy decisions seem to differ from the governing bodies of schools in their views about the appropriate medium of instruction. In contrast to the prevalence of English as medium of instruction, according to the Pansalb report (2001), only 12% of the respondents (who were 16 years of age and older) indicated that they preferred English as medium of instruction, whereas 37% preferred instruction through their primary language (a Bantu language), and 39% preferred that English and their primary language be used jointly (p. 10). Strydom (2003) obtained similar responses in Atteridgeville and Mamelodi, finding that 75.3% of the respondents in Mamelodi preferred the use of a Bantu language in addition to English as medium of instruction in the primary schools, and 71.3% in the secondary schools, whereas the respective percentages for Atteridgeville were 94% and 88% . In Mamelodi, 20% (primary school) and 28% (secondary school) opted for English as medium of instruction, whereas in Atteridgeville the support for English was only 3.3% (primary school) and 12% (secondary school).

A possible explanation for the difference between the views of black South Africans and the school governing bodies can be found in research by Ngcobo (2001), among Zulu-speaking teachers in Durban, the major urban area in KwaZulu/Natal. Ngcobo found that 76% of his respondents preferred to send their own children to English-medium schools, whereas 71% indicated (where a Bantu language was the medium of instruction in the initial school years, with a switch to English later on) that the switch from the Bantu language to English should preferably occur from Grade 2. That is, the teachers' views are similar to those of the schools' governing bodies. Perhaps the views are so different between teachers and governing bodies on the one hand and members of communities on the other because English has become an instrument of elite closure, and the black middle class uses it to protect its own interests and privileges.

There are many reasons why the Department of Education in South Africa should pay serious attention to the medium-of-instruction issue. Besides poor educational development generally, and inadequate English language proficiency specifically, there is general agreement among sociolinguists and educational linguists that the use for educational purposes of a language that is not known adequately constitutes a barrier to educational development, and could even lead to a form of culture shock for entrance-level learners. As Caesar (2001) argues, using a language that learners know insufficiently well as medium of instruction can lead to "a form of anxiety accompanied by the loss of generally acceptable signs and symbols for social interaction" (p. 136) leading to frustration and uncertainty about appropriate behaviour, an inability to interpret classroom interaction and emotional insecurity. Thus, many learners do not become a meaningful part of the educational process. Furthermore, many educational linguists believe that the use of a second language as medium of instruction can only be effective in contexts where conceptual skills in the home language have already been developed, where the home language is widely used in the community, and where it has acquired higher social and economic value than the second language. Where first language literacy skills have not been meaningfully developed and where the home language has a lower social and economic value than the second language, as in South Africa, the use of a second language as medium of instruction is not advisable.

Sociolinguists in South Africa also generally find it difficult to understand why policy makers do not take seriously their arguments about medium of instruction, despite strong supporting evidence from African research (see Bamgbose, 1991). The reason is probably that politicians and government officials have different primary interests and goals, with politicians and state officials being more concerned with effective administration and control. The only possible way in which one can still hope to influence decision makers in South Africa is by providing hard empirical evidence in a specifically local context (see Webb & Grin, 2000).

CONCLUSIONS

This analysis of language policy in post-apartheid South Africa has identified both positive and negative features of the effort to develop and implement a comprehensive and progressive language policy. Negative features include the following: increasing Anglicisation of the public sector, in direct contradiction of constitutional provisions; skewed medium-of-instruction choices; relatively slow progress in language-planning development; insufficient funding of Pansalb; and apparent lack of a serious commitment to multilingualism among decision-makers and administrators responsible for policy implementation. Other disturbing features include the low level of the language debate in the country in general, with few new ideas being expressed at the numerous language-policy conferences; the inadequate availability of relevant research findings; a continuing tendency to follow an approach of advocacy rather than data analysis; the undersupply of language planning specialists; and a seeming lack of understanding of the complexity of language planning, with most people in authority assuming that any intelligent person can handle the task effectively. This last aspect is particularly disturbing, because there is generally an inadequate grasp of the language-planning process and little understanding of the complex interrelationship between language and society at the macrolevel. Persons involved in language-planning work, for example, often wrongly assume that simple language-promotion programmes (such as literary competitions, the production of dictionaries and grammars, and term creation) will lead to the linguistic realisation of the national ideals of transformation, reconstruction, and development.

On the positive side, the first important achievement is the establishment of the necessary regulatory infrastructure for a plurilingual language plan. This infrastructure includes the promulgation of the constitutional language stipulations, the Langtag process, the development of the South African Languages Bill, the establishment of a directorate for language planning in the Department of Arts, Culture, Science and Technology (the department officially tasked with language planning), and the establishment of the Pan South African Language Board. Second, there is extensive scholarly involvement in the field: Several conferences (see for example Webb, 1995) and workshops have been held, and serious research is being undertaken across the country (see Webb 1998), strongly supported by the country's National Research Foundation, which recently presented a workshop directed at the development of multilingualism as a niche area of research. Third, clear support for multilingualism and the use of primary languages (in particular the Bantu languages) has been expressed by key government leaders (including the Minister of Education and the Minister of Arts, Culture, Science and Technology), and there has also been grass-roots support for the Bantu languages (see Pansalb, 2000, 2001). Also positive is the willingness of the government to consult with language planning experts, as in the Langtag process and in the appointment of the committee charged with developing a proposal for a national language plan. A final encouraging development is the gradual emergence of positive ethnolinguistic awareness among the general public, especially regarding the Bantu languages.

The eventual state of language planning in South Africa can ultimately only be evaluated within the context of the response to what is arguably the two most important challenges to language planning in South Africa, namely changing language attitudes (or, in another formulation, combating economic, political, and sociocultural globalisation, which leads to the continued marginalisation of minority language communities), and the development of cost-effective language-policy proposals. The latter issue is especially important, because one cannot realistically expect the government to support a policy proposal unless it is demonstrably affordable and will not place undue stress on the government's resources, particularly in the context of the country's serious problems (including HIV/AIDS, poverty, housing, and crime).

Many important questions about language policy in South Africa remain unanswered: Will the country succeed in its implementation of the policy of 11 official languages? Would failure in South Africa imply that progressive language policies elsewhere in similar contexts are also doomed to failure? What can language planners elsewhere learn from the South African experience and thus, what contribution can language planning in South Africa make to the field in general? Although positive and negative trends are beginning to emerge, it is too soon to predict the outcome of the South African language-planning endeavour.

REFERENCES

Bamgbose, A. (1991). *Language and the nation: The language question in sub-Saharan Africa.* Edinburgh, Scotland: Edinburgh University Press.

Beukes, A. (2000, September). The language policy and plan for South Africa. Paper presented at the Language Summit, Pretoria, South Africa.

Caesar, N. J. (2001). *Die medium van onderrig vir Xhosamoedertaal leerders (sic) in 'n Engels- en Afrikaansmedium sekondêre skool in die Wes-Kaap: 'n gevalle studie (sic) in 'n wetenskaples.* [The medium of education for Xhosa-speaking learners in an English- and Afrikaans-medium secondary school in the Western Cape: A case study in a Science class]. Unpublished mini-thesis, University of the Western Cape, Belville, South Africa.

Calteaux, K. (1996). *Standard and non-standard African language varieties in the urban areas of South Africa: Main report for the Stanon research program*. Pretoria, South Africa: Human Sciences Research Council Publishers.

Cummins, J. (1979). Linguistic interdependence and the educational development of bilingual children. *Review of Educational Research, 49*, 221–251.

Department of Arts, Culture, Science and Technology. (1996). *Towards a national language plan for South Africa. Final report of the Language Plan Task Group*. Pretoria, South Africa: Author.

Department of Arts, Culture, Science and Technology. (2000). *Language policy and plan for South Africa. Final draft*. Pretoria: Author.

Department of Education. (1997). *Education statistics.* Pretoria, South Africa: Author.

du Plessis, T. (1999, July). Multilingualism and government in South Africa. Unpublished paper presented at an annual conference of the Linguistics Society of Southern Africa. Pretoria, University of South Africa.

Government of the RSA. (1996). *Constitution of the Republic of South Africa*. Pretoria, South Africa: Government Printer.

Granville, S. (1998). English with or without gu(i)lt: A position paper on language in education policy for South Africa. *Bua! 4*, 254–272.

Kubchandani, L. M. (1984). Language modernization in the developing world. *International Social Science Journal, 36*(1), 169–188.

Le Roux, N., & Schollar, E. (1996). *A survey report on the reading and writing skills of pupils participating in READ programmes*. Braamfontein, South Africa: READ Educational Trust.

Macdonald, C. (1989). *Crossing the threshold into std. 3*. Pretoria: HSRC.

National Committee for Higher Education. (1996). *A framework for transformation*. Pretoria, South Africa: HSRC Publishers.

Nfila, B. (2002). *Standard Setswana in Botswana*. Unpublished master's thesis, University of Pretoria, Pretoria, South Africa.

Ngcobo, S. (2001). *IsiZulu (sic)-speaking educator's (sic) attitudes towards the role of isiZulu in education in Durban*. Unpublished mini-thesis, University of Natal, Durban, South Africa.

Pan South African Language Board [Pansalb]. (2000). *Language use and language interaction in South Africa: A national sociolinguistic survey*. Pretoria, South Africa: Author.

Pan South African Language Board [Pansalb]. (2001). *Language use and language interaction in South Africa: A national sociolinguistic survey. Summary report. Pansalb Occasional Paper No. 1*. Pretoria, South Africa: Author.

Republic of South Africa. (1996). *No. 84 of 1996. South African Schools Act*. Pretoria, South Africa: Government Printer.

Ryan, C. (1996, June). *The RDP Quarterly Report*, p. 3.

South African Institute of Race Relations. (2000). *Race relations survey, 1999/2000: Millennium issue*. Johannesburg, South Africa: SA Institute of Race Relations.

Strauss, J. P., & Burger, M. A. (2000). *Results of the Monitoring Learning Achievement (MLA) project, North West*. Bloemfontein, South Africa: Research Institute for Education Planning, University of Orange Free State.

Strydom, H. A., & Pretorius, J. L. (1999, October). Language policy and planning: How do local governments cope with multilingualism? Paper presented at the conference on Multilingual cities and towns in South Africa—challenges and prospects, Pretoria, South Africa.

Strydom, L. (2003). *A sociolinguistic profile of Atteridgeville and Mamelodi, Pretoria.* Unpublished doctoral dissertation. Pretoria, South Africa: University of Pretoria.

van Rensburg, C. (2000). Unpublished workshop report on the unit for language skills development. Pretoria, South Africa: University of Pretoria.

Webb, V. N. (Ed.). (1995). Language in South Africa: An input into language planning for a post-apartheid South Africa. *The LiCCA (SA) Report.* Pretoria, South Africa: University of Pretoria.

Webb, V. N. (1996). English and language planning for South Africa: The flip-side. In V. de Klerk (Ed.), *Varieties of English around the world: Focus on South Africa* (pp. 175–190). Amsterdam/Philadelphia: John Benjamins.

Webb, V. N. (1998). Mutilingualism as a developmental resource: Framework for a research program. In N. M. Kamwamgamalu (Ed.), *Aspects of multilingualism in post-apartheid South Africa. A special issue of Multilingua, 17*(2–3; pp. 125–154). Berlin, Germany: Mouton de Gruyter.

Webb, V. N. (1999). Multilingualism in democratic South Africa: The over-estimation of language policy. *Journal of Educational Development, 19,* 351–366.

Webb, V. N. (2000, September). Constitutional principles and challenges for language policy and language planning in tertiary education. Keynote lecture at the seminar on language policy at the tertiary level. Potchefstroom University for Christian Higher Education, Vaal Triangle Campus, van der Bijl Park, South Africa.

Webb, V. N. (2002a). English as a second language in South Africa's tertiary institutions: A case study at the University of Pretoria. *World Englishes: Special issue on English in South Africa, 21*(1), pp. 49–61.

Webb, V. N. (2002b). *Language in South Africa: The role of language in the transformation, reconstruction and development of South Africa.* Amsterdam/New York: John Benjamins.

Webb, V. N., & Grin, F. (2000). *Language, educational effectiveness and economic outcomes: A research proposal.* Centre for Research on the Politics of Language, Pretoria, South Africa: University of Pretoria.

Webb, V. N., & Kembo-Sure. (Eds.). (2000). *African voices: An introduction to the languages and linguistics of Africa.* Cape Town: Oxford University Press South Africa.

12

Indigenous Language Education in Bolivia and Ecuador: Contexts, Changes, and Challenges

Kendall A. King
Georgetown University

Carol Benson
Stockholm University

The Andean countries of Ecuador and Bolivia hold much in common. Both have sizable indigenous populations, many of which have successfully retained their unique languages and cultures, albeit to varying degrees, throughout more than 500 years of Spanish colonial and post-colonial oppression. Both are home to vast numbers of speakers of Quechua, the largest indigenous language in South America with over 10 million speakers. And both have been overshadowed to some extent by Peru, the largest, most economically powerful Andean nation, and former seat of the Inca empire. Peru is home to the greatest number of indigenous language speakers in South America (6 million), and was the first Andean nation to institute a national bilingual education policy in 1972–1973 (Hornberger & King, 2000).

Although they have received less international attention, Ecuador and Bolivia have more recently undergone significant shifts in language and

241

education policy. These shifts, taking place in the 1980s in Ecuador and the 1990s in Bolivia, reflect greater recognition and respect for the languages and cultures of indigenous groups, as evidenced by educational reforms in which bilingual intercultural education (BIE) is a significant feature. Luykx (2000a, p. 1) notes that these reforms have been "cut from the same cloth," as responses to pressure from indigenous organizations as well as international donors concerned with promoting more democratic and inclusive educational systems. By explicitly including indigenous languages and cultures in public schooling, these new policies reflect the intent to increase indigenous integration into national societies that have long been dominated by Spanish-speaking sectors and to promote pluralistic values among their citizenries.

Despite significant policy shifts, long-term social inequalities have yet to be substantially redressed in the region, in part due to the significant lag in implementation of these measures. As von Gleich observed in the early 1990s, "the gap between even the modest legal status [for Quechua] and implementation is deep" (1992, p. 62). Such gaps exist for other indigenous languages as well; for example, field observations in Bolivia have consistently found significant differences between the innovative, pluralistic discourse of educational reforms involving Quechua, Aymara, and Guaraní and the reality of monolingual Spanish classrooms (Mengoa, 1999).

This chapter explores recent shifts in language education planning in Ecuador and Bolivia, and analyzes reasons for the existing gaps between policy and implementation. Such gaps are of course not unique to the Andean context; indeed, many of the issues addressed by Fishman (1982) in the 1980s concerning the social and educational problems of using nonstandardized languages in education remain relevant today including, for example, the low status of the languages, the lack of adequate materials, and the shortage of trained teachers. Our discussion picks up on many of these themes, with specific attention to how recent bilingual education reforms have influenced pedagogical practice in Andean regions, where the school has long been an exclusively Spanish domain. Specifically, we argue that discontinuities between official policy and everyday practice can be traced to ideological tensions, technical implementation problems, and resource constraints. We begin with some general comments regarding inequality in the Andes before outlining policy shifts specific to each country. We continue with a discussion of reasons for the continued predominance of Spanish-language educational models despite research, theory, and national policy to the contrary, and conclude by discussing directions for the future.

THE ANDEAN CONTEXT

Bolivia and Ecuador share a colonial heritage that has greatly influenced the attitudes of indigenous peoples as well as Spanish-speaking educated elites and *mestizos* (individuals of mixed indigenous and Spanish heritage). Urban Spanish speakers have long dominated culturally, politically, and economically, even while representing a numerical minority in many areas. For instance, Haboud's research (1998) suggests that many (non-indigenous) Ecuadorians consider indigenous languages not part of contemporary Ecuadorian identity, but rather symbols of the past. In Bolivia, Albó (1999) notes that the national society has not yet succeeded in overcoming Spanish colonial structures in which segregation and exclusion persist, and from which indigenous people often feel their only escape is to renounce their indigenous backgrounds and assimilate.

Gaps between recent progressive policies and actual educational practice are intertwined with these attitudinal and identity issues in both countries. Hornberger notes that official use of indigenous languages in school contexts invokes a paradox for educational planners:

> Specifically, there are tensions and contradictions inherent in transforming what has been and continues to be a tool for standardization and national unification into, simultaneously, a vehicle for diversification and emancipation. The paradox is a fundamentally ideological one about roles and responsibilities for multiple languages and their speakers within one national society. (2000, p. 174)

Conflicting ideologies regarding schools, languages, and the role of indigenous people in general are visible throughout our discussion of educational language policy and practice in Ecuador and Bolivia. Equally evident is tension concerning how "bilingual" and "intercultural" education are to be defined and toward which populations these programs should be directed.

The task of implementing reform that provides meaningful education for indigenous students is further complicated by lack of basic resources. Schools throughout the region are characterized by inequalities between urban and rural areas, between Spanish-speaking and indigenous populations, and between boys and girls. These problems are common in ex-colonial countries but are compounded in the Andes, where high altitudes result in extreme temperatures, low crop yields, inadequate sanitation, and distances that are difficult to traverse. As an example, many rural schools suffer from the "Wednesday teacher" syndrome, where teachers who commute weekly from towns are frequently absent due to lack of transportation, low salaries, illness, administrative obligations, or political activities, and in effect may only teach on Wednesdays (d'Emilio, 2001).

Although Ecuador and Bolivia share these and other features, they have followed somewhat distinct trajectories in terms of reform policy, development of BIE, and use of indigenous languages as media of instruction. Their individual characteristics, including key demographic data, are outlined in the next sections.

Ecuador

Roughly one quarter of Ecuador's total population, estimated at 12 million, self-identifies as indigenous (CONAIE, 1989; Haboud, 1998). By far the most widely spoken indigenous language of the country, and indeed the only indigenous language of the highlands, is Quichua. (*Quechua* is the term used to refer to the varieties spoken in Peru, Bolivia, and parts of northern Chile; it is also the cover term for all varieties of the language. In contrast, *Quichua* is used exclusively for varieties in Ecuador.) Eight other indigenous languages are found in much smaller numbers in lowland and coastal regions. As noted previously, indigenous populations have long been economically, culturally, and politically marginalized; there are, however, indications that this is changing in Ecuador. Greater numbers of indigenous persons assume public office and attend institutes of higher education, for example, while simultaneously maintaining indigenous dress (Belote & Belote, 1997; King, 2000). Another clear change is the substantial growth of identity-based political movements. Ecuador has long been home to one of the stronger indigenous organizations in South America, the Confederación de Nacionalidades Indígenas del Ecuador (CONAIE). This political organization was formed in 1986 and officially recognized by the government soon after, hence uniting the distinct indigenous groups across the country and mobilizing cultural and linguistic resistance (von Gleich, 1992).

Due in large part to the efforts of CONAIE in conjunction with pressure from international aid agencies, indigenous language education policy has undergone substantial changes in recent decades. Prior to the 1960s, formal schooling in Ecuador was Spanish-only in terms of medium of instruction and cultural orientation. Aside from resulting in irrelevant curricula and largely ineffective pedagogy, this system also abetted indigenous language shift and cultural assimilation (DINEIB, 1994; PEBI, n.d.). The first official step toward government-supported bilingual education took place in January, 1981, when Decree No. 000529 made BIE official in primary and secondary schools serving predominantly indigenous populations. The second important development took place in 1983, when Article 27 was added to the constitution stipulating that in indigenous regions, the principal language of instruction would be the indigenous language (Yánez Cossío, 1991).

However, despite this new legal footing, there were few specific programs and policies in place to support the practice of bilingual education. It was not until the lack of accord between official policy (which mandated BIE) and educational practice (which apart from a few experimental programs remained unchanged) was repeatedly brought to public attention by CONAIE (among other groups) that serious reforms were implemented

(Moya, 1991). The first of these was the establishment of the Dirección Nacional de Educación Intercultural Bilingüe (DINEIB) in November, 1989. DINEIB was charged with administering schools in areas in which the population is more than half indigenous, and with guaranteeing the unity, quality, and efficiency of indigenous education throughout Ecuador (DINEIIB, 1991).

When DINEIB was established, all educational programs targeting indigenous peoples fell under its jurisdiction; the most important of these programs was the bilingual project known as Proyecto de Educación Bilingüe Intercultural (PEBI), which also operated in Peru (Hornberger, 1988) and in Bolivia under the name PEIB. This project, supported by the German Agency for Technical Cooperation (GTZ), began in Ecuador in 1986 and by 1993 was working in seven Quichua-speaking provinces with 53 pilot schools and about 4000 students (PEBI, n.d.). PEBI emphasized the affirmation of the students' first language and ethnicity, along with the development of intercultural and communicative competence in interacting with other groups. The project used both Spanish and Quichua in the first 6 years of schooling, with heaviest use of the mother tongue in the first 2 years and equal use of Quichua and Spanish from 3rd grade on (Krainer, 1996). Although PEBI ended in 1993, it left behind a wealth of scholastic texts, technical information, and pedagogical experience that continue to shape DINEIB's implementation of BIE in Ecuador.

Bolivia

Bolivia has a proportionately larger indigenous population than Ecuador or any other Andean nation (López, 1995). Of a total population of 8 million, 70% of Bolivians are estimated to be indigenous (Albó, 1995; ETARE, 1993). More than 30 ethnolinguistic groups have been identified, the largest of which are Quechua (2.5 million), Aymara (1.6 million), and Guaraní (60,000; MDH, 1995). The Spanish-speaking *mestizo* population, although a numerical minority, dominates nearly all sectors of society, although some inroads have been made by indigenous peoples, as demonstrated by their participation in higher levels of organization and greater recognition of indigenous issues in national discourse (UNICEF, 1998). However, it is estimated that 70% of the population live in poverty, and that poverty, rural subsistence farming, and indigenous background are highly correlated (ETARE, 1993).

Schooling in Bolivia has traditionally been geared to the needs of Spanish monolinguals; although the indigenous population officially gained access to public education in 1931 (Olstedt, 1995), in practice only a small fraction of the indigenous population attended (Luykx, 1998). An educational reform in 1955 extended schooling to a greater portion of the population, and especially to rural and indigenous peoples, yet failed to take into account their cultural and linguistic diversity (Hyltenstam & Quick, 1996). Until very recently, *castellanización*, meaning the linguistic and cultural assimilation of indigenous peoples into mainstream Spanish-speaking ways, has been an explicit goal of public schooling (ETARE, 1993).

Bilingual schooling in Bolivia, as in many parts of the world, started first with isolated projects such as missionary efforts to teach native-language literacy. According to d'Emilio and Albó (1991), there were a number of isolated experiments in bilingual schooling prior to 1983, but these lacked consistent institutional backing, and were hindered by the social climate. In 1983, the ruling party attempted to address low levels of formal education among indigenous peoples by passing the National Education Plan, which emphasized the need for BIE in the first 8 years of schooling (Hyltenstam & Quick, 1996). According to d'Emilio and Albó (1991), this policy improved the general climate for BIE, but did not result in any concrete changes. As Muñoz Cruz points out, even a 1985 document entitled "Policies and Plan for Rural Bilingual Intercultural Education" failed to connect ideology with methodology, overall objectives with strategies for action, and enthusiasm with capacity to implement change in the classroom (1997). However, this climate of change precipitated planning for a more wide-scale reform.

Parallel to these developments, an experiment known as Proyecto de Educación Intercultural Bilingüe (PEIB) was conducted as part of the PEBI project mentioned previously. This project operated in 140 schools and involved approximately 9,000 primary students, providing mother-tongue instruction in Quechua, Aymara, and Guaraní, and second-language instruction in Spanish (UNICEF, 1998). PEIB attracted numerous researchers and evaluators, many of whom later became involved in implementing BIE when, in 1995, it became part of the educational reform (Gottret, del Granado, Soliz, Perez, & Barreta, 1995; Muñoz Cruz, 1997). As in Ecuador, many of the experiences from the PEIB project have fed into reform implementation, especially in the areas of language standardization, materials development, and teacher training.

These and other efforts culminated in the Educational Reform of 1994, an extremely progressive piece of legislation that calls for BIE for all societal sectors (Benson, 2002; UNICEF, 1998). The reform stresses official recognition of all Bolivian languages (ETARE, 1993) and the need for mutual respect among all Bolivians (CEBIAE, 1998) through bilingual intercultural education. The intercultural aspect has been promoted as a means of increasing mutual understanding, equality, and democracy among students. The accompanying Law of Popular Participation, also in effect from 1994, involves community and indigenous organizations in educational decision-making, sometimes creating new organizations to replace pre-existing ones, and decentralizes school management. This legislation provides the architecture of the Bolivian Education Reform that is presently undergoing implementation.

INDIGENOUS LANGUAGES AS MEDIA OF INSTRUCTION

Within the field of language planning, policies regarding the medium of instruction are perhaps most clearly a form of acquisition planning. Acquisition planning can be distinguished from status and corpus planning by the means employed to attain particular language-planning goals; specifically, acquisition planning is accomplished by creating or improving the opportunities and/or incentives to learn a language (Cooper, 1989). Within Hornberger's integrative framework (1994), acquisition planning goals potentially involve policy planning (targeting education/school, literature, religion, or mass media) or cultivation planning (with the aim of reacquisition, maintenance, foreign/second language learning, or shift). Concomitantly, medium-of-instruction policies potentially incorporate both status planning (e.g., BIE policies can address issues of language maintenance and language status) and corpus planning (e.g., use of indigenous languages in school often entails language standardization). In the Andean context, use of indigenous languages as media of instruction is often a tool for maintaining or even revitalizing indigenous languages. For instance, Ecuador's DINEIB specifies that a major aim of BIE involves "cultivating and recuperating the mother tongue" (DINEIIB 1991, p. 36, translation ours).

Adoption of a medium of instruction that students comprehend is also effective pedagogy, independent of language-planning goals. This perspective rests on a number of widely cited principles including the efficacy of first-language literacy instruction (Skutnabb-Kangas, 2000); the transferability of skills from the first language to the second (Cummins, 2001; Krashen, 1996); and the interdependence of first- and second-language competence (Ramírez, Yuen, & Ramey, 1991; Thomas & Collier, 2002). Taken together, these principles indicate that the best pedagogical approach for monolingual indigenous language speakers in the Andes would be to teach beginning literacy and content in the first language; to gradually introduce Spanish as a second language; and to continue developing the mother tongue in parallel with Spanish throughout primary school. These principles are evident in BIE policy documents; for example, the Bolivian Educational Reform promotes a "maintenance and development" model that includes continued study of the mother tongue for academic reasons even after transitioning to content instruction in Spanish (UNICEF, 1998).

Despite substantial policy, theory, and research supporting systematic, meaningful, and extensive use of students' first language, there is a tendency worldwide, and perhaps especially in post-colonial countries with limited technical and economic resources, to circumvent established models of bilingual education and take a "short cut" to the official language, transitioning to the prestige language after 1 or 2 years (Benson, 2002). This tendency is bolstered by popular wisdom and public opinion as both parents and policymakers prioritize use of the official language in school and believe wholeheartedly in its necessity for students' futures (Stroud, 2002). Choice of such short cut models often rests on the "time-on-task" myth (i.e., greater exposure equals greater competence). Although there is ample research that exposes this myth (Krashen, 1996), the pedagogical principles of bilingual education appear counterintuitive to many, and indeed, often must be seen to be believed.

CHALLENGES TO INDIGENOUS LANGUAGES AS MEDIA OF INSTRUCTION

As noted previously, the gap between public policy and political rhetoric on the one hand, and pedagogical implementation on the other, is often substantial. In the next section, we outline what we see to be the major challenges to full implementation of indigenous media of instruction, including the dearth of resources available for indigenous languages, questions of language standardization, divergent interpretations of "bilingual" and "intercultural," and complications surrounding decentralization and local authority over indigenous schools. This overview is not intended to be comprehensive, but rather to provide examples of key obstacles to meaningful use of indigenous languages in the Andes. It is our hope that this discussion will shed light on some of the counterproductive forces at work, as well as the means to overcome them.

Human and Material Resources

A central issue in expanding the use of indigenous languages in education in the region is the cultivation of qualified bilingual teachers (Abram, 1989). In Ecuador, for example, this has long been recognized as a major challenge. In response, CONAIE, DINEIB, and PEBI have established intensive, accelerated programs to train teachers (Yánez Cossío, 1991). This is similar to the situation in Bolivia, where the PEIB project extensively promoted bilingual teacher training, sending many trainers to a regional bilingual center in Puno, Peru (López, 1995). However, wide-scale implementation of BIE requires a critical mass of trained bilingual teachers, something that neither country, despite these and other significant efforts, has yet succeeded in cultivating.

The lack of qualified bilingual teachers is not surprising considering the traditionally low status and levels of formal education associated with indigenous sectors, as well as the limited salaries earned by rural teachers in general. The Bolivian Ministry of Education has recently taken measures to address this problem by introducing monetary supplements for teaching in rural areas, for teaching multi-grade classrooms, and for teaching bilingually (Benson, 2001; Öström, Benson, & Vargas, 2001). For most bilingual teachers, two or three of these supplements apply, substantially increasing their incomes. In addition, to address the severe shortage of trained bilingual teachers, which results in widespread employment of *interinos* (untrained "emergency" teachers), the Ministry is piloting a *Bachillerato Pedagógico* (a high school degree in education), designed to simultaneously provide secondary schooling and teacher training, and to attract future teachers with indigenous backgrounds (Albó, 2000; Moya, 1999; Öström, Benson, & Vargas 1998).

Even where basic training and recruitment issues are addressed, ideological forces potentially undermine use of the indigenous language in the classroom. As Dauenhauer and Dauenhauer (1998) note, there is often disparity between expressed ideals and actual support for indigenous languages, which in their view often results from deeply embedded ideologies concerning the language. Indigenous teachers might sharply recall their own punishment and embarrassment for using their language in school. Bilingual teachers also may harbor doubts about the suitability of the language for academic use, or feel insecure about their own language skills. Other teachers may question, as Luykx does (2000a), the assumption that formal school initiatives are key to indigenous language maintenance, and instead believe that home transmission is more appropriate.

Even among teachers who support BIE, there is often a lack of full understanding of how to use indigenous languages for beginning literacy and content instruction (Arnold, Yapita, & López, 1999), as well as teaching methods in Spanish as a second language (Moya, 1999). As an evaluator of the Bolivian PEIB experiment noted, failure to fully develop both languages limits the potential transfer of skills (Muñoz Cruz, 1997). These misunderstandings can be at least partially attributed to the fact that indigenous teachers are products of submersion models, where Spanish was used for all school teaching, where use of the mother tongue was prohibited and punishable, and where students had to "sink or swim" through repetition and memorization (Skutnabb-Kangas, 2000). Confusion over the teaching of Spanish as a first or second language is evident in Bolivia, for example, where there has been disagreement among educational technicians regarding whether the same set of Spanish materials can be used for native speakers and second-language learners (Moya, 1999).

This issue remains current in Bolivia; at a conference on the teaching of Spanish as a second language in August 2000, input was requested from international experts on this and other questions. Hornberger describes the conference as an unprecedented open discussion and debate, and remarks that curricula developers chose a "richly communicative and literature-based...design" (2002, p. 4). She also expresses the concerns of many present that the materials lack consideration of second-language development processes. Benson, who also attended the conference, concurs but was concerned that Ministry technicians charged with developing Reform materials were both pressured for time and challenged to process the large amount of input they received during the conference. During a visit to Bolivia 6 months after the conference, Benson found that the discussion remained at the same level: Some still felt one set of Spanish materials would suffice for all students, while others were busy writing supplementary materials for the bilingual teachers whom they felt would be unable (without extensive training) to make use of the materials to teach Spanish as a second language (Benson, 2001; Öström et al., 2001). Although these technicians are highly competent in many respects, it seems that general lack of experience with second-language methodology influences implementation even at these high levels.

Standardization and Unification of Indigenous Languages

A second important challenge to greater use of indigenous languages as media of instruction in the region stems from complications with the standardization of indigenous languages and development of pedagogical materials. The example of Quichua in Ecuador is illustrative. The process of standardizing Quichua was formally initiated in 1981 when representatives of the different Ecuadorian varieties of Quichua agreed on a unified variety (Montaluisa, 1980, as cited in von Gleich, 1994). Quichua language planners, most of whom were indigenous political and education leaders, made decisions in two areas: a unified writing system, consisting of 20 consonants and 3 vowels; and lexical modernization and purification, primarily through replacement of Spanish loan words with neologisms. These decisions were codified in subsequent dictionaries and grammars (CONAIE, 1990; MEC, 1982) and constituted a major step toward the standardization of Ecuadorian Quichua, known as *Quichua Unificado,* whose aims included facilitating the development of Quichua materials, and contributing to the maintenance and even revitalization of the language. Despite the new written standard, it was expected that the regional varieties would continue to exist in their spoken forms (CONAIE, 1990). In practice, however, these aims have proved elusive. For instance, King (1999b, 2000) reports that as Quichua materials have been introduced into some Quichua-Spanish bilingual communities in the southern highlands, two distinct Quichua varieties have emerged. The Quichua pedagogical materials promote the nationally standardized variety (*Quichua Unificado*); this stands in contrast to what is commonly referred to as *Quichua auténtico,* spoken by elderly and rural dwellers. Because children and young adults studying *Quichua Unificado* have not mastered the phonological system or the lexicon of the local variety, they learn not only to read but to speak *Quichua Unificado*. Although the varieties are mutually intelligible to most, there are clashes and gaps in communication between the older and younger Quichua speakers; such tensions undermine Quichua use and exacerbate generational and social divisions.

In the case of Bolivian Quechua, debates have, until recently, proceeded parallel to those of neighboring countries and have focused on issues such as whether Quechua has three vowels or five (Quiróz, 2000). At the Second International Congress of Aymara and Quechua Languages and Cultures (November 2000), one resolution was to seek "local consensus" before working for regional (Andean) consensus, so that linguistic efforts continue to support BIE in practical ways (UNICEF, 2000). Indeed, materials production has proceeded as part of the Reform, and local authors are currently preparing materials in a number of minority languages of the Bolivian Amazon (L.E. López, personal communication, 2000). Benson (2002) has pointed out the general need for bilingual programs to move ahead with materials development and not wait for linguists to agree. In a similar vein, Luykx questions the assumption that standardization of the written form is essential to Quechua's expanded use (2000a). She maintains that in practice the emphasis on standardization tends to shift resources away from those domains that are Quechua's stronghold, toward those where its disadvantage relative to Spanish is greatest; to prioritize concerns of linguists over those of most Quechua speakers; and to link dialectal variation with status and class hierarchies. The result is that standardization tends to undermine meaningful use of indigenous languages in communities and schools. Although standardization has long been viewed as an important means to improving status and prestige (Hornberger & King, 1996; Stewart, 1968), it seems appropriate to question whether it is essential to the establishment of successful bilingual education programs.

Interpretations of Bilingualism and Interculturalism

A third issue in relation to the challenges of using indigenous languages as media of instruction pertains to the considerable lack of clarity concerning how "bilingual" and "intercultural" are operationalized. These tensions have played out differently in the two nations, although common threads exist.

Not unlike early formulations of bilingual education policy in the United States (Crawford, 1999), legislation in Ecuador provides few specifics concerning how bilingual education should be defined and how Spanish and Quechua should be balanced within and across grades. For instance, DINEIB outlines the primary goal of BIE as "contributing to the affirmation of the cultural identity of people of Ecuador," altering the relationships and attitudes among peoples and groups, and contributing "to the development of a process of reflection which is the basis of a sustained and creative dialogue between cultures" (DINEIIB, 1991, p. 25, translation ours). DINEIB does not specify media of instruction, but rather states that "the process of indigenous education involves cultivating and recuperating the mother tongue and learning the second language as a means of intercommunication with other cultures" (DINEIIB, 1991, p. 36, translation ours).

According to Krainer, in the Ecuadorian context, the use of the word "bilingual" reflects recognition of the fact that within the society there are diverse forms of expression and communication. Thus, "the process of bilingual education supports the teaching and use of indigenous languages and Spanish in a manner which develops both languages lexically and stylistically with the aim of converting them into multifunctional languages" (1996, p. 26, translation ours). From this perspective, "bilingual" education is concerned not only with the use and instruction of indigenous languages within schools, but as noted earlier, with the corpus and status development of indigenous and Spanish languages.

Likewise, "intercultural" education is also open to interpretation. Krainer (1996) defines intercultural education as that which affirms one's social and conceptual universe, but also permits the selective and critical appropriation of cultural elements of other groups. Haboud (2000) argues that interculturalism refers to relations and interactions between two separate cultures, as well as the political task of constructing an egalitarian society. However, as Haboud (2000) and Hornberger (2000) have noted, interculturalism in Ecuador has generally been treated as an issue that is exclusive to the indigenous population.

In Bolivia, interculturalism is an explicit aim of the Reform policy, which mandates intercultural training for all. Unfortunately, this component has yet to be operationalized or implemented, although there are a number of excellent proposals for how to do so (Albó, 1999; CEBIAE, 1998; Mengoa, 1999; Moya, 1999). Teaching indigenous languages as second languages to Spanish speakers could be effective in increasing sensitivity; and indeed it could be argued that if a more democratic and equitable society is to be promoted by the schools, it is precisely the Spanish speakers who require such training. There have been a few moves in this direction; for instance, a small number of public schools in Bolivia have replaced French with Quechua for second/foreign language instruction, and Quechua classes are required for university majors such as law, medicine, and agronomy (A. Luykx, personal communication, January 27, 2002). Unfortunately, there is a distinct lag in implementation of bilingual programs in the larger towns and cities (Moya, 1999), even where there are higher concentrations of indigenous language speakers. In response to criticisms of this nature, Reform advocates explain that the priority is on rural indigenous areas where educational quality is arguably lowest. However, it is clear that although BIE is intended to promote respect for the worldviews and cultural practices of nondominant social groups (Luykx, 2000a), there is no demand from the dominant social group for this type of teaching; as Abram has observed in Ecuador, "there is not the slightest interest among *mestizos* in learning Quichua" (1989, p. 423).

Decentralization, Democratization, and Local Authority

A final issue relates to the delegation of authority to indigenous groups to control their own schools, which is part of the move to decentralize and democratize government administration. In Ecuador, in the months after the establishment of DINEIB, an agreement of technical cooperation allocated high-level DINEIB positions to CONAIE representatives. In collaboration with CONAIE, DINEIB's responsibilities include developing bilingual intercultural education curricula, designing education programs for the indigenous population, promoting the production and use of didactic materials, and supporting the maintenance and spread of *Quichua Unificado* (DINEIIB, 1991). In order to administer the diverse and numerous indigenous schools across the country, DINEIB established 21 provincial directorates responsible for locally administering indigenous schools. The allocation of funds and authority to DINEIB marked the first time "in the educational history of Latin America that a Hispanic government allowed and supported the establishment of an independent educational administration" (von Gleich, 1994, p. 96). However, these shifts have created new tensions at the local level; King (2000) reports, for instance, that in certain regions this has resulted in power struggles among regional indigenous political organizations, in some cases inhibiting the implementation of effective BIE.

Also important to note is that greater local control of indigenous schooling and increased numbers of indigenous teachers do not necessarily or immediately translate into substantial use of indigenous languages in the classroom. King's (2000) study of two communities in southern Ecuador suggests that although Quichua is employed regularly in schools for symbolic purposes (e.g., greetings, taking attendance), it is taught only occasionally and can in no way be considered a medium of instruction. One dynamic that seems to be in play is that the frequent symbolic use of Quichua in school, in contrast to its total absence prior to the reforms, obfuscates the limited academic and communicative use of the language.

In the case of the Bolivian Reform, despite the democratic aims of decentralization and popular participation, the Ministry of Education maintains a tight hold on most aspects of the transformation of traditional schools to Reform schools, although indigenous individuals are highly involved at many levels. One avenue for indigenous participation is through the four CEPOs (*Consejos Educativos de los Pueblos Originarios*), which were formed during the 1990s to represent Quechua, Aymara, Guaraní, and speakers of various Amazonian languages in national educational concerns. The CEPOs have been instrumental in garnering community support for BIE, promoting linguistic development and training of teachers and writers, and organizing the Reform-mandated school boards at the school, district, and departmental levels. However, their relationship to the Ministry of Education is undefined; their autonomous status simultaneously protects them from government politics and leaves them at the mercy of international donors for salaries and support, and the Ministry is not required to incorporate their advice (Albó, 2000; Moya, 1999).

In addition, decentralization according to the 1994 Law of Popular Participation in Bolivia has altered the organization of public services at local levels. Each municipal prefecture has a designated representative for various social issues including education, and the prefecture budget must demonstrate spending within each social category including education (UNICEF, 1998). This is designed to allow for greater local control of government resources and increased local administrative capacity (Öström et al., 1998, 2001). In terms of the Education Reform, participation takes the form of local *juntas escolares* or school boards whose representatives participate in municipal and departmental *juntas* as well (UNICEF, 1998). These boards decide on a wide range of issues, including curriculum development and personnel. However, formation of the *juntas* has often been mandated from above and proved extremely bureaucratic. In addition, where *juntas* exist, there are inevitable power struggles among parents, teachers, school directors, and other community members, none of whom are sure how far their power extends (Moya, 1999).

Despite these moves toward decentralization, the Bolivian Education Reform has remained heavily centralized, for instance, in orchestrating teacher training and curriculum development. At Ministry offices, three bilingual technicians (one each for Guaraní, Quechua, and Aymara), one technician for Spanish as a second language, and a few pedagogical technicians are worked beyond their capabilities (Benson, 2001; Moya, 1999), designing curricula, writing materials, and traveling widely to train teachers. Their whirlwind training tours are designed to impart the goals of the Reform, for which they feel great responsibility and ownership (Benson, 2001). Sharing this feeling of ownership with others could be their greatest challenge.

Although it is clear that indigenous groups are gaining ground, it seems equally clear that there are limits to their power in the schools. In Ecuador, there are long-standing complaints that too little support is given to DINEIB programs, and that the indigenous population "has remained on the outside of public administration" (Yánez Cossío, 1991, p. 63). In Bolivia, some important public spaces for indigenous participation have also been created, but indigenous groups like the CEPOs continue to struggle for definition (Benson, 2001; Moya, 1999). In addition, it appears that lack of experience with a democratic, decentralized administrative system may render popular participation an elusive goal.

FUTURE DIRECTIONS

In this chapter, we have provided a number of examples of reform efforts, as well as conditions that frustrate their implementation. One could ask at this point whether the educational language policies in Ecuador and Bolivia represent real shifts truly aimed at equalizing educational access and social relations, or are merely rhetorical ploys (cf. Hornberger, 2000; Luykx, 1996). The most pessimistic interpretation would suggest that these policies were introduced to satisfy demands of indigenous groups and international donors while maintaining the status quo through under-resourcing implementation, thus implying conscious effort to demonstrate good will, while systematically undermining progressive goals. We do not believe this is the case, given the many well-intentioned policies and people in both countries who are dedicated to the principles of democratic reform and to inclusion of indigenous peoples, cultures, and languages. Also noteworthy in this regard is the fact that these policy reforms are part of broader shifts taking place in the Andean nations and beyond. As Luykx notes, BIE can be understood as "but one manifestation of a wider political current that embraces a nebulous constellation of 'progressive' issues: cultural and linguistic pluralism, various criticisms of capitalism and racism, freedom of personal and political expression, revision of academic canons, etc." (2000b, p. 152).

We believe that there are many reasons to continue to support BIE programs, not the least of which are that they are the most pedagogically sound and that they potentially facilitate indigenous language and cultural maintenance. A major issue is overcoming diverse sources of opposition and adverse conditions so that BIE can function pedagogically and politically. As we have seen, opposition comes from many different fronts, including not only Spanish-speaking elites, but also indigenous people who value schooling in Spanish and see it as their escape from further discrimination, and teachers who may have divergent views concerning the appropriate contexts for indigenous language use and need for training and experience. Nonetheless, slow but steady progress has been made in many arenas, and in particular can be seen in the growing access of indigenous organizations to power in decision-making; the greater visibility of indigenous languages and cultures; and the increasing pride indigenous peoples have for their own languages and cultures. These trends are clearly intertwined; as von Gleich notes, increased indigenous organization in Ecuador has meant "an increase of Quichua loyalty, [and] a higher degree of linguistic consciousness reflected in the use of the unified standard in oral mass media and by school teachers" (1992, p. 57).

Despite some real gains in educational outcomes (cf. d'Emilio, 2001; Hyltenstam & Quick, 1996; Muñoz Cruz, 1997), there is a sense of urgency among reform advocates, in part motivated by a fear of backlash. In Bolivia, for example, the Reform has thus far survived three political administrations, demonstrating that some continuity is possible (Contreras, 1999, p. 47); however, there is concern that more progress must be made to guarantee success of the Reform (Moya, 1999; Reforma Educativa, 2000; UNICEF, 2000), and that there is danger of losing critical political or ideological momentum. For example, Hovens (2003) observes that in Niger, bilingual schools that were once successful have been kept in experimental status for more than 20 years and allowed to deteriorate, so that the consequent poor quality of schools has largely eroded parents' support (see Alidou, chap. 10, this volume). On the other hand, Peru provides a now classic example of attempting to go too far too fast, when in the 1970s sweeping reforms officialized Quechua and made its instruction mandatory for Spanish speakers, resulting in such a negative reaction from the Spanish-speaking majority that the idea was immediately dropped (Hornberger & King, 2000). Although balancing between these two extremes is difficult, Hornberger has recently urged linguists, educators, and researchers to "work hard alongside language planners and language users to fill the ideological and implementational spaces opened up by multilingual language policies" (2002, p. 19), correctly implying that these spaces will not always be available.

In summary, although there are innumerable challenges to indigenous language education in the Andes, advocates of bilingual intercultural education—and of access, democracy, and pluralism—should not be disheartened. Indigenous groups and individuals are increasingly taking on leadership roles and administrative responsibilities in reform efforts. Many indigenous languages have written forms and are now used in literacy and basic schooling. Increasing numbers of indigenous people are becoming literate in their mother tongues or learning the mother tongues of their grandparents, while the presence of indigenous languages in a once exclusively Spanish domain confers prestige on both the languages and their users. Although the gaps between policy and practice remain frustratingly wide, many important small steps have been made, and continued progress into this new, uncharted territory seems likely to follow. In the words of the poet, Antonio Machado:

Caminante, no hay camino:
Se hace camino al andar

Traveler, there is no road:
The road is made by walking

(excerpt from the poem "Caminante ... " by Antonio Machado,
1875–1938; see Machado, 1994).

ACKNOWLEDGMENTS

This chapter draws on King's research on language policy and ideology
as they relate to educational practice in Ecuador (1999a, 1999b, 2000),
and Benson's extensive experience in teacher training and evaluation of
bilingual programs in Bolivia (1999, 2001, 2002). We thank Nancy
Hornberger and Aurolyn Luykx for their thoughtful comments on an
earlier version of this chapter.

REFERENCES

Abram, M. (1989). El papel de las organizaciones indígenas en la educación [The
role of indigenous organizations in education]. In E. Lopez & R. Moya (Eds.),
Pueblos indios, estados, y educación [Indian peoples, states, and education] (pp.
309–326). Lima: PEB/PEBI/PERA.
Albó, X. (1995). Bolivia plurilingüe. Guia para planificadores y educadores [Pluri-
lingual Bolivia. Guide for planners and educators]. *Cuadernos de Investigación*,
44(1–2). La Paz: UNICEF/CIPCA.
Albó, X. (1999). *Iguales aunque diferentes* [Equal but different]. La Paz, Bolivia:
Ministerio de Educación/UNICEF/CIPCA.
Albó, X. (2000). *Evaluación del componente "Apoyo a la educación intercultural bilingüe
en tierras bajas de Bolivia"* [Evaluation of the component "Support for bilingual
intercultural education in the lowlands of Bolivia"]. La Paz, Bolivia: CIPCA.
Arnold, D., Yapita, J., & López, G. R. (1999). Leer y escribir en aymara bajo la Reforma
[To read and write in Aymara under the reform]. *T'inkazos, 2*(3), 103–115.
Belote, J., & Belote, L. (1997). *The Saraguros, 1962–1997: A very brief overview.* Re-
trieved from http://www.saraguro.org/overview.htm
Benson, C. (1999). *Informe final sobre la asistencia técnica al Proyecto de EIB, UNICEF*
[Final report concerning technical assistance to the EIB UNICEF project]. La Paz,
Bolivia: UNICEF.
Benson, C. (2001). *Internal report on the EIB Project.* La Paz, Bolivia: Sida.
Benson, C. (2002). Real and potential benefits of bilingual programmes in developing
countries. *International Journal of Bilingual Education and Bilingualism, 5*(6), 303–317.
Centro Boliviano de Investigación y Acción Educativas. (1998). *Diversidad cultural y
procesos educativos* [Cultural diversity and educational processes]. La Paz,
Bolivia: CEBIAE.

Confederación de Nacionalidades Indígenas del Ecuador. (1989). *Las nacionalidades indígenas en el Ecuador: Nuestro proceso organizativo* [The indigenous nationalities of Ecuador: Our organizational process]. Quito, Ecuador: Tincui/Abya-Yala.

Confederación de Nacionalidades Indígenas del Ecuador. (1990). *Ñucanchic shimi 1* [Our language 1]. Quito, Ecuador: MEC/DINEIIB/CONAIE.

Contreras, M. (1999). El conflicto entre maestros/as y gobierno [The conflict between teachers and the government]. *T'inkazos, 2*(4), 47–54.

Cooper, R. L. (1989). *Language planning and social change.* Cambridge, UK: Cambridge University Press.

Crawford, J. (1999). *Bilingual education: History, politics, theory, and practice.* Los Angeles: Bilingual Education Services.

Cummins, J. (2001). *Language, power and pedagogy: Bilingual children in the crossfire.* Clevedon, UK: Multilingual Matters.

Dauenhauer, N. M., & Dauenhauer, R. (1998). Technical, emotional, and ideological issues in reversing language shift: Examples from Southeast Alaska. In L. A. Grenoble & L. J. Whaley (Eds.), *Endangered languages: Current issues and future prospects* (pp. 57–116). Cambridge, UK: Cambridge University Press.

d'Emilio, L. (2001). *Voices and processes toward pluralism: Indigenous education in Bolivia.* Stockholm, Sweden: Sida.

d'Emilio, L., & Albó, X. (1991). Las lenguas en la educación formal y no formal en Bolivia. [Languages in formal and informal education in Bolivia]. *Arinsana, 13,* 43–63.

Dirección Nacional de Educación Intercultural Indígena Bilingüe. (1991). La educación intercultural bilingüe en el Ecuador [Bilingual intercultural education in Ecuador]. *Pueblos Indígenas y Educación, 17,* 31–67.

Dirección Nacional de Educación Intercultural Bilingüe. (1994). Modelo de educación intercultural bilingüe [The model of bilingual intercultural education]. *Pueblos Indígenas y Educación, 29–30,* 5–142.

ETARE (Equipo Técnico de Apoyo a la Reforma Educativa). (1993). *Reforma Educativa. Propuesta* (Cuadernos de la Reforma Educativa) [Educational reform. Proposal (Notes on the Educational Reform)]. La Paz, Bolivia: ETARE.

Fishman, J. (1982). Sociolinguistic foundations of bilingual education. *The Bilingual Review/La Revista Bilingüe, 9*(1), 1–35.

Gottret, G., del Granado, T., Soliz, W., Perez, B., & Barreta, B. (1995). *Proyecto de Educación Intercultural Bilingüe. Evaluación longitudinal* [The bilingual intercultural education project. Longitudinal evaluation] . La Paz, Bolivia: Servicio de Investigación Pedagógica.

Haboud, M. (1998). *Quichua y Castellano en los Andes Ecuatorianos: Los efectos de un contacto prolongado* [Quichua and Spanish in the Ecuadorian Andes: The effects of prolonged contact]. Quito, Ecuador: Ediciones Abya-Yala.

Haboud, M. (2000). *Interculturalidad y sordera visual.* [Interculturalism and visual deafness]. Unpublished document.

Hornberger, N. (1988). *Bilingual education and language maintenance.* Providence, RI: Foris Publications.

Hornberger, N. (1994). Literacy and language planning. *Language and Education, 8*(1–2), 75–86.

Hornberger, N. (2000). Bilingual education policy and practice in the Andes: Ideological paradox and intercultural possibility. *Anthropology and Education Quarterly, 31*(2), 173–201.

Hornberger, N. (2002). Multilingual language policies and the continua of biliteracy: An ecological approach. *Language Policy, 1*(1), 27–51.

Hornberger, N., & King, K. (1996). Language revitalisation in the Andes: Can the schools reverse language shift? *Journal of Multilingual and Multicultural Development, 17*(6), 427–441.

Hornberger, N., & King, K. (2000). Reversing Quechua language shift in South America. In J. Fishman (Ed.), *Can threatened languages be saved? Reversing language shift revisited* (pp. 166–194). Clevedon, Avon, UK: Multilingual Matters Press.

Hovens, M. (2003). *Enseignment primaire bilingue: Deux expériences ouest-africaines* [Primary bilingual education: Two West African experiences]. Niamey, Niger: Albasa/GTZ.

Hyltenstam, K., & Quick, B. (1996). *Fact finding mission to Bolivia in the area of bilingual primary education.* Stockholm, Sweden: Sida.

King, K. (1999a). Language revitalization processes and prospects: Quichua in the Ecuadorian Andes. *Language and Education, 13*(1), 17–37.

King, K. A. (1999b). Inspecting the unexpected: Language corpus and status shifts as aspects of language revitalization. *Language Problems and Language Planning, 23*(2), 109–132.

King, K. (2000). *Language revitalization processes and prospects: Quichua in the Ecuadorian Andes.* Clevedon, UK: Multilingual Matters Press.

Krainer, A. (1996). *Educación intercultural bilingüe en el Ecuador* [Bilingual intercultural education in Ecuador]. Quito, Ecuador: Ediciones Abya–Yala.

Krashen, S. (1996). *Under attack: The case against bilingual education.* Culver City, CA: Language Education Associates.

López, L. E. (1995). *La educación en áreas indígenas de América Latina: Apreciaciones comparativas desde la educación bilingüe intercultural.* [Education in indigenous areas of Latin America: Comparative observations of bilingual intercultural education]. Guatemala City, Guatemala: Centro de Estudios de la Cultura Maya.

Luykx, A. (1996). From *indios* to *professionales*: Stereotypes and student resistance in Bolivian teacher training. In B. Levinson, D. Foley, & D. Holland (Eds.), *Cultural production and the educated person: Critical ethnographies of schooling and local practice* (pp. 239–272). Albany, NY: SUNY Press.

Luykx, A. (1998). *The citizen factory: Schooling and cultural production in Bolivia.* Albany, NY: SUNY Press.

Luykx, A. (2000a). *Diversity in the new world order: State language policies and the internationalization of Quechua.* Paper presented at the 2nd Spencer Early Career Institute in Anthropology and Education: Globalization and Education. Chicago, IL.

Luykx, A. (2000b). Gender equity and *interculturalidad*: The dilemma in Bolivian education. *The Journal of Latin American Anthropology, 5*(2), 150–178.

Machado, A. (1994). *Poesías completas* [Complete poetic works]. Edición Manuel Alvar. Madrid, Spain: Espasa Calpe.

Ministerio de Desarrollo Humano (1995). *Reforma Educativa. Nuevos programas de estudio de la Reforma Educativa* [The Educational Reform. New research studies of the Educational Reform]. La Paz, Bolivia: MDH/SNE/UNSTP/UNICOM.

Ministerio de Educación y Cultura (1982). *Caimi ñucanchic Shimiyuc-Panca* [Our Quichua language dictionary]. Quito, Ecuador: MEC/PUCE.

Mengoa, N. (Ed.). (1999). *Interculturalidad y calidad de los aprendizajes en ámbitos urbanos* [Interculturalism and learning quality in urban contexts]. La Paz, Bolivia: CEBIAE.

Montaluisa, L. O. (1980). El vocabulario general de la lengua Quichua para el Ecuador [General vocabulary of Ecuadorian Quichua]. *Revista de la Universidad Católica, 25*, 99–119.

Moya, R. (1991). Un decenio de educación bilingüe y participación indígena: Ecuador [A decade of bilingual education and indigenous participation]. *Pueblos Indígenas y Educación, 17*, 4–25.

Moya, R. (1999). *Informe para el gobierno de Suecia sobre la evaluación de la Reforma Educativa de la gestión de 1999: Componente de Educación Intercultural Bilingüe* [Report for the Swedish government on the evaluation of the Education Reform during 1999: Bilingual intercultural education component]. La Paz, Bolivia: Sida.

Muñoz Cruz, H. (1997). *De proyecto a política de estado: La Educación Intercultural Bilingüe en Bolivia, 1993* [From project to state policy: Bilingual intercultural education in Bolivia, 1993]. La Paz, Bolivia: UNICEF.

Olstedt, A. C. (1995). *Studie av undervisningssektorn i Bolivia* [Study of the Bolivian education sector]. Stockholm, Sweden: Sida.

Öström, N., Benson, C., & Vargas, G. (1998). *Appraisal of UNICEF project proposals for rural development in Bolivia 1999–2001. Mission report.* Stockholm, Sweden: Sida.

Öström, N., Benson, C., & Vargas, G. (2001). *Monitoreo de proyectos de UNICEF apoyados por Suecia en Bolivia.* [Monitoring of UNICEF projects supported by Sweden in Bolivia]. *Mission report to Ministry of Education, UNICEF/Sida.* Stockholm, Sweden: Stockholm Group for Development Studies.

PEBI (Proyecto de Educación Bilingüe Intercultural) (n.d.). Proyecto de Educación Bilingüe Intercultural [The bilingual intercultural education project] (Informative brochure). Quito, Ecuador PEBI.

Quiróz, A. (2000). *Gramática Quechua* [Quechua Grammar]. La Paz, Bolivia: UNICEF.

Ramírez, J., Yuen, S., & Ramey, D. (1991). *Executive summary: Final report: Longitudinal study of structured English immersion strategy, early-exit and late-exit transitional bilingual education programs of language-minority children (Contract No. 300-87-0156).* Washington, DC: US Department of Education.

Reforma Educativa. (2000). *Programa de Reforma Educativa. Donación de Suecia. Julio 2000-Diciembre 2003* [Educational Reform program: Swedish support July 2000–December 2003]. La Paz, Bolivia: Viceministerio de Educación Inicial, Primaria y Secundaria.

Skutnabb-Kangas, T. (2000). *Linguistic genocide in education. Or worldwide diversity and human rights?* Mahwah, NJ: Lawrence Erlbaum Associates.

Stewart, W. (1968). A [...] lingualism. In J. Fish[...] The Hague, Netherla[...]

Stroud, C. (2002). *Towar[...] education division d[...]

Thomas, W. P., & Collier, [...] *nority students' long-te[...]

UNICEF (1998). *Propuesta [...] posal for bilingual int[...] UNICEF.

UNICEF (2000). *Conclusi[...] Aymara y Quechua* [Su[...] and Aymara languages [...]

von Gleich, U. (1992). Chan[...] & M. Hellinger (Eds.), *S[...] de Gruyter.

von Gleich, U. (1994). Lang[...] republics of Bolivia, Ecu[...] *Language, 107*, 77–113.

Yánez Cossío, C. (1991). The [...] dor. *International Review o[...]*

13

Medium of Instruction in Slovenia: European Integration and Ethnolinguistic Nationalism

James W. Tollefson
University of Washington

In recent years, medium-of-instruction policies have become particularly important in the new states emerging from the breakup of the Soviet Union and the end of communist control of Eastern Europe. A number of language-policy analysts have noted that both dominant and nondominant ethnolinguistic groups in these new states have been affected by two competing forces (see Blommaert, 1996; Phillipson, 2000). One force is *globalization*, a general term referring to economic, political, cultural, and social changes that result in increasing integration. In Europe, integration is particularly advanced, with the adoption of a common currency and financial system, an integrated media network, and increasingly powerful institutions of the European Union. A second, contradictory force has also arisen, however, partly in a response to the movement toward integration. This second force is the rise of ethnolinguistic nationalism, manifest in movements by ethnolinguistic groups seeking official status and protection for their language varieties as well as in the dissolution of multi-ethnic and multilingual states. Particularly important examples of dissolution are the Soviet Union and Czechoslovakia (which broke up relatively peacefully) and Yugoslavia (which suffered enormous violence). Other examples include movements for autonomy or independence among ethnolinguistic minorities in Spain, Bulgaria, Romania, Slovakia, Turkey, and elsewhere.

Existing states have responded to these centrifugal movements with a variety of policies, including reassertion of the dominant language in education (e.g., the United Kingdom), official-language laws (e.g., Slovakia), immigration restrictions and ultranationalist movements (e.g., France, Italy), martial law (e.g., Kosovo in the 1980s and 1990s), and military repression (e.g., Turkey). Institutions of a united Europe have been active in encouraging various forms of pluralism as an appropriate response to ethnolinguistic nationalism. The Council of Europe has been particularly vocal in arguing that pluralist policies are an effective strategy for managing conflict in states buffeted by the combined forces of globalization and ethnolinguistic nationalism, and it has encouraged a discourse of language rights in cultural and educational policy of member states as well as those seeking membership.

The new state of Slovenia, formed from the breakup of Yugoslavia, has been especially outspoken about the importance of pluralist language policies. With Slovenia's Declaration of Independence from Yugoslavia in June, 1991, Slovenes for the first time in history gained control of their own state. Indeed, the independent state of Slovenia is a direct result of the ethnolinguistic nationalism that has characterized Europe and Central Asia since the 1980s. Although Slovenia is an example of the triumph of a minority language group at the state level, its population of only 2 million citizens has limited political and economic power to respond to the forces of globalization and integration. Moreover, although the Slovene language has historically been linked with Slovene ethnolinguistic identity, Slovenia's continuing survival has required a shift away from long-established policies designed solely to protect the Slovene language.

This chapter examines medium-of-instruction policies in Slovenia, focusing on the tension between the processes of integration and ethnolinguistic nationalism. It begins by summarizing policies during the post-World War II period, particularly the rise of pluralism and efforts to protect the Slovene language within a united Yugoslavia. The chapter then examines conflict over medium-of-instruction policies that developed during the breakup of Yugoslavia; this section argues that Serb efforts to rescind pluralism were part of a strategy for creating social conflict to further Serbian political interests, and that the public discussion of language-in-education helped to define options for the political future of the country. Finally, the chapter examines new language policies in Slovenia that are designed to achieve the goals of integrating the country into a united Europe while also protecting the Slovene language as a key symbol of Slovene ethnolinguistic nationalism. In Slovenia, as elsewhere in Europe, these two goals are not easily combined. The challenges facing Slovenia exemplify those facing other new nation-states grappling with the educational and political agendas of medium-of-instruction policies.

PLURALISM IN YUGOSLAVIA, 1945–1986

Pluralism refers to an approach to language policy that encourages linguistic diversity and has as a central value tolerance for different languages and ethnolinguistic groups (Schmidt, 1998). Pluralism is often associated with a discourse of equality, though it also may be justified with reference to national unity.

During the period of rule by President Josip Broz Tito (1945–1980), language policies in Yugoslavia generally were characterized by increasing pluralism. Beginning in the 1950s, a pluralist approach to language became a central component in Tito's strategy for maintaining a united state and managing the demands of the large number of ethnolinguistic groups in the federation of six republics in united Yugoslavia (Serbia, Croatia, Slovenia, Macedonia, Montenegro, and Bosnia-Hercegovina). Serbs were the largest group, making up about 40% of the population, whereas Croats comprised about 20%, Moslems about 10%, and Slovenes, Albanians, and Macedonians between 6% and 8% each. (In Tito's Yugoslavia, "Moslem" was an ethnic rather than a religious term in the federal census figures.) Montenegrins and Hungarians made up less than 5% each, and a dozen other nationalities made up the rest of the population (see Table 13.1).

These groups have important historical differences. Slovenia and Croatia were part of the Austro-Hungarian Empire, whereas Serbs, Albanians, Macedonians, and other southern groups were under Turkish rule. Croats and Slovenes are primarily Roman Catholic, whereas Serbs are Orthodox. Moslems, which are both an ethnolinguistic and religious group, reside mostly in Bosnia. Slovene and Croatian are written in the Latin alphabet, whereas Serbian and Macedonian are written in Cyrillic. Serbian and Croatian are mutually intelligible, but there are distinct differences between them phonologically, lexically, and grammatically; these differences are linked with ethnolinguistic identity. Varieties of Serbian and Croatian were the most commonly spoken second language in united Yugoslavia and widely used for intergroup communication. Distinct languages that are mutually unintelligible are spoken by Slovenes, Macedonians, Albanians, Hungarians, and smaller groups such as Italians in border regions of Slovenia and Croatia.

The Titoist system of decentralized authority (called *self-management*) included a distinction between two sets of ethnolinguistic groups. The "nations" were the indigenous national groups associated with and numerically dominant in the six republics (i.e., Serbs, Croats, Slovenes, Macedonians, Montenegrins, and Moslems [the dominant group in

TABLE 13.1
The Major Nations and Nationalities of Yugoslavia Before the Breakup (in thousands)

	Yugoslavia	Bosnia	Montenegro	Croatia	Macedonia	Slovenia	Serbia	Vojvodina	Kosovo
Serb	8136	1320	20	532	45	42	4861	1107	210
Croat	4428	758	8	3454	3	56	31	109	8
Moslem	2000	1629	78	24	39	13	151	5	59
Slovene	1754	3	1	25	1	1712	8	3	0
Albanian	1731	4	37	6	378	2	72	4	1277
Macedonian	1341	2	1	5	1281	3	29	19	1
Montenegrin	577	14	399	10	4	3	77	43	27
Hungarian	427	1	0	25	0	9	5	385	0
Yugoslav	1216	326	31	379	14	26	271	167	1

Source: Statistički koledar Jugoslavije, 1988.

266

Bosnia]). The "nationalities" consisted of all other groups not considered to be indigenous; these groups had ethnolinguistic association with dominant groups in other countries, although they were long-standing residents of Yugoslavia and often comprised majorities in particular regions (e.g., Italians in areas of Slovenia and Croatia). Two nationalities held special, intermediate status: Hungarians were granted "semi-autonomous" status in the province of Vojvodina in Serbia where they ranked second in size, next to the Serbs, and Albanians were granted similar status in the province of Kosovo in Serbia where they were the largest group.

In order to ensure the continued commitment of the diverse nations and nationalities to a united Yugoslavia, official discourse encouraged both "state loyalty" and "national loyalty" (Joó, 1991). State loyalty was focused on the need for a unified political state to ensure economic development, protection from the Soviet threat, and peaceful coexistence of the national groups; it was associated with a discourse of national unity and democracy. National loyalty expressed the value of linguistic diversity and language rights, and was associated with a discourse of equality. Pluralism in language policy was justified with both discourses: It was essential for maintaining peace, stability, and unity, and it offered protection against the potential for domination by a single ethnolinguistic group. (For an extended discussion, see Tollefson, 2002b.)

From important constitutional changes that marked the end of Stalinist centralism in the early 1950s until the important new constitution of 1974, which devolved virtually all policymaking authority to the republics, Tito's Yugoslavia steadily expanded legal protection for the various ethnolinguistic groups, including the right to medium of instruction in their languages. The Titoist ideology of language and nationality supported detailed policies spelled out at the federal, republic, and communal (local) levels. These policies were designed to guarantee language maintenance and use in education for a wide variety of languages, including Serbian, Croatian, Slovene, Macedonian, Albanian, Hungarian, and Italian.

Yet constitutional guarantees of language rights in education were not unlimited: they were tied to territory. The nations could exercise their right to medium of instruction at all educational levels in their home republics, but they could not expect mother-tongue medium of instruction if they moved to different republics (although in practice such instruction was available in some areas).

This limitation in the right to mother-tongue medium of instruction affected different groups unequally. For instance, approximately 95% of all Slovenes resided in Slovenia, and thus attended Slovene-medium schools (*Statistički koledar Jugoslavije 1988*, 1988). (Data are from the 1980 census, the last one before the crisis.) In contrast, only 60% of all Serbs lived in Serbia proper (i.e., areas of the Republic of Serbia not including Kosovo and

Vojvodina). In general, nations and nationalities from the southern regions of the country, which were less developed economically, were more dispersed, due to internal migration for employment. As the most developed region, Slovenia enjoyed the most stable indigenous population, little affected by the pressure to migrate for employment.

Similarly, the nationalities could expect medium of instruction only in their semi-autonomous provinces and local communes. For instance, Italian primary and secondary schools operated in the Italian–Slovene bilingual regions along the border with Italy, and most families speaking Italian at home sent their children to those schools (Tollefson, 1981). Particularly important were policies ensuring medium of instruction for Albanians in Kosovo and Hungarians in Vojvodina, although these two semi-autonomous provinces remained ultimately subject to Serbian authority. In Kosovo, 1.3 million Albanians comprised more than 80% of the population, and attended Albanian-medium schools at elementary, secondary, and tertiary levels. In Vojovdina, 385,000 Hungarians were a minority of the 1.8 million citizens, but they attended Hungarian-medium schools. For all groups—nations and nationalities—the right to medium of instruction was legally protected only in the group's specific republic, semi-autonomous province, or commune.

Operating within this system, Slovenes were primarily concerned with ensuring that the Slovene language was protected from the much larger population of speakers of Serbo-Croatian in other republics. This concern involved both corpus and status issues. In the schools, spoken and written forms of standard Slovene were used from the beginning of elementary school. Because Slovene is characterized by significant dialect diversity, the role of the schools in promulgating the standard variety was crucial (see Herrity, 2000; *Slovenski pravopis*, 2000). In status planning, Slovene republic authorities were firm in their insistence that Slovene should be the medium of instruction at all levels of education, including universities. Slovene-medium of instruction was constitutionally protected, and implemented through a range of educational statutes (for details, see Tollefson, 1997).

Yet it is crucial to recognize that the desire to protect Slovene medium of instruction did not result in limits on varieties that were official minority languages in the Republic of Slovenia. In fact, like Slovene schools, Hungarian and Italian-medium schools were constitutionally protected. This constitutional provision was implemented through special funding for Italian elementary and secondary schools in the areas of Slovenia along the Italian border, and in Hungarian elementary and secondary bilingual schools along the border with Hungary. Institutions of higher education were solely in Slovene, however, although special programs provided for some students to attend tertiary institutions in Italy and Hungary. Protection for Italian and Hungarian-medium schools remained strong from the mid-1950s through the crisis of the late 1980s. Indeed, there is reason to believe that Slovene authorities saw the protection of Italian and Hungarian as part of an overall strategy to protect Slovene by ensuring language rights for all nations and nationalities (Tollefson, 1981).

Yet the concern with protecting Slovene-medium of instruction did not mean that the Slovene schools adopted a narrow vision of language in education. In fact, multilingualism was highly valued in Slovenia (Tollefson, 1981). Serbo-Croatian was effectively taught in the schools, so that virtually all Slovenes were fluent in Serbo-Croatian. In the Italian and Hungarian bilingual areas, Slovene speakers were expected to learn the minority language, and evidence suggests that many did so effectively (see Mejak & Novak-Lukanovič, 1991; Novak-Lukanovič, 1993). In fact, Italians, Hungarians, and many Slovenes were trilingual in Slovene, Serbo-Croatian, and the local minority language. Many also learned German, English, or another European language, although measures of level of proficiency are uncertain (Tollefson, 1981).

In summary, when it was part of united Yugoslavia, Slovenia followed a pluralist approach to medium of instruction that protected language diversity, and specifically ensured instruction in Slovene, Italian, and Hungarian, as well as widespread learning of Serbo-Croatian and other languages. Pluralist medium-of-instruction policies were so central to the commitment of most Slovenes to a united Yugoslavia that the Serbian effort to rescind pluralism was viewed as a fundamental threat to the future of the state.

THE PROCESS OF DISSOLUTION

Debates about medium of instruction often reflect broader conflicts between groups involved in a struggle over political power or economic resources (Schmidt, 1998). Indeed, when ethnolinguistic groups mobilize around language issues, medium-of-instruction policies may come to symbolize broader concerns about power and control, and public debates may reflect and help shape the broader political struggle. In such circumstances, pedagogical concerns about medium of instruction may be overwhelmed by political agendas.

In addition, language policies are one mechanism by which state authorities can create and sustain sociopolitical conflict (Cluver, 1992). In Yugoslavia from 1984 until 1992, language policies in education were one arena for the struggle between those who sought to reduce the potential for social and political conflict, and those for whom conflict offered major political advantages (Levinger, 1994). As the debate over language policies in education developed during this period, alternative medium-of-instruction policies came to symbolize fundamentally incompatible visions for the future of Yugoslavia.

Unity Through Uniformity: Nationalism and Centralism In Serbia

Until the early and mid-1980s, a pluralist approach to language in education persisted throughout Yugoslavia. Many languages continued to be used as media of instruction. At the republic level, Slovene, Serbian, Croatian, and Macedonian continued to enjoy official status and widespread use as media of instruction. In Kosovo, Albanian continued to be the dominant language of education at all levels, whereas in Hungarian speaking communities, Hungarian was either the sole medium of instruction or used along with Serbian, Croatian, or Slovene in bilingual programs. In local communes, Italian, Hungarian, and other languages continued to be used.

In the mid-1980s, however, Serb authorities led by Slobodan Milošević proposed that pluralism should be replaced by a new centralism highlighting the role of Serbian history, culture, and language. (For an extended discussion of this change, see Tollefson, 2002b). In a variety of forums, Serb nationalists began to advocate concrete alternatives to pluralism. Serbian was proposed as the medium of instruction throughout Serbia, including Kosovo (Vučelić, 1991). Other proposals were for the Cyrillic system of writing to be granted official status throughout the country, thereby becoming the only national orthography; and for the Serbian standard for Serbo-Croatian to become the basis for a unified Serbo-Croatian. By 1988, Serb national leaders argued that Serbian should become the sole medium of instruction in all areas of Serbia, Croatia, Bosnia, Kosovo, and elsewhere that included Serb minorities. In some contexts, the rationale for such proposals was limited to technical matters, such as a concern that continued dialect variation, sustained by pluralist medium-of-instruction policies, would eventually lead to the development of mutually unintelligible varieties (Ivić, 1992). But as the movement for Serbian nationalism intensified, the rationale for rescinding pluralism increasingly focused on alleged injustices against Serbs under Tito, who had been keen to ensure that none of the nations or nationalities rose to prominence, and under the continued policy of pluralism. In Serbian nationalist discourse, pluralism came to be blamed for a wide range of problems, including economic stagnation and politically ineffective state authority, and ultimately genocide against Serbs; the demise of pluralism was justified as essential for protecting Serbs and preserving the integrity of the state of Yugoslavia.

For example, the Memorandum of the Serbian Academy of Sciences and Arts, released in September, 1986, created a storm of controversy throughout Yugoslavia by linking pluralism with cataclysmic changes affecting the country: "Malignant disintegration ... in the economy and society [have taken] on alarming proportions ... Vindictive policy towards Serbia ... has grown ever stronger, to the point of genocide" (Mihailović & Krestić, 1995, pp. 102, 125). A primary argument of the Serbian Memorandum was that pluralism was the cause of the economic and political crisis facing Yugoslavia in the 1980s, and that limits must be imposed on the regional and local autonomy of Slovenes, Croats, Bosnians, Albanians, Hungarians, and other nations and nationalities. The Memorandum criticized pluralist medium-of-instruction policies, alleging that they promoted "regional" cultures rather than a "universal" Yugoslav culture (Mihailović & Krestić, 1995, p. 114). Croatian efforts to promote a distinct Croatian variety of Serbo-Croatian were interpreted as attacks against the Serb minority in Croatia. Policies in Kosovo to promote standard Albanian in the schools were viewed as threats to the Serb minority in Kosovo. It was with the claim of genocide against Serbs that Serbian authorities rescinded the semi-autonomous status of Kosovo in 1988–1989. Albanian was banned as a medium of instruction in Kosovo, replaced by Serbian throughout the educational system. Albanian school authorities and teachers were purged, and the Albanian-medium educational system effectively ended. Thus, the alternative to pluralism, emphasizing the primacy of Serbian national interests, offered a vision of unity through linguistic uniformity.

Unity Through Diversity: Pluralism in Slovenia

The Serbian proposals met with resistance in many areas outside Serbia. In Kosovo, for example, linguists and other educators in the mid-1980s feared that Albanian would gradually be pushed out of the schools, as indeed occurred (Zymberi, 1992). In Bosnia, linguists feared that local varieties would become stigmatized, and so they proposed an alternative policy of official recognition of separate linguistic norms based in each republic (Dunatov, 1987). Perhaps the most well organized and clearly articulated resistance to the movement to rescind pluralism took place in Slovenia. For example, in a review of the status of Slovene and Serbo-Croatian in Slovenia in 1989, Toporišič (1992) complained that Serbo-Croatian was "the most equal among equals" (p. 111). Expressing great concern for the "dangerously intensified" situation (p. 111), Toporišič called not only for a continuation of pluralism, but extension of laws to protect Slovene and other language varieties against Serbian centralism.

An influential popular expression of public resistance to Serbian centralism was a series of columns about language that appeared in the Slovene publication 7D between July, 1987, and July, 1989. Written by the Slovene linguist Velemir Gjurin, the columns advocated continued use of the Slovene language in all domains, including education (Gjurin, 1991; also see Paternost, 1997; Tollefson, 2002a). Gjurin's columns used technical discussions of language as a means to argue for continued protection of language diversity in Yugoslavia, and to resist increasingly strident Serb nationalism.

Over the 2-year period in which the columns appeared, Gjurin became increasingly confident of his position, examining language policies not only in education, but also in the Yugoslav army, where Serbo-Croatian was the dominant language. Despite the risks involved, particularly in criticizing the army, Gjurin's columns became a popular forum for the discussion of language policy. As time passed, his increasingly bold statements in support of Slovene language rights offered a rationale first for confederation and then for Slovene independence. Thus, Gjurin's columns helped to lead popular opinion toward independence, and also reflected, in their increasingly explicit statements, the success of the Slovene independence movement as an alternative to Serbian centralism. Indeed, Slovene government leaders, including those in the Slovene League of Communists, finally came to accept the goal of Slovene independence. Along with other language specialists, Gjurin responded to pro-Serbian language policies by using language issues to shape public opinion in support of a pluralist vision of unity through diversity, and, when that vision could no longer be realized in a united Yugoslavia, for mobilizing virtually the entire population of Slovenia in support of independence (Tollefson, 2002a).

INDEPENDENT SLOVENIA

With independence, Slovenes were faced with crucial decisions about language policies in education. Should Slovene be the sole medium of instruction? Should the right to medium of instruction be preserved for the Italian and Hungarian minorities? What should be done about the thousands of immigrants and refugees from other regions of Yugoslavia?

The Slovene constitution, adopted in December 1991, declares that Slovene is the official language of the educational system, and also that the Italians and Hungarians have a right to mother-tongue education. Thus, the constitution continues the pre-independence system of language rights. Two approaches to minority-language medium of instruction are used in areas with Italian and Hungarian populations. In Italian districts, separate Italian-medium schools operate from preschool through secondary school; Slovene is a compulsory subject in these schools. In Slovene-medium schools in these districts, Italian is a compulsory subject for the Slovene-speaking students. In Hungarian districts, bilingual education is the preferred approach, with Slovene and Hungarian children attending classes together, using both Slovene and Hungarian as media of instruction. Enrollment data suggest that community support for Italian and Hungarian-medium of instruction—first established decades ago—has generally remained constant in recent years. At the primary level, for example, the number of students enrolling in Italian-medium schools has increased by approximately 5% since 1980 (Ministry of Education and Sport, 1996).

As in the earlier period, Italians and Hungarians retain their rights only in the officially bilingual districts. In those districts, state policy declares that knowledge of both Slovene and the minority language "is not only an obligation of members of national communities, but also of members of the [Slovene] majority nation" (Republic of Slovenia, 2000, article 4, paragraph 2–20). A 1993 Council of Europe investigation into language rights in Slovenia concluded: "Slovenia, in our opinion, fully respects the rule of law and fundamental rights and freedoms. The way it protects the rights of [Italian and Hungarian] minorities is a model and an example for many other European states both east and west" (Council of Europe, 1993). (For a complete list of regulations affecting the special rights of Italians and Hungarians in Slovenia, see Republic of Slovenia, 2000, annex II).

The broad guarantee of the right to medium of instruction in Slovene, Italian, and Hungarian has been implemented within an educational system undergoing major reform. The educational reforms recently carried out in Slovenia are the result of a 1995 government study of Slovene education that led to new laws covering all levels of the educational system. This study was the *White Paper on Education in the Republic of Slovenia*.

The White Paper on Education in Slovenia

First published in 1995, the White Paper (Ministry of Education and Sport, 1995, 1996) was a comprehensive review of education, with particular attention to comparison with educational systems elsewhere in western and central Europe. Although the report acknowledged that education in Slovenia had undergone significant liberalization during the 1980s and 1990s, eliminating influence by the League of Communists, it argued that major reforms remained to be carried out, in order to ensure that the new nation's system of education conformed to standards and practices common elsewhere in Europe. Following issuance of the report, the Slovene parliament adopted legislation that legally incorporated its recommendations into Slovene educational statutes.

The report specifically highlighted changes aimed at encouraging a "plural system of values" and helping Slovenia "join processes of European integration" (Ministry of Education and Sport, 1996, p. 7). The rationale for this change was that it would "prepare people for [European] integration demanding the ability to communicate in foreign languages" (Ministry of Education and Sport, 1996, p. 17). Although language policies in pre-independence Slovenia were primarily aimed at Slovene language maintenance and resistance to Serbo-Croatian, the new educational system has abandoned concern with Serbo-Croatian, instead emphasizing European integration: "Attention should be drawn to the fact that sharp delineation between 'our' and 'their' ... civilization ... is questionable" (p. 37). Thus, education is charged with a dual purpose: to form and disseminate Slovene "national culture" and also to ensure that Slovenes engage fully in "the processes of European integration, migration, political changes, etc." (Ministry of Education and Sport, 1996, p. 37). The focus on internationalism in education is part of a wider discourse of internationalism that has dominated Slovene political culture since the 1980s (see Tollefson, 2002b).

The key to integrating Slovenia in Europe, according to the White Paper, is language education to ensure that Slovenes can communicate effectively in foreign languages: "This is extremely important for us, since we belong to a group of smaller European countries" (p. 38). Indeed, a major focus of recent changes in educational statutes has been language education.

To implement this shift in priorities, the White Paper proposed many specific changes. Compulsory foreign language education now begins in the 4th grade, 2 years earlier than previously, with a second foreign language added in the 7th grade; even earlier study of foreign languages is encouraged, beginning as young as the age of 5. In the elementary curriculum, the time spent studying foreign languages comprises at least 10% of class time, with every school offering foreign languages. At the secondary level, two foreign languages have become compulsory; the total annual hours of classroom time devoted to their study (840 hours) is greater than any other subject in the curriculum (e.g., Slovene language/literature-560 hours; mathematics-560 hours). By comparison, in bilingual regions, Hungarian and Italian language receive 560 hours of class time, equivalent to that devoted to Slovene.

In addition to required language classes, the White Paper encouraged the expansion of optional classes in English, German, and other languages. During the 1990s, the number of optional English classes was surpassed only by special assistance classes in Slovene language arts and mathematics (Statistical Office of the Republic of Slovenia, 1994). In addition, new language curricula were introduced in 1996 for English, French, and Italian (Godunc, 2001).

The White Paper also argued for a new cadre of trained language teachers to take over language education from the regular classroom teachers, beginning in the 4th grade. Until that change becomes feasible, Slovenia relies on various stopgap measures, such as a language assistants scheme in which undergraduates from elsewhere in Europe spend a year in Slovenia helping to teach languages in the schools. Although generally well received, this program operates with a limited number of assistants, who cannot be expected to meet the language needs of the country (see Beloglavec & Straus, 2001). Finally, in perhaps the most important change to ensure that schools give priority to language education, foreign languages have become compulsory (along with Slovene and mathematics) in the "Matura" secondary examination.

Yet this emphasis on language education is not unqualified. Acknowledging that giving higher priority to foreign languages could undermine the status of Slovene, the White Paper included recommendations to preserve Slovene-medium of instruction. In particular, it explicitly did not favor increasing foreign language study at the expense of Slovene; in fact, the report proposed that the amount of time dedicated to Slovene should be increased. It also urged adoption of new national tests to assess Slovene language ability from the early elementary years. Moreover, the report recommended that Slovene citizens should not be permitted to enroll during the years of compulsory schooling in private international schools using English or other languages as media of instruction. As the report states: "It is in Slovenia's national interest that primary schooling of Slovene citizens be carried out in the Slovene language or the languages of national minorities [Italian and Hungarian]" (Ministry of Education and Sport, 1996, p. 240). In perhaps the clearest statement of official commitment to maintaining Slovene-medium of instruction, the Slovene government initiated an Office for the Slovene Language (directed by a sociolinguist), charged with developing the Slovene language and ensuring that it is fully implemented as the official language.

As a result of the White Paper's emphasis on maintaining Slovene as the medium of instruction, new statutes on education explicitly declare Slovene the official medium of instruction, along with Italian and Hungarian in the bilingual districts (specifically, in new laws on education, preschool, gymnasium, matura examinations, higher education, and organization and financing of schools). These statutes permit only limited use of other languages for particular purposes. For example, the Law on Gymnasium permits individual subjects to be taught in a foreign language "for the purpose of international comparison or preparation for an international baccalaureate" (article 8); the Law on Higher Education specifies that study programs may be conducted in a medium of instruction other than Slovene only when the purpose of the program is to teach a language, when visiting scholars are involved, or when a similar program is also offered in Slovene (article 8). Such exceptions to Slovene-medium of instruction must follow special regulations issued by the Minister of Education.

These efforts to protect the Slovene language reflect continuing concern for the future of the language within an increasingly integrated Europe. Of particular concern is the spread of English and German into domains previously reserved for Slovene (Toporišič, 1997). Thus, some Slovenes have argued for restrictions on the use of foreign terms and idioms in school textbooks, whereas others have expressed concern about the use of English in the informal interactions among children at school and the increasing use of foreign borrowings in classroom materials and exercises (see Toporišič, 1991, 1993, 1997). Thus, although the Slovene language now enjoys the protection of state policy, there is growing concern that the forces of integration may ultimately threaten the use of Slovene in education.

Other Languages in Slovenia

Medium-of-instruction policies have not been developed for Romany residents of Slovenia or for immigrants and refugees from other regions of former Yugoslavia. Since independence, the Slovene government has begun to recognize the Romany minority as an autochthonous group deserving legal protection and assistance. For instance, the Slovene Office for Nationalities is charged with protecting the rights of the Romany community, along with Hungarians and Italians. Nevertheless, the right to Romany-medium of instruction has not been legally established.

Bosnians, Serbs, Croats, and other groups from former Yugoslavia are handled by a separate Office for Immigration and Refugees, which was established in part to handle refugee centers set up during the wars. For these groups, there is no statutory guarantee of medium of instruction in their home languages. Small programs, however, have been established under the Primary School Act for supplementary mother-tongue classes, taught by native speakers, for children attending Slovene-medium schools. The first programs, offering 3 to 5 hours per week of instruction, were established in Macedonian, Albanian, and Arabic.

The continuing issue of immigrants and refugees residing in Slovenia has not been resolved. In part, the medium-of-instruction question has been mitigated by progressive legislation that permitted immigrants and other long-term residents of Slovenia to gain citizenship. The Citizenship Act, adopted at the time of independence, permitted individuals meeting specific length-of-residence and employment criteria to acquire Slovene citizenship; approximately 170,000 individuals used this provision to do so. One result is that official figures on the number of residents speaking languages other than Slovene probably underestimate the total number of speakers of other languages (see Republic of Slovenia, 2000). Although the White Paper recommended new policies and programs to meet the educational needs of these groups, the report did not recommend medium of instruction in their native languages.

CONCLUSION: MINORITY LANGUAGES IN EUROPE

Because minority language issues are a permanent feature of Europe, policymakers in virtually every state must decide which language varieties should be used as media of instruction. As in Yugoslavia, these decisions have important pedagogical and political consequences. One challenge in developing medium-of-instruction policies is that language minorities in Europe vary considerably in their circumstances and needs.

One category of minority language consists of regional varieties that lack a full range of legal protections. These languages include Corsican and Breton (France), Sorbian (Germany), Frisian (Netherlands), Catalan and Basque (Spain and France), and Welsh (Britain). With as many as 20 to 40 million people speaking such varieties, institutions in Europe face significant pressure to increase protection for speakers of these languages (Dandridge, 1997). A second category of minority language consists of varieties that have official status in border states. Examples include German in France, Poland, and Romania; Hungarian in Slovakia, Croatia, and Slovenia; Slovene in Italy and Austria; and Italian in Slovenia. In some cases, these languages are linked with ongoing border disputes and other international conflicts involving border states. A third category of minority language consists of languages spoken by "guestworkers," temporary (although often long-term) residents and their families who have migrated from their home country for employment. For example, the 3 million Turks in Germany (only 2.5% of whom have become German citizens) continue to use Turkish along with German; medium-of-instruction policies vary widely from one region to another within Germany (Klau, 1997). Although estimates are difficult (due to lack of agreement about the definition of *minority language*), according to the Federal Union of European Nationalities, the total number of minority language varieties falling into all categories may be as many as 200, spoken by nearly 100 million people in western and central Europe and the Baltic states (Dandridge, 1997).

With growing awareness of the language issues facing a united Europe, the Council of Europe has written two legal documents that advocate pluralism for reducing the potential for ethnolinguistic conflict: the European Charter for Regional and Minority Languages, which does not apply to dialects of official languages or to the languages of migrants, and the Framework Convention for the Protection of National Minorities, the first legally binding multilateral document in Europe devoted to protecting national minorities. Although many member states have not ratified these instruments, the Council of Europe continues to push for their adoption; for example, ratification of the Framework Convention is a condition of membership for new states seeking to join the Council of Europe. (Slovenia has ratified both instruments.)

Despite its discourse of pluralism, the Council of Europe has not followed Slovenia's model of guaranteeing indigenous language minorities the right to medium of instruction in their native languages. The European Charter for Regional and Minority Languages, for example, focuses on protecting language as a symbol of culture; the Charter is not a minority-rights document. It recommends possible measures for providing instruction in regional and minority languages, including using them as media of instruction or teaching them as part of the curriculum (Council of Europe, 1992, article 8), but the recommendations permit states to strictly limit the use of minority languages in education. The Framework Convention for the Protection of National Minorities, written in 1995, recommends a set of principles that states should follow for protecting national minorities, but the Framework does not support a right to medium of instruction in minority languages. It specifies only a "right to learn" one's own language (article 14) and a right to establish private schools using minority languages (article 13), and it includes a general statement encouraging states to consider "as far as possible and within the framework of their education systems ... adequate opportunities for being taught the minority language or for receiving instruction in this language" (article 14). Thus, the Framework presents only a weak case for medium of instruction in minority languages. One of the major sources of difficulty in debates over these documents is that national governments do not agree on which languages deserve protection, nor on which languages exist within particular state boundaries (Council of Europe, 2001). These uncertainties provide an opening for states to block debate over the right to medium of instruction for some groups.

Although general statements encouraging minority-language medium of instruction can contribute to awareness of medium-of-instruction issues, state policies must address the particular needs of specific ethnolinguistic groups. For instance, many Turks in Germany plan to return to Turkey, and therefore Turkish children may need to be educationally prepared for this move, as well as for succeeding in German schools. In contrast, other minorities (e.g., Catalan) are indigenous residents in their home communities. In addition, the politics of language vary considerably from one language to another. Whereas Catalan and Welsh, for example, enjoy wide recognition and some legal protection, other varieties (e.g., Corsican) are dismissed as dialects or corrupt versions of standard varieties, and therefore deserving of no recognition or protection. In addition, although some varieties (e.g., Catalan in Spain) are spoken by middle- and upper-class individuals who have access to political power and policymaking authority, other varieties (e.g., Turkish in Germany) are spoken by working class populations suffering significant economic distress and enjoying little opportunity to influence language policy. Thus medium-of-instruction policies must be shaped not only by general concerns for human rights, but also by understanding of the local context for speakers of particular language varieties.

One of the major effects of globalization is that minority groups must deal with market forces. That is, efforts to extend minority language use are constrained by the limited economic value of minority languages within the European (and global) market. For example, in a 1996 Council of Europe review of cultural policy in Slovenia, experts concluded that Slovene cultural institutions using the Slovene language (e.g., theater groups) could not compete with similar institutions in neighboring Austria and Italy; therefore the report recommended that dance and visual arts, in which language plays a minor role, should receive priority funding in efforts to attract an international audience (Council of Europe, 1996). Similarly, in a unified Europe, an educational system using Slovene as the medium of instruction may not be able to compete with schools using English or other dominant languages. As a consequence, although private schools in Slovenia are still prohibited by law from educating most Slovene citizens in English or another foreign language, it is possible that the Slovene public will demand changes in this policy. Should that happen, Slovene medium of instruction would no longer be assured. Thus, advocates of minority-language medium of instruction must confront community concerns for the economic consequences of alternative policies.

Although the pressures of integration clearly threaten many minority languages, dominant groups nevertheless must deal with minorities in a fair manner or risk inciting ever-stronger demands for autonomy. As the recent history of Yugoslavia suggests, if minority demands for pluralism are not met, then some groups will support claims for autonomy or independence. Indeed, for several years during the 1980s, Slovenes (and Bosnians) resisted the breakup of Yugoslavia, but Serb refusal to protect pluralism left them with a stark choice: seek independence, or risk losing Slovene language and culture in a system dominated by Serbs and the Serbian language. The case of Yugoslavia demonstrates that centralism can have disastrous results, and that in many contexts, dominant groups must support pluralism if conflict is to be channeled into political rather than military forms. Managing the tension between integration and ethnolinguistic nationalism will continue to be one of the greatest challenges facing Europe. Medium-of-instruction policies are a key arena for meeting this challenge.

REFERENCES

Beloglavec, D., & Straus, B. (2001). The language assistants scheme in Slovenia. In J. C. Anderson, K. Pižorn, N. Žemva, & L. Beaver (Eds.), *The language assistant scheme in Slovenia: A baseline study* (pp. 9–21). Ljubljana, Slovenia: Ministry of Education, Science and Sport of the Republic of Slovenia and the British Council.

Blommaert, J. (1996). Language planning as a discourse on language and society: The linguistic ideology of a scholarly tradition. *Language Problems and Language Planning, 20*(3), 199–222.

Cluver, A. D. de V. (1992). Language planning models for a post-apartheid South Africa. *Language Problems and Language Planning, 23*(2), 133–156.

Council of Europe. (1992). *European Charter for Regional or Minority Languages.* Retrieved July 15, 2002, from http://conventions.coe.int/Treaty/EN/Treaties/Html/148.htm

Council of Europe. (1993, March 22). *Report of the Committee on Legal Affairs and Human Rights in Slovenia*. AS/Jur (44)55.

Council of Europe. (1996). *The cultural policy review in Slovenia*. Strasbourg, France: Council of Europe.

Council of Europe. (2001, January 29). *Right of national minorities*. Report of the Committee on Legal Affairs and Human Rights. Strasbourg, France.

Dandridge, B. (1997, March/April). Protecting languages proves a challenge for EU officials. *European Dialogue, 2*, 1–3.

Dunatov, R. (1987). A note on the nature and the status of the standard Serbo-Croatian in Bosnia-Herzegovina. *Slovene Studies, 9*(1–2), 75–78.

Gjurin, V. (1991). *Slovenščina zdaj!* [Slovene now!]. Ljubljana, Slovenia: Art agencija.

Godunc, Z. (2001). The education system in Slovenia. In J. C. Alderson, K. Pižorn, N. Žemva, & L. Beaver (Eds.), *The language assistant scheme in Slovenia: A baseline study* (pp. 1–8). Ljubljana, Slovenia: Ministry of Education and Sport of the Republic of Slovenia and the British Council Slovenia.

Herrity, P. (2000). *Slovene: A comprehensive grammar*. London: Routledge.

Ivić, P. (1992). Language planning in Serbia today. In R. Bugarski & C. Hawkesworth (Eds.), *Language planning in Yugoslavia* (pp. 101–110). Columbus, OH: Slavica.

Joó, R. (1991). Slovenes in Hungary and Hungarians in Slovenia: Ethnic and state identity. *Ethnic and Racial Studies, 14*, 100–106.

Klau, T. (1997, March/April). Germany's Turks face feeling of isolation. *European Dialogue, 2*, 8.

Levinger, J. (1994). Language war—war language. *Language Sciences, 16*(2), 229–336.

Mejak, R., & Novak-Lukanovič, S. (1991). *The participation of parents, schools and the social surrounding in the implementation of the concept of bilingual education*. Ljubljana, Slovenia: Institute for Ethnic Studies.

Mihailović, K., & Krestić, V. (1995). *Memorandum of the Serbian Academy of Sciences and Arts: Answers to criticisms*. Belgrade, Serbia: Serbian Academy of Sciences and Arts.

Ministry of Education and Sport. (1995). *Bela knjiga o vzgoji in izobraževanju v Republiki Sloveniji*. Ljubljana, Slovenia: Author.

Ministry of Education and Sport. (1996). *White paper on education in the Republic of Slovenia*. Ljubljana, Slovenia: Author.

Novak-Lukanovič, S. (1993). The role of the minority language in the educational system: Results of the case study. In S. Devetak, S. Flere, & G. Seewann (Eds.), *Small nations and ethnic minorities in an emerging Europe* (pp. 219–222). Munich, Germany: Slavic Verlag Dr. Anton Kovac.

Paternost, J. (1997). Recent sociolinguistic struggles for language sovereignty among the Slovenes. *International Journal of the Sociology of Language, 124*, 185–200.

Phillipson, R. (2000). Integrative comment: Living with vision and commitment. In R. Phillipson (Ed.), *Rights to language: Equity, power, and education* (pp. 264–278). Mahwah, NJ: Lawrence Erlbaum Associates.

Republic of Slovenia. (2000). *Report submitted by the Republic of Slovenia pursuant to article 25 paragraph 1 of the Framework Convention for the Protection of National Minorities*. Ljubljana, Slovenia: Author.

Schmidt, R. J. (1998). The politics of language in Canada and the United States: Explaining the differences. In T. Ricento & B. Burnaby (Eds.), *Language and politics in the United States and Canada* (pp. 37–70). Mahwah, NJ: Lawrence Erlbaum Associates.

Slovenski pravopis. (2000). Ljubljana, Slovenia: SAZU and ZRC.

Statistical Office of the Republic of Slovenia. (1994). *Primary and secondary schools at the end of the school year 1992–93 and at the beginning of the school year 1993–94.* Ljubljana, Slovenia: Author.

Statistički koledar Jugoslavije, 1988 (1988). Belgrade, Yugoslavia: Zvezni zavod za statistiko.

Tollefson, J. W. (1981). *The language situation and language policy in Slovenia.* Washington, DC: University Press of America.

Tollefson, J. W. (1997). Language policy in independent Slovenia. *International Journal of the Sociology of Language, 124,* 29–49.

Tollefson, J. W. (2002a). The language debates: Preparing for the war in Yugoslavia, 1980–1991. *International Journal of the Sociology of Language, 154,* 1–18.

Tollefson, J. W. (2002b). Language rights and the destruction of Yugoslavia. In J. W. Tollefson (Ed.), *Language policies in education: Critical issues* (pp. 179–199). Mahwah, NJ: Lawrence Erlbaum Associates.

Toporišič, J. (1991). *Družbenost slovenskega jezika: Sociolingvistična razpravljanja* [The social aspect of Slovene: Sociolinguistic studies]. Ljubljana, Slovenia: Državna založba Slovenije.

Toporišič, J. (1992). The status of Slovene in Yugoslavia. In R. Bugarski & C. Hawkesworth (Eds.), *Language planning in Yugoslavia* (pp. 111–116). Columbus, OH: Slavica.

Toporišič, J. (1993, February 2). Gospoda in raja ob Slovenskem pravopisu [Gentlemen and the mob on the Slovene orthography]. *Delo, 10.*

Toporišič, J. (1997). Slovene as the language of an independent state. *International Journal of the Sociology of Language, 124,* 5–28.

Vučelić, M. (1991). *Conversations with the epoch.* Belgrade, Yugoslavia: Ministry of Information of the Republic of Serbia.

Zymberi, I. (1992). Albanian in Yugoslavia. In R. Bugarski & C. Hawkesworth (Eds.), *Language planning in Yugoslavia* (pp. 130–139). Columbus, OH: Slavica.

14

Contexts
of Medium-of-Instruction Policy

James W. Tollefson
University of Washington

Amy B. M. Tsui
The University of Hong Kong

Although decisions about medium of instruction are often justified with pedagogical rationales, medium-of-instruction policies are not formed in isolation, but rather emerge in the context of powerful social and political forces, including globalization, migration and demographic changes, political conflict, changes in government, shifts in the structure of local economies, and elite competition. A major purpose of this collection of chapters is to explore the connections between medium-of-instruction policies and these broader sociopolitical issues.

KEY ISSUES IN MEDIUM-OF-INSTRUCTION POLICY

This chapter presents an integrative summary of key issues examined in the articles in this collection. Although the authors of the articles write about a wide range of situations in which medium-of-instruction policies are shaped by divergent social and political forces, a number of generalizations may be drawn. This chapter summarizes those generalizations and explores the connections that exist across the separate chapters. In particular, this chapter emphasizes the role of medium-of-instruction policies in mediating the tension between, on the one hand, the centralizing forces of globalization and state mandated policies and, on the other hand, demands for language rights by ethnic and linguistic minorities. In this role, media of instruction policies often reflect competing educational and political agendas.

Medium-of-Instruction Policies as Ideological and Discursive Constructs

As McCarty argues, medium-of-instruction policies are both ideological and discursive constructs. As ideological constructs, policies often reflect the interests of groups that dominate the state policymaking apparatus, and thus, they reproduce unequal relationships of power within the larger society. McCarty's historical examination of language policy in the United States, for example, shows that medium-of-instruction policies for ethnolinguistic minorities have largely served the interests of dominant groups seeking to expand their geographical and political control. Similarly, medium-of-instruction policies in India support the interests of English-speaking elites, in part by reflecting widely held beliefs about the necessity of learning English. In sub-Saharan Africa, policies often reflect the continuing domination of education (and other public institutions) by European economic and political interests. In Ecuador and Bolivia, the goal of many advocates of Spanish-only instruction is the continued marginalization of speakers of Quechua and other indigenous languages.

At the same time, however, language policies offer an arena within which marginalized ethnolinguistic groups may assert their claim for rights and privileges. For instance, the recent expansion in the number of schools using American Indian languages as media of instruction is linked with the wider movement for indigenous control of institutions that affect the lives of American Indians. In New Zealand, the growth in the number of Māori-medium schools since the 1980s not only reflects wider interest in Māori-medium education, but also an important change in the position of the Māori community in New Zealand's sociopolitical system. In South Africa, the policy of 11 official languages, although not fully implemented, is aimed in part at increasing the political participation of speakers of languages other than English and Afrikaans, and undoing the harmful effects of apartheid. In Ecuador, state support for bilingual education programs entails formation of an independent educational administration for schools in areas in which the population was more than half indigenous; this independent administration has been able to further the educational and economic interests of speakers of indigenous languages. Thus, in many contexts, the narrow issue of medium of instruction is an arena for achieving greater autonomy for linguistic minorities and for broader movements for social change.

As discursive constructs, medium-of-instruction policies are linked with a range of social issues in which language may play an important symbolic role. The processes by which language policies are produced and legitimized reveal complex social relations among ethnolinguistic communities, social classes, and other groups engaged in the struggle for political power and economic resources. For instance, the growth of Māori-medium schooling in recent years is made possible by—and also furthers—the movement to guarantee protection of Māori "treasures," including language and culture. Shifts in medium of instruction in New Zealand's schools are part of the larger process of reinvigorating Māori social institutions, and support for—or opposition to—Māori-medium instruction is fundamentally linked to broader social issues. Thus, by examining public debates over the process of medium-of-instruction policymaking, we gain insight into broader social struggles.

In liberal democratic states, most public discussion of medium-of-instruction policies assumes that their aim is to ensure that students gain the language skills necessary for successful subject content instruction, equal educational opportunity, and future employment. Indeed, in many settings, one of the most effective discursive moves to legitimize particular policies is to associate them with a discourse of "opportunity" or "equality" (Schmidt, 1998). In the United States, for instance, suppression of indigenous languages has been justified since the 19th century as a necessary step for creating economic opportunity for indigenous peoples. In Wales, anglicization in 19th century Welsh schools was considered to be necessary for both the "moral progress and commercial prosperity" of speakers of Welsh (Roberts, 1998, p. 204, cited in Jones & Martin-Jones, chap. 3, this volume). In India today, English is associated with expectations of economic opportunity not only among the urban middle class, which has long enjoyed access to English-medium instruction, but also increasingly among the rural poor, who associate English with urban opportunities. A similar discourse of opportunity has favored English in New Zealand, Singapore, and Philippines; Spanish in Ecuador and Bolivia; French in Mali, Niger, and Burkina Faso; and dominant languages in many other settings. Like a discourse of opportunity, a discourse of "equality" is also widely used to justify medium-of-instruction policies. In Yugoslavia beginning in the late 1980s, for example, equality for Serbs living outside Serbia was Milošević's central rationale for rescinding policies that had successfully maintained a united Yugoslavia since 1945. More recently, supporters of the official-English movement in the United States argue that official-English laws will ensure equal treatment for all citizens. Thus, medium-of-instruction policies must be understood as discursive constructs emerging from broader social struggles; and rationales for policies must be seen in light of ideological assumptions about the symbolic role of language in particular contexts.

The Gap Between (Pluralist) Discourse
and (Monolingual) Practice

Language-policy researchers have long recognized that the consequences of language policies may differ significantly from stated aims. In the words of King and Benson, there is often a "discontinuity" between official policy and everyday practice. Traditional neoclassical analysis (Tollefson, 1991) assumes that this gap between rhetoric and reality is largely due to difficulties in implementing language policies (e.g., Eastman, 1983). For example, Webb's analysis of the process of language policymaking in South Africa traces the enormous complexity involved in implementing a new medium-of-instruction policy to achieve the national ideals of democracy, unity, human rights, and tolerance.

In addition to difficulties in implementation, the gap between policy and practice may have other explanations. A historical–structural approach to language policy analysis assumes that policymakers, while paying lip-service to equality and opportunity, usually represent the interests of dominant groups, and thus adopt policies designed to further those interests, often at the expense of ethnolinguistic minorities. Therefore a historical–structural approach to language policy analysis critically examines the stated goals of alternative policies, the discursive processes by which policies are legitimized, and the different consequences of policies for various social groups. For example, Jones and Martin-Jones argue that an account of Welsh–English bilingual schools requires a critical, historical perspective that takes into account the link between medium of instruction and the subjugation of the Welsh population and, more recently, the role of the bilingual schools in the Welsh national revival. Similarly, May argues that recent shifts in New Zealand's medium-of-instruction policies can only be understood within the broad historical framework of the "repositioning" of social identity and language rights in New Zealand, and the national effort to redress the country's legacy of colonialism. In India, Annamalai argues, the favored position of English, although it is widely seen as the language of opportunity, in fact provides economic advantage for only a tiny minority of the population.

Despite powerful discursive attention to "opportunity" and "equality," the primary goal of state policies in some contexts may be to block full and open access to education and employment for particular ethnolinguistic groups. One such example is the United States, where the exclusion from most schools of the languages of American Indians, immigrants, and ethnolinguistic minorities such as African Americans has had the effect of lowering school performance of linguistic minority children and restricting employment opportunities, despite the widely held belief that the policy ensures equal educational and employment opportunity for these students (see Wiley, 2002). Similarly, in sub-Saharan Africa, the continued use of English, French, and other colonial languages as media of instruction not only favors foreign textbook publishers, but also helps to preserve the privileged social, political, and economic position of African elites who speak the former colonial languages. Also striking is the gap between the pluralist discourse of language education in Bolivia and the reality of monolingual Spanish classrooms. In India, a discourse of opportunity through English persists, despite the fact that two thirds of all adults have not completed middle school and literacy remains largely out of reach of many individuals. Thus, a pluralist discourse may mask the consequences of policies that channel speakers of minority languages into monolingual classrooms and eventually into marginal employment in the peripheral economy (see Tollefson, 1989).

The Importance of Resources

Although some linguistic minority communities are able to mount successful educational programs using local minority languages as media of instruction, many such communities lack the resources needed to support ongoing programs. As a result, state support or significant external aid is usually essential. In New Zealand, for example, the critical shortage of Māori-medium materials and resources has required an official state response. As May notes, however, state budgetary support also entails state control. In sub-Saharan Africa, Alidou describes the influential role of the World Bank and various development agencies in medium-of-instruction decisions. With national budgets inadequate for bilingual programs that use local languages, outside providers of funding ensure that medium of instruction continues to be offered almost exclusively in colonial languages. Control of resources, in other words, often means control of medium-of-instruction policy. Similarly, programs seeking to offer medium of instruction in American Indian languages in the United States have been plagued by the constant struggle to obtain new funding from government agencies. As McCarty reports, Indian leaders spend far too much time in the never-ending search for funding, rather than focusing on curriculum, textbooks and materials, teacher training, and other essential aspects of classroom instruction. In Ecuador and Bolivia, inadequate resources threaten to overwhelm even the most committed advocates of medium of instruction in indigenous languages. As conflicts over medium-of-instruction decisions often become struggles over budgets, the challenge for advocates of medium of instruction in the languages of linguistic minorities is to find ways to fund programs and also to retain local control. In this effort, possible models are those of the Māori-controlled schools in New Zealand and indigenous-controlled schools in the U.S. Southwest (see also schools in the Solomon Islands [Gegeo & Watson-Gegeo, 1995]).

The Relationship Between Ethnolinguistic Diversity and Social Conflict

Until the 1980s, Yugoslavia and India shared important features: significant ethnolinguistic diversity, educational systems that ensured the use of a large number of local languages, and a public discourse committed to multilingualism and multiculturalism. Despite striking similarities in their policies and their ethnolinguistic configurations, debates over medium of instruction in the 1990s moved in fundamentally different directions in the two countries. In Yugoslavia, Serbian efforts to promote Serbian medium of instruction were widely perceived as central components in the effort to achieve Serbian hegemony; in India, medium-of-instruction debates have been a source of reassurance that the state will protect a wide range of languages in education and restrict efforts by any group to attain hegemony in the educational system. Indeed, mother-tongue promotion in India continues to be associated with linguistic and cultural rights, whereas in Yugoslavia in the 1980s and 1990s, Serbian mother-tongue promotion policies were essentially efforts to rescind the rights of other ethnolinguistic groups.

In other settings, multilingualism may be viewed as a "resource," although medium-of-instruction policies may not necessarily protect the right to mother-tongue education. In Singapore, for instance, language is linked with globalization, which is seen not merely as a process requiring knowledge of English, but also as one in which multilingualism and multicultural competence are important. In rural areas of Philippines, although English is widely perceived as having economic value, local indigenous languages are also effectively maintained, although they are excluded from the schools, thus far with little public protest or resistance to current policies. Thus, the chapters in this collection show that the particular configuration of medium-of-instruction policies within local and regional diglossia may vary widely, with varying consequences for social conflict.

The Potential Impact of Language Rights in Education

As several chapters in this collection illustrate, a system of language rights can provide a framework within which ethnolinguistic minorities may seek recognition of their languages in the educational system. In New Zealand, for example, recent changes in Māori-Pākehā relations have been linked to the reinvigorated Treaty of Waitangi and the introduction of the principles of biculturalism and equality into the law and public discourse. With the Māori language legally recognized as an official language of the state since 1987, Māori communities have been able to achieve significant gains in Māori-medium education. These gains are made possible and can be sustained in part through the support of language-rights guarantees. In Yugoslavia, before the recent wars, a complex system of language rights, particularly in education, was the key to four decades of peace; and the Serbian-led effort to rescind that system of language rights was a major cause of the breakup of the country. More recently, Slovenia's guarantee of the right to medium of instruction in Italian and Hungarian has been an important component in the country's movement to gain membership in the institutions of a united Europe.

More profoundly, the articles in this collection raise a fundamental question about language rights in education: What should be the basis for language rights? One possibility is territory, that is, a system in which the right to instruction depends on membership in groups whose rights are assured within particular geographical regions. The appeal of linking language rights to the territory in which particular groups reside is that such a system seems practical. In Yugoslavia and India, for example, territory and language have been linked, due in part to the particular geographical distribution of ethnolinguistic groups. Indeed, in most settings, pragmatic concerns limit the right to medium of instruction in the home language to regions where the minority language is widely spoken. Welsh-medium schooling, for instance, is possible in Wales, but not elsewhere in the United Kingdom; in the United States, American Indian community-controlled schools are possible in regions of the Southwest, but politically difficult in most major cities, where Indian populations also reside. Although the pragmatic connection between territory and the right to medium of instruction is understandable, there are risks in basing claims for language rights on territory. As in Yugoslavia in the 1990s and the United States in the 1800s, territorially based language rights may encourage states to create "new facts on the ground," through the forced movement of ethnolinguistic populations. Moreover, territory and ethnolinguistic identity are rarely perfectly matched. Thus, opinion leaders can exploit concerns for individuals living outside their "home" territory, and thereby use language to create and sustain social conflict.

A second basis for language rights is ethnolinguistic identity, that is, a system in which individuals who identify themselves as members of recognized groups may be able to exercise particular rights to medium of instruction. One difficulty with such a system is that identity is increasingly fluid. Migration, intermarriage, and other forces lead individuals to develop multiple and changing identities that a direct association of language and identity may not be able to accommodate. An additional problem is that such a system may be inherently unjust, in so far as individuals who are not members of officially recognized groups will be unable to exercise equal language rights.

A third basis for language rights is citizenship, that is, a system in which citizenship entails the ability to exercise specified language rights, such as the right to instruction in particular languages. The link between language and citizenship varies from one setting to another. In the United States, a popular view is that learning English is a central duty of all citizens, although this view has not generally become the basis for law. Indeed, Bureau of Indian Affairs (BIA) policy for many decades expressed this particular link between language and citizenship, as expressed by the title of the BIA English-teaching publication, *I am a Good Citizen* (Williamson, 1954, cited in McCarty, chap. 4, this volume). In contrast, New Zealand in recent years has moved toward a more complex notion of citizenship, in which historical relations among dominant and minority groups, legal rulings and treaties, and a reinvigorated discourse of equality and partnership support a multilingual citizenry. In South Africa, support for 11 official languages, although initially the result of a pragmatic political compromise between the African National Congress and the ruling National Party of the apartheid government, has now become associated with constitutional support for equality and human rights, as well as efforts to promote a climate of tolerance and national unity. Although English retains major economic advantages, it has not become exclusively linked with notions of South African citizenship; and other languages—once linked by the apartheid government with "tribalism" and disadvantage—have come to be seen as symbols of the new South Africa.

The effort to develop conceptions of citizenship that accommodate fluid and changing relations between language and identity is an important counterforce to the rise in ethnolinguistic nationalism, as well as to the homogenizing effect of globalization. In some settings, particularly in Eastern Europe and Central Asia, medium-of-instruction policies are increasingly affected by the claim that nation-states must express the authentic national roots of groups having a single ethnolinguistic identity. In Western Europe, ultranationalist movements in Italy, Germany, France, and elsewhere have argued that medium-of-instruction policies must be formulated in light of the mythic history of a unified dominant people (see Anderson, 1983). One challenge for proponents of a right to medium of instruction in one's home language is to develop notions of citizenship that acknowledge the social functions of ethnolinguistic identity, but do not lead to the creation of unequal groups of citizens having different rights and responsibilities (see Kymlicka, 1995).

The Tension Between Global and Local Concerns

As Alidou's examination of medium of instruction in sub-Saharan Africa demonstrates, the colonial period exerted a powerful influence over language in education; and in the post-colonial period, the development of global economic structures, global mass media, and global political institutions has an equally powerful impact on medium-of-instruction policies. Medium-of-instruction policies in countries such as Mali, Niger, and Burkina Faso are largely determined by international financial institutions such as the World Bank and by international aid agencies. In Singapore and Malaysia, medium-of-instruction policy is directly linked to the national goal of full integration into the global economy. In South Africa, training the labor force for the new economy is a major goal, influencing the trend toward English-medium instruction. In the Philippines, language attitudes favoring English are shaped by public perception of the value of English in the economy of the 21st century. In Hong Kong, the shift to Chinese-medium schooling since 1997 has been partially undermined by the association of English with globalization. In many settings, globalization, with its increasing cultural homogenization, threatens the continued use of local languages in education, as well as in other domains.

Yet local concerns also shape medium-of-instruction debates in profound ways. For instance, although political stability in Singapore rests in part on agreement that widespread English-knowing bilingualism is in the national interest, ethnic values associated with languages other than English, as well as with local varieties of English, are equally important for the country's long-term stability. In Malaysia, support for Bahasa Malaysia remains strong, particularly among the educational elite, as a symbol of Malay nationalism. Indeed, local responses to globalization vary widely. In many settings, as individuals feel a growing inability to influence the economic, political, and social forces that control their lives, ethnolinguistic identity has taken on renewed importance. In New Zealand, Wales, and the United States, indigenous language education is, in part, an effort to regain a sense of belonging, by rediscovering and, to some extent, recreating the ethnolinguistic group that, before globalization, was central to individual identity. A very different kind of local concern is at work in Hong Kong, where the political effort to reestablish linguistic, cultural, and social ties with China has shaped the movement away from English and toward Chinese-medium instruction.

Particularly important is the most local site of all—the classroom. Effective medium-of-instruction policies require attention to the daily concerns of teachers and students: curriculum and materials, class size, schedules for language study and other subjects, pre-service and in-service training for teachers, and a host of other factors that affect the quality of education. Efforts to develop bilingual medium of instruction in Ecuador and Bolivia, for example, are restricted by teachers' struggle to understand how to use indigenous languages for beginning literacy. In Mali, Niger, and Burkina Faso, teachers in bilingual programs often lack adequate skills in writing in the local language. In Malaysia, a return to English-medium education is partly a result of perceived inadequacies of Bahasa Malaysia in science and technology, and failure of the Bahasa Malaysia-medium classes to prepare learners for higher education in English. In Wales, as elsewhere, students and teachers, often with varying degrees of language proficiency, face complex communicative challenges as they use multiple languages to study math, history, and other subjects. Across sub-Saharan Africa and the Andes, teachers and students struggle for literacy in languages still subject to intense debates over language standardization and the development of writing systems. Everywhere, the success of language-in-education policies depends on concrete efforts to improve teachers' working conditions and students' learning environments. Policies that do not consider the specific challenges facing teachers and students in their daily lives are not likely to be successful.

PEDAGOGY AND POLITICS IN MEDIUM-OF-INSTRUCTION POLICIES

As this collection demonstrates, medium-of-instruction policies reflect the dual importance of pedagogy and politics. In analyzing medium-of-instruction policies, it is always important to include both pedagogical and political perspectives. The central pedagogical question is: What are the consequences of instruction in various combinations of students' native language(s) and languages of wider communication? This question highlights the importance of medium of instruction as a factor in students' subject-content learning, language learning, and overall school performance. The political perspective highlights the crucial role of medium-of-instruction policies in shaping relationships of power among different social groups. Indeed, debates over alternative medium-of-instruction policies are often struggles to legitimize the minority group itself and to affect its relationship to the state. In New Zealand, for example, Te Kōhanga Reo and Kura Kaupapa Māori are not only creating renewed interest in Māori language and culture, but they are central to the survival of Māori culture and, more broadly, to ongoing efforts to further social justice in New Zealand.

Yet, as sub-Saharan Africa and Yugoslavia suggest, medium-of-instruction policies also offer opportunities for political leaders or dominant groups to further their own interests at the expense of others. Thus, in some settings, a central political question is: How might medium-of-instruction policies create or sustain social conflict, perhaps by maintaining or exacerbating various forms of social, political, or economic inequality? Yugoslavia is perhaps the best example of a state in which leaders used medium-of-instruction policy to instigate conflict, in this case, so that they could hold onto political power at a time when the rest of Eastern Europe was undergoing a fundamental change in leadership. Alternatively, medium-of-instruction policies can be used to mitigate conflict, in part by convincing both dominant and minority groups that their needs can be met within the existing educational system. Such a goal is part of medium-of-instruction debates in New Zealand, Wales, post-apartheid South Africa, Singapore, Philippines, Ecuador, and Bolivia. In all settings, it is important to recognize that pedagogical debates may mask political agendas. As in Hong Kong, political agendas—even if they are not openly acknowledged—are crucial to medium-of-instruction policies; and educational concerns receive special prominence precisely when they converge with political agendas.

Thus, it is always important to examine the underlying agendas of alternative medium-of-instruction policies. In order to do so, and to adequately understand the complex interplay of politics and pedagogy, researchers must incorporate a classroom (and playground) perspective as well as a broader historical–structural perspective. As Jones and Martin-Jones argue, research within a classroom (and playground) perspective should investigate the bilingual discourse practices with which teachers and students face their daily communicative challenges. Research within a historical–structural perspective should place individuals' language practices within the social, cultural, and political context in which they occur. Through such complex, multilayered research, we can better understand the processes of cultural and linguistic reproduction that are central to schools: the processes by which teachers and students together negotiate language practices within institutional settings in which medium-of-instruction policies have substantial and concrete consequences.

REFERENCES

Anderson, B. (1983). *Imagined communities: Reflections on the origin and spread of nationalism.* London: Verso.

Eastman, C. M. (1983). *Language planning: An introduction.* San Francisco: Chandler & Sharp.

Gegeo, D. W., & Watson-Gegeo, K. A. (1995). Understanding language and power in the Solomon Islands: Methodological issues for educational intervention. In J. W. Tollefson (Ed.), *Power and inequality in language education* (pp. 59–72). Cambridge, UK: Cambridge University Press.

Kymlicka, W. (1995). *Multicultural citizenship.* Oxford, UK: Oxford University Press.

Schmidt, R. J. (1998). The politics of language in Canada and the United States: Explaining the differences. In T. Ricento & B. Burnaby (Eds.), *Language and politics in the United States and Canada* (pp. 37–70). Mahwah, NJ: Lawrence Erlbaum Associates.

Tollefson, J. W. (1989). *Alien winds: The reeducation of America's Indochinese refugees.* New York: Praeger.

Tollefson, J. W. (1991). *Planning language, planning inequality: Language policy in the community.* London: Longman.

Wiley, T. G. (2002). Accessing language rights in education: A brief history of the U.S. context. In J. W. Tollefson (Ed.), *Language policies in education: Critical issues* (pp. 39–64). Mahwah, NJ: Lawrence Erlbaum Associates.

Author Index

Subject Index